Islanders and Empire

Islanders and Empire examines the role smuggling played in the cultural, economic, and sociopolitical transformation of Hispaniola from the late sixteenth to seventeenth centuries. With a rare focus on local peoples and communities, the book analyzes how residents of Hispaniola actively negotiated and transformed the meaning and reach of imperial bureaucracies and institutions for their own benefit. By co-opting the governing and judicial powers of local and imperial institutions on the island, residents could take advantage of, and even dominate, the contraband trade that reached the island's shores. In doing so, they altered the course of the European interimperial struggles in the Caribbean by limiting, redirecting, or suppressing the Spanish crown's policies, thus taking control of their destinies and that of their neighbors in Hispaniola, other Spanish Caribbean territories, and the Spanish empire in the region.

Juan José Ponce Vázquez is Assistant Professor of History at the University of Alabama.

CAMBRIDGE LATIN AMERICAN STUDIES

General Editors
KRIS LANE, Tulane University
MATTHEW RESTALL, Pennsylvania State University

Editor Emeritus
HERBERT S. KLEIN
Gouverneur Morris Emeritus Professor of History, Columbia University and Hoover
Research Fellow, Stanford University

Other Books in the Series

121. *Islanders and Empire: Smuggling and Political Defiance in Hispaniola, 1580–1690*, Juan José Ponce Vázquez

120. *Our Time is Now: Race and Modernity in Postcolonial Guatemala*, Julie Gibbings

119. *The Sexual Question: A History of Prostitution in Peru, 1850s–1950s*, Paulo Drinot

118. *A Silver River in a Silver World: Dutch Trade in the Rio de la Plata, 1648–1678*, David Freeman

117. *Laboring for the State: Women, Family, and Work in Revolutionary Cuba, 1959–1971*, Rachel Hynson

116. *Violence and The Caste War of Yucatán*, Wolfgang Gabbert

115. *For Christ and Country: Militant Catholic Youth in Post-Revolutionary Mexico*, Robert Weis

114. *The Mexican Mission: Indigenous Reconstruction and Mendicant Enterprise in New Spain, 1521–1600*, Ryan Dominic Crewe

113. *Corruption and Justice in Colonial Mexico, 1650–1755*, Christoph Rosenmüller

112. *Blacks of the Land: Indian Slavery, Settler Society, and the Portuguese Colonial Enterprise in South America*, Weinstein/Woodard/Montiero

111. *The Street Is Ours: Community, the Car, and the Nature of Public Space in Rio de Janeiro*, Shawn William Miller

110. *Laywomen and the Making of Colonial Catholicism in New Spain, 1630–1790*, Jessica L. Delgado

109. *Urban Slavery in Colonial Mexico: Puebla de los Ángeles, 1531–1706*, Pablo Miguel Sierra Silva

(Continued after the Index)

Islanders and Empire

Smuggling and Political Defiance in Hispaniola, 1580–1690

JUAN JOSÉ PONCE VÁZQUEZ

University of Alabama, Tuscaloosa

CAMBRIDGE
UNIVERSITY PRESS

University Printing House, Cambridge CB2 8BS, United Kingdom

One Liberty Plaza, 20th Floor, New York, NY 10006, USA

477 Williamstown Road, Port Melbourne, VIC 3207, Australia

314–321, 3rd Floor, Plot 3, Splendor Forum, Jasola District Centre,
New Delhi – 110025, India

79 Anson Road, #06–04/06, Singapore 079906

Cambridge University Press is part of the University of Cambridge.

It furthers the University's mission by disseminating knowledge in the pursuit of
education, learning, and research at the highest international levels of excellence.

www.cambridge.org
Information on this title: www.cambridge.org/9781108477659
DOI: 10.1017/9781108477659

© Juan José Ponce Vázquez 2020

This publication is in copyright. Subject to statutory exception
and to the provisions of relevant collective licensing agreements,
no reproduction of any part may take place without the written
permission of Cambridge University Press.

First published 2020

A catalogue record for this publication is available from the British Library.

Library of Congress Cataloging-in-Publication Data
NAMES: Ponce Vázquez, Juan José, 1978– author.
TITLE: Islanders and empire : smuggling and political defiance in Hispaniola,
1580–1690 / Juan José Ponce Vázquez, University of Alabama, Tuscaloosa.
DESCRIPTION: Cambridge, United Kingdom ; New York, NY : Cambridge University
Press, 2020. | Series: Cambridge Latin American studies | Includes bibliographical
references and index.
IDENTIFIERS: LCCN 2020018691 | ISBN 9781108477659 (hardback) |
ISBN 9781108477659 (ebook)
SUBJECTS: LCSH: Smuggling – Hispaniola – History – 16th century. | Smuggling –
Hispaniola – History – 17th century. | Hispaniola – Commerce – History – 16th
century.| Hispaniola – Politics and government – 16th century. | Spain – Colonies –
America – Administration – History – 16th century. | Hispaniola – History – 16th
century. | Hispaniola – Commerce – History – 17th century. | Hispaniola – Politics and
goverment – 17th century. | Spain – Colonies – America – Administration – History –
17th century. | Hispaniola – History – 17th century.
CLASSIFICATION: LCC HF3312 .P66 2020 | DDC 364.1/33609729309032–dc23
LC record available at https://lccn.loc.gov/2020018691

ISBN 978-1-108-47765-9 Hardback

Cambridge University Press has no responsibility for the persistence or accuracy of
URLs for external or third-party internet websites referred to in this publication
and does not guarantee that any content on such websites is, or will remain,
accurate or appropriate.

Para Julie, Santiago y Alejandro.

Contents

List of Figures and Tables	*page* viii
Acknowledgments	x
Introduction	1
1 Colonial Origins: Hispaniola in the Sixteenth Century	22
2 Smuggling, Sin, and Survival, 1580–1600	56
3 Repressing Smugglers: The Depopulations of Hispaniola, 1604–1606	98
4 Tools of Colonial Power: Officeholders, Violence, and Exploitation of Enslaved Africans in Santo Domingo's *Cabildo*	134
5 "Prime Mover of All Machinations": Rodrigo Pimentel, Smuggling, and the Artifice of Power	172
6 Neighbors, Rivals, and Partners: Non-Spaniards and the Rise of Saint-Domingue	223
Conclusion	263
Glossary of Spanish Terms	269
Bibliography	273
Index	289

vii

Figures and Tables

FIGURES

0.1 Main Spanish Caribbean ports in the late sixteenth and early seventeenth century (Alexander Fries, University of Alabama Cartographic Research Laboratory).   *page* xvi

1.1 Francis Drake's attack on Santo Domingo, in Baptista Boazio, *Map and views illustrating Sir Francis Drake's West Indian voyage, 1585–6.* [London?: s.n., 1585]. Library of Congress, Rare Book and Special Collections Division.   24

1.2 Map of Santo Domingo defenses, 1619 (detail). Ministerio de Cultura y Deportes, AGI, Mapas y Planos, Santo Domingo, 29.   48

1.3a *Casa del Cordón* (Cord House). Photo by the author.   51

1.3b Main facade of the cathedral of Santa María de la Encarnación, Santo Domingo. Photo courtesy of Getty Images.   51

1.3c Church of the Dominican order. Photo by the author.   51

1.3d Church of Regina Angelorum. Photo by the author.   51

2.1 Map of the fields between Santo Domingo and the mouth of River Haina, 1679. Ministerio de Cultura y Deportes, AGI, Mapas y Planos, Santo Domingo, 77B.   57

2.2 Main towns and villages of Hispaniola by the end of the sixteenth century (Alexander Fries, University of Alabama Cartographic Research Laboratory).   62

2.3 Building of the *Audiencia* of Santo Domingo. Photo courtesy of Getty Images.   76

List of Figures and Tables

3.1 Main towns and villages of Hispaniola after the 1604–6
Depopulations (Alexander Fries, University of Alabama
Cartographic Research Laboratory).   111

4.1 Ruins of the monastery of San Francisco in Santo Domingo.
Photo by the author.   135

5.1a *Puerta de Atarazanas* (Shipyard Gate) seen from outside
the city walls. Photo by the author.   189

5.1b *Puerta del Río* (River Gate), also known as San Diego,
seen from within the city walls. Photo by the author.   189

5.2 Rodrigo Pimentel's self-aggrandizing plaque. Convent
of Santa Clara, Santo Domingo. Photo by the author.   220

6.1 Main Spanish and French towns and villages of Hispaniola
in the 1680s (Alexander Fries, University of Alabama
Cartographic Research Laboratory).   233

TABLES

4.1 Rural properties in Hispaniola divided by type, 1606
(Osorio's census).   143

4.2 Distribution of enslaved African laborers by occupation
in Hispaniola, 1606 (Osorio's census).   143

5.1 Provenance of *Audiencia* cases received in Santo Domingo
with powers of attorney addressed to Rodrigo Pimentel
before 1652, by city of origin. Source: AGI, Escribanía,
23 C.   187

Acknowledgments

Thanking people in the front matter of academic books is a genre in itself, one that could be considered invariably and unavoidably performative. At the same time, it can also be a powerful act in which you gather your own band of friends and dear ones who have supported you along the way, so this is what I plan to do here.[1] I do not see myself capable of avoiding all (or most of) the clichés, so please allow me at least to embrace those that are dearest to me and try to make them mine as I assemble my super team.

I have been terrified about writing this section for a long time, in part because I know that even though I have tried to keep track of all the people who have come to my aid, I know that I will forget some of them and that I will forever regret it. If that is your case, I am really sorry. Some of you have contributed in multiple ways. Please forgive me if, for the sake of brevity, you are only mentioned once.

The only reason I was able to write this book is that I have received assistance and kindness from an endless number of people. Since this book came out of my doctoral dissertation, I feel a moral obligation to start by showing my gratitude and affection to my dissertation advisor, Kathleen Brown. She trusted me and gave this intellectual orphan a chance when others thought I should have left graduate school. She has unwaveringly supported my professional career ever since, a career I would not have without her. Along with Kathy, my dream team of advisors, mentors, and now friends, includes Antonio Feros and

---

[1] Emily Callaci, "On Acknowledgments." *The American Historical Review*, vol. 125, n. 1 (February 2020): 126–31.

Acknowledgments

Tamara J. Walker. Their thoughtful guidance and advice through the years has been invaluable to me.

I would be remiss if I did not acknowledge the mentoring role that other faculty at the University of Pennsylvania had, especially Professors Ann Farnsworth-Alvear, Sheldon Hackney, Yolanda Martínez-San Miguel, Daniel K. Richter, and Barbara Savage. They all had a profound impression on me, and their teachings and support have stayed with me in one way or another.

Despite the talent and kindness of these professors, the rigors of graduate school would have been too much to bear without a strong cohort of friends that made the hard work we did tolerable. Friends like Sarah Van Beurden, Francesca Bregoli, D'Maris Coffman, Jo Cohen, Tina Collins, Nicholas DiLiberto, Andrew Heath, Matt Karp, Laura Keenan-Spero, Larissa Kopytoff, William Kuby, Andrew Lipman, Sarah Manekin, Agnieszka Marczyk, Erik Mathisen, Ben Mercer, Vanessa Mongey, Catalina Muñoz, Adrian O'Connor, Brian Rouleau, Alison Scheiderer, and Patrick Spero, among others. A very special thanks to Clemmie Harris, my brother in arms, for being always there, a phone call away, after all these years.

A few institutions trusted me and supported this project, and they have my endless gratitude. The University of Pennsylvania first made available funds to do some reconnaissance in the Dominican Republic in the conceptualization phase of this project. Many thanks to the John Carter Brown Library for their José Amor y Vázquez Fellowship, which allowed me to spend the first and only resident fellowship of my career to date. The late Pepe Amor himself was extraordinarily kind to me. My time at the JCB was not only productive, but enchanting, especially thanks to the skillful guidance of their staff, and the company and comradeship of fellows like Marie Arana, Adrian Finucane, Jason Sharples, and Natalia Sobrevilla. I also owe a debt of gratitude to the Dominican Studies Institute at the City University of New York, where I spent two weeks reading and writing thanks to the 2017 Archives and Library Research Awards Program. Special thanks to Sarah Aponte, Ramona Hernández, Anthony Stevens-Acevedo, and the fantastic group of student workers that they train and employ at the center. The startup funds of the University of Alabama allowed me to spend two weeks at the Archivo General de Simancas, following the elusive trace of Hispaniola in such an incredible repository. Archivist Isabel Aguirre Landa was very generous with her time, expertly guiding me through such a massive collection. A semester-long ASPIRE fellowship at the University of Alabama allowed me to focus on writing without other academic distractions. I must also thank the publishers who allowed me to use some materials published elsewhere.[2]

I was able to formally workshop a couple of chapters thanks to the generosity of some institutions and academics. My thanks to Cecile Accilien, Santa Arias, and Robert Schwaller at the University of Kansas for their invitation to share Chapter 2, as well as their wonderful suggestions to improve this chapter and the project as a whole. Special thanks to Marie G. Brown, whose insights during this visit helped me reconceptualize this whole project at a crucial stage of its development. Attendees of the 2018 Southwest Seminar also provided invaluable feedback: Ryan Crewe, Jessica Criales, Max Deardorff, Kevin Gosner, Mark Hanna, Jay Harrison, Ryan Kashanipour, Kittiya Lee, Mark Lentz, Bianca Premo, Joaquín Rivaya-Martínez, Christoph Rosenmüller, and Dana Velasco-Murillo, provided thoughtful commentary which had quite an impact on Chapter 3.

Not all institutions are able to support financially researchers, but I will never forget the kindness of those who opened their doors and resources to me. In my hometown of Sevilla, the *Archivo General de Indias* became my second home in the city during the almost two years I spent there doing research for this book. Their archivists and staff were always extraordinarily helpful and courteous in that special Sevillian way. In the Dominican Republic, I must thank the staff of the Archivo General de la Nación, as well as its director, Roberto Cassá, for their invitation to give a talk about part of this book, their generous gifts of books, and the availability to answer my research questions. I owe a special debt of gratitude to Genaro Rodríguez Morel, a great specialist in the early history of the Hispaniola, and someone who has aided me and encouraged me to carry on with this project since we first met as students in the *Universidad de Sevilla*.

Writing a book would be impossible without the heroic (and often unrecognized) work that librarians do curating collections and

---

[2] A few passages and ideas from Chapter 3 were previously published in "Casting Traitors and Villains: The Historiographical Memory of the 1605 Depopulations of Hispaniola," in Marina Llorente, Marcella Salvi, Aída Díaz de León, eds., *Sites of Memory in Spain and Latin America: Trauma, Politics, and Resistance*. Lanham: Lexington Books, 2015, 151–66. Parts of Chapter 4 draw on the article "Unequal Partners in Crime: Masters, Slaves and Free People of Color in Santo Domingo, c.1600–1650," *Slavery & Abolition*, 37:4 (2016), 704–23. Also, sections of Chapter 6 were previously published as "Atlantic Peripheries: Diplomacy, War, and Spanish French Interactions in Hispaniola, 1660–1690," in D'Maris Coffman, Adrian Leonard, and William O'Reilly, eds., *The Atlantic World*. Routledge, 2014, 300–18.

Acknowledgments   xiii

providing us with the resources we need to conduct our research. At Penn I had the incredible help of Joe Holub (who also employed me when all other sources of funding had been exhausted); at St. Lawrence University, Paul Doty often paddled his way to my rescue; and at the University of Alabama, Alex Boucher exercised unlimited patience with my constant stream of emails asking him to purchase books for the library and my own research. Their work made mine possible.

Books cannot exist without an editor to nurture them in their early stages and make them the best piece of material culture they can be. I was fortunate enough to work with two. First, my appreciation to Deborah Gershenowitz for believing in this project and giving it such a great home. Second, thank you to Cecelia Cancellaro for making this project her own with such enthusiasm and turning it into something I am very proud of. Rachel Blaifeder was also crucial to make me understand the subtleties of the editing process. Many thanks to Kris Lane and Matthew Restall, who were the best faculty editors one can dream of.

I have been extraordinarily lucky in every academic job I have had. I have always been surrounded by incredible teachers and superb scholars who have made me feel like a valuable part of the team, and despite the distance, they have become friends for life. From Rutgers University, I must thank Aldo Lauria Santiago, who has never stopped mentoring me and pushing me to be a better historian. At St. Lawrence University, Donna Alvah, Matthew Carotenuto, Anne Csete, Judith DeGroat, Elun Gabriel, Howard Eissenstat, Evelyn Jennings, Liz Regosin, Melissane Schrems, and Mary Jane Smith were a formidable team and role models of what teachers and scholars should be. Special thanks to Mindy Pitre for being such an incredible friend and academic rockstar.

Work is always labor even when it is pleasurable, but going to work every day at the University of Alabama to be alongside many colleagues and friends who also represent the best in each of their fields is a rare privilege that I have never taken for granted. Scholars like John F. Beeler, Steven Bunker, Charles Clark, Teresa Cribelli, Kari Frederickson, Andrew Huebner, Lesley Gordon, Sharony Green, Holly Grout, Heather Miyano Kopelson, Margaret Peacock, Erik L. Peterson, Joshua D. Rothman, Sarah Steinbock-Pratt, and Janek Wasserman. My conversations with them and their support of me and my family have shaped this project in multiple ways. I cannot thank them enough.

I would also like to show my appreciation to the graduate students I have had the privilege to teach and spend time with. They are still the reason most universities with graduate programs function, since they

xiv *Acknowledgments*

teach the majority of the classes, and yet they are one of the most unprotected and poorly paid groups in academia. Their daily work as teaching assistants, research assistants, and graders, as well as their struggles to keep up with their own work, are a constant reminder of my own experience as a graduate student. Their enthusiasm and dedication has always been an inspiration to me, and our classes together have given me the chance to reread and relearn many classic and new works that have left their mark on these pages. I would like to thank two of them by name: Logan James' work as a grader gave me some extra time to dedicate to writing these pages, and Chase McCarter was a fantastic and enthusiastic grader and suggested some sources for this book.

Doing research on this book has been an infallible way to meet amazing scholars and make long-lasting friendships. Friends like Fernanda Bretones Lane, Frances Ramos, Stuart B. Schwartz, Erin Stone, and Robert D. Taber made their own works available to me. Karen Graubart generously shared with me the draft of two chapters of her unfinished manuscript, as well as a lot of bibliographical suggestions. Many others helped me with their support, advice, suggestions, and friendship, like José Luis Belmonte Postigo, John Belzis-Selfa, Bradley Benton, Kristen Block, Asmaá Bouhrass, Clarisa Carmona, Caroline P. Cook, Caroline Cunill, Gregory Cushman, James Dator, Magdalena Díaz Hernández, Julia Gaffield, Ignacio Gallup-Díaz, Natalia González, Alexander Keese, Katy Kole de Peralta, David Lafevor, Xochitl Marsilli-Vargas, Juan Negrón Ayala, Esteban Mira Caballos, Francisco Moscoso, Isabel María Povea Moreno, Meliza Reynoso Montás (and her entire family), Elena A. Schneider, John F. Schwaller, Beatriz Valverde Contreras, William Van Norman, David Wheat, and Bárbara Zepeda Cortés. There are some whom I have never met in person, but via Twitter they selflessly aided me when I asked for help. People like Manuel Barcia, Chad Black, Lisa Krissoff Boehm, Sara J. Brenneis, Adriana Chira, William F. Connell, Lisa Covert, Pol Dalmau, Julia López Fuentes, Jorge L. Giovannetti, Mary Lewis, Juan Andrés Suárez, and many others.

In editing this book, I also had great assistance from colleagues and friends who carefully questioned my choices and my English, improving them both in the process. Carrie Gibson went through many of the early versions of this book, correcting my English and making questions about my narrative in all the right places. Her dedication and skill as a writer and historian are unparalleled. Anne Eller also read some chapters and the Introduction and spent a lot of time pushing me to go deeper and to be

Acknowledgments xv

a better historian. Someday, I will be half the scholar she is today. I met both of them in the archives in Sevilla, and they have been constant companions in the process of researching and writing this book. A lifetime of thanks will not be enough to repay them.

But many others helped, too. Rebecca Goetz read an early version of Chapter 2. William Booth, Jesse Cromwell, Casey Schmitt, and others mentioned elsewhere read the Introduction and gave me numerous ideas on how to improve it. Jorge Cañizares-Esguerra read an early version of the introduction and the six chapters of this book twice and gave very insightful feedback on how to sharpen my arguments. Special thanks to Marc Eagle and an anonymous reader, who acted as Cambridge University reviewers and gave me much food for thought on how to improve the manuscript as a whole. Apart from being a wonderful friend, Esther González helped me with the paperwork to get some of the images included within. Kristin Cahn von Seelen generously edited Chapter 3, and all she asked in return was a copy of this book. Sarah Moore kindly proofread the whole thing, again, one more time. She has a sixth sense for editing, and I am delighted she accepted to help me with her superpowers.

I will end with a word of sorrow and a word of happiness. My biggest lament surrounding this project is that my father, José Ponce Camacho, passed well before he was able to see this book published. I grieve his absence every day. He and my mother, Elvira Vázquez Rodríguez, have always been phenomenally supportive of all my choices, even if they led me to live half a world away. I could have never initiated this project without their unconditional love. My sister Elvira, *mis padrinos* Pepín and Luisa, and my extended Sevillian family have been a great source of comfort to me. I miss them terribly. Finally, finishing this book would not have any meaning without my American family. My parents-in-law Roger and Jane Bannerman are the kindest and most generous people I have ever known. My best friend and partner Julie is the better person and scholar in our family, and I am thankful every day for having her in my life. She makes me want to be a little better every day. Our sons Santiago and Alejandro were born while I wrote this book, and they have given new meaning to everything I do. This book is dedicated to the three of them.

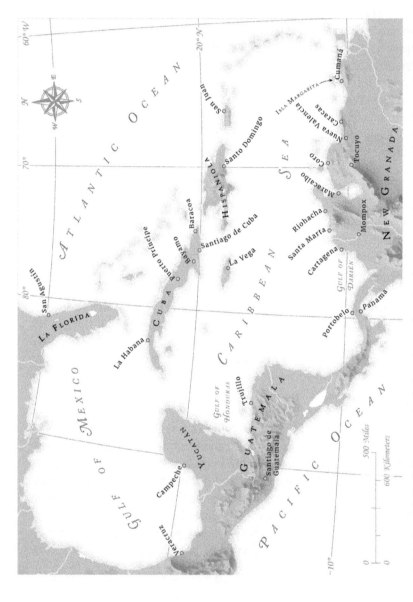

FIGURE 0.1 Main Spanish Caribbean ports in the late sixteenth and early seventeenth century (Alexander Fries, University of Alabama Cartographic Research Laboratory).

Introduction

This book focuses on the peoples of Hispaniola and their deep, intimate, and persistent embrace of smuggling, and situates their story at the crossroads of the fields of colonial Latin American, Caribbean, and Atlantic history. Hispaniola residents traded extralegally in order to circumvent the increasingly marginal space the island occupied within the Spanish colonial system, one which left them on the fringes of lawful commercial connections. During the long seventeenth century (which I define as the years between the 1580s and 1690s), the Atlantic world was a growing network of interconnected port towns and cities and their hinterlands that developed simultaneously to the integration of those port cities into their own imperial systems. With this twin dynamic in mind, I argue that the inhabitants of the Spanish colony of Hispaniola overcame their peripheral status within the Spanish empire by embracing the possibilities that the people, networks, and goods of the nascent new Atlantic world provided. Elites wove themselves into the fabric of the trade and dominated it as they could; other residents also made their lives through the trade. By carefully navigating around Spanish imperial monopolistic expectations – or simply ignoring them – Hispaniola's residents turned the island into an Atlantic center in its own right. They pursued their short-term and intermediate social and economic goals, while also embracing cross-imperial contraband as an economically viable and morally acceptable livelihood for their own personal prosperity. In the process, steeped in the contraband networks that ruled the colony, Hispaniola residents transformed the

2   *Islanders and Empire*

political dynamics that ruled their relationship with the Spanish monarchy, giving themselves great control over the decision-making progress of the island as well as a good part of the Spanish Caribbean region.

This book offers a ground-up reconstruction of transimperial and interregional illicit trade, politics, and institutional history. Hispaniola residents instantiated what Jesse Cromwell, inspired by E. P. Thompson, identifies as a moral economy of smuggling.[1] In Hispaniola, just as in coastal Venezuela, this social ethos also cut across race and class, unifying the great majority of society into a communal pact that normalized their practice of and benefits from contraband trade, while maintaining a deeply hierarchical society in which enslaved and free people of color, either willingly or forcedly, participated in the trade often as cogs within a smuggling machinery controlled by white elites. This process appeared in Hispaniola in the second half of the sixteenth century, over a century earlier than in Venezuela, and shows the deep roots of smuggling in coastal Caribbean communities. *Islanders and Empire* details efforts of local residents at every social level: those enslaved on plantations and in towns, free town residents, and especially the social and political machinations of the elite, who manipulated and benefitted most from the trade. It considers actions of the Spanish state – often ineffectual, sometimes brutal – the considerations of the Catholic Church, the dynamics of local rivalry, and the impact of non-Spanish networks and residents on the island, a factor that only continued to grow.

Next, and equally as important as the social and economic relationships related to illicit commerce, this study of the social ethos of smuggling in Hispaniola also reveals a progressive institutionalization of smuggling at the highest levels of colonial governance, which led to intimate and mutually beneficial interactions between colonial bureaucrats and some (but certainly not all) local inhabitants. Throughout the seventeenth century, Hispaniola elites' accumulated influence as smugglers permitted them to exert increasingly tight control over the reins of all local institutions. This local control not only allowed them to practice their illicit dealings without being prosecuted or punished for their actions, but gave them an outsized influence in the *Audiencia* of Santo Domingo. Local leverage over the machinery of power within the *Audiencia* allowed them

---

[1] Jesse Cromwell, *The Smugglers' World: Illicit Trade and Atlantic Communities in Eighteenth-Century Venezuela* (Williamsburg, Omohundro Institute of Early American History and Culture; Chapel Hill: University of North Carolina Press, 2018), 15–16.

Introduction

in turn to establish mutually beneficial connections with other renowned Caribbean smuggling regions such as Venezuela and New Granada. They did this with almost complete impunity, while using the royal treasury to finance their actions.

Local control over the *Audiencia* also had an important geostrategic dimension both for the island as part of the Spanish empire and for the region as a whole. During the late seventeenth century, the Caribbean became a heavily contested imperial frontier among European empires that were fighting to realize their own imperial ambitions while imposing commercial supremacy over the region. The ability of Hispaniola residents to steer the *Audiencia* of Santo Domingo and royal officials on the island to protect and expand their ability to conduct extralegal commerce had a significant impact on the implementation of Spanish imperial policy across a large part of the Caribbean, rendering most efforts from Madrid secondary to the interests of Hispaniola's power networks. At times, the Spanish crown managed to squash local efforts to cultivate multinational and transimperial contraband networks. In the depopulations of 1604–6, for example, the crown destroyed the smuggling villages of the north and west of the island: Puerto Plata, Montecristi, Bayahá, la Yaguana, and San Juan. The king's men destroyed all local resistance and caused considerable loss of life and property. Their actions resulted in great dislocation to both enslaved and free local inhabitants, who in the eyes of the crown were not only breaking the commercial laws, but were also dangerously confraternizing with proselytizing Lutherans. Despite the crown's punctual successes after 1606 in stifling unsanctioned commerce, Hispaniola – and the majority of the Spanish Caribbean possessions during the seventeenth century – established an early and increasingly fierce independence from Madrid's mandates. The marginal space that Hispaniola occupied in the mind of Spanish bureaucrats gave local peoples great latitude to mold imperial rule to their own ends, embracing what was useful for their own socioeconomic prosperity, absorbing institutional power, and disregarding some of the most onerous aspects of colonial governance.

This book opens with a chapter on the history of Hispaniola or Ayiti, as the indigenous Arawak people called it, from Cristóbal Colón's arrival to the second half of the sixteenth century.[2] The main narrative, however, begins in the 1580s when plantation agriculture had been in decline for at

---

[2] I have chosen to use Christopher Columbus' Spanish name instead of its anglicized version. I will do the same with the names of kings and queens like Isabel and Fernando, Carlos, Felipe, etc.

least thirty years and contraband had increased as an alternative economic activity. *Islanders and Empire* ends with the Treaty of Ryswick in 1697, with Spanish recognition of French dominion over Hispaniola's western lands. The treaty divided the island into the two polities of French Saint-Domingue and Spanish Santo Domingo, and despite the tensions over land and plunder, people from both sides had enjoyed a thriving contraband activity for more than a decade by this point. This illicit trade became one of the defining features in the relationship between the two colonies in the next century and beyond.

Although *Islanders and Empire* reflects the participation in contraband trade of all residents of Hispaniola, it highlights the paths of the members of the local Hispaniola-born elites. They dominated the overt smuggling on the island, even as many other actors participated. Portuguese and other foreigners, enslaved and free peoples of African descent, and Spanish officials also engaged in the consumption and trade of contraband goods, which included the purchase of African captives. In the beginning of this prosperous contraband trade in the second half of the sixteenth century, people of all ranks and backgrounds actively participated in exchanges with foreign traders along the sparsely populated shores and bays of Hispaniola. The depopulations of 1604–6 marked a watershed moment in the ability of a great part of the population to participate in the extralegal trade: access to smuggled goods became limited to a small group of individuals who took advantage of their location and/or their rank within the island's political and military structure to restrict access to these goods, thus becoming gatekeepers. This position allowed them to benefit economically from their access, while at the same time creating important patronage networks that allowed their members to obtain these goods, as well as African captives, and the wealth associated with these exchanges. By the end of the seventeenth century, the unequal access to smuggled goods created a social and political hierarchy on the island. Both crown officials and local municipal leaders in towns like Santo Domingo and Santiago de los Caballeros became direct providers of smuggled goods and centers of powerful (and often competing) contraband networks. This overt local economic defiance of imperial rules established a pattern that would continue until the end of the Spanish colonial period.

Islanders and Empire brings to bear important implications for the wider understanding of Spanish colonialism beyond the island. Despite the best attempts of the Spanish monarchy to curb contraband trade and reassert control of Santo Domingo's commerce and institutions, its efforts were ultimately thwarted by local interests bent on pursuing the path that

Introduction

suited their social and economic ambitions. The study of a colonial periphery such as Hispaniola in the seventeenth century demonstrates how local peoples actively negotiated and transformed the meaning and reach of imperial bureaucracies and institutions for their own benefit. In Santo Domingo, local actors managed to undermine and co-opt the powers of imperial bureaucracies, either by absorbing them into their own patronage networks or by confronting them with the strength that their colonial isolation granted them. Smuggling became a common activity in which all sectors of society directly or indirectly participated, including those who, at least theoretically, represented the crown's interests.

Additionally, *Islanders and Empire* demonstrates that improvisation and resistance to the mandates of Madrid occurred even in seats of empire as embattled and contradictory as the early colonial Caribbean. Besieged by Spanish enemies, the crown needed to control this region to ensure its transatlantic communication with the bullion-rich mainland of Mexico and Peru. Yet during most of the sixteenth and seventeenth centuries, from a colonial standpoint, the Caribbean remained largely unprofitable and very far down on the list of priorities of the Spanish crown. During this long seventeenth century, Spain formally retained control of Hispaniola, but in practice, it was the alliance of colonial administrators and local groups that controlled the destiny of the island, even as they performed their loyalty to the king in letters and treatises to Madrid. Local groups accommodated Spanish rule not just because of historical inertia (doing what their parents did before them) or abject loyalty – they did so because Madrid rarely interfered with local designs. When it did, local dominance of imperial institutions rendered most of those attempts unsuccessful. Even when the crown managed to impose its will, local peoples rendered these triumphs moot and short-lived. Hispaniola thus provides a model to study most Spanish imperial peripheries during this period, which is to say, most of the Spanish empire.

By co-opting the governing and judicial powers of local and imperial institutions on the island and prioritizing their own short- and medium-term goals (including wealth acquisition, social recognition, and privileges), the residents of Hispaniola were able to take advantage of and even dominate the contraband trade that reached the island's shores. In doing so, they altered the course of European interimperial struggles in the Caribbean by limiting, redirecting, or suppressing the Spanish crown's policies, while seeking to advance their own social and economic interests. Hispaniola's decline in state-sanctioned commercial importance and the demise of its plantation agriculture ruined the social, political, and

6   *Islanders and Empire*

economic backbone of the island's economy. Smuggling represented a viable livelihood and even an opportunity for a certain level of prosperity and conspicuous consumption for Hispaniola residents. It often involved the co-optation of institutions and individuals with the power to punish contraband as an illicit activity. Thinking about the history of Hispaniola in this way allows for an examination of the pursuits of individual actors with in the otherwise abstract process of imperial and economic decline. The island's seventeenth-century past also elucidates the meaning and impact of that so-called decline, as well as its effects in colonial governance, from an on-the-ground peripheral perspective.

NARRATIVE EXCLUSIONS

The Spanish Caribbean islands in general, and Hispaniola in particular, have often been sidelined from the main historical narratives of the Caribbean and Atlantic world during the seventeenth century. This omission has multiple explanations. One is that the history of the Caribbean during this period has traditionally been told with an emphasis on those aspects that scholars identified as defining features of the region in later periods, such as the importance of sugar and the rise of plantation societies. As a result, the study of the seventeenth-century Caribbean has often been filtered by scholarly interest in the plantation societies that flourished, at horrible human costs, in the late seventeenth and eighteenth centuries. In United States academia in particular, this has led to an expansive historiographical production concerning plantation societies in the Caribbean and Atlantic world and their connection to the rise of Western (mostly English, French or Dutch) capitalism. Unfortunately, such an approach has also led to completely ignoring entire regions of the Caribbean that did not fit into this teleological narrative.[3] Ironically, Hispaniola was home to the first plantation society in the Americas, but this first plantation cycle failed to be

---

[3] For more on this critique, see Alejandro de la Fuente (with the collaboration of César García del Pino and Bernardo Iglesias Delgado), *Havana and the Atlantic in the Sixteenth Century* (Chapel Hill: University of North Carolina Press, 2008), 226; David Wheat, *Atlantic Africa and the Spanish Caribbean, 1570–1640* (Chapel Hill: University of North Carolina Press, 2016), 8; Alberto Abello Vives and Ernesto Bassi Arévalo, "Un Caribe por fuera de la ruta de plantación," in *Un Caribe sin plantación*, ed. Alberto Abello Vives (San Andrés: Universidad Nacional de Colombia, 2006), 11–43. For a wonderful roundup of recent contributions to refute the plantation teleology and redirect the study of the Caribbean, see Jesse Cromwell, "More Than Slaves and Sugar: Recent Historiography of the Trans-imperial Caribbean and Its Sinew Populations," *History Compass*, vol. 12, n. 10 (2014): 770–83.

Introduction

included with what historians have identified as the definitive rise of plantations in the Caribbean by the end of the seventeenth century, no doubt contributing to the island's historiographical obscurity.[4] Academic interest in the study of the island after 1550s has been even more scarce, possibly due to the decline of the sugar plantations. Many African and indigenous enslaved captives escaped the Spanish farms and formed maroon communities, while many of those who stayed in bondage found a form of freedom associated with subsistence agriculture and cattle ranching instead of plantation work.[5] In most general histories of the region, the people living in the Spanish islands of the Caribbean are only described as active participants in the earliest stages of colonization. As soon as the English, French, and Dutch settlers arrive, Spanish settlers recede to the background, where they appear to remain exclusively as victims of pirates and other forms of North European aggression. Pirate narratives celebrate north-coast smugglers only obliquely. In this telling, the European nations and their Atlantic extensions were the real protagonists in the rise of the Caribbean to preeminence as one of the central nodes of the early modern Atlantic world.[6]

---

[4] There are some exceptions, like Genaro Rodríguez Morel, *Orígenes de la economía de plantación de La Española* (Santo Domingo: Editora Nacional, 2012); Genaro Rodríguez Morel, "The Sugar Economy in Hispaniola in the Sixteenth Century," in Stuart B. Schwartz, ed., *Tropical Babylons: Sugar and the Making of the Atlantic World, 1450–1680* (University of North Carolina Press, 2003), 85–114. Lynne A. Guitar, "Cultural Genesis: Relationships Among Indians, Africans, and Spaniards in Rural Hispaniola, First Half of the Sixteenth Century" (Ph.D. diss., Vanderbilt University, 1998).

[5] This is something that Raymundo González has observed for the eighteenth century, but it was certainly happening since the late sixteenth century. Raymundo González, *De esclavos a campesinos: vida rural en Santo Domingo colonial* (Santo Domingo: Archivo General de la Nación, 2011).

[6] An early example of this historical narrative turn can be found in Eric E. Williams, *From Columbus to Castro: The History of the Caribbean 1492–1969* (New York: Harper & Row Publishers, 1970), but more recent histories of the Caribbean and the Atlantic repeat the same model. See, for instance, James Ferguson, *A Traveller's History of the Caribbean* (Northampton: Interlink, 2008); Jan Rogozinski, *A Brief History of the Caribbean: From the Arawak and Carib to the Present* (New York: Plume, 2000), B. W. Higman, *A Concise History of the Caribbean* (New York: Cambridge University Press, 2011); Gad Heuman, *The Caribbean: A Brief History* (New York: Bloomsbury Academic, 2014). A welcome exception to this trend is Stephan Palmié and Francisco Scarano, eds. *The Caribbean: A History of the Region and Its Peoples* (Chicago: Chicago University Press, 2011). General books about the Atlantic word also tend to follow the same path. See, for instance, Douglas Egerton, Alison Games, et al., eds., *The Atlantic World, A History, 1400–1888* (Wheeling: Harlan Davidson, 2007); Jack P. Greene and Philip D. Morgan, eds., *Atlantic History, A Critical Appraisal* (New York: Oxford University Press, 2009); Thomas Benjamin, *The Atlantic World: Europeans, Africans, Indians, and Their Shared History, 1400–1900* (New York: Cambridge University Press, 2009). Ida Altman and

8   *Islanders and Empire*

Focusing more narrowly on the historiography of the Spanish colonial world, scholars interested in Hispaniola have spent most of their energies on the first fifty years of European colonization of the Americas. Known sometimes as the Caribbean phase of Spanish colonial expansion, this period has attracted the attention of academics interested in the origins of European colonization of the New World, as well as its earlier protagonists.[7] The European exploration and colonization of the Caribbean basin, the exploitation and enslavement of indigenous peoples, and the introduction of African enslaved men and women continue to be some of the most active areas of research of the early colonial period of the region.[8] In these studies, Hispaniola society (with Santo Domingo as its most important urban center) has featured prominently as the center of this expanding Spanish early colonial world in the Americas.

David Wheat have made a similar point recently about the reluctance of historians to see the sixteenth-century Caribbean beyond mere backdrop for the rise of other Western empires. Ida Altman and David Wheat, eds., *The Spanish Caribbean & the Atlantic World in the Long Sixteenth Century* (Lincoln: University of Nebraska Press, 2019), xvi.

[7] The historiography on Colón is vast. See, for instance, Consuelo Varela Bueno and Isabel Aguirre Landa, *La caída de Cristóbal Colón: el juicio de Bobadilla* (Madrid: Marcial Pons, 2013) and Troy S. Floyd, *The Columbus Dynasty in the Caribbean, 1492–1526* (Albuquerque: University of New Mexico Press, 1973); for early colonization, see Roberto Cassá, *Los taínos de la Española* (Santo Domingo: Editorial Caribe, 1974); Samuel Wilson, *Hispaniola: Caribbean Chiefdoms in the Age of Columbus* (Tuscaloosa: University of Alabama Press, 1990); Francisco Moscoso, *Caguas en la conquista española del siglo 16* (Puerto Rico: Gaviota, 2016); Esteban Mira Caballos, *El indio antillano: repartimientos, encomienda y esclavitud, 1492–1542* (Sevilla: Editorial Muñoz Moya, 1997); Esteban Mira Caballos, *Nicolás de Ovando y los orígenes del sistema colonial español, 1502–1509* (Santo Domingo: Patronato de la Ciudad Colonial de Santo Domingo, 2000); Ida Altman, "Marriage, Family, and Ethnicity in the Early Spanish Caribbean." *The William and Mary Quarterly*, vol. 70, n. 2 (2013): 225–50; Frank Moya Pons, *Después de Colón: Trabajo, sociedad y política en la economía del oro* (Madrid: Alianza, 1987).

[8] Apart from some of the examples and authors cited in previous note, see also Altman and Wheat, *The Spanish Caribbean*; Ida Altman. "The Revolt of Enriquillo and the Historiography of Early Spanish America." *The Americas*, vol. 63, n. 4 (2007): 587–614; Corinne Hofman et al., "Stage of Encounters: Migration, Mobility, and Interaction in the Pre-Colonial and Early Colonial Caribbean." *World Archaeology*, vol. 46 n. 4 (2014): 599–600; Fernando Santos-Granero, *Vital Enemies: Slavery, Predation, and the Amerindian Political Economy of Life* (Austin: University of Texas Press, 2009); Molly A. Warsh, *American Baroque, Pearls and the Nature of Empire, 1492–1700* (Chapel Hill: University of North Carolina Press, 2018); Erin Woodruff Stone, "America's First Slave Revolt: Indians and African Slaves in Española, 1500–1534." *Ethnohistory*, vol. 60, n. 2 (Spring 2013): 195–217; Erin Stone, "Slave Raiders Vs. Friars: Tierra Firme, 1513–1522." *The Americas*, vol. 74, no. 2 (2017): 139–70.

Introduction

Just as Madrid focused most of its energies and resources in the exploitation and development of their expanding mainland viceroyalties of Mexico and Peru, most historians seem to have abandoned the Spanish Caribbean for those new Spanish lands and their inhabitants. Santo Domingo, Hispaniola, and most of the first cities that were so important in the initial Spanish expansion through the Caribbean became marginalized in histories of the region. Starting in the late sixteenth century, Spanish Caribbean ports cities were described as a chain of poorly administered, supplied, and defended garrison towns besieged by corsairs and pirates.[9] This view is not necessarily erroneous, but its focus solely on Spanish imperial needs ignores the internal processes of these colonial societies, the lives of their inhabitants, and how, beyond their defensive needs, the peoples of these locales had an impact upon Spanish imperial plans in the hemisphere. Even Dominican and Spanish scholars seem to have taken this view of seventeenth century decline as a reason to sideline the study of this period. When forced to provide an analysis of Hispaniola society during this century, they merely join the chorus of voices that decry the poverty of the period with little insightful analysis of local society beyond these tropes.[10] This is evident in almost every collection of primary sources and general histories of the Dominican Republic that tries to tackle the seventeenth century, making them very limited in their ability to provide an extensive portrait of Hispaniola society during this period.[11]

Other scholars have focused on the history of Hispaniola in the eighteenth century, studying the configuration of island society, economy, the role of smuggling, the lives and struggles of African enslaved labor, its status as an imperial frontier with the French colony of Saint Domingue,

---

[9] For instance, Paul E. Hoffman, *The Spanish Crown and the Defense of the Caribbean, 1535–1585* (Baton Rouge: Louisiana University Press, 1980), or Bibiano Torres Ramírez, *La armada de Barlovento* (Sevilla: Escuela de Estudios Hispano-Americanos de Sevilla, 1981).

[10] One of the few exceptions to this rule is Juana Gil-Bermejo García, *La Española. Anotaciones históricas (1600–1650)*, (Sevilla: Escuela de Estudios Hispanoamericanos, 1983).

[11] Frank Moya Pons, *The Dominican Republic, a National History* (Princeton: Markus Wiener Publishers, 2010); Frank Moya Pons, coord., *Historia de la República Dominicana* (Madrid: Consejo Superior de Investigaciones Científicas, 2010); Eric Paul Roorda, Lauren Derby, and Raymundo González, eds., *The Dominican Republic Reader: History, Culture, Politics* (Durham: Duke University Press, 2014); Ernesto Sagás and Orlando Inoa, *The Dominican People, A Documentary History* (Princeton: Markus Wiener, 2003). Frank Moya Pons did write a colonial history of Santo Domingo, but he was limited to the sources available in the Dominican Republic at the time. Frank Moya Pons, *Historia Colonial De Santo Domingo* (Santiago: UCMM, 1976).

10 *Islanders and Empire*

and the consequences of the Haitian Revolution on the Spanish side of the island. The lack of attention to the seventeenth century has forced many of these historians to start their work *in media res*, without having an appropriate context cemented in the earlier period. Reading some of these works, Hispaniola seems to be an island without an immediate past and with only a remote and somewhat mythical memory of the sixteenth century. In this historiography, the division of the island into the Spanish and French colonies also appears as a fait accompli without process or change over time.[12]

SANTO DOMINGO: IMPERIAL PERIPHERY, IMPERIAL FRONTIER

The existing historiography of the Spanish Caribbean in the seventeenth century is scarce, with most of the existing work focusing on Havana and/or Cartagena. Both of those cities have been at the center of an extraordinary historiographical renaissance in recent years that reflect their status as central nodes of the Spanish monarchy.[13] That these recent

[12] Some classic works on Hispaniola during this period are Antonio Gutiérrez Escudero, *Población y Economía en Santo Domingo (1700–1746)* (Sevilla: Diputación Provincial, 1985); *Mª Rosario Sevilla Soler, Santo Domingo Tierra de Frontera (1750–1800)* (Sevilla: Escuela de Estudios Hispanoamericanos, 1980). See also Christine D. Rivas, "Power, Race, Class and Gender in Colonial Santo Domingo: An Analysis of Spanish Dominican Marital Patters in the Archbishopric of Santo Domingo, 1701–1801." (Ph.D. diss. Carleton University, 2008). Regarding the study of slavery and Afrodescendants in eighteenth-century Santo Domingo, the work of José Luis Belmonte Postigo is critical. See, for example, Jose Luis Belmonte Postigo, "Sobre esclavitud y otras formas de dominio. Gradaciones de libertad y estatus social en Santo Domingo a fines del periodo colonial," in José Antonio Piqueras e Imilcy Balboa Navarro, eds., *Gente de color entre esclavos* (Granada: Editorial Comares, 2019), 159–78; José Luis Belmonte Postigo, "Tratando de gobernar lo ingobernable. Leyes y proyectos esclavistas en Santo Domingo durante la centuria ilustrada," in Scarlett O'Phelan and Margarita Rodríguez, coord., *El ocaso del Antiguo Régimen en los imperios ibéricos* (Lima: Pontificia Universidad Católica del Perú, Fondo Editorial, 2017), 205–30; José Luis Belmonte Postigo, "Bajo el negro velo de la ilegalidad. Un análisis del mercado de esclavos dominicano, 1746–1821," *Nuevo Mundo Mundos Nuevos* (online publication, 2016). See also González, *De esclavos a campesinos.* For the ramifications of the Haitian Revolution in the Spanish colony, and especially in Afrodescendants and the institution of slavery, see Graham T. Nessler, *An Islandwide Struggle for Freedom: Revolution, Emancipation, and Reenslavement in Hispaniola, 1789–1809* (Chapel Hill: The University of North Carolina Press, 2016); José Luis Belmonte Postigo, "Esclavitud y status social en Santo Domingo y Puerto Rico durante la diáspora de la Revolución Haitiana," in Jonis Freire and María Verónica Secreto, eds. *Formas de Liberdade. Gratidâo, condicionalidade e incertezas no mundo escravista nas Americas* (Rio de Janeiro: Ed. Mauad, 2018), 71–102.

[13] See Pablo Gómez, *The Experiential Caribbean: Creating Knowledge and Healing in the Early Modern Atlantic* (Chapel Hill: University of North Carolina Press, 2017);

Introduction

works position Havana and Cartagena as colonial centers and Santo Domingo (among other Spanish port cities) as periphery is relevant here, because it raises the question: what does it mean to be a periphery? I follow here the definition provided by Amy Turner Bushnell, in which an early modern periphery or frontier is described as "a geographic area contested by two or more nations, each of which is engaged in a process of polity formation in which control is tenuous and continuously negotiated."[14] Some of these regions, like Havana in the late sixteenth century, became colonial centers over time, but this process of transformation from center to periphery was far from linear, and it was always subject to regression. However, Santo Domingo – both the capital city and the colony as a whole – represents a colonial space that transitioned from colonial center in the early stages of Spanish colonization to a borderland in the last decades of the sixteenth century and throughout the seventeenth century. This relative positioning of Santo Domingo within the Spanish monarchy was neither predetermined nor permanent. One of the aims of this book is to ascertain the impact of the island's actors had on Spanish colonial policies and their application on the ground.

From the perspective of the Spanish monarchy in the seventeenth century, Hispaniola and the rest of the Spanish Caribbean islands were territories to protect from falling into the hands of other European powers and little else. But being peripheral to Madrid's immediate imperial interests does not necessarily make a region or its peoples unimportant in

---

Guadalupe García, *Beyond the Walled City: Colonial Exclusions in Havana* (Oakland: University of California Press, 2016); Wheat, *Atlantic Africa*; Nicole von Germeten, *Violent Delights, Violent Ends: Sex, Race, & Honor in Colonial Cartagena de Indias* (Albuquerque: University of New Mexico Press, 2013); Kristen Block, *Ordinary Lives in the Early Caribbean: Religion, Colonial Competition, and the Politics of Profit* (Athens: University of Georgia Press, 2012); de la Fuente, *Havana and the Atlantic*; José Serrano Álvarez, *Ejército y fiscalidad en Cartagena de Indias. Auge y declive en la segunda mitad del siglo XVII* (Bogotá: El Ancora, 2006); Antonino Vidal Ortega, *Cartagena de Indias y la región histórica del Caribe, 1580–1640* (Sevilla: Consejo Superior de Investigaciones Científicas, 2002); Antonino Vidal Ortega, "Barcos, velas y mercancías del otros lado de mar. Cartagena de Indias a comienzos del siglo XVII" in *Colombia y el Caribe: XIII Congreso de Colombianistas* (Barranquilla: Universidad del Norte, 2003), 45–60.

[14] Amy Turner Bushnell and Jack P. Greene, "Gates, Patterns, and Peripheries: The Field of Frontier Latin America," in Christine Daniels and Michael V. Kennedy, eds., *Negotiated Empires: Centers and Peripheries in the Americas, 1500–1820* (London: Routledge, 2002), 18. Other useful and classic conceptualizations of the terms "center" and "periphery" can be found in David J. Weber, *The Spanish Frontier of North America* (New Haven: Yale University Press, 1992), 10–13; James Lockhart and Stuart B. Schwartz, *Early Latin America: A History of Colonial Spanish America and Brazil* (New York: Cambridge University Press, 1983).

understanding how the empire functioned as a whole. The lack of work on Spanish Caribbean peripheries like Hispaniola has led historians to replicate and amplify Spanish imperial voices and agendas, relegating these territories to almost complete marginality in historical narratives. Yet as John Jay TePaske has reminded us, peripheries were "integral parts of an organic whole."[15] In the Caribbean, peripheries were often defined not only by their remoteness from imperial regional centers. They were also imperial frontiers, contact zones with other imperial polities, and spaces of negotiation and conflict in which these societies at the edge of empire enjoyed a great degree of independence to determine the terms of such encounters.[16] This was certainly the case for Hispaniola. Apart from being a periphery in the last decades of the sixteenth century, by the mid-seventeenth century the island also became an imperial borderland, fighting off both pirates and French settlers in the island's western lands. In many ways, the power of individuals and societies in the periphery to define their place in the empire and that of their neighbors was as great as (or even greater than) individuals located in imperial centers, where colonial powers had a more solid footing. In colonial fringes like Hispaniola, Spanish authorities depended on the acquiescence of enslaved and free men and women, whose actions on the ground and pressure on colonial officials (as well as the latter's personal agendas) decisively influenced the implementation of the royal orders.[17] *Islanders and Empire* demonstrates that despite the weaknesses of Spanish rule in the outskirts of its empire, its nominal control remained extraordinarily stable because local people benefitted from the crown's weakness and used it to their own advantage.

It is also possible to conceptualize early Spanish-American places as both center and periphery at the same time, depending on what social, political, or economic aspect is being considered. In the case of Hispaniola, the city of Santo Domingo preserved certain characteristics

---

[15] John Jay TePaske, "Integral to Empire: The Vital Peripheries of Spanish America," in Daniels and Kennedy, eds., *Negotiated Empires*, 36.

[16] For an excellent summary of the history of the concept of frontiers and borderlands, see Fabricio Prado, "The Fringes of Empires: Recent Scholarship on Colonial Frontiers and Borderlands in Latin America." *History Compass*, vol. 10, n. 4 (2012): 318–33. The expression "imperial frontier" was first coined by Juan Bosh, *De Cristobal Colón a Fidel Castro: el Caribe, frontera imperial* (Madrid: Alfaguara, 1970).

[17] For an example of a recent work that highlights the importance of Caribbean peripheries in both interimperial and transimperial competition, see Casey Schmitt. "Centering Spanish Jamaica: Regional Competition, Informal Trade, and the English Invasion, 1620–62." *The William and Mary Quarterly*, vol. 76, no. 4 (2019): 697–726.

Introduction

that made it a relatively important administrative center within the Spanish imperial structure. Even though the size of the *Audiencia* of Santo Domingo's jurisdiction as a court of appeals shrunk during the sixteenth and seventeenth centuries, it still extended throughout the better part of the Spanish Caribbean islands and the coast of Venezuela. People from the district of the *Audiencia* made regular visits to the city to follow their legal appeals, hoping for a positive resolution of criminal and civil disputes. The governor of Santo Domingo also elected interim governors for the entire district of the *Audiencia*.[18] Powerful local groups were aware of the importance of the *Audiencia* and its influence across the Spanish Caribbean, and did everything in their power to influence royal officials, benefitting themselves and their allies in the process.

Despite their power as *oidores* (judges) of the *Audiencia* of Santo Domingo, these royal officials understood their post as peripheral. This *Audiencia* was the least prestigious of all the Spanish American high courts. In most cases, it was the first judicial post of these officials in the Americas, and most of them spent their time on the island writing letters to Madrid asking to be transferred, complaining about their poverty, health, and living conditions. Such complaints were part of a complex performance by subjects before the king, and therefore should be taken with a grain of salt. Yet there is little doubt that most royal officials could not wait to be on their way up to the next post in the American judicial bureaucracy, to *Audiencias* in places such as Quito or Guatemala. Historians have traditionally considered these high courts peripheral, but from the perspectives of these officials, they represented an enormous improvement in their careers and quality of life. It was precisely this sense of isolation, not to mention financial shortfalls, that drew royal officials to seek alliances with local residents. This reliance in turn allowed local groups to influence the *Audiencia* to such a degree that the court often defended local interests more ardently than those of the Spanish monarchy. This duality, as a Caribbean administrative and judicial center on the one hand and a colonial fringe on the other, is one of the central themes of this book. It reveals the complexities of colonial peripheries when analyzed in detail.

---

[18] As the seventeenth century wore on, Santo Domingo governors found increasing resistance from the residents in the district to accept their picks as interim governors, like Caracas in 1677. *Fiscal* Juan Garcés de los Fayos to the Council of the Indies, August 24, 1677. Archivo General de Indias (AGI), Santo Domingo (SD.) 63, R. 3, n. 36. Thanks to Marc Eagle for this reference.

Islanders and Empire

The tensions between Santo Domingo and the countryside in Hispaniola (between urban and rural life and between urban and rural slavery) also comprise important cornerstones in several chapters of this work. At the ground level, a center-periphery model can also be very useful to understand internal dynamics within Hispaniola, in particular the relationships between the residents of Santo Domingo and those who lived in the villages, farms, and ranches of the interior and the northern coasts. From a commercial and economic perspective, Santo Domingo was only marginally connected to Spanish commercial networks. Only a few merchants maintained businesses in Santo Domingo during the seventeenth century, and they did so, despite the risks, because they knew they had a pool of captive customers from whom they could extract high prices. It was precisely this price gouging, coupled with the limited availability of cargo space to export local produce, that drove inhabitants in the interior of the island to supply themselves with clothes and enslaved laborers through the practice of contraband trade.

During the late sixteenth century, the towns and villages in the northern and western coasts of Hispaniola such as Bayahá and La Yaguana defied Santo Domingo's economic and political primacy and developed their own smuggling networks that often connected them with northern European markets. Throughout the seventeenth century, there is some evidence of Hispaniola's inhabitants commanding their own small vessels across the Caribbean, to buy and sell in defiance of Spanish monopolistic practices. In the second half of the century, with Santo Domingo controlling most of the smuggling operations on the island for more than seventy years, the presence of French settlers in western Hispaniola allowed the inhabitants of the interior to create new contraband networks with their neighbors. This was a direct challenge to the local and ruling elites of the capital, and also an example of the potential growth that some sectors of the interior and northern coast would experience during the eighteenth century as the commercial relationship with their French neighbors grew.

SMUGGLING, ILLICIT PRACTICES, AND CORRUPTION

This work argues that the seventeenth-century Caribbean world created a blueprint for transimperial dealings and contacts, a sociopolitical *praxis* for Spanish Caribbean subjects to interact with royal officials and institutions, and a set of expectations about their ability to operate away from colonial oversight. These sets of habits were in part those that the eighteenth-century Bourbon state would try to reject, with mixed results,

Introduction 15

as it attempted to reclaim lost control over its colonial subjects.[19] And yet, the role of smuggling in the socioeconomic construction of the seventeenth-century Spanish Caribbean islands remains a mystery, even as it was a time of profound negotiations and competition between the Spanish, French, English, and Dutch for land and economic primacy. Spanish Caribbean colonial subjects in the region were forced to grapple with the increased presence of northern European traders and settlers in the region, and they found ways to benefit from the increasing uncertainty in their world.

The study of Caribbean smuggling has received some attention over the years, although relatively little considering the importance of the practice in the entire region across space and time. Most of these studies have focused on New Granada and the southern Caribbean from the aftermath of the War of Spanish Succession (1701–14) to the Age of Revolutions, with specialists from Colombia and Venezuela leading the way, followed by scholars in the United States in recent decades.[20] Other regions of Spanish America, such as the Rio de la Plata, have a long tradition of studies centered around smuggling and, with some exceptions, the eighteenth century, which have received a continued interest from specialists.[21]

---

[19] Jesse Cromwell also makes this point clear. Cromwell, *The Smugglers' World*, 33–59.

[20] Some renowned examples in this trend are Celestino Andrés Araúz Monfantes, *El contrabando holandés en el Caribe durante la primera mitad del siglo XVIII*, 2 vols. (Caracas: Academia Nacional de la Historia, 1984); Ramón Aizpurua, *Curazao y la costa de Caracas: introducción al estudio del contrabando de la provincia de Venezuela en tiempos de la Compañia Guipuzcoana, 1730–1780* (Caracas: Academia Nacional de Historia, 1993). More recently, some important works worth highlighting are Wim Klooster, *Illicit Riches: Dutch Trade in the Caribbean, 1648–1795* (Leiden: KITLV Press, 1998); Linda M. Rupert, *Creolization and Contraband: Curaçao in the Early Modern Atlantic World* (Athens: University of Georgia Press, 2012); Cromwell, *The Smugglers' World*; Jesse Cromwell, "Illicit Ideologies: Moral Economies of Venezuelan Smuggling and Autonomy in the Rebellion of Juan Francisco De León, 1749–1751." *The Americas*, vol. 74, n. 3 (2017): 267–97; Casey S. Schmitt, "Virtue in Corruption: Privateers, Smugglers, and the Shape of Empire in the Eighteenth-Century Caribbean." *Early American Studies, An Interdisciplinary Journal*, vol. 13, n. 1 (2015): 80–110; Ernesto Bassi, *An Aqueous Territory: Sailor Geographies and New Granada's Transimperial Greater Caribbean World* (Durham: Duke University Press, 2016).

[21] See for example Sergio R. Villalobos, *Comercio y contrabando en el Río de la Plata y Chile: 1700–1811* (Buenos Aires: Editorial Universitaria de Buenos Aires, 1965); Zacarías Moutoukias, *Contrabando y control colonial en el siglo XVII: Buenos Aires, el Atlántico, y el espacio peruano* (Buenos Aires: Centro Editor de América Latina, 1988); Fabricio Prado, *Edge of Empire: Atlantic Networks and Revolution in Bourbon Rio de la Plata* (Oakland: University of California Press, 2015); Tyson Reeder, *Smugglers, Pirates, and Patriots: Free Trade in the Age of Revolution* (University of Pennsylvania Press, 2019).

16 *Islanders and Empire*

The most recent works in these two regions emphasize what some authors have described as the rise of a "transimperial" or intimately intertwined world, in which the circulation of information, people (including African captives), ideas, and at the center of it all, illicit commercial exchanges played a crucial role in reshaping the Atlantic throughout the eighteenth century.[22] The relative abundance and accessibility of eighteenth-century sources, compared with earlier periods, as well as a renaissance in studies focused on the Age of Revolutions in recent years, might explain this renewed interest in the eighteenth century. In many ways, however, the Caribbean during the seventeenth century was no less entangled and transimperial than the eighteenth century, but it has barely been studied.[23]

Islanders and Empire situates extralegal trade at the center of the formation of the Hispaniola human landscape during this crucial period of reinvention of the island's economy and society. A close look at this colony provides ample evidence of the ways Spanish subjects interacted with their regional counterparts within and beyond Spanish imperial borders. Smuggling and the relationship that local smugglers formed with royal officials and foreigners defined early modern Atlantic empires. It established the personal connections that bound together interimperial and transimperial relationships, thus linking these competing empires. Just as the scholars of the Rio de la Plata and the southern Caribbean have identified the rise of these regions as transimperial centers for the eighteenth century, this book argues that those already existed in the seventeenth century, with Hispaniola being one of the earliest ones in the Caribbean.

[22] See Bassi, *An Aqueous Territory*; Prado, *Edge of Empire*; Adrian Finucane, *Temptations of Trade: Britain, Spain, and the Struggle for Empire* (Philadelphia: University of Pennsylvania Press, 2016); Elena A. Schneider, *The Occupation of Havana: War, Trade, and Slavery in the Atlantic World* (Williamsburg: Omohundro Institute of Early American History and Culture; Chapel Hill: University of North Carolina Press, 2018); Gregory E. O'Malley, *Final Passages: the Intercolonial Slave Trade of British America, 1619–1807* (Williamsburg: Omohundro Institute of Early American History and Culture; Chapel Hill: University of North Carolina Press, 2014); Shannon Lee Dawdy, *Building the Devil's Empire: French Colonial New Orleans* (Chicago: University of Chicago Press, 2008); Michael J. Jarvis, *In the Eye of All Trade: Bermuda, Bermudians, and the Maritime Atlantic World, 1680–1783* (Williamsburg: Omohundro Institute of Early American History and Culture; Chapel Hill: University of North Carolina Press, 2010).

[23] For a few examples that already expose the transimperial nature of the Caribbean world and its peoples before the eighteenth century, see Block, *Ordinary Lives*; Jorge Cañizares-Esguerra, ed., *Entangled Empires, The Anglo-Iberian Atlantic, 1500–1830* (Philadelphia: University of Pennsylvania, 2018); Schmitt, "Centering Spanish Jamaica."

Introduction 17

Smuggling was, from the Spanish crown's point of view, an illicit practice, and it is closely associated in the historiography with the mechanics of corruption. It not only involved local residents, but also royal officials. The latter benefitted directly or indirectly from these practices either by facilitating illicit exchanges, looking away when they happened, or mediating to free those captured while engaged in contraband trade. These were all extralegal practices, but could they be considered corruption? The answer to this question is thornier than it might seem. Scholars have moved from seeing corruption permeating every fissure of the Spanish monarchy in the seventeenth century to a middle ground in which they acknowledge that corruption existed more generally during the early modern period. More recent scholarship also sometimes avoids the term because of its loaded modern associations, preferring the contemporary phrase *mal gobierno*. Others have resorted to new terms to refer to corruption, such as "malfeasance."[24] Even though the literature on corruption is vast, coming up with a definition or even a list of practices that can be considered "corrupt" in the early modern Spanish Atlantic has proven very difficult. At times, the idea of corruption fits awkwardly within patrimonial societies in which the relationship of early modern state officials with each other and their immediate community was shaped by personal ties, and not by institutional ones. Although from the perspective of the Spanish monarchy's interests, smuggling was undoubtedly illicit, it is harder to pin such an adjective on some of the client relationships that formed around the practice of contraband trade.

Officers in Madrid viewed practices such as bribery, gambling, falsification of documents, offerings of gifts and lodging, influence-peddling, abuses of power, or extortion as objectionable. But in Hispaniola, many of the worst offenders in all these categories escaped castigation, even when accused by specially appointed judges, or when those cases were appealed to the Council of the Indies and reviewed by those closest to the monarch. In other parts of the empire, however, such acts were prosecuted, and the culprits paid for their infractions. What accounted for the disparity of outcomes for the same crime? First, even though many men

---

[24] For two recent summaries of the state of the field, see Christoph Rosenmüller, ed., *Corruption in the Iberian Empires: Greed, Custom, and Colonial Networks* (Albuquerque: University of New Mexico Press, 2017); Francisco Andújar Castillo and Pilar Ponce Leiva, eds., *Debates sobre la corrupción en el mundo ibérico, siglos XVI-XVIII* (Alicante: Biblioteca Virtual Miguel de Cervantes, 2018). The term "malfeasance" is used by Marc Eagle in "Portraits of a Bad Officials: Malfeasance in Visita Sentences from Seventeenth-Century Santo Domingo," in Rosenmüller, ed. *Corruption*.

18 *Islanders and Empire*

who became *oidores* had legal training, in most cases the judge's educational background (or lack thereof) was only one among many other factors in taking up this post: others were family connections, wealth, or previous services to the crown. Second, the idea of justice was far from universal. As Bianca Premo has shown, before the eighteenth century, magistrates tended to choose laws that applied to a specific situation and gave each side "its rightful due," that is, according to the time, place, social context, the *calidad* of the parties, etc.[25]

When thinking about smuggling at the ground level in colonial peripheries like Hispaniola, ideas about corruption varied case by case, as did the application of the law itself depending on the social, personal, and moral standing of the parties as perceived by the judges. Illicit behavior was something social actors ascribed either to those socially (and often racially) inferior or to social/political rivals, and they used the crown's legal expectations for their own political ends. Smugglers, however, did not believe that their practice of contraband was illegitimate. At times they defied the crown's authority violently; more often, they simply ignored its mandates. From the point of view of colonial officials engulfed in these accusations of misconduct, they understood that the support of a powerful cadre of local residents who tolerated and encouraged such illicit behavior was more important than a rigid understanding of the law. Communities and institutions were not separate entities. Locals and bureaucrats formed "bundles of relationships" in which power dynamics were "intermittent, incomplete, and complicated by many conflicting obligations and loyalties."[26] With local support, crown officials could count on friendly witnesses who would testify to their good performance, thus opening the doors to career promotions. Those who accused crown officials of illicit behavior could be easily dismissed as enemies in any legal proceeding. Locals used accusations of corruption as a way to seek revenge against rivals, colonial officials who had wronged them, or as a threat to keep these bureaucrats under control. The study of Hispaniola in the seventeenth century serves as an example of how the perpetuation of corruption, malfeasance, or illicit behavior did not happen as the result of

---

[25] Tamar Herzog, *La administración como un fenómeno social: la justicia penal de la ciudad de Quito, 1650–1750* (Madrid: Centro de Estudios Políticos y Constitucionales, 1995), 51–54, 133–34; Bianca Premo, *The Enlightenment on Trial: Ordinary Litigants and Colonialism in the Spanish Empire* (New York: Oxford University Press, 2017), 65.

[26] William B. Taylor, "Between Global Process and Local Knowledge: An Inquiry into Early Latin American Social History, 1500–1900," in Olivier Zunz, ed., *Reliving the Past: The Worlds of Social History* (Chapel Hill: University of North Carolina Press, 1985), 145.

Introduction 19

individuals' desire for wealth and privileges, but it was in fact an insepar-
able aspect of the ways patrimonial societies blurred the lines separating
personal and institutional relations, which was, to paraphrase Alejandro
Cañeque, the very essence of political power.[27]

METHODOLOGY AND SOURCES

In this age of great sweeping trans-Atlantic and circum-Atlantic history
works, this book is decisively, and may I say, unapologetically, cis-
Atlantic in its approach.[28] My main goal is to highlight the social and
political realities that people in Hispaniola helped to shape within their
own immediate surroundings, as well as in the Caribbean and the Atlantic
world, whenever possible. While my historical lens is close to the ground
for most of this book, only at very specific times would I label this book's
method microhistorical. My attempt here is to conduct a sociopolitical
study through a deep analysis of available sources to provide an understanding of local dynamics that other Atlantic historical approaches
would tend to disregard in favor of Hispaniola's transnational connections. These transnational links are obviously there, and I address them
whenever possible. As important as those links are, however, I am much
more interested in centering Hispaniola within an international commercial web. I analyze how this international context defined the local community, how local changes reverberated regionally within the Spanish
empire, and finally, how the local had an impact at the Atlantic level, in
that order. Following William Taylor's warning, I have tried to focus on
a community and locale without losing sight of the systems they inhabit.[29]

The fragmentary nature of early modern Caribbean sources also presents unique challenges for historians, but their use is far from impossible.
When I was first considering a project about the Spanish Caribbean, an
eminent professor in the field of colonial Latin American history told me
that I should consider a different topic because the weather had likely
destroyed most of the Caribbean documents I would need to use. This is
a typical warning offered by academics who specialize in densely populated or urban areas in the mainland of Latin America, and I can only

[27] Alejandro Cañeque, *The King's Living Image: The Culture and Politics of Viceregal
Power in Colonial Mexico* (New York: Routledge, 2004), 13.
[28] David Armitage, "Three Concepts of Atlantic History," in David Armitage and Michael
J. Braddick, eds., *The British Atlantic World, 1500–1800* (New York: Palgrave
McMillan, 2002), 11–27.
[29] Taylor, "Between Global Process and Local Knowledge," 120.

imagine how many scholars have been steered away from the Spanish Caribbean toward what some believe to be more lush historical pastures. Even though it is now clear to me that this advice was terribly misguided, it did contain a certain element of truth. Researching Hispaniola's colonial history, when compared with other Latin American regions, does present serious challenges. Unlike other places in the mainland, where *Cabildo* and *Audiencia* records dating back to the sixteenth century have been preserved, records of Hispaniola have not been so durable. *Cabildo* records are nonexistent on the island for the seventeenth century, even for Santo Domingo. All of the documentation of the *Audiencia* during the entire colonial period has been lost, as well as all notarial records. Most of the evidence in this book is drawn from documents available in the *Archivo General de Indias* in Sevilla (Spain), where much still remains to be uncovered. My main sources are the correspondence of *oidores*, governors, archbishops, clergymen, soldiers, and local people written to the Council of the Indies in Spain, as well as *Audiencia* court cases appealed to the Council, *juicios de residencia*, *visitas* and royal decrees sent to the island and saved in Spain in draft form. Research at the *Archivo General de Simancas* (Spain) and the John Carter Brown Library in Providence (Rhode Island) complemented some of my earlier finds.

These sources present numerous challenges to constructing an adequate portrait of local society. In the case of the correspondence of people in Santo Domingo with the Council of the Indies, the authors of these sources performed the role of the faithful servant who looked out for crown interests above all and therefore expected a reward appropriate for their social rank and service. Actively lying and distorting their reports to fit this overall narrative was not beyond the pale for many of these historical actors, and without other local sources to contrast the information, the historian is often left with contradictory accounts. Crown officials and local residents alike were depicted as saviors and villains in parallel accounts of the same events. *Juicios de residencias* and *visitas* are far from objective assessments of a crown official's performance either. To deal with these challenges, I analyze them as reflections of the social networks that these officials had managed to form during their tenure of the island. They reveal much of the underlying tensions within Hispaniola's social fabric and say very little about the officials' merits. In order to untangle these webs of deception, whenever possible, I have tried to uncover the local context to understand the motivations and personal relationships embedded in these accounts. Whenever this local context proved elusive, I have tried to be as transparent as possible about my own doubts regarding the sources.

Islanders and Empire recenters our conversation about what it meant to be a subject of the Spanish monarchy around the men and women who lived in Caribbean towns and fields. Royal agents regularly regarded Hispaniolans as frontier people who inhabited a remote borderland at the edge of the empire. Hispaniola residents used the benign neglect of imperial officials to their advantage: they established mutually beneficial, yet extralegal, commercial relationships with enemies of the crown, which led them to restructure their own colonial society in the process. At the same time, they also took control of the royal institutions designed to govern them, thus redefining the significance and reach of their colonial pact with Madrid and reshaping Spain's ability to influence events in the Caribbean.

I

Colonial Origins: Hispaniola in the Sixteenth Century

Witnessing a few sails on the horizon approaching the port of Santo Domingo on January 10, 1586, inhabitants of the island would not have imagined that they were about to be attacked by the English privateer Sir Francis Drake. On the day the sails appeared, the governor of Santo Domingo placed the city on high alert nonetheless, and the soldiers in the fortress kept their eyes on the vessels still cruising at a prudent distance from the Spanish cannons. The fortress was well protected with artillery, but the powder was of very low quality, a fact the governor hoped to conceal by ordering his men not to open fire unless it was absolutely necessary. The city's defenders even went so far as to sink some smaller Spanish vessels in the mouth of the port to prevent the enemy ships' entry. A damaged galley repurposed with artillery was placed in the river blocking any incoming ships. The city breathed a sigh of relief knowing that the port was well secured. Its residents knew that the cliffs along the coast around Santo Domingo would prevent any land invasion, with the exception of a small cove near the city, called Guibia, which was also guarded throughout the day and night.[1]

Francis Drake's expedition had left England in 1585 with the purpose of attacking Spanish possessions in the Caribbean. Unbeknownst to the Spaniards in Santo Domingo, Drake had at his disposal not seventeen, but twenty-five ships and approximately 2,300

---

[1] "The *Audiencia* of Santo Domingo to the Council of the Indies, February 24, 1586," in J. Marino Incháustegui, ed., *Reales Cédulas y Correspondencia de Gobernadores de Santo Domingo. De la Regencia del Cardenal Cisneros en adelante*, vol. III (Madrid, 1958), 679–80.

Colonial Origins: Hispaniola in the Sixteenth Century 23

men. Drake had chosen Santo Domingo as his first target of the expedition because of "the glorious fame of the Citie of S. Domingo, being the ancientest and chief inhabited place in all that tract of country thereabouts."[2] This fantasy that Drake and his captains shared – of Santo Domingo as a prosperous Caribbean city – differed markedly from the impressions of the sailors of a small frigate also bound for the city that the English captured on their way to Santo Domingo. That vessel's pilot warned the English that their desired target was actually "a barren haven."[3] The English disregarded such warnings, and the pilot of the frigate guided Drake and his men to a safe landing spot further down the coast. While seventeen ships headed straight to Santo Domingo with the aim of attracting attention, the remaining ships sailed to the mouth of the River Haina, a few miles west of Santo Domingo, where a force of around 1,400 men landed and began their march into the city in the early hours of January 11, 1586 (see Figure 1.1).

The city's defenders had spent the night expecting a naval attack, so by noon they were shocked to hear that a party of heavily armed men was rapidly advancing toward the western part of the city – an area that lacked walls and was completely unprotected. Panic spread among the residents. Many quickly gave up any attempt to defend the city and started scattering through its streets, gathering their most prized possessions, and escaping toward the countryside, following the path that the city's women and children had taken only hours before. Despite the exodus, the authorities were able to gather nearly 200 men willing to try to repel the attackers. Forty horsemen charged against the invading force, with musketeers riding in the rear, but they were turned back by the firepower of the highly organized English forces. The remaining Spaniards were soon overwhelmed by the English fire, both from the infantry and the artillery of the ships, leaving them little option but to turn and run, allowing the English to enter the city unopposed.

By the time Drake and his men left the ransacked and burned city, the last vestiges of Santo Domingo's prosperity had completely disappeared.

---

[2] Walter Bigges, *A summarie and true discourse of Sir Francis Drakes West-Indian voyage. Accompanied with Christopher Carleill, Martin Frobusher, Francis Knollis, with many other captains and gentlemen. Wherein were taken, the townes of Saint Jago, Sancto Domingo, Cartagena and Saint Augustine* (London: Roger Ward, printer, 1589), 25–33.

[3] Ibid.

FIGURE 1.1 Francis Drake's attack on Santo Domingo, in Baptista Boazio, *Map and views illustrating Sir Francis Drake's West Indian voyage, 1585–6*. [London?: s.n., 1585]. Library of Congress, Rare Book and Special Collections Division.

Despite the attempts of colonial officials to maintain the city as the social, political, and economic center of the island, Drake's sacking accelerated an economic decline that had begun decades earlier. As later testimonies made clear, the city that Drake encountered was far from the wealthy and prosperous capital that he had expected. Indeed, the bounty he collected was a disappointment due in part to the social, political, and economic transformations that had taken place throughout the sixteenth century. In this chapter, I aim to offer a brief overview of the multiple transformations that the island went through with the rise and fall of the colonial economy, as it cycled through gold and then sugar, all the while exploiting indigenous and African labor. Ginger cultivation and cattle ranching followed as the most important economic activities the century's final two decades. By then, Francis Drake's dreams of sacking the prosperous and historic Santo Domingo belied a far more complex reality, evoking the city's and island's past but not its current state.

Colonial Origins: Hispaniola in the Sixteenth Century 25

COLÓN, GOLD, AND INDIAN EXPLOITATION

From the very beginning of the European presence in the New World, Hispaniola became the epicenter of the efforts to consolidate and expand Spanish control over the entire region. Cristóbal Colón made Hispaniola the regional center of his explorations and the destination for the colonists he brought with him on his second voyage, in 1494. Hispaniola's most important native group was the Arawak-speaking Taínos, who were "among the most densely settled prestate sedentary societies of the New World."[4] They were organized in a complex hierarchical structure with centralized power in the hands of a male or female *cacique* and assisted by the *niTaíno* or elite groups, over a relatively large non-elite population. At the time of Colón's initial arrival in 1492, there were five Taíno *cacicazgos,* or chiefdoms, in Hispaniola, each of them led by a powerful *cacique.*

Soon after their arrival, Colón and his men discovered gold deposits across Hispaniola. Any friendly relations Colón was able to inspire in his early interactions with the Taíno communities in the northern part of the island soon turned into open hostility as Castilians abused the native population in search of food, labor, and gold. Colón unleashed his men on the island in an effort to control Taíno communities, while imposing onerous labor and crippling taxes as well as enslaving a good number of natives to sell in the Iberian Peninsula. During Colón's governorship (1492–1500), at least 2,000 Hispaniola natives were sold in Europe as

---

[4] William H. Hodges, Kathleen Deagan, and Elizabeth J. Reitz, "The Natural and Cultural Settings of Puerto Real," in Kathleen Deagan, ed., *Puerto Real: The Archaeology of a Sixteenth-Century Spanish Town in Hispaniola* (Gainesville: University Press of Florida, 1995), 65. The size of the native population before Colón has produced one of the most heated debates in Hispaniola historiography, with numbers that have oscillated wildly from a very conservative estimate of 100,000 people to several millions. The truth may well be somewhere in the middle, with a population between 400,000 and less than a million. For a discussion of Native American demography, see, for instance, Karen Frances Anderson-Córdova, *Surviving Spanish Conquest: Indian Fight, Flight, and Cultural Transformations in Hispaniola and Puerto Rico* (Tuscaloosa: The University of Alabama Press, 2017), 78–86; Samuel M. Wilson, *Hispaniola: Caribbean Chiefdoms in the Age of Columbus* (University of Alabama Press, 1990), 91–92; Frank Moya Pons, "La población taína y su desaparición," en Frank Moya Pons, ed., *Historia de la República Dominicana* (Madrid: Consejo Superior de Investigaciones Científicas, 2010), 19; Massimo Livi-Bacci, "Return to Hispaniola: Reassessing a Demographic Catastrophe." *The Hispanic American Historical Review,* vol. 83, n. 1 (2003): 3–51; Frank Moya Pons, *Después de Colón. Trabajo, sociedad y política en la economía del oro* (Madrid: Alianza Editorial 1987), 181–89; Noble David Cook, "Disease and the Depopulation of Hispaniola, 1492–1518." *Colonial Latin American Review,* vol. 2, n. 12 (1993): 213–45.

26 *Islanders and Empire*

slaves.[5] War, slavery, forced labor, disease, and famine led to the spiraling decline of the Taíno population starting during these years. These destructive forces remained unabated into the early decades of the sixteenth century. Meanwhile, Colón's desire to keep a tight control over indigenous labor and resources created internal division among the Castilian colonists, and a group of them rebelled against his authority. The admiral's unpopularity, as well as the desire of the crown to secure the resources of these new territories, led to Colón's removal from power and his arrest. He was taken to the Iberian Peninsula in irons.[6]

In the years following Colón's departure, the Castilian crown consolidated its control over the island during the governorship of Nicolás de Ovando (1501–9), while trying to maintain and increase its gold production. The Castilians declared open war against the last remaining pockets of Taíno resistance, who were considered rebels against royal authority, sold as slaves, and thus deprived of the limited rights they might have been entitled to as free (but forced) laborers in the new colonial world. As part of the Castilian settlement project in Hispaniola, Ovando established Castilian villages near every gold deposit, which were also areas of possible conflict with the native inhabitants.

A Royal Decree of December 20, 1503, granted the freedom of the Taínos as royal vassals, which now made them responsible for paying tribute. At the same time, however, it explicitly accepted the policy of forcing indigenous people to work for the colonists, thus sanctioning what had become a common practice on the island from the earliest years of the settlement. The creation of the *encomienda* system shaped this mountain of contradictions into an institutional framework in which natives were forced to pay taxes to the crown. They also worked for part of the year for their *encomenderos*, who were entrusted with their evangelization, but in practice, treated them as slaves. Despite any Christian piety inherent in Queen Isabel's edicts to protect and evangelize her new vassals, the realities of colonization for both the crown and the Spanish colonists demanded the island's inhabitants labor for the benefit of the Castilians.

Ovando used the distribution of indigenous labor to strengthen his political authority and reward his closest collaborators, creating a new elite class on the island. Some of them led expeditions of conquest into

---

[5] Juan Gil and Consuelo Varela, "La Conquista y la implantación de los españoles," in *Historia general del pueblo dominicano*, tomo I, Genaro Rodríguez Morel, coord. (Santo Domingo: Academia Dominicana de la Historia, 2013), 272.

[6] Moya Pons, *Después de Colón*, 22–27.

Colonial Origins: Hispaniola in the Sixteenth Century   27

other territories of the Caribbean. Conquistadors like Diego Velázquez, the future governor of Cuba, and Juan Ponce de León, the future governor of Puerto Rico, became wealthy *encomenderos* under Ovando. Many others stayed on the island, building sumptuous stone houses in Santo Domingo with their families ruling local life for generations.[7] For these colonists to become wealthy, many other Castilians had to be deprived of their native workers. With little to tie them to the land, some colonists may have considered seeking their fortune elsewhere in the Americas. In 1508, an expedition leaving for Tierra Firme recruited at least 600 men from the island. This expedition started the cycle of exploration and conquest of other Caribbean islands and circum-Caribbean territories, placing Hispaniola at the center of the Spanish expansion in the region. This also possibly contributed to the redirecting of impoverished and disaffected colonists to other parts of the Americas and to the consolidation of power on the island into the hands of a small number of families. The expeditions created a steady business for local residents, who supplied many of the voyages that either originated from the island or stopped in Santo Domingo to stock themselves with supplies and horses. Expeditions like the one manned by Pánfilo Narvaez to the western coast of Florida and the Gulf Coast of Mexico in 1527 stopped on their way from Spain in Santo Domingo for more than a month to supply themselves with horses and other necessary provisions. While in Santo Domingo, lured by promises of economic opportunities, 140 of his men (over a third of all of Narvaez's men) decided to stay in Hispaniola. Almost twenty years after the expedition to Tierra Firme, the sharp decline of Spanish colonists in Hispaniola and the abandonment of many of Governor Ovando's original settlements were now driving locals to entice visitors to stay at all cost.[8]

Meanwhile, the pressure on indigenous workers only increased as they died of famine, exhaustion, or malnourishment. *Encomenderos* pushed natives to work harder and longer in the gold mines to produce the same results. They also coerced *caciques* to extract more work and tribute from their communities, thus becoming unwilling enforcers of colonial rule. By 1508, there were approximately 60,000 natives left on the island, an

---

[7] Ibid., 41–48; Esteban Mira Caballos, "La consolidación de la colonia," in *Historia general del pueblo dominicano*, vol. I, Genaro Rodríguez Morel, coord. (Santo Domingo: Academia Dominicana de la Historia, 2013), 325, 330.

[8] Genaro Rodríguez Morel, *Orígenes de la economía de plantación de La Española* (Santo Domingo: Editora Nacional, 2012), 44; Álvar Nuñez Cabeza de Vaca, *The Narrative of Cabeza de Vaca*, edited, translated, and with introduction by Rolena Adorno and Patrick Charles Pautz (Lincoln: University of Nebraska Press, 2003), 48.

28   *Islanders and Empire*

astounding fall, even from a conservative lower estimate of 400,000 for 1492. In order to increase the number of forced workers, colonists requested permission to organize expeditions to raid and capture the indigenous populations of neighboring islands. Some colonists, like the ones in the prosperous towns of Concepción, Santiago, and Santo Domingo, joined their capital and formed companies to raid nearby islands such as Cuba and the Bahamas.[9] For a few years, from 1508 to 1511, the availability of native workers increased dramatically, with 26,000 Lucayos brought to Hispaniola in 1510 alone. Prices for enslaved workers remained relatively low, which allowed for the continued exploitation of the mineral deposits with the use of this new captive force.[10]

Unsurprisingly, such an abundance of workers did little to improve labor conditions, and the native population continued to die in dramatic numbers, with less than 27,000 natives left in 1514. Many perished from European diseases, malnutrition, and brutal work conditions. Exploitation also took many subtle forms, and it hid behind what might have appeared as mutually beneficial relations between Taínos and Spaniards. Spanish wills from 1510s to 1530s show native women and their children often as the main beneficiaries after the death of Spanish *encomenderos*. Spanish-Taíno formal marriages were encouraged by the crown from 1501, and some Spaniards did marry Taíno women, especially the daughters of *caciques*, thus gaining access to workers that the *caciques* had the power to mobilize. Sexual abuse by Spanish colonizers abounded amidst such skewed power dynamics, but stable (although rarely Church-sanctioned) unions that produced children were also common. Out of the spoils of war, and the violence, inequality, and contradictions of Hispaniola colonial society, Spanish and Taíno people managed to form mixed families. As Jane Mangan has pointed out for the Andes, Spaniards could be conquistadors as well as caring fathers of both their legitimate and illegitimate children. Indigenous women were at the same time victims of the colonial system and committed mothers.[11] As the native societies of the

---

[9] Moya Pons, *Después de Colón*, 50–51.

[10] Erin Woodruff Stone, "America's First Slave Revolt: Indians and African Slaves in Española, 1500–1534." *Ethnohistory*, vol. 60, n. 2 (2013): 201; Erin Stone, "War and Rescate: The Sixteenth-Century Circum-Caribbean Indigenous Slave Trade," in Ida Altman and David Wheat, eds., *The Spanish Caribbean & the Atlantic World in the Long Sixteenth Century* (Lincoln: University of Nebraska Press, 2019), 48–50. Thanks to Dr. Stone for sharing her scholarship with me. See also, Carlos Esteban Deive, *La Española y la esclavitud del indio* (Santo Domingo: Fundación García Arévalo, 1995), 89–108.

[11] Lynne Guitar, "Willing It So: Intimate Glimpses of Encomienda Life in Sixteenth Century Hispaniola." *Colonial Latin American Historical Review*, vol. 7, n. 3 (1998): 244–63;

Colonial Origins: Hispaniola in the Sixteenth Century   29

island disappeared, many children of these unions, who early on might have been labeled as *mestizos*, came to be considered Spaniards, thus erasing their mixed origin from the archival record.[12]

The exploitation and calamitous decrease of the native population of the island, despite the repeated raids on neighboring islands, became an increasing source of concern for a handful of university-educated friars of the Dominican order headed by friar Pedro de Córdoba, who arrived on the island in 1510. Their strict discipline, devotion to study, prayer, poverty vows, and emphasis on penance placed them in clear contrast with other religious orders like the Franciscans, who had focused exclusively on mass conversion early on, and later limited themselves to the instruction of native elites and Spanish colonizers. The Franciscan approach enabled members of the order to benefit from their proximity to the island's colonial powers. Dominican friars clashed with a society thoroughly focused on reaping earthly rewards and the extraction of wealth. On December 21, 1511, Dominican friar Antonio de Montesinos delivered the first of two provocative sermons denouncing the excesses of the Spanish exploitation of native peoples, warning the Spaniards that, by their actions against the innocent natives, they had placed themselves in mortal sin. Most *encomenderos*, however, were outraged and unmoved by the friar's discourse and pressured him to leave the island. Montesinos (accompanied by young friar Bartolomé de las Casas) and Córdoba did so in the following years to lobby for native rights in the Spanish royal court.[13]

The death of King Fernando in 1516 and the rise of Archbishop of Toledo Cardinal Francisco Jiménez de Cisneros as crown regent brought important changes to the leadership in Hispaniola. Cisneros welcomed the defense of native rights that the Dominicans had been championing, but knew that naming the Dominican friars to lead those reforms in

---

Jane E. Mangan, *Transatlantic Obligations, Creating the Bonds of Family in Conquest-Era Peru and Spain* (New York: Oxford University Press, 2016); the last sentence is paraphrased from Mangan, 5. See also, Ida Altman, "Marriage, Family, and Ethnicity in the Early Spanish Caribbean." *The William and Mary Quarterly*, vol. 70, n. 2 (2013): 225–50.

[12] For more on racial categories in the early Caribbean, see Stuart B. Schwartz, "Spaniards, 'Pardos,' and the Missing Mestizos: Identities and Racial Categories in the Early Hispanic Caribbean." *New West Indian Guide/Nieuwe West-Indische Gids*, vol. 71, n. 1–2 (1997): 5–19. Thanks to Dr. Schwartz for providing the reference and a copy of his work.

[13] Lauren Elaine MacDonald, "The Hieronymites in Hispaniola, 1493–1519" (MA thesis, University of Florida, 2010), 50–59.

30   *Islanders and Empire*

Hispaniola, where they were hated by the colonial elites, would be pointless. Cisneros followed Las Casas and Montesinos' advice, choosing three friars from the more obscure but, he hoped, more neutral Order of Saint Jerome to carry out the plans for reforms. Three friars of the order were appointed governors of Hispaniola and given full powers to implement a very ambitious plan that included the continuation of the colonial project in Hispaniola, but also the preservation of native lives, the liberation of all natives in servitude, the dismantling of the *encomienda* system as it existed, and the settling of natives in villages supervised by priests. Once in Hispaniola, however, such lofty plans met with the impossibility of being carried out without upending colonial society, which had been built on the exploitation of the natives. The friars encountered the opposition of the local elites, but more importantly, the first smallpox epidemic of the New World hit Hispaniola by the end of 1518, killing thousands. Only 3,000 natives survived the disease on the island.

SUGAR AND AFRICAN ENSLAVED LABOR

Historians agree that the most enduring legacy of the Jeronymite friars' government was to encourage and facilitate of the transition from a failing gold-mining economy to a plantation sugar economy.[14] The *encomenderos* were aware that the gold deposits were almost depleted and the colony's survival depended on developing a new economic model, and, with that in mind, they started looking for alternatives to gold. Agriculture, which had been completely disregarded in the early colony, became an area of experimentation. As early as 1515, there is evidence that some Spaniards in the town of Concepción built small mills and made sugar for local consumption. One *vecino* and physician named Gonzalo de Vellosa brought specialists in the sugar-refining process from the Canary Islands.[15] Sugar cane soon became one of the preferred crops of the elites,

---

[14] For example, see Frank Moya Pons, *Historia colonial de Santo Domingo* (Santiago: UCMM, 1976), 68–71; Miguel D Mena, *Iglesia, espacio y poder: Santo Domingo (1498–1521), experiencia fundacional del Nuevo Mundo* (Santo Domingo: Archivo General de la Nación, 2007), 316–18; Rodríguez Morel, *Orígenes*, 25; Erin Stone, "Slave Raiders Vs. Friars: Tierra Firme, 1513–1522." *The Americas*, vol. 74, n. 2 (2017): 156.

[15] Atlantic islands like the Canary Islands for the kingdom of Castilla, and the Azores, Madeira, and Cape Verde for the Portuguese, became important sugar-producing colonies in the fifteenth century. The use of African enslaved labor, and in the case of the Canary Islands, native enslaved labor, was commonplace. These islands became important area of experimentation, and it is from these islands that sugar experts and refining

Colonial Origins: Hispaniola in the Sixteenth Century 31

especially the judges of the *Audiencia* and members of the local *Cabildos,* who started using their wealth to construct costly sugar mills. By 1517, the Jeronymite governors were also aware of the need to support these experiments and came to believe sugar would be the best alternative for the economy of Hispaniola, in response to growing European demand.[16]

With that in mind, the Jeronymite friars first encouraged investments in the planting of cane and manufacturing sugar using loans made with royal funds to *vecinos* willing to build mills. Soon the crown followed the friars' lead and took the initiative, distributing thousands of gold *pesos* to those *vecinos* who agreed to build their mills and repay the loan within two years. At least thirty-two individuals received loans, and although not all of them finished their mills or even returned their loans, the policy allowed the creation of a nascent plantation economy, concentrated mostly in the area surrounding Santo Domingo and near the town of Azua, west of the capital. Other forms of aid to would-be planters included land, pastures, and river access for the construction and operation of the water-powered mills necessary for sugar processing. The crown also allowed tax incentives and exemptions for the importation and smelting of local copper for sugar refining, meaning that the earliest sugar plantations could also benefit from the exploitation of the mineral deposits of the island – and do so with strong crown support. At the same time, the rise of King Carlos to the seat of Holy Roman Emperor in the early 1520s allowed some of his European allies to make their way to the Americas. Genoese, German, and Flemish merchants invested heavily in the Hispaniola sugar economy, and, in partnerships with local planters, they built many more sugar mills. By 1527, there were already nineteen water mills and six smaller, animal-powered mills (known as *trapiches*) operating on the island, and their numbers continued growing throughout the first half of the sixteenth century.[17]

Since the native population had reached a nadir, the turn to intensive agriculture and plantations could not be achieved without finding new sources of forced laborers. Even before the smallpox epidemic of 1518, the

---

techniques were first introduced in the Americas, with Santo Domingo as the entry point into the hemisphere. See Philip D. Curtin, *The Rise and Fall of the Plantation Complex: Essays in Atlantic History* (New York: Cambridge University Press, 1990), 17–28.

[16] Genaro Rodríguez Morel, "The Sugar Economy of Española in the Sixteenth Century," in Stuart B. Schwartz, ed., *Tropical Babylons: Sugar and the Making of the Atlantic World, 1450–1680* (Chapel Hill: University of North Carolina Press, 2003), 87.

[17] Ibid., 90–93; Moya Pons, *Historia colonial,* 73, 79; Moya Pons, *Después de Colón,* 174–75.

32   *Islanders and Empire*

Jeronymite friars looked to free the natives from the abuses they were subjected to when working for the colonizers. They forbade any further slave raids into neighboring islands, though they did authorize the capture and barter of people they called "Caribs" or cannibals in Tierra Firme. The crown, supported by the expert yet interested testimony of merchants, slavers, and elites in Santo Domingo, allowed for the legal expansion of the Indian slave trade. Native resistance only gave more credence to the Spanish testimonies of Carib rebelliousness and savagery, thus perpetuating the myth of the savage cannibal Caribs in the Caribbean. From 1514 to 1524, at least sixty-eight expeditions of slave raiders left Hispaniola, enslaving at least 1,000 Indians who were then sold in Santo Domingo.[18]

Despite this surge in Indian slavery, their numbers were not sufficient enough to adequately operate the new sugar mills. In this context, the idea of importing enslaved Africans to provide the majority of the labor force took hold of colonists, colonial officials, and finally the crown. Free and enslaved Africans had nonetheless been present in Hispaniola since the early stages of colonization, the first known one being a man named Juan Moreno or Juan Prieto, a servant of Cristóbal Colón in the 1492 and 1493 trips.[19] Throughout the following decade, enslaved and free Christianized Africans arrived or were brought to Hispaniola. They undertook a wide array of tasks, from gold mining to domestic duties. As early as 1501, there is evidence that two men of African origin named Andrés García and Pedro were hired by two separate employers in Sevilla to dig gold in Hispaniola and provide other services in exchange for a salary.[20] One of the best-known West Africans who resided in Santo Domingo during these years was Juan Garrido, a black conquistador who would later join Cortés in his expedition against the Mexica empire. Garrido possibly arrived in Santo Domingo around 1510 and lived there until 1517.[21]

---

[18] Since many expeditions left without permits and the natives they brought went unaccounted for in official records, these numbers represent low estimates. Erin Woodruff Stone, "Indian Harvest: The Rise of the Indigenous Slave Trade and Diaspora From Española to the Circum-Caribbean, 1492–1542" (Ph.D. diss., Vanderbilt University, 2014), 144–47; Rodríguez Morel, *Orígenes*, 52.

[19] Consuelo Varela Bueno and Isabel Aguirre: *La caída de Cristóbal Colón. El juicio de Bobadilla* (Madrid: Marcial Pons, Ediciones de Historia, 2006), 155. Cited in CUNY Dominican Studies Institute, *First Blacks in the Americas: The African Presence in the Dominican Republic*, accessed April 18, 2020. http://firstblacks.org/en/summaries/arrival-01-free-and-enslaved/#page-1.

[20] CUNY Dominican Studies Institute, *First Blacks in the Americas*.

[21] Peter Gerhard, "A Black Conquistador in Mexico." *The Hispanic American Historical Review*, vol. 58, n. 3 (1978): 452; Ricardo E. Alegría, *Juan Garrido, el conquistador negro en las Antillas, Florida, Mexico y California* (San Juan: Centro de Estudios

Colonial Origins: Hispaniola in the Sixteenth Century

Most Africans arriving to Hispaniola during these early years were probably enslaved Christian converts brought initially via Sevilla or Lisbon, since the crown was concerned about the introduction of non-Christians in the Americas. King Fernando sent the first group of enslaved Africans to the town of Puerto Real in 1505 to start a copper mine.[22] Many of these early enslaved Africans were *ladinos*; that is, they were familiar with Spanish (or Portuguese) language and customs. The Jeronymite friars added to their reports the recommendation of introducing more enslaved Africans to work in the plantations. They echoed the wishes of many landowners and colonists who had been requesting more enslaved laborers for some years, while the wealthiest miners and landowners had managed to introduce small groups of enslaved Africans with royal licenses. The first massive introduction of enslaved Africans directly from Africa, and therefore unfamiliarized with Iberian culture (which led to them being known as *bozales*) possibly took place in 1518, when 200 enslaved Africans entered the port of Santo Domingo.[23] From that point, the African population of Santo Domingo increased at the same precipitous rate as the sugar plantations that appeared in the island's countryside. The crown facilitated the issuing of licenses, and African enslaved laborers became a central part of Hispaniola's social, cultural, and economic life. By the 1530s, there were approximately 20,000 enslaved Africans working in the mills, ranches, and households on the island, reaching a peak in the 1540s with nearly 30,000 men and women. In contrast, the lack of other economic opportunities, in part due to the monopolization of sugar by the planter class, led to the European population shrinking to 5,000 people during the same decade, with many colonists migrating to other parts of the Caribbean and, especially, the new mainland colonies. Towns and villages in the interior lost their populations rapidly, and the crown's edicts prohibiting migration outside the island had little effect. Only Santo Domingo, the commercial and institutional center of

---

Avanzados de Puerto Rico y El Caribe, 2004); Jane G. Landers, "Cimarrón and Citizen: African Ethnicity, Corporate Identity, and the Evolution of Free Black Towns in the Spanish Circum-Caribbean," in Jane Landers and Barry M. Robinson, eds., *Slaves, Subjects, and Subversives: Blacks in Colonial Latin America* (Albuquerque: University of New Mexico Press, 2006), 113.

[22] William H. Hodges and Eugene Lyon. "A General History of Puerto Real," in Kathleen Deagan, ed., *Puerto Real: The Archaeology of a Sixteenth-Century Spanish Town in Hispaniola* (Gainesville: University Press of Florida, 1995), 96.

[23] Genaro Rodríguez Morel, "El sector azucarero," in *Historia general*, 396; MacDonald, "Hieronymites in Hispaniola," 87.

34 *Islanders and Empire*

the island preserved its population of approximately 3,000 people. German, Genoese, and Portuguese ships loaded with hundreds of African enslaved men and women continued to arrive at its port, while much of the increasing sugar crop of the island left for Spain.[24]

NATIVE AND AFRICAN RESISTANCE

The drive of Spanish colonizers to subjugate both indigenous and African peoples was met with repeated and, at times, successful forms of resistance. Taíno polities fought Colón and his successors for years. When the Spanish finally destroyed the recalcitrant Taíno societies left on the island under governor Ovando, many of them fled to the mountains, along with native peoples brought from other islands. With the arrival of the first enslaved Africans to the island, both groups resisted and rebelled against Spanish rule together. As early as 1503, Governor Nicolás de Ovando reported that the *ladino* enslaved Africans working in the mines were escaping, joining the natives in the mountains, and transmitting all sorts of bad habits to them.[25] Ovando's negative judgment aside, it is clear that natives and Africans learned a great deal from each other and adapted to each other's practices. Spanish chronicler (and Hispaniola colonist) Gonzalo Fernández de Oviedo criticized enslaved Africans' habit of smoking tobacco, a custom that they learned from the natives as a way to stifle hunger and fatigue.[26] Enslaved Africans also learned the geography of the island from the natives with whom they worked, and when it came the time to flee, they often did it together and then formed mixed communities in the mountains.

The most successful and longest-lasting open rebellion against Spanish authority on the island occurred precisely because of the alliance of African and Indian fugitives. In 1519, a *cacique* known by his Christian name of Enrique fled his *encomienda* in the town of San Juan de la Maguana with his wife and several followers and hid in the Bahoruco

---

[24] Franklin J. Franco: *Historia del pueblo dominicano*, vol. I (Santo Domingo: Instituto del Libro, 1992), 80, 92; Moya Pons, *Historia colonial*, 75, 77. For a summary on the slave trade in this early period, see Mark Eagle, "The Early Caribbean Trade to Spanish America: Caribbean Pathways, 1530–1580," in Altman and Wheat, eds., *The Spanish Caribbean*, 139–60.

[25] Stone, "America's First Slave Revolt," 203.

[26] Kris E. Lane, "Africans and Natives in the Mines of Spanish America," in Matthew Restall, ed., *Beyond Black and Red: African–Native Relations in Colonial Latin America*, (Albuquerque: University of New Mexico Press 2005), 166.

Colonial Origins: Hispaniola in the Sixteenth Century   35

mountains (see Figure 2.2).[27] Enrique was born possibly between 1498 and 1500, and was a descendant of powerful *caciques* of the southwestern region of Jaragua that the Spaniards encountered on the island when they first arrived. The Franciscan friars of the monastery of Verapaz baptized and probably gave him his Christian name. The order had founded a school to teach the native nobility, and Enrique attended their school and learned to read and write in Spanish, making him understand Spanish culture and customs in ways that the previous generation of *caciques* were never able to do.[28] Beyond his personal reasons for fleeing, Enrique's escape to the mountains may well have been due in part to complex transformations that were undermining the role that *caciques* played as intermediaries between native and colonial societies.[29] Forced relocations, separation of communities from their ancestral lands, gods, and ancestors, and their subjection to increasing labor demands in this fast-changing colonial world might have induced men like Enrique to leave for the mountains.[30]

Enrique was not the first native to flee to the Bahoruco mountains or the last. From the earliest years of the Spanish colonization, this range of mountains in the southwest of Hispaniola served as a refuge for both indigenous and African enslaved peoples escaping Spanish exploitation. It is likely that Enrique joined an existing group of runaways, and he probably played an important role organizing them. Africans and native peoples established stable mixed communities away from Spanish control, and as the sugar plantations appeared in countryside, more Indian and enslaved Africans joined them. In 1521, twenty slaves identified as being Wolof people from West Africa rebelled at the sugar plantation belonging to Diego Colón, and this is considered to be the first major rebellion of African enslaved people in the Americas. The group gained

---

[27] Enrique is known by the historiography and sources by the diminutive "Enriquillo." I have decided to follow the example of Ida Altman and use his baptism Christian name, Enrique, without modifiers. Ida Altman, "The Revolt of Enriquillo and the Historiography of Early Spanish America." *The Americas*, vol. 63, n. 04 (2007): 587–614.

[28] Stone, "America's First Slave Revolt," 205.

[29] Some historians have pointed out that Enrique may have resented the treatment that he was receiving from his *encomendero* and other Spanish officials in the town of San Juan de la Maguana, and this became the catalyst for his escape. See Ida Altman, "The Revolt of Enriquillo," 594–96; Lynne A. Guitar, "Cultural Genesis: Relationships among Indians, Africans, and Spaniards in Rural Hispaniola, First Half of the Sixteenth Century" (Ph.D. diss., Vanderbilt University, 1998), 224.

[30] For a full and elegant articulation of this argument, see Stone, "America's First Slave Revolt," 199–200, 204–06.

36   *Islanders and Empire*

another twenty followers (some of them Guanches, natives from the Canary islands, and some Muslims from northwest Africa) and raided nearby plantations. The Spaniards organized a party to stop them and managed to kill at least six and injure another few, but most of the rebels survived and made it to the Bahoruco mountains, where they likely joined Enrique's group.[31]

The authorities of Santo Domingo did not formally declare hostilities against Enrique and his people until 1523, in what they described as the "War of Bahoruco." The Spanish authorities organized at least four major expeditions against Enrique, in 1523, 1525, 1526, and 1529, all of them ending in failure. Meanwhile the natives and Africans in the Bahoruco mountains continued their assault on the plantations, destroying machinery, taking provisions, and attracting new recruits while also at times killing the inhabitants. In 1533, new negotiations began between representatives of the crown and Enrique. Instead of trying to defeat him with weapons, the Spanish tried diplomacy and granted Enrique and his men a full pardon. With the intercession of a Franciscan friar known by Enrique, and even Bartolomé de las Casas himself, the *cacique* agreed to lay down his arms after twelve years of resistance. He received the title of "Don" and gained full amnesty for his followers, who settled with him in an Indian town on the outskirts of the town of Azua. Enrique died one year later, leaving his wife Doña Mencia and his nephew as leaders of his community.[32]

The conclusion of the War of Bahoruco only put an end to one of the many groups of escaped people operating in Hispaniola during those years. In the late 1520s, groups of Indian runaways led by men such as Tamayo, Ciguayo, Murcia, and Hernando el Tuerto fought for their independence and attacked sugar mills and farms in the countryside, forcing many residents to seek refuge in Santo Domingo.[33] Only a few years after the peace treaty with Enrique, the Bahoruco Mountains once again became a refuge of maroons, and it would be so for the rest of the colonial period, despite repeated attempts to capture them. Runaway Africans and Indians also established independent communities in remote areas that the Spanish had depopulated in recent years. In the 1540s and 1550s, African maroon leaders like Lemba (who fought with Enrique until

---

[31] Ibid, 196; Guitar, "Cultural Genesis," 229–20.
[32] Stone, "America's First Slave Revolt," 210–11.
[33] Carlos Esteban Deive, *Los guerrilleros negros: esclavos fugitivos y cimarrones en Santo Domingo* (Santo Domingo: Fundación Cultural Dominicana, 1989), 39.

Colonial Origins: Hispaniola in the Sixteenth Century 37

he came to terms with the Spanish), Diego de Guzmán, Diego de Ocampo, or Juan Vaquero led the offensive against Spanish settlements, plantations, and people. As the war against Enrique had done before, these maroons leaders forced the Spanish officials to mobilize considerable amounts of resources and people to keep them at bay.[34]

The African enslaved population continued to grow, and so did Spanish fears of an islandwide insurrection, forcing colonists to increase the resources used to capture and silence the most active maroon groups. With the exception of Diego de Ocampo, who reached an agreement with the Spanish colonists to abandon the fight and become a maroon hunter himself, most of these famous runaway leaders were captured or killed. The Spanish made common use of terror to force the enslaved population of the island to submit to their control. Violent executions of maroon leaders, like the quartering of Juan Vaquero's body on Palm Sunday in Santo Domingo, or the display of Lemba's head on the city's gates, became commonplace.

Michel Foucault has argued that the aim of public executions "is not so much to re-establish a balance [of power] as to bring into play, at its extreme point, the dissymmetry between the subject who has dared to violate and the all-powerful sovereign who displays his strength."[35] In this particular colonial setting, with the Spanish dwindling in numbers and a vastly larger enslaved population, these gruesome rituals of power by the colonial state and its bureaucracy hints at desperation, a ruthless attempt by colonists and bureaucrats to instill fear and deter other African slaves from running away. Despite these tactics, African and Indian workers continued to flee from Spanish control. Isolated attacks on Spanish settlements and farms never disappeared completely, but from the second half of the sixteenth century onwards, most runaways were able to escape to uninhabited areas away from Spanish control. Violent confrontations like the ones led by Lemba or Juan Vaquero decreased and disappeared almost completely, not because the public executions succeeded in instilling fear in the minds of the enslaved: They disappeared because as the Spaniards migrated to other parts of the Caribbean and the island depopulated, both

[34] Ibid., 43–53. Robert C. Schwaller has argued that maroon activity in Hispaniola was a form of conquest in itself, and that the raids of Spanish property followed patterns of West African warfare. Robert C. Schwaller, "Contested Conquests: African Maroons and the Incomplete Conquest of Hispaniola, 1519–1620." *The Americas*, vol. 75, n. 4 (2018): 609–38.

[35] Michel Foucault, *Discipline and Punish: The Birth of the Prison* (New York: Pantheon Books, 1977), 48–49.

38   *Islanders and Empire*

Indians and African maroons changed tactics.[36] In their attempt to preserve their freedom, runaways tried to keep their communities and places of habitation as hidden as possible from the Spanish. On an island as sparsely populated as Hispaniola was by the second half of the sixteenth century, staying away from the Spanish proved to be the best possible strategy for the survival of runaway communities.[37]

BUILDING AND MANAGING PLANTATIONS

The apex of active violent resistance by Indian and African workers against the Spanish happened at the same time that the colonial powers in Hispaniola were fully embracing the cultivation of sugar as the main economic activity on the island. This process started during the rule of Jeronymite friars and continued into Diego Colón's second governorship, this time as viceroy. His tenure was short (1520–3), but those years were crucial to the transformation of the island into a sugarocracy. The great *encomenderos* like Colón had seen the writing on the wall regarding the depletion of the island's gold deposits and used their wealth and political influence as members of the municipal councils, or *Cabildos,* in the towns across the island to acquire land and loans to build sugar mills.

Once Colón was recalled to Spain in 1523, the *oidores* (judges) of the *Audiencia* of Santo Domingo became the highest authority on the island. They were all sugar-mill owners, and their social, political, and economic interests lined up with those of other local elites. The first president of the *Audiencia*, in charge of defending the royal interests on the island, did not arrive in Santo Domingo until 1528. By then sugar had become the main source of wealth on the island. The crown protected and encouraged its growth with numerous incentives such as exemptions on the tithe on sugar, patronage rights – which granted plantation owners control over chapels built inside their plantations – or tax exemptions on the importation of copper to build the boilers. Perhaps the most important of all was the right to form *mayorazgos,* or entails, which allowed plantation owners to pass their property to their eldest son without having to follow

---

[36] For a study of the performative aspects of state bureaucracies and public executions such as the *auto de fe*, see Irene Silverblatt, *Modern Inquisitions: Peru and the Colonial Origins of the Civilized World* (Durham: Duke University Press, 2004), 79–84.

[37] Manuel Barcia has noted a similar change of tactics for slaves in Cuba during the nineteenth century, avoiding direct confrontation and instead practicing new forms of resistance. Manuel Barcia Paz, *The Great African Slave Revolt of 1825: Cuba and the Fight for Freedom in Matanzas* (Baton Rouge: Louisiana University Press, 2012), 147.

Colonial Origins: Hispaniola in the Sixteenth Century 39

Castilian inheritance law that forced the division of estates among all heirs. *Mayorazgos* also prevented the expropriation of property by any court to pay a family's debts.[38]

Acquiring and managing debt was an important part of building these plantations. Many of these mills required immense investments. Diego Caballero spent 15,000 *ducados* to build his plantation, which included sixty stone houses in addition to extensive lands to cultivate food for enslaved laborers. The price of construction of these plantations only increased throughout the sugar boom, and many planters came together to form companies to build plantations. Genoese and German merchants often allied themselves with local residents to start up sugar enterprises, although often these companies dissolved when one member purchased the part belonging to the partners, thus allowing the consolidation of plantations in the hands of those with the most economic resources.[39]

During the central decades of the sixteenth century, most of the population was concentrated in the countryside as the island went through a ruralization process that would become the main feature of the life in Hispaniola for the entire colonial period and beyond. With the exception of Santo Domingo, which remained the main port and political, institutional, and economic center of the colony, most of the other urban centers lost population or simply disappeared. At the same time, plantations became economic and demographic centers in their own right.[40] Because the sugar mills in Hispaniola used hydraulic power to crush the cane, the most important plantation areas were concentrated on the shores of some of the mightiest rivers in the south and west of the island. Apart from the Ozama River, which flowed straight into Santo Domingo, most of the plantations were in fluvial systems west of the capital, such as the Haina, Nizao, Nigua, Ocoa, and Cozuí rivers. Plantations were also built in more remote places, such as near the village of San Juan, northwest of the Bahoruco mountains; in the environs of Higüey, in the southeast of the island; and near the village of Puerto Plata on the northern coast.

These plantations used the forced labor of both indigenous and African laborers throughout the first half of the sixteenth century. By the 1530s, an average plantation with a water-powered sugar mill would have an enslaved population of at least 100 laborers, but they could easily reach 200 or 300 laborers, depending on the available land. A

---

[38] Moya Pons, *Historia colonial*, 76–77.
[39] Rodríguez Morel, "The Sugar Economy of Española," 96–97.
[40] Moya Pons, *Historia colonial*, 76.

40 *Islanders and Empire*

census from 1545 found that the average number of laborers was even higher, with seven plantations having more than 100 enslaved laborers, five with more than 200, eight with over 300, four more than 400, three more than 500, and one with more than 600 enslaved laborers. Some Spaniards owned several plantations, which held combined enslaved populations of over 1,000 laborers.[41]

From the 1520s to the 1540s, plantations went through important transformations in the composition of their workforce. In the early years, some of the most specialized work was carried out by salaried white Europeans, but they were soon replaced by enslaved Africans who took on most (if not all) labor on the plantation. As the availability of enslaved labor and their familiarity with the sugar-producing process increased, African forced laborers were trained to undertake all the major tasks of producing sugar. It is quite possible that the second-generation enslaved laborers became important sources of knowledge in the sugar process, and plantation owners simply took advantage of this. For example, in the plantation Santiago de la Paz, which was auctioned in 1547, the list of laborers indicates how, with the exception of the overseer, every position of responsibility on the plantation was carried out by enslaved African men, with the exception of one female African slave who was listed as a strainer, meaning she participated in the crystallization process. Some of the wealthiest Spanish plantation owners continued using Portuguese specialists, but it became the exception rather than the rule.[42]

At the same time that the work on the plantations was placed on the shoulders of African enslaved laborers, the island experienced a minor resurgence in the numbers of small white landowners. Due to the mass emigration of white settlers to Mexico and Peru that the island suffered in the 1520s and 1530s, the crown gave land grants, special tax exemption, and other accommodations to peninsular farmers who would come and establish themselves on the island. It is uncertain if many Iberian farmers embraced the proposal, but many former salaried plantation laborers who were losing their jobs did. It provided them with a way to stay in the colony, on land where they subsequently produced corn,

---

[41] Rodríguez Morel, *Orígenes*, 184–94; Lynne Guitar, "Boiling It Down: Slavery on the First Commercial Sugarcane Ingenios in the Americas (Hispaniola, 1530–45)," in Jane G. Landers and Barry M. Robinson, eds., *Slaves, Subjects, and Subversives: Blacks in Colonial Latin America* (Albuquerque: University of New Mexico Press, 2006), 48.

[42] Rodríguez Morel, ibid; Guitar, ibid., 59–60.

Colonial Origins: Hispaniola in the Sixteenth Century   41

yams, sweet potatoes, legumes, small quantities of tobacco, and, in the second half of the sixteenth century, ginger. These small farmers usually lacked the resources to buy enslaved Africans, so they normally worked small plots of land surrounding the larger plantations, which were their main customers. For example, the plantation known as Samate, owned by Juan de Villoria and located in the village of Higüey, was surrounded by small properties owned by forty Castilian farmers. The plantation owned by the Trejo family, also in Higüey, had another twenty-five Castilian farmers in its vicinity.[43] With the increasing availability of foodstuffs, plantation owners might have used more of their land to plant sugar cane, especially at times of very high prices. Most plantations, however, continued to use some of their valuable land to grow food in order to be as self-sufficient as possible.

Little information survives about the lives of the enslaved in the Hispaniola plantations, and most what does is extrapolated from the experiences of African slaves in other plantation societies. What seems certain is the Spanish slaveowners may have been particularly concerned with their workers' tendency to abandon the plantations temporarily, from a few days to even years at a time in the most extreme cases. The slave ordinances of 1528, 1535, 1542, and 1544 put an increasing emphasis on trying to keep enslaved Africans on the plantations. Penalties were also stiffened with each reiteration of the laws for both the enslaved and, theoretically, their owners, for failing to control their bound laborers. The constant repetition of this point in the ordinances hints at their failure to limit the mobility of the enslaved, who used their time away to trade, hire themselves out to earn extra money, or visit relatives and friends enslaved in nearby plantations, which even included maroons in the mountains, with whom they probably had fluid relations.[44] These cases of *petit marronage*, added to the multitude of runaway slaves, and other forms of daily resistance, perhaps goes some way to explaining the low levels of productivity despite the large numbers of enslaved people on Hispaniola's plantations. Even in the 1540s, at the height of the maroon rebellions and violence – and a time when witnesses wrote of the Spanish population living in terror – Spanish colonists continued requesting thousands of new African slaves for their plantations. Historian Lynne Guitar has suggested that these new workers might have been necessary for the Spanish to

---

[43] Ibid.; Robert S. Haskett, "Santiago De La Paz: Anatomy of a Sixteenth-Century Caribbean Sugar Estate." *UCLA Historical Journal* 1 (1980): 58–59.
[44] Guitar, "Boiling It Down," 51–52.

42 *Islanders and Empire*

continue expanding sugar production, but in light of the numerous acts of resistance that she mentions, they could also have needed the extra slave labor simply to continue producing sugar at the same level.[45]

FROM SUGAR TO GINGER AND HIDES

By the second half of the sixteenth century, Hispaniola saw a slow decline of the sugar industry, followed by a sharp crisis in the last decades of the century. The challenges for the sugar plantations in Hispaniola were both internal and external. Among the external factors, the most important one was the rise of new, larger, sugar-producing colonies in the Atlantic basin such as Brazil, which brought sugar prices down and forced Hispaniola producers out of the market. Between 1550 and 1560, the Portuguese colony of Bahía entered the Atlantic sugar economy and, by 1587, it already boasted fourteen sugar mills, nearly as many as were in Santo Domingo at the same time.[46]

In addition, the second half of the sixteenth century saw the consolidation of the bi-annual fleet system between Spain and the Indies. This became the only avenue for legal trade with the Iberian peninsula. The newly established routes of these fleets skipped Santo Domingo, the only port on the island authorized to trade, and this fact considerably reduced the naval traffic to the city. Merchants in Sevilla had long resented the competition from other Iberian ports in regions such as Galicia and the Canary Islands, which tended to reduce prices and, therefore, their own profit margins. They repeatedly petitioned the crown to prohibit the presence of those merchants on the island. In turn, the crown acquiesced in part because it was also immersed in the process of centralizing its mercantile operations with its American colonies. Sevilla became the only authorized Spanish port of origin and destination for American products. Limited to trade with Sevilla but unable to access the annual fleet merchants and cargo to carry the local products to the Iberian Peninsula, Hispaniola was placed at the mercy of the few Sevillian merchants willing to sail to Santo Domingo.

---

[45] Ibid., 63.

[46] About the rise of Brazilian plantation economy, see Stuart B. Schwartz, *Sugar Plantations in the Formation of Brazilian Society: Bahia, 1550–1835* (Cambridge University Press, 1985), 71, 92. About the prohibition of merchants from other Iberian ports to sail to Santo Domingo, see Genaro Rodríguez Morel, *Cartas del Cabildo de la ciudad de Santo Domingo en el siglo XVI* (Santo Domingo: Centro de Altos Estudios Humanísticos y del Idioma Español, 1999), 42.

Colonial Origins: Hispaniola in the Sixteenth Century 43

These merchants knew that their products and cargo space in the hull of their ships would not have any competition.[47]

Another step toward the reorganization of the trade was the standardization of the currency throughout the Caribbean islands with that of Spain, making their value the same and bringing uniformity to the specie throughout the empire. This had a negative effect on the commerce of Hispaniola: before 1550s, the *real* on the island had been valued at 44 *maravedís* instead of 34, as was customary in Castilla. Since all taxes were paid in *maravedís*, local and visiting merchants conducting business on the island were rewarded with a 23 percent tax reduction in all their transactions, while the importation of goods from the peninsula had a 23 percent discount. After the standardization of the currency, the appeal of doing business in Santo Domingo vanished for some merchants. All the silver currency disappeared from the markets and was replaced by copper currency, commonly known as *cuartos*. The introduction of this low-grade currency eliminated Santo Domingo's competitive advantage, making it very difficult for local residents to compete with wealthier Caribbean ports.

High prices had always been a problem for the residents of Hispaniola, but since the currency was worth very little, the cost of goods skyrocketed. Unlike in Havana, where the *Cabildo* of the city regularly supervised local markets and regulated prices on some basic products, the *Cabildo* of Santo Domingo could not, even though it had requested the crown's permission to do so at least since the 1530s.[48] The price of imported staples like wine, olive oil, and flour rose, while products such as European textiles, or, indeed, enslaved Africans, were prohibitively expensive for all but the elites. Although the standardization of Hispaniola's currency with the rest of the empire emptied the pockets of most locals, it may have benefited the wealthiest residents who had *censos* (mortgages on some of their properties to religious orders) and, with the

---

[47] Some classic works on the organization and consolidation of the fleets are Clarence H. Haring, *Trade and Navigation between Spain and the Indies in the Time of the Hapsburgs* (Cambridge, 1918); Guillermo Céspedes del Castillo, "La avería en el comercio de Indias," in *Anuario de Estudios Hispanoamericanos*, 9 (1954), 617–703; for a social history of the fleets, see Pablo E. Pérez-Mallaína, *Spain's Men of the Sea; Daily Life on the Indies Fleets in the Sixteenth Century*, trans. Carla Rahn Phillips (Baltimore: Johns Hopkins University, 1998). For specifics on the commercialization of Santo Domingo sugar, see Justo del Río Moreno, "Comercio y transporte en la economía del azúcar antillano durante el siglo XVI." *Clío*, 179 (enero-junio 2010): 15–54.

[48] Esteban Mira Caballos, "Otros sectores productivos y económicos," in *Historia general*, 433.

44 *Islanders and Empire*

reduction of the value of the local currency, saw their mortgage payments sliced by almost 25 percent.[49]

With the death of most of the native population of the island by 1550s, the Spanish inhabitants of Hispaniola progressively became dependent on a constant influx of African enslaved laborers, Simultaneously, the gradual marginalization of the island from Iberian commercial routes also meant a drop in the arrival of slave ships. The limited number of slaves, and the high demand for them, added to the existing inflation on the island, raising the price of slaves to levels that were not affordable for most inhabitants. Many local residents, like the *fiscal* of the *Audiencia* of Santo Domingo, Juan de Larrieta, complained about the dearth of the slaves because the Africans were now "the only farmers of the land ... because there are not any Indians and the Spaniards do not want to serve." For Larrieta, the lack of replacements was the reason for the economic decline of Hispaniola.[50] Realistically, the lack of enslaved ships was likely another symptom, rather than the root cause of this decline.

As the age of the great sugar estates in Hispaniola waned during the second half of the sixteenth century, ginger became an alternative crop. By the late 1580s, only a few large sugar producers remained, while most landowners had transitioned to planting ginger or cattle ranching. Ginger required less capital to grow, and its price was on the rise in Spain. Ginger as a crop was also attractive because, unlike sugar, which was heavily regulated and subject to a long-established tithe, the lack of regulations around ginger allowed many planters initially to easily evade attempts by the local church to tithe their production, at least for a while. Archbishop Alonso López Davila complained numerous times about the irregular payment of the tithe by the ginger planters during the early 1580s.

---

[49] For an explanation of how this process of currency standardization unfolded in Havana, see Alejandro de la Fuente, *Havana and the Atlantic*, 59–61. Dominican historians have traditionally viewed this process as a devaluation of the local currency, an attempt of the crown to cut its bureaucratic expenses on the island (which was paid in *maravedís*), or a way for the crown to provide an incentive to Sevillian merchants at the cost of Hispaniola's local economy, which is, quite possibly, also true. See, for instance, Genaro Rodríguez Morel, *Cartas del Cabildo*, 32–38; Frank Moya Pons, *La Otra Historia Dominicana* (Santo Domingo: Buho, 2008). For a careful examination of the currency of Hispaniola in the sixteenth century, see Pilar González Gutiérrez, "Importación y acuñación de moneda circulante en la Española durante el siglo XVI." *Estudios de historia social y económica de América*, 13 (1996): 25–45.

[50] "los labradores de la esta tierra son negros porque indios no los hay ni blancos quieren servir, y para todas granjerías y labores de ingenios y estancias y ganados son necesarios y forzosos y vienen muy pocos." Juan de Larrieta to the Council of the Indies. February 27, 1581. AGI, SD. 51, R. 4, n. 53. All translations are the author's.

Colonial Origins: Hispaniola in the Sixteenth Century   45

Despite these complaints, in 1588, the Council of the Indies decided to slash the ginger tithe in half from 10 percent to 5 percent of production, most likely to encourage its planting, but such a move dismayed the archbishop and local prebendaries, who depended on that income.[51]

Possibly encouraged by the reduction of the ecclesiastical tax, landowners across Hispaniola turned to ginger. The subsequent overproduction flooded the market, causing prices to drop, so some landowners found ways to limit the number of those who could benefit from the plant. In 1587, the prebendaries of the bishopric of La Vega and members of its ecclesiastic *Cabildo* informed the crown that the *Audiencia* had prohibited the inhabitants of their diocese, which encompassed the north and west of the island, from planting ginger to the detriment of those residents and the Catholic church in those territories. The *Audiencia*'s order was probably influenced by the desire of Santo Domingo landowners to reduce the ginger production, increase prices, and engross the benefits from its cultivation of ginger. It is doubtful that, as a result of the *Audiencia*'s decree, ginger disappeared from the fields of northern and western Hispaniola. The prebendaries of the archdiocese of Santo Domingo certainly believed that planters were abandoning the cultivation of ginger. Although a certain decrease in production was likely, it is also worth considering the possibility that many producers turned to smuggling with foreign traders as a way to maximize their profits.[52]

From 1576 to 1594, Hispaniola sent more than 22,000 *quintales* of ginger to Sevilla, which amounted to 70 percent of the ginger that arrived there from the Antilles.[53] By the end of this period, however, Hispaniola's legal exports had declined precipitously. In the year 1594, Hispaniola

---

[51] Justo L. del Río Moreno, and Lorenzo E. López y Sebastián, "El Jenjibre: historia de un monocultivo caribeño del siglo XVI." *Revista Complutense de Historia de América* 18 (1992): 73. For the complaints of the archbishop of Santo Domingo, see AGI, SD. 93, R. 1, n. 27, and AGI, SD. 80, R. 2, n. 33. The reduction of the tithe can be found in the letter of the prebendaries of the archdiocese of Santo Domingo to the Council, May 27, 1588. AGI, SD. 94, R. 2, n. 54.

[52] The prebendaries of the diocese of La Vega to the Council of the Indies. January 24, 1587. AGI, SD. 94, R. 2, n. 51; AGI, SD. 94, R. 2, n. 54.

[53] A *quintal* is a unit of weight equal to 100 pounds. Del Río Moreno and López y Sebastián, "El Jenjibre." These numbers only reflect legal exports. They don't include illicit exports to Sevilla or those smuggled onto foreign vessels. See also Eufemio Lorenzo Sanz, *El comercio de España con América en la época de Felipe II*, tomo 1 (Valladolid: Diputación Central de Valladolid, 1979), 606–08; Juana Gil-Bermejo García, *La Española: anotaciones históricas (1600–1650)* (Sevilla: Escuela de Estudios Hispanoamericanos, CSIC, 1983), 65–69; Bethany Aram. "Caribbean Ginger and Atlantic Trade, 1570–1648." *Journal of Global History*, vol. 10, n. 3 (2015): 412–15.

46   *Islanders and Empire*

account for only 30 percent of all the ginger sent from the Antilles to Sevilla. The neighboring island of Puerto Rico had become a ginger powerhouse, and its shipments to Sevilla amounted to almost 70 percent of the total. This reversal in the trend might indicate that landowners around Santo Domingo succeeded in pressuring planters in the north of the island out of ginger cultivation. The inability of landowners in the north and west of Hispaniola to sell their ginger through Santo Domingo may have pushed them to pursue other activities to achieve their social and economic aspirations. Cattle ranching grew during these years more intensely than before and, as will be discussed in the following chapter, many turned to contraband trade as their only viable alternative. Although it is difficult to prove due to the covert nature of smuggling and the lack of evidence about the ginger production in the remote farms of Hispaniola, it is likely that some of these landowners from the interior did not abandon ginger cultivation. They may simply have rerouted their shipments to northern European ships searching for trade on the northern shores of Hispaniola, thus benefiting from the increasing demand of ginger in European ports like Antwerp and London and sharply decreasing the ginger exports to Sevilla.[54]

After sugar and ginger, cattle ranching was the next most important economic activity in the island's early colonial history. Initially, Governor Ovando promoted its growth for the maintenance of the Spanish population, and imported pigs, cows, and sheep became an important part of the island's landscape. Lacking natural enemies and with abundant land for pasture, cattle managed to reproduce at a prodigious rate. Many escaped their owners and lived free in the unpopulated areas of Hispaniola. By 1526, one wealthy Hispaniola resident, Rodrigo de Bastidas, owned nine cattle ranches with more than 8,000 head. By 1547, he had 25,000 head of cattle, and many of his neighbors easily owned between 7,000 and 20,000 head. The archdiocese of Santo Domingo itself owned several thousand head, and the individual members of the ecclesiastical *Cabildo* also invested their own income in cattle ranching, acquired through the tithe.[55]

The proliferation of cattle meant that meat was very cheap. Many plantation owners used the ranches to feed their families and their enslaved laborers, as well as supply tallow for candles and soap, and

---

[54] Chapter 2 includes some examples of smugglers taking ginger to the northern shores to sell to foreigners, so we do have some evidence of this illicit rerouting of ginger.

[55] Lorenzo E. López y Sebastián and Justo L. del Río Moreno, "La ganadería vacuna en la isla Española (1508–1587)." *Revista Complutense de Historia de América* 25 (1999): 31.

Colonial Origins: Hispaniola in the Sixteenth Century   47

cattle hides for local use, and more importantly, for export to Europe. Hides were in high demand for the manufacturing of a myriad goods, from clothing and boots to weapons, tools, saddles, and bridles. Between 1530s and 1550s, local producers were sending an average of 30,000 hides yearly to Sevilla.[56] Most of the cattle on the island were not kept in pens, but roamed free. Their owners hunted them down when they wanted to sell their hides and left most of the meat behind to rot. Throughout the second half of the sixteenth century, cows were killed for their hides and sold either legally through Santo Domingo, or most likely, to foreign traders on the northern coasts of the island. The indiscriminate killing of the cattle to sell their hides led to a rapid decrease of the herds and a scarcity of meat in Santo Domingo in the early decades of the seventeenth century, but cattle ranching survived and continued to be one of the most important economic activities of the island throughout the colonial period.

THE CITY OF SANTO DOMINGO

Despite the reversal of fortune in the island's economy, a sailor, merchant, or traveler arriving in Santo Domingo in the early 1580s encountered a relatively prosperous Spanish Caribbean port city of its time. In his *General History of the Indies* (first published in 1535), Gonzalo Fernández de Oviedo bragged about the city's solid construction, arguing that, with the exception of Barcelona, there was no better city in the Iberian peninsula.[57] Even though this was clearly an exaggeration, the city was indeed well built, with the majority of its houses and official buildings made out of stone and tiled roofs in the Castilian tradition. Originally settled on the eastern side of the mouth of the river Ozama, the city was moved a few years later to the western bank, allowing Santo Domingo to face east toward its port on the river side of the city, while its southern side, overlooking the Caribbean sea, remained protected by ragged cliffs and rock formations.

The first structure that the crew of any ship entering the port would have seen was the fortress, located in the mouth of the river (see Figure 1.2). Built by Governor Ovando (probably with forced Taíno laborers), its medieval square-shaped tower became an effective tool to protect the

---

[56] Ibid., 32.
[57] Gonzalo Fernández de Oviedo y Valdés, *Historia general y natural de las Indias, islas y Tierra Firme del mar Océano* (Asunción: Guaranía, 1944), 162.

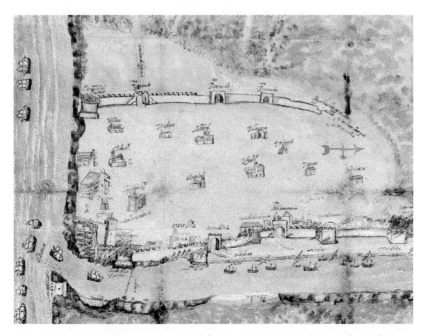

FIGURE 1.2 Map of Santo Domingo defenses, 1619 (detail). The walls on the west side of the island (top of the image) were just an embankment with gates at this point. The map also includes some of the most important secular and religious buildings of the city. Ministerio de Cultura y Deportes, AGI, Mapas y Planos, Santo Domingo, 29.

river. In the second half of the sixteenth century, a city wall was added to the entire river front, with extra bastion and cannon platforms added in the following decades. Despite this impressive display of defensive architecture, the rest of the city remained without walls, especially its western part, which made it vulnerable to land attacks. Drake's assault in 1586 took full advantage of this lack of fortifications, which would not be completed until the late seventeenth century.

From the water, the sailors of any ship passing the fortress would see the facade and roof of the building of the *Audiencia* of Santo Domingo, which also doubled as the official residence of the governor. Advancing a few hundred paces north up the river, the ship would arrive in the harbor, home to the *Reales Atarazanas* (royal shipyard). Reigning over the port on elevated ground, newcomers could look at the palace that viceroy Diego Colón built upon his arrival on the island, a beautiful mixture of the late gothic and renaissance styles in vogue in the Iberian Peninsula at the time.

Both buildings, the palace and the *Audiencia*, were constructed around a square that brought together the original administrative center of the city. Upon disembarking and walking through the city gates into the plaza, the newcomers might have encountered some of the homes of the city's elite, the early settlers who managed to survive the social, political, and economic uncertainty of the early years of the colony. These houses, built with enslaved native and African enslaved labor and with beautiful stone carvings and coats of arms decorating their facades, signaled the wealth that their owners accumulated during the cycles of gold and sugar production. The importance of the *Audiencia* and the port remained constant throughout the colonial period, but, as the city expanded, a second center of power appeared.

Travelers and mariners seeking spiritual comfort or eager to give thanks for their safe arrival to Santo Domingo could have walked a couple of city blocks to the Plaza Mayor, or central square of the city, where the cathedral of Santa María de la Encarnación stood. The construction of the plaza and the cathedral were linked: the former appeared as a result of the building of the latter, completed during the 1540s, on the southern side of the plaza. The cathedral's facade, however, did not face the plaza, but run parallel to it, with one of the long sides of its basilica forming the southern side of the Plaza Mayor. The cathedral's facade faced its own atrium, in the southwestern corner of the Plaza Mayor. Also surrounding the plaza, a traveler could not have missed the building of the *Cabildo*, sitting in the northwest corner of the square, and the local prison, on its eastern side. The construction of this second hub of secular and ecclesiastical power in the city, rivaling the royal nexus around the *Audiencia*, speaks to its evolution from early settlement to a more complex political space where local interests gained importance in the power dynamics of Santo Domingo and the region as a whole. The number of wealthy householders around the square signaled the rise and continued prominence of this new focal point in the life of the city.[58]

The religious institutions of Santo Domingo, however, were not limited to its central plaza. From the perspective of the secular church, the cathedral was the main parish of the city. A second parish was delineated in the northernmost corner of the city, housed in the church of Santa Bárbara, which at this time was likely still a very humble building with a thatched roof. As for the regular church, three of the most important

---

[58] Eugenio Pérez Montás. *La ciudad del Ozama: 500 años de historia urbana* (Santo Domingo: Patronato de la Ciudad Colonial de Santo Domingo, 1998), 78.

50 *Islanders and Empire*

mendicant orders of the time erected their own monasteries in different corners of city. The Franciscan Order built the largest of the monasteries in the north, which was the highest point of the city and near the quarry, the source of most of the local building stone. The Dominican Order built their monastery southwest of the Plaza Mayor. Finally as the last to arrive, the Order of Mercy erected their monastery in the western suburbs. Two additional female convents also existed: Regina Angelorum, under the Dominican Order and annexed to the Dominican monastery, and the Franciscan convent of Santa Clara, located in the southeastern corner of the city, across from the fortress. Other smaller chapels were distributed across the city, including the chapel housed in the hospital of San Nicolás, the chapel of San Andrés, or the very modest chapel of San Miguel. Private chapels also existed, like the one built by wealthy resident Francisco Davila in his house directly in front of the *Audiencia*'s main entrance.

The city also had two educational institutions. The Gorjón school was built and endowed by indebted sugar planter Hernando Gorjón as a way to avoid payment to his creditors and maintain his social and economic standing.[59] This became a primary school for the children of the local elites, although it struggled to survive throughout the sixteenth and seventeenth century due to constant abuses in the management of its endowment. The city also had a university, hosted in the Dominican convent and staffed by university-trained priest, friars, and other residents.

SANTO DOMINGO AS A STAGE

As the center of political and religious power on the island, Santo Domingo became an important staging ground for social expressions of cultural belonging within the Spanish Atlantic world. Specific days of the Catholic calendar, such as Holy Week, became important markers of social cohesion and religious expression. Starting in the 1540s, there were at least two annual processions. The first one took place on the night between Holy Thursday and Holy Friday, and featured men processing through the city with their faces covered and flogging their own bare backs. It was known as *los disciplinantes* (the flagellant). A second smaller and more restrained procession departed from the Dominican convent on Easter Sunday and paraded in the plaza outside the convent. The tradition

---

[59] Emilio Cordero Michel. "Hernando Gorjón, hombre de empresa y de presa." *Clío*, 155 (1996): 93–113.

FIGURE 1.3a *Casa del Cordón* (Cord House). One of the first Spanish stone houses in the Americas. Photo by the author.
b Main facade of the cathedral of Santa María de la Encarnación, Santo Domingo. Photo courtesy of Getty Images.
c Church of the Dominican Order, Santo Domingo. Photo by the author.
d Church of Regina Angelorum, part of the Dominican female convent. Photo by the author.

of carrying sacred sculptures as part of the procession started in Santo Domingo in the late sixteenth and to a greater extent in the seventeenth century. By then, Santo Domingo had religious confraternities most days of Holy Week, each with their own procession. Some of these were formed exclusively by people of African descent, such as the one of the confraternity of Nuestra Señora de la Candelaria, formed in the sixteenth century by Africans identified with the ethnonyms "biafaras" and "mandingas," or the confraternity of los Remedios del Carmen, founded in 1592.[60]

---

[60] Fray Vicente Rubio and María Ugarte, *Semana Santa en la ciudad colonial de Santo Domingo* (Santo Domingo: Commission Permanente Para la Celebración del Quinto Centenario del Descubrimiento y Evangelización de América, 1992); José Luis Sáez, *La*

52 *Islanders and Empire*

In addition to marking the holy days of the Catholic calendar, residents of Santo Domingo enthusiastically celebrated exceptional events and news from Spain. For instance, in 1583, the reports of the impressive naval victory of Álvaro de Bazán, Marquis of Santa Cruz, against the Anglo-French fleet in the Battle of Ponta Delgada near the Azores a year earlier was celebrated with great pomp. The governor ordered the city to come together in a solemn general procession in which the residents displayed their richest gold and silver adornments, silks, satins, velvets, and taffetas. Afterwards, the city gathered for bullfights and *juegos de cañas,* both present in many secular celebrations in the Iberian Peninsula during the late medieval and early modern period.[61] Three days later, the city celebrated a masquerade, in which a richly ornamented carriage carried the god Apollo, surrounded by the nine muses. According to the script of the event, the gods had been sent by the almighty Jupiter, who had rejoiced and celebrated the great Spanish victory in the skies and wanted to announce it to the governor of Santo Domingo as representative of King Felipe. The carriage, pulled by tame oxen and escorted by fifty horsemen with torches, rolled down the street as fireworks exploded overhead. Musicians accompanying the procession sang and played vihuelas and flutes. Upon reaching the palace of the *Audiencia* and with the governor, his wife, and many other ladies watching from the balcony, the musicians played songs especially composed for the occasion, praising the king, the heroic deeds of the Spanish in the battle, and the president of the *Audiencia.* Even the god Mercury, adorned with wings on his helmet and feet, descended from a hidden structure within the carriage and went up the stairs of the *Audiencia,* where the president received him. In the end, the musicians played and sang a *chacota,* a humorous and playful song. Mercury returned to Apollo's carriage, the knights galloped down the street, and the masquerade dissolved into the streets of Santo Domingo, possibly to continue in another corner of the city.[62]

Iglesia y el negro esclavo en Santo Domingo: una historia de tres siglos (Santo Domingo: Patronato de la Ciudad Colonial de Santo Domingo, 1994), 50; Cipriano de Utrera, *Santo Domingo. Dilucidaciones Históricas,* tomo 1 (Santo Domingo: Imprenta de Dios y Patria, 1927), 327–30.

[61] Of Moorish origin, *juegos de cañas* were mock battles in which horse riders displayed their skill engaging elaborate maneuvers and feigning attacks to an invisible enemy. See Teófilo F. Ruiz, *The King Travels. Festive Traditions in Late Medieval and Early Modern Spain* (Princeton: Princeton University Press, 2012), 212–20.

[62] Archivo General de Simancas (AGS), Guerra y Marina (GYM), 152, n. 189.

Colonial Origins: Hispaniola in the Sixteenth Century

Triumphal culture involving parades, heroic entrances, and even ephemeral architecture were an important part of the Iberian Renaissance and Baroque culture on both sides of the Atlantic.[63] These public spectacles, beyond their entertainment value, became crucial tools to legitimize and bolster the power of the monarchy, as represented by the crown officials. As the residents of Santo Domingo gathered to commemorate the Spanish victory, they were also celebrating their loyalty and membership to a transatlantic Spanish community. At the same time, this solemn general procession with citizens richly dressed reveals the exclusionary nature of part of the celebration, in which the wealthy and the powerful on display mirrored the local social hierarchy. It is unclear the level of voluntary participation of certain residents of the city, such as enslaved or free Africans, in either part of the ceremony. In any case, the celebration of such an event in Santo Domingo indicated active participation and involvement in the news coming from Spain and in the power of the Spanish monarchy. The lavish celebration also signaled the city's continued prosperity amid the progressive decline that most sugar producers were experiencing.[64]

AN ISLAND IN TRANSITION

The Spanish colony of Hispaniola reinvented itself multiple times throughout the sixteenth century: the relentless exploitation of the Taíno population of the island in the gold mines during the early years, accompanied by war and disease, led to the irrevocable disappearance of Taíno communities by the middle of the sixteenth century. Their substitution with native labor from the surrounding islands only led to the eradication of many other communities across the Caribbean. As the gold mines became depleted by the late 1510s, some colonists invested the wealth they had accumulated and created sugar plantations across the

---

[63] See for example, Teófilo F. Ruiz, *Spanish Society, 1400–1600* (Harlow, UK; New York: Longman, 2001), 129–30; Ruiz, *A King Travels*, 1–33; Fernando Checa Cremades and Laura Fernández-Gonzalez, eds. *Festival Culture in the World of the Spanish Habsburgs* (Burlington: Ashgate, 2015); Carolyn Dean, *Inka Bodies and the Body of Christ: Corpus Christi in Colonial Cuzco, Peru* (Durham: Duke University Press, 1999); Linda A. Curcio-Nagy, *The Great Festivals of Colonial Mexico City: Performing Power and Identity* (Albuquerque: University of New Mexico Press, 2004).

[64] These early years of 1580s coincide with a boom in the exportation of ginger to Spain, and planters possibly enjoyed record prices for their harvest. Del Río Moreno and López y Sebastián, "El jenjibre," 63–88.

south of the island. They did so by obtaining credit provided by the crown and private Spanish and Genoese merchants, thus perpetuating their families in the social and economic apex of the island's society.

Planters purchased thousands of African enslaved workers, who toiled and struggled in the plantations alongside the remaining natives from Hispaniola and neighboring islands. They worked, resisted, and often fled the plantations together. Enrique's rebellion in 1519 constituted the longest-lasting movement of resistance against the Spanish on the island, but the final peace agreement between Enrique and the crown in 1533 did not mean the end of the maroons in Hispaniola. In the mountains, numerous groups continued to oppose the colonists, sometimes violently, sometimes by the mere act of surviving and creating free communities away from Spanish control. Despite native and African resistance, some Spanish colonists on the island prospered and became wealthy. A few lucky ones were able to invest the fortunes they acquired as miners into sugar plantations. Most, however, were unable to do so, and they either survived by turning to cattle ranching, or sought their fortunes in other parts of the Americas.

By the 1570s, Hispaniola was a colony once again in transition. As the sugar plantations languished, new crops such as ginger replaced them, but this economic bonanza lasted only a few years, as the rest of Spanish Caribbean colonies started producing ginger as well, sinking the prices in the Spanish markets and forcing planters to search for new alternatives. Cattle ranching and subsistence agriculture became a viable option for those with limited resources. Meanwhile, despite the economic challenges, Santo Domingo continued to be the main commercial and political center of the island, a site of conspicuous consumption where residents still managed to display vestiges of their old wealth and rank, while living in the houses that their forebearers had built with the wealth generated by natives and Africans.

This world came to a screeching halt on 1586 when the English privateer Francis Drake and his men assaulted Santo Domingo. Drake and his forces stayed in the city for about two weeks, gathering 16,000 *ducados* from the royal treasury in addition to pillaging every building. In the words of a Santo Domingo resident to the Council of the Indies, "I can't talk to Your Majesty about the destruction of this city or the ills that your servants and vassals have experienced without tears in my eyes. Because it is not just the losses and deaths, but it hurts to have seen our enemies trample and

Colonial Origins: Hispaniola in the Sixteenth Century 55

burn our images, churches, and blaspheme our Christian religion without us poor wretches being able to stop them."[65]

The English tried to ransom the city for a million *ducados*, but they soon realized that the legendary prosperity of Santo Domingo was well in the past, and such a price was beyond the reach of its residents. They then lowered the ransom to the still princely sum of 100,000 *ducados*. When the residents struggled to gather even a fraction of such an amount, the English started burning the city. This required far more than setting a few fires – Drake had to dedicate a team of 200 sailors, working from dawn to 9 am (before the day's heat was too intense), to burn and destroy houses. Despite such dedication, they only managed to burn between a third and half of the city, at which point they settled with the Spanish to ransom the other half of the city for a discounted 25,000 *ducados*. In addition, they took all valuable goods, such as elegant clothing, every gold and silver item they could find, the church bells, the artillery of the fortress, and many African enslaved laborers left behind by their masters.[66]

The sacking of Santo Domingo not only ruined the lives of many of the residents of the city, but it is also likely that it had a cascading effect in exposing the population of Santo Domingo in very personal ways to the harsh realities of the economic crisis reigning on the island. Deprived of most of their savings, housing, and their most prized possessions – including many of their enslaved laborers – the city's residents faced the gloomy prospect of rebuilding their lives at a time in which the island's economic prospects were at a crossroads. Sugar was no longer a reliable source of wealth. Ginger and cattle ranching were promising as long as planters and ranchers could find reliable markets for their products. As the next chapter will show, this struggle to find alternative commercial partners led many residents to make their own arrangements with foreign traders, with important consequences for the island's future.

---

[65] "No se puede decir sin lágrimas la destrucción de esta ciudad de Vuestra Majestad o los males que a sus criados y vasallos de Vuestra Majestad nos han venido, porque no solo han sido pérdidas de haciendas y muertes. Mas lo que más duele haber visto a nuestros enemigos pisar y quemar las imágenes, iglesias, y blasfemar de nuestra religion cristiana, y nosotros miserables sin poderles resistir." Rodrigo Fernández de Rivera to the Council of the Indies. June 30, 1586, in Incháustegui, *Reales Cédulas*, 688.

[66] Bigges, *A summarie*, 32; Incháustegui, *Reales Cédulas*, 682.

2

Smuggling, Sin, and Survival, 1580–1600

During the celebration of Corpus Christi in Santo Domingo in 1588, the prebendary and teacher Cristóbal de Llerena and his students performed a short play or *entremés* as part of the day's festivities. The play opened with a conversation between the simpleton Cordellate, who was fishing without much success, and an unnamed character, who suggested that the simpleton engage in a much more profitable "fishery": to go to the mouth of the River Haina, a few miles to the southwest of Santo Domingo and exchange the copper coin circulating on the island for silver currency at a more advantageous rate than the one offered in the city (see Figure 2.1). This unnamed character did not say with whom Cordellate would be exchanging copper coins, but the audience, composed of Santo Domingo residents, likely would have assumed that referred to some form of illicit trade with Spanish, Portuguese, or northern European traders.

The play revolved around Cordellate giving birth to a monster who, the modern reader might suspect, represented the population of Santo Domingo at large. The monster, in the classic tradition of the grotesque, had a woman's head, a horse's neck, a bird's body, and a fish's tail. All the play's characters, including two *alcaldes ordinarios* (local judges) of the *Cabildo* of Santo Domingo agreed that, since the monster was born on the island at this particular moment, his birth must have been a sign of the times. To interpret the meaning behind the apparition of this beast, different classical figures appeared on stage to share their insights. Oedipus, King of Thebes, interpreted the monster's features as symbols of femininity and as a warning against the dissolute lives led by the women of Santo Domingo. The god Proteus, another of the classical characters,

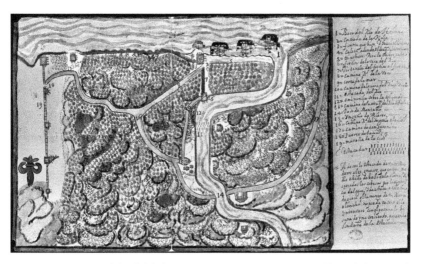

FIGURE 2.1 Map of the fields between Santo Domingo city walls and the mouth of River Haina, 1679. Most of the defenses depicted, including the city walls, did not exist in the late sixteenth century. Ministerio de Cultura y Deportes, AGI, Mapas y Planos, Santo Domingo, 77B.

saw the features of the monster as signs of the ills of the Republic, namely, impudent women (again), corrupt royal officials (which one of the *alcaldes* character resented), and the abusive prices and shipping fees charged by merchants operating in the city. It was the augur Calchas, however, who was granted the last word. In his view, the birth of the monster forewarned tempestuous times for the island in the form of war and warships sent against Santo Domingo and thus signaled the women to escape the city and to get all the local horses and vessels ready to flee.

With these words, the playwright Llerena possibly reminded his audience of the horrors of Francis Drake's destruction of the city two years earlier when, in the testimony of a witness, "women, children, nuns, friars and disabled people [were] scattered through mountains and roads," and warned them of a second invasion.[1] In reply to these interpretations by these classical characters and despite the calls for prudence by the second *alcalde*, who advised everyone to consider these interpretations seriously, the first *alcalde* dismissed them all as folly, pointed out the strong defenses

---

[1] "mujeres y niños, monjas y frailes y personas impedidas descarriadas por los dichos montes y por los caminos." Letter of *oidor* Francisco de Aliaga to the Council of the Indies. January 13, 1586. AGI, SD. 9, n. 84.

58   *Islanders and Empire*

of the city, the galleys guarding the port, and hurried his colleague to a gathering of the *Cabildo* of the city for an official interpretation of what the monster would mean.[2]

As the oldest existing European theatre piece written in the Americas, Cristóbal de Llerena's *entremés* has been studied by scholars of literature and theater, but its importance goes beyond the literary.[3] It represents a scathing critique of Hispaniola's society and the local and colonial administration on the island at the end of the sixteenth century. It was interpreted as such by the authorities of the island who, according to the archbishop Alonso López Dávila, were annoyed by the play's inferences about the city's poor defenses. As a consequence, they exiled Llerena from the island without a trial and put him on a boat bound to Riohacha, located in today's eastern Colombia. Through his characters, Llerena voiced some of the problems troubling the residents of the island: namely, the economic difficulties of Hispaniola, the changes in the local currency, the abuses of merchants doing business in the city, the threat of foreign ships to the island shores, a sense of moral fragility, and the importance of contraband in people's daily lives.

In this chapter, I will focus the issues highlighted by Llerena, namely, the contraband culture that developed in Hispaniola in response to the economic challenges the island faced during the last decades of the sixteenth century. This is what Jesse Cromwell, inspired by E. P. Thompson, has described for eighteenth-century Venezuela as "the moral economy of smuggling."[4] I argue that, although smuggling had existed in some

---

[2] The play is attached to a letter of the Archbishop Alonso López Dávila to the Council of the Indies, dated July 16, 1588. AGI. SD. 93, R. 1. Published in Pedro Henríquez Ureña, *La cultura y las letras coloniales en Santo Domingo* (Buenos Aires: unknown press, 1936), 153–57. A transcription of the play is also available online in the Biblioteca Virtual Miguel de Cervantes at www.cervantesvirtual.com/nd/ark:/59851/bmc4x557 (Last accessed, April 29, 2020).

[3] Some of the works that Llerena's *entremés* has generated are Anthony M. Pasquariello, "The Entremes in Sixteenth-Century Spanish America." *The Hispanic American Historical Review*, vol. 32, n. 1 (Feb., 1952), 44–58; Abelardo Vicioso, *Santo Domingo en las letras coloniales, 1492–1800* (Santo Domingo: Universidad Autónoma de Santo Domingo, 1972), 162–75; Julie Greer Johnson, "Cristóbal De Llerena and His Satiric Entremés." *Latin American Theatre Review Fall* (1988): 39–45; Raquel Chang-Rodríguez, "Colonial Voices of the Hispanic Caribbean," in Albert James Arnold et al., eds., *A History of Literature in the Caribbean, volume 1, Hispanic and Francophone Regions* (Philadelphia: John Benjamins Publishing Company, 1994), 111–40.

[4] Jesse Cromwell, *The Smugglers' World: Illicit Trade and Atlantic Communities in Eighteenth-Century Venezuela* (Chapel Hill: University of North Carolina Press, 2018), 15–16.

Smuggling, Sin, and Survival, 1580–1600 59

measure throughout the earlier years of the colony, contraband as a widespread phenomenon in Hispaniola involving all of the island's social groups appeared during the second half of the sixteenth century and had its origins in the lack of official trade with Sevilla and the search by local residents for alternatives.

By the early seventeenth century, contraband had become an intrinsic part of Hispaniola's culture, and that of many other parts of the Spanish Caribbean. Many island residents organized their lives around the trade with foreign merchants. They created an alternative marketplace, a parallel system to the one sponsored by the Spanish crown, that peoples from all corners of society, including members of the royal administration and the clergy, participated in and benefited from either knowingly or inadvertently. The easy and cheap access to European commodities prolonged the sense of prosperity and comfort in the day-to-day lives of the island's inhabitants and made the hardships of living in a progressively marginal and isolated territory of the Spanish Monarchy tolerable.

On the other hand, this contraband culture raised the suspicions of some authorities and members of the clergy who feared the consequences that such close relations with foreign Protestant traders might have for the economic and spiritual life of the local residents. These concerned observers made no distinctions between French or English merchants. They were all seen as a threat to the economy of the island and the faith of its residents. This chapter also reveals the complete inability of the Spanish bureaucracy to curb illicit trading. Even when the *Audiencia* judges were not members of local patronage networks involved in smuggling, they rarely managed to catch illicit merchants and make an example out of them. Special prosecutors (*visitadores*) sent from Spain encountered increasing resistance and a hostile environment to carrying out their mission in Hispaniola, and their convictions were often ignored. All attempts by the crown to curb the contraband trade failed, and by the early seventeenth century, Hispaniola was firmly established as one of the most important contraband centers in the Caribbean.

SMUGGLING WITH NORTHERN EUROPEAN TRADERS

As seen in the previous chapter, the sugar plantation economy of Hispaniola entered into a progressive decline in the second half of the sixteenth decade from which it would not recover. The cultivation of ginger and cattle ranching expanded as alternative economic activities, but the rearticulation of the Spanish colonial economy around the fleet

60   *Islanders and Empire*

system left Hispaniola outside the legal shipping circuit. In Santo Domingo, the dependence of its residents upon Sevillian merchants became a serious hurdle to local producers. The very limited traffic of vessels in the port of Santo Domingo emboldened merchants in the city to raise shipping fees and prices of imported products at will. Only those landowners with ships of their own were able to circumvent the onerous conditions that these merchants imposed on local residents. Writing in 1581, Juan López Melgarejo, the *alguacil mayor* of the *Audiencia,* expressed his dissatisfaction with commerce on the island, pointing out that, in 1580, the merchants from Sevilla sent only two ships with extremely expensive merchandise and demanded one box of sugar as payment for every box they freighted to Spain.[5]

The *Audiencia* of Santo Domingo agreed with Melgarejo a year later, and claimed that the diminished number of vessels had been a calculated move by the Sevillian merchants to sell their remaining stock at high prices.[6] These allegations may not have been gratuitous. In circumstances in which their monopolistic position was challenged in any way, the merchants did not hesitate to complain to the governor or to the Council of the Indies in Spain, denouncing irregularities and violations of the law. This happened in 1584, when Governor Cristóbal de Ovalle allowed entry to the port to some ships forced to reroute during a voyage to Brazil by a storm that damaged the vessels. In his defense, the governor claimed that the arrival of the ships into the port did not cause any harm to the inhabitants but instead benefited the island and the royal coffers, since the products sold on the island provided needed tax revenue. The only parties annoyed by the entry of the ships in the port, the governor added, "are two or three merchants that do not do anything in the service of Your Majesty, and all they do is robbing the *vecinos* of this city."[7] Ovalle's response highlights the tensions between peninsular merchants, who were interested in keeping Santo Domingo an exclusive market for Sevillian ships, and local residents, who welcomed merchants who could provide them with goods at more competitive prices.

---

[5] Juan López Melgarejo to the Council of the Indies, November 17, 1581. AGI, SD. 80, R. 1, n. 19.

[6] The *Audiencia* of Santo Domingo to the Council of the Indies, February 26, 1581. AGI, SD. 51, R. 4, n. 52.

[7] "los que se agravian de esto son dos o tres mercaderes que no tratan de cosa que convenga al servicio de Vuestra Majestad sino de saltear a los vecinos de esta ciudad." Governor Cristóbal de Ovalle to the Council of the Indies, February 4, 1584. AGI, SD. 51, R. 7, n. 75.

The unscheduled arrival of ships to the port, known as *arribadas,* did leave room for many irregularities. Shipmasters sometimes claimed to have been taken off course in order to sell their merchandise in a port where they did not have permission to anchor. The *Audiencia* needed to tax these ships as much as the residents of the city wanted or needed their products since, during these years and until the end of the century, the salaries of the members of the *Audiencia* were paid from the revenue generated by the royal treasury of the island in duties from commerce and sentences of individuals processed in its court. The reduction of port traffic thus created some problems for the *Audiencia,* and the arrival of unscheduled ships became a welcome addition to the royal coffers as well as to the city's markets. The newly arrived products lowered local prices and, for a little while, freed local residents from the terms established by the Sevillian merchants. At the same time, shipmasters of the incoming vessels offered bribes, deep discounts, or privileged access to products to the *oidores* and other members of the *Audiencia.* Sevillian merchants conducting business on the island complained that these abuses were commonplace. As discussed later, the interest of the *Audiencia* as a body to maintain high levels of activity in the port of Santo Domingo was not in contradiction with the fact that many *oidores,* in the performance of their duties and despite their writings to Spain, allowed the smuggling activity on the northern coasts of the island, benefited from it, and did little to stop it.

Just as merchants and landowners in or near Santo Domingo found a silver lining to the decreased commercial traffic in all these welcome irregularities, in the north and western shores of Hispaniola, local inhabitants were also forced to seek new alternatives to place their products into the Atlantic markets, supply themselves with African enslaved labor, and procure desired manufactured goods, notably textiles, at more affordable prices. Smuggling became a necessity for the majority of island residents, and a great opportunity to accumulate wealth, despite the risks, for a few. Situated far from Santo Domingo and royal officials, the unpopulated harbors in the north and west of the island became the preferred areas of exchange with foreign traders, in the proximity of the towns of La Yaguana, Bayahá, Montecristi, and Puerto Plata (see Figure 2.2). With the signing of the treaty of Cateau-Cambrésis between France and Spain in 1559 and its policy of "no peace beyond the line," French ships started frequenting Caribbean waters for trade and plunder without fear of their actions undermining diplomatic relations between the two countries in Europe. Before 1580s, French ships were the main visitors to

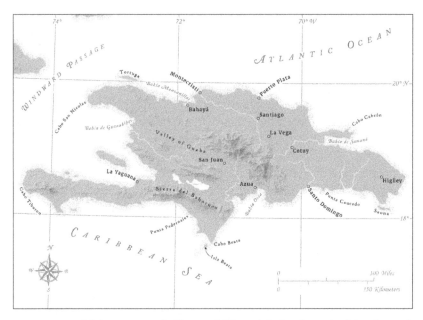

FIGURE 2.2 Main towns and villages of Hispaniola by the end of the sixteenth century (Alexander Fries, University of Alabama Cartographic Research Laboratory).

the remote northern coasts of Hispaniola. Portuguese vessels, whose presence was already commonplace to the slave trade, also increased with the union of the crowns of Castilla and Portugal under Felipe II in 1580. Francis Drake's sack of Santo Domingo in 1585 signaled an increase of hostilities between Castilla and England in the last two decades of the sixteenth century and led to an increasing presence of English piratic and commercial activity in the Caribbean and in Hispaniola. By the turn of the century, probably coinciding with the founding of the West India Company, many Dutch merchants started conducting business in the northern ports of the island. The increased presence of northern Europeans in Caribbean waters coincided with the island's commercial woes, and the rise of commercial partnerships between local producers and foreign traders ensued.[8]

---

[8] Kenneth R. Andrews, *The Spanish Caribbean: Trade and Plunder, 1530–1630* (New Haven: Yale University Press, 1978), 136, 156, 180–81; Paul E. Hoffman, *The Spanish Crown and the Defense of the Caribbean, 1535–1585: Precedent, Patrimonialism, and Royal Parsimony* (Baton Rouge: Louisiana State University Press, 1980), 109–14; Mark Hanna, *Pirate Nests and the Rise of the British Empire, 1570–1740* (Chapel Hill: University of North Carolina Press, 2015), 38–39.

Smuggling, Sin, and Survival, 1580–1600   63

In some cases, these relationships were the result of more or less fortuitous coastal encounters between a foreign merchant who arrived in Hispaniola looking to trade their merchandise and local inhabitants willing to trade. According to Jerónimo de Torres, *escribano de cámara* of the *Audiencia* and once resident in the town of La Yaguana, when a French merchant anchored in a bay, he "shoots once or twice, and thus is heard in the nearby ranches three or four *leguas* away ... and from one rancher to the next, the whole region of Puerto Real and Montecristi is notified." The cannon shot was the sign that a ship willing to trade was nearby. The merchants rarely went to land because of the great risk to their safety, and when they did, they asked for hostages to ensure that their men were not harmed and that all previous agreements were respected. In 1593, a group of *vecinos* from Bayahá traded with a French ship for twelve enslaved Africans. Two Spaniards stayed in the French ship as hostages while a French boat went to land with the captive Africans. A witness testified that the French were very close to hanging one of the hostages because they considered that the Spaniards had not fulfilled their part of the deal. Foreign traders understood that fortuitous exchanges with locals were based on a very fragile balance of forces between the merchant and the local inhabitants.[9]

Depending on the people involved and local circumstances, a commercial exchange could very quickly turn into a pillaging expedition. A 1569 anonymous French document translated into Spanish provides an example. A French ship from Dieppe (near Rouen, in northern France) entered the port of Artibonite, in the northwest of Hispaniola. The captain went on land to meet the locals and both groups exchanged hostages to ensure the safety of both parties. Once the exchange was finished and the captain was ready to return to his ship, the captain returned the Spanish hostages. The Spaniards, taking advantage of their moment of strength and anticipating great profits, attacked the captain and his men, killing at least eight, capturing part of the crew and forcing the captain to ransom them in

---

[9] A *legua* equals approximately 2.7 miles. "En surtiendo el francés, tira una o dos piezas y óyenlo en los hatos de vacas comarcanos que estan a dos y tres y cuatro leguas ... y de unos a otros avisase todo el término de Puerto Real y el de Montecristi." Jerónimo de Torres, "Relación sobre cosas de la isla Española," May 29, 1577. Transcribed in E. Rodríguez Demorizi, *Relaciones Históricas de Santo Domingo*, vol. II (Santo Domingo: Montalvo, 1945), 135. The commercial exchange with hostages is from the testimony of Juan Cardenas, barber and resident of Santo Domingo, in the investigation of Judge Alonso de Acevedo. 1594. AGI, Escribanía de Cámara de Justicia (Escribanía), 17A. For another description of the possible itinerary of foreign merchants seeking trade with local residents, see Hoffman, *The Spanish Crown*, 119–20.

64   *Islanders and Empire*

exchange for much of the merchandise in his ship. Events like this one, either truthful or invented, might have played a role in the way many foreign merchants conducted business in Hispaniola and other ports.[10]

In order to avoid risks and maintain an upper hand in the deals, foreign merchants normally waited on their ships for the inhabitants of the neighboring lands to come to the beach with their products, and then "they deal with them as if they were in Cádiz." Francisco Díaz, a Portuguese sailor, also testified in 1594 that on a beach near the town of Montecristi, people arrived loaded with hides and left with cloth "as if they went to the market." When the exchanges took place in a secluded port, white inhabitants participated directly, although it was not unusual for free and enslaved peoples of African descent to be commissioned by their patrons or owners to act as intermediaries between merchants and *vecinos*. This way, white landowners and masters stayed out of harm's way and protected themselves against any possible prosecution from the royal justice.[11]

On other occasions, these exchanges were the result of solidly established partnerships between northern European merchants and local inhabitants. In 1584, some witnesses in a smuggling investigation identified Francisco Tostado de Vargas, member of one of the oldest families on the island, as "an agent for Lutheran ships" who introduced smuggled merchandise into the city of Santo Domingo through a prebendary of the cathedral of Santo Domingo. In 1597, Francisco Jiménez, a well-known smuggler, was identified by many witnesses as an agent representing French merchants. He was a *vecino* of the village of Bayahá, who during 1596 had been appointed as *alcalde ordinario* of the town, and in 1597 he purchased the office of the town's *alguacil mayor* (high constable) to be able to trade with foreigners undisturbed. French merchants came every year to load their ships with the products that Jiménez had assembled. He, his brother Cristóbal Jiménez, and his brother-in-law Juan Cid, both also residents in Bayahá, had a network of associates, clients, relatives, and enslaved people who helped them in their deals. They (or possibly, their enslaved workers) traveled the land on pack animals and brought ginger

---

[10] "Discurso verdadero de las crueldades de españoles contra franceses así en Perú, Tierra Firme como en las islas," 1569. AGI, SD, 87.

[11] "y tratan con ellos como si fuese en Cádiz." Memorial by Jerónimo de Torres, in Rodríguez Demorizi, *Relaciones*, vol. II, 130; "iban y venían como quien va a la feria." Testimony of Francisco Díaz, 1594. AGI, Escribanía, 17A. Carlos Esteban Deive, *Tangomangos: Contrabando y Piratería en Santo Domingo, 1522–1606* (Santo Domingo: Fundación Cultural Dominicana, 1996), 107–18.

Smuggling, Sin, and Survival, 1580–1600

and hides from places as distant as Cotuy and La Yaguana directly to the ports in the north to speed up the loading of the ships and reduce their risk of being captured. Jiménez was seen entering French ships on numerous occasions, sometimes carrying the baton that identified him as a royal official, and he even held banquets on the beach for his French associates.

Although this close relationship with foreign traders carried the risk of visibility that might attract the island's authorities, it also contained ample benefits for the local smuggler. In exchange for the local production, Jiménez asked the French merchants to supply specific merchandise on subsequent trips to the island so that he would be able to sell these difficult-to-source goods at higher prices. Also, these local smugglers protected their contacts with foreign partners from being known to others, thus ensuring themselves as the only point of access to the much-desired merchandise.[12]

During these years, Portuguese sailors were frequently found among the crews of these ships from northern Europe. Apart from their skills and knowledge of the navigation routes, they were also great intermediaries with local merchants and residents, some of whom were of Portuguese descent themselves. From the first half of the sixteenth century, many Portuguese merchants had maintained business on the island. They participated in an active contraband trade, bringing enslaved Africans from Senegambia and introducing them through Hispaniola's northern shores or the harbors around Santo Domingo like Ocoa, thus avoiding detection from the authorities. These and many other merchant ships also brought Portuguese sailors who remained and settled in Hispaniola as well as in every Spanish port city in the Caribbean. The Spanish captain Iñigo de Lecoya affirmed that every year at least three hundred Portuguese (and Italians) made it to the Indies in the annual fleet, and only a few returned. "It is a marvel," he added, "to find there a boatman, small innkeeper, grocer, doctor, or apothecary who is not Portuguese."[13] The continuous arrival of Portuguese immigrants, added to the emigration of Spanish

---

[12] Testimony of Juan González Campuzano. June 4, 1584. AGI, SD. 80, R. 2, n. 69; testimony of Deputy Judge Antonio Orozco to judge Francisco Varela, 1597. AGI, SD. 24, n. 57; AGI, Escribanía, 17A.

[13] AGI, Indiferente General, 2673, memorandum of Captain Íñigo de Lecoya, ca. 1575. Cited in Pablo E. Pérez-Mallaína, *Spain's Men of the Sea: Daily Life on the Indies Fleets in the Sixteenth Century.* Translated by Carla Rahn Phillips (Baltimore: Johns Hopkins University Press, 1998), 61. For examples of Portuguese migration to Santo Domingo and other Caribbean ports at this time, as well as their links to the transatlantic slave trade, see David Wheat, *Atlantic Africa and the Spanish Caribbean* (Chapel Hill: University of North Carolina Press, 2016), 104–41; Andrews, *The Spanish Caribbean*, 38–39.

66   *Islanders and Empire*

settlers to other parts of Spanish America in the 1560s and 1570s, made
the population of Portuguese descent much more conspicuous to the eyes
of royal officials, who continuously reported their presence. *Visitador*
(royal inspector) Rodrigo Ribero, who was on the island in the early
1580s, talking about the connection between contraband ships and the
Portuguese population of the island, complained that every French
ship arriving to the island's shores brought a Portuguese pilot and
added that "there are more Portuguese inhabitants than Castilians.
Many of them live in the interior [meaning the north] near the sea and
they are rich ... Nowadays it is felt that they are more concerned by the
things of Portugal than if they lived in Rua Nova in Lisbon. The main
smugglers are Portuguese."[14]

Governor Cristóbal de Ovalle did not subscribe to such a negative view
of the Portuguese community, but he did remain uncertain about their
intent. Many Portuguese residents, he pointed out, were merchants and
had married and settled on the island. Others were constantly coming in
and out of the island with merchandise and enslaved African laborers. The
governor suggested that, for the prosperity of the island, they should not
be excluded. However, when approached by the local Portuguese community asking him to help them with the founding of an all-Portuguese
religious confraternity in honor of St. Anthony, the governor took their
documents and signatures, but ordered them not to pursue it. He suggested to them that if they were so fond of the saint, they should instead
dedicate masses and good works to him. For Governor Ovalle, it was one
thing to allow Portuguese merchants to live on the island and benefit
Hispaniola's economy with their trade, but a very different one to support
a Portuguese institution that enabled them to gather privately without any
Spanish supervision.[15]

The deep ambivalence that these two peninsular public officials, Ribero
and Ovalle, about the Portuguese population stemmed from the geographic and social mobility of some Portuguese, which was perceived as

---

[14] "... muchos de ellos son vecinos de la tierra adentro en puertos de mar y ricos ... hoy se
siente de ellos tienen más vivas y en el alma las cosas de Portugal que si actualmente
estuviesen avecindados en la Rua Nova de Lisboa, y los principales rescatadores son
portugueses." Rodrigo Ribero to the Council of the Indies. December 24, 1581. AGI, SD.
70, R. 1, n. 16. For more on Portuguese emigration to Hispaniola during the sixteenth
century, see Marcel Bataillon, "Santo Domingo 'Era Portugal,'" in Bernardo Garcia, ed.,
Historia y sociedad en el mundo de habla española. Homenaje a José Miranda (México:
Colegio de México. Centro de Estudios Históricos, 1970), 113–20.
[15] Governor Cristóbal de Ovalle to the Council of the Indies. November 15, 1583. AGI, SD.
51, R. 6, n. 73.

Smuggling, Sin, and Survival, 1580–1600

troubling in a Spanish world where a sense of community rooted to a particular space – such as the city, town, or region – ruled its social, political, and religious life. Even in cases where these Portuguese merchants were solidly established in the community, they were still viewed with suspicion and perceived as outsiders. The influence that Portuguese residents had over the local markets by the late sixteenth century during a time of economic hardships did not improve their popularity in the eyes of many Spanish residents, and the suspicion of connections with northern European traders also fueled this mistrust.[16]

Some of these merchants took advantage of their wide network of associates throughout the Atlantic to conduct their business. If these associations involving English merchants became public, they could bring down the entire operation, especially in the period between 1585 and 1604, when Spain had issued an embargo against trade with England. In 1594, the Portuguese sailor Tomé Rodríguez was apprehended in the town of Bayahá, where he had arrived as the *contador* (accountant) of an English ship called *Luna Creciente* (Crescent Moon). This was his third visit to the island. Rodríguez originally arrived in Hispaniola for the first time in 1590 on a Spanish ship. In 1592 he arrived with an English ship to the town of La Yaguana, where he sold all the merchandise he had left from his previous stop in Cumaná. On this third visit, he was arrested by order of the governor of Santo Domingo soon after his ship anchored in Bayahá. An *oidor* of the *Audiencia* released him on bail, and he went back to Bayahá and warned his shipmates. By the time a judge sent to the island to prosecute contraband cases heard of this, the ship had left the port with its cargo of local products. Tomé Rodríguez was found soon afterwards walking down a street in Santo Domingo and was again detained and condemned to death.[17] In exchange for the commutation of his death

---

[16] For a study of the Portuguese nation and their increasing role in the emerging Atlantic economy of the sixteenth and seventeenth century, see Daviken Studnicki-Gizbert, *A Nation Upon the Ocean Sea: Portugal Atlantic Diaspora and the Crisis of the Spanish Empire, 1492–1640* (Oxford University Press, 2007), 34–39. For more on this mistrust of Portuguese residents in the Caribbean, see Brian Hamm, "Between Acceptance and Exclusion: Spanish Responses to Portuguese Immigrants in the Sixteenth-Century Spanish Caribbean," in Ida Altman and David Wheat, eds., *The Spanish Caribbean & the Atlantic World in the Long Sixteenth Century* (Lincoln: University of Nebraska Press, 2019), 113–35. See also, Ignacio Chueca Saldías. "El Caribe portugués: sobre políticas imperiales, redes planetarias y la presencia de portugueses en el Caribe durante el gobierno de Felipe III (1598–1621)." *Iberoamérica Social*, volumen especial 2 (2018): 27–45; Wheat, *Atlantic Africa*, 104–41.

[17] List of charges found by the licentiate Fernando Varela against the *oidor* Simón de Meneses, October 26, 1597. AGI, 51, R. 20, n. 162.

68　　　　　　　　*Islanders and Empire*

sentence, Rodríguez revealed to the judge the existence of two trade licenses granted to two residents in the city by England and United Provinces. In the house of Duarte Riberos, a Portuguese *vecino* and merchant, an *oidor* found the documents hidden in the ceiling, which named other Portuguese residents like Simón de Herrera, a known merchant in the city, who this time managed to escape to Puerto Rico. The other members of the company were immediately detained and their properties, valued at more than 30,000 *ducados*, were expropriated.[18] High profile cases such as this one against Tomé Rodríguez and his partners show the complex and far reaching Atlantic networks in which some of the merchants were active participants. Spanish residents were likely aware of many of these deals, participated actively in them, and possibly learned from some Portuguese merchants. In the early 1590s, Diego de Ovalle, a resident in the town of La Yaguana, went to England where he formed a company with English merchants and came back to the Caribbean, visiting the island of Margarita and the town of La Yaguana with a ship loaded with European merchandise, which he exchanged for local products.[19]

CONTRABAND, CHURCH, AND SIN

As discussed in Chapter 1, Francis Drake's attack on Santo Domingo in early 1586 was a profound shock for the city's residents. The English privateer landed a force of 1,200 men on the coast near Ocoa and headed for the capital, where defenders were poorly organized. Most *vecinos* were more concerned about saving their own possessions than with defending the city. As a consequence, the city was taken without any meaningful opposition. The city was sacked, almost half of it was burned, and the parts still standing were saved only after paying Drake and his men a ransom of 25,000 *ducados*.[20]

---

[18] Letter of *oidor* Dr. Quesada to the Council of the Indies. March 28, 1596. AGI, SD. 51, R. 17, n. 145. Tomé Rodríguez became a collaborator and in exchange for being taken to Spain (while his father was kept in prison in his place), he offered to reveal sensitive information regarding individuals who illegally traded with Dutch, English, and German merchants, and whose properties in Spain were valued more than 500,000 *ducados*. He even offered himself to go to Hamburg to convince certain merchants to send some ships and thus capture them, but it is unlikely that the Council accepted his proposal. He was probably sent to Spain in late 1598. AGI, SD. 51, R. 17, n. 164.

[19] Verdict issued by Fernando Varela against *oidor* Simón de Meneses. October 26, 1597. AGI, SD. 70, R. 1, n. 41.

[20] For collections of documents that narrate the events surrounding Drake's attack of Santo Domingo, see Rodríguez Demorizi, *Relaciones*, vol. II (Ciudad Trujillo: Editora

Smuggling, Sin, and Survival, 1580–1600 69

For years after the sack of the city, letters describing the damages that the Elizabethan privateer and his men caused to houses, religious buildings, and the economic well-being of many residents deluged the Council of the Indies in Spain. Despite these complaints and cries for royal assistance, which were rarely granted, this event did not alter the attitudes of many inhabitants with regard to dealing with foreigners. In fact, possibly driven by the impoverished conditions in which many residents of Santo Domingo were left after the invasion, their involvement in contraband activities and in the purchase of smuggled goods only increased. The sale of contraband goods (especially cloth, as well as other accessories like hats, handkerchiefs, but also enslaved Africans) also attracted the local elites in Santo Domingo. Most of the products smuggled through the northern and western coasts of the island ended up in Santo Domingo, the population and consumption center of the island. In the city, the products were sometimes mixed with those bought from Sevillian merchants to hide their provenance. Also, many smugglers had connections not only with residents, but with royal officials in the city, who bought their merchandise or sold it in their stead. Gonzalo Suárez, a resident in Santo Domingo, testified in 1594 in front of a judge about his trip a few days earlier outside the city walls, during which he had taken a boat to cross to the other side of the river Ozama. During the crossing, the boatman had complained to him about the previous night's disrupted rest; Diego Carrasco Barrionuevo, *regidor* of Santo Domingo, had asked him to take six *bozales* enslaved people from Angola into the city from the other side of the Ozama. The fact that the enslaved people were sneaked into the city in the middle of the night was all Suárez needed to know to conclude that they had been smuggled, and this was what he reported to the judge when he was asked. The seemingly casual retelling of the story by the boatman indicates the normalcy of events such as this one in the life of Hispaniola residents.[21]

For those interested in buying cloth in the city and used to the abusive prices of Sevillian merchants, low prices were a sure indicator of the provenance of the fabrics, or at least a cause for suspicion. Gonzalo

---

Montalvo, 1945), 7–108; Joaquín Marino Incháustegui Cabral, *Reales cédulas y correspondencia de gobernadores de Santo Domingo de la regencia del cardenal Cisneros en adelante*, tomo III (Madrid, 1958), 677–94.

[21] *Bozal* (pl. *bozales*) was a term used to refer to enslaved peoples brought directly from Africa, and therefore they were not familiar with Iberian cultural practices or language. Testimonies given to the contraband judge Alonso de Acevedo, 1594. AGI, Escribanía, 17A.

70   *Islanders and Empire*

Suárez narrated how in the parish of Santa Bárbara, in Santo Domingo, it was rumored that Cristóbal de Talavera, again in the name of the *regidor* Diego Carrasco Barrionuevo, was selling textiles at very low prices. When he went to Talavera's house, he found him selling linen at six *reales* a yard, even though its regular price was between thirty or forty *reales*. He immediately suspected the fabric's illicit origin, and, seeing himself in the moral predicament of possibly buying smuggled goods, he went to consult with his confessor. The priest eased his mind, saying that since he did not know for sure how the textiles had been acquired and since Cristóbal de Talavera was a respected member of the community and a *vecino* of the city, he could buy without worry. Reassured, Gonzalo Suárez returned to purchase the textiles. This event is very revealing on many levels. It shows that despite the wide acceptance of the practice of contraband and the purchase of smuggled goods, some residents were worried about the moral and religious repercussions of buying such products. Suárez also told the judge how two daughters of Diego de Montesdeoca, another *vecino* of the city, bought cheap linen cloth in the house of Francisco Tostado de Vargas; when they found out that it had been smuggled, they went to see the archbishop to seek absolution.[22]

Even though smuggling was an integral part of life in Hispaniola, many people living in Santo Domingo only came into contact with contraband at the marketplace. Some residents of Santo Domingo viewed the purchase of contraband goods not only as illegal, but as sinful. The fact that neither Suárez nor the two daughters of Montesdeoca returned the cloth when they found out it was smuggled, and instead looked for absolution is not necessarily a sign of insincerity. Instead, it speaks of the power of the clergy to ease the conscience of inhabitants over illegal interactions and to ameliorate questionable moral acts related to smuggling. The previous examples also reveals that the clergy's condemnation of smuggling was far from unanimous. As we saw in the case of Gonzalo Suárez, his moral misgivings about buying contraband goods were in sharp contrast with the unconcerned approach of his confessor, for whom ignorance about the origin of the textiles and the theoretical respectability of the seller as a member of good standing in the community were good enough. Most members of the lower clergy (priests) and the mendicant orders were born on the island and had a sizable web of relatives and acquaintances. Some of them either participated actively within contraband networks, or

[22] Ibid.

Smuggling, Sin, and Survival, 1580–1600

excused the participation of their neighbors, perhaps benefiting from it as a way to complement their limited income.[23]

The local clergy was deeply divided on the sinfulness of contraband trade. Many of those who arrived from Spain (although certainly not all) to serve in the archdiocese of Santo Domingo as prebendaries of the cathedral chapter condemned contraband as an immoral and sinful act. Other members of the high clergy, however, many of them born and raised on the island, promoted and benefitted from smuggling. In 1594, Simón de Alcázar, a *vecino* of Santo Domingo, was traveling to Santo Domingo from Montecristi. A few miles outside the town, Alonso de Cobo, prebendary of the cathedral of Santo Domingo, caught up with him. Cobo was in a hurry, and told Alcázar that he was on his way to see Francisco Tostado de Vargas, a known smuggler. The prebendary described how the captain of a French ship anchored near Montecristi demanded 1,500 *ducados* that Tostado owed him, and if Tostado did not pay, the Frenchman would not release the *regidor* of Santo Domingo Alonso de Cáceres Carvajal. Cobo, a close collaborator of Tostado de Vargas, had been seen aboard the French ship himself, and through him, Tostado introduced large quantities of merchandise into Santo Domingo. Also, the fact that a prebendary of the cathedral went all the way to Montecristi, a common smuggling port on the northern shore, when royal officials and judges normally complained about such a long trip through difficult and sparsely inhabited terrain even when paid to do so, shows the close ties that Cobo had with local contraband networks.[24]

Like Cobo, prebendaries of the cathedral of Santo Domingo who had been born on the island were often well connected with the most notable families of Hispaniola. Usually, they also owned land. By the end of the sixteenth century, more than half of the prebendaries of the cathedral were born in Hispaniola. As island production decreased and landowners found ways to evade paying the tithe, it became increasingly difficult for peninsular prebendaries, whose meager salaries depended on the tithe, to maintain themselves, and thus peninsular priests declined the

---

[23] Juana Gil-Bermejo García, *La Española: anotaciones históricas (1600–1650)* (Sevilla: Escuela de Estudios Hispanoamericanos, CSIC, 1983), 15.

[24] Judicial inquiries against Francisco Tostado de Vargas, 1594. AGI, Escribanía, 17A; testimony of Juan González Campuzano, *alguacil* of the judge Sancho Angulo's commission to investigate smuggling. June 4, 1584. AGI, SD. 80, R. 2, n. 69.

72   *Islanders and Empire*

appointment. By the middle of the seventeenth century, all the prebendaries in Santo Domingo were *criollos*.[25]

The archbishops of Santo Domingo tended to interpret local relationships with foreign merchants as the worst possible thing that could happen to the Catholic faith in Hispaniola. Regardless of their nationality, foreign traders were always assumed to be Protestants who fiercely tried to spread their false religion throughout the Indies while mocking the pope, Catholic institutions, and beliefs. In his letters to Madrid, Archbishop Fray Nicolás de Ramos (1592–9), showed his deep concern with the possible repercussions that smuggling could have on the spread of heretical ideas and behaviors in the population. In 1594, he wrote: "this island is about to be lost for Christianity as far as the faith in Christ is concerned, because in six or seven of its ports ... *vecinos* from those ports and even many from this city buy, sell and even eat meat with them [foreign traders] on prohibited days. And while they are all drunk, the heretics scoff at the authority of the pope and sneer at the Sacraments of the Holy Church."[26] According to the archbishop, the English merchants who came to the shores of Hispaniola to smuggle, challenged the authority of the king of Spain in the Indies, while claiming the island for the queen of England. The prelate claimed that "this evil has been planted in the land and spread among some in this island to such an extent that it has been necessary for me to preach from the pulpit that His Majesty is as much king of the Indies as he is of Castilla and León, and the rest."[27] Through their trade with the island residents, smugglers were winning the religious and ideological battle for the souls of the island inhabitants, and at the same time eroding the claim of the king of Spain to the island of Hispaniola.

---

[25] For a discussion on the clergy in Santo Domingo and their origin, see Genaro Rodríguez Morel, *Cartas de los Cabildos eclesiásticos de Santo Domingo y Concepción de la Vega en el siglo XVI* (Santo Domingo: Patronato de la Ciudad Colonial de Santo Domingo, 2000), 32–42.

[26] "Esta isla va por la posta a perderse así en la Cristiandad de las obras como en lo que toca a la fe de Cristo, porque en seis o siete puertos que hay en ella ... los vecinos de aquellos puertos y aun muchos de esta ciudad tratan con ellos, compran y venden y hartas veces comen carne con ellos en días vedados, estando los unos y los otros en sus borracheras, y los herejes mofando de la autoridad del papa y escarneciendo de los Sacramentos de la Santa Madre Iglesia." In Rodríguez Demorizi, *Relaciones*, vol. II, 145.

[27] "Hase sembrado esta maldad y corrido entre algunos de esta isla tanto que me ha sido necesario predicar en el púlpito que es Su Majestad tan rey de las Indias como de Castilla y León y lo demás." Ibid.

Ramos' concerns were not unfounded. In 1594, the *Cabildo* of Santo Domingo reported that in the previous year, more than twenty ships had been seen in the northern coasts of Hispaniola trading, and at that moment there were more than eleven vessels anchored in northern ports. "As they give what it is worth six for one, many of those who live in those parts, with little fear of God or Your Majesty, trade with them everything they bring, and to be able to pay, they kill all their cattle, so in very little time the island will be left without its main product."[28] With letters like this one, the members of the *Cabildo* of Santo Domingo rhetorically distanced themselves from the practices of the residents to the north. Even though many *regidores* in Santo Domingo were as guilty as their northern neighbors of participation in this illicit trade, a letter like this one might indicate a division in the body of the *Cabildo* and the need to maintain an official position that was in tune with those of the religious authorities on the island and with the official position of the crown about contraband trade with foreigners. The *Cabildo* members portrayed their northern neighbors as dissolute people led by greed, or even worse, easily tricked by heresy into foolish exchanges in which they bargained their fortunes. The letters warned about the dangers of trade with foreigners and the disappearance of all the cattle of the island, which would irrevocably lead to the ruin of the colony. They also exposed the vulnerability of the inhabitants of the north of the island to the heretical influence of foreign traders, which would risk religious contamination and losing the island for the Catholic faith.

Other prelates such as Ramos' successor, Agustín Dávila Padilla (1599–1604) had a much more nuanced vision of the realities of contraband trade. Dávila Padilla was also concerned about the religious contamination that northern residents were exposed to in their dealings with foreigners. He unequivocally denounced its practice: "not only breaking the laws of God and Your Majesty, but also, by communicating with heretics, they are at risk of being stained by the filth they deal with."[29] In a *visita* or inspection he commissioned to the interior of the island, the

---

[28] "y como dan lo que vale seis por uno, muchos de los que viven en aquella parte con poco temor de Dios y de lo que deben al servicio de Vuestra Majestad les mercan cuanto traen, y para podérselo pagar matan y disipan todo el ganado ... de manera que muy en breve quedará la isla sin su principal sustento." The *Cabildo* of Santo Domingo to the Council of the Indies. May 20, 1594. AGI, SD. 81, R. 4, n. 52.

[29] "no solamente quebrantando las leyes de Dios y de Vuestra Majestad pero comunicando con herejes y andando en peligro de que los manche la pez con que tratan." Archbishop Agustín Dávila Padilla. November 6, 1601. AGI, SD. 93, R. 1, n. 48.

74 *Islanders and Empire*

prebendary in charge found more than three hundred Lutheran bibles and burned them in the plaza next to the cathedral of Santo Domingo.[30] Dávila Padilla's critique, however, extended to the local clergy as well. He denounced the ignorance of local priests, who comprised the large majority of the clergy on the island. Their lack of a solid religious formation, Dávila Padilla believed, was the reason behind the leniency that many of them showed those participating in the contraband trade. The island residents, claimed Dávila Padilla, "have false prophets brought up in the ignorance and lack of study of these lands, and [these priests] tell them they can redeem their hardships and that their needs do not know any laws."[31]

On the other hand, Dávila Padilla understood that the contraband trade was in part the result of Santo Domingo being the only port on the island allowed to conduct trade with Sevilla and other American ports and of the lack of legal trade arriving to the northern and western regions of the island. He saw the consequences of such trade restrictions for the residents of the northern and western regions of the island as far reaching and dire.

> If the people from the region around Lisbon did not have the ships to export its production and import the goods from other regions but instead, they [the residents of Lisbon] had to go by land to Sevilla to load their products and buy whatever they needed from the Indies, they would take the great risk of making deals with the heretics that arrived at their ports. And that is the way things are in these lands. Those of us in the southern coast are like Sevilla, and those in the north are like Lisbon.[32]

In the same letter, the archbishop advocated for the crown to send ships with an escort to the northern ports to stimulate legal trade, but his

[30] The episode of the Lutheran bibles can be found in multiple sources. See, for instance, Luis Jerónimo de Alcocer, "Relación de la Isla Española," in Rodríguez Demorizi, *Relaciones*, vol. I, 262. There are references of similar findings in Cuba. Luis Martínez-Fernández, *Key to the New World: A History of Early Colonial Cuba* (Gainesville: University of Florida Press, 2018), 89.

[31] "porque tienen falsos profetas criados en la ignorancia y falta de estudio de esta tierra, que les dice que pueden redimir su vejación y que la necesidad carece de ley." Archbishop Agustín Dávila Padilla to the Council of the Indies. November 20, 1601. AGI, SD. 93, R. 1, n. 48. His predecessor, Nicolás de Ramos, also held local-born Spaniards with extreme contempt.

[32] "Si los de Lisboa no tuviesen navíos en su puerto que les sacasen de allí sus frutos y les llevasen los de otras tierras, sino que hubiesen de venir por tierra a Sevilla a cargar sus frutos y lo que hubiesen menester de las Indias, en gran peligro estarían de hacer este trato con herejes si a su puerto llegasen. De esta suerte están las cosas en esta tierra, y los que estamos a la banda del sur somos los de Sevilla, y los del norte como los de Lisboa." Ibid.

proposal was ignored or deemed inadequate. He even suggested arming two galleys to patrol the coasts of Hispaniola and hunt pirate ships, but as we will see later, this idea had already been tried with very limited success. It is unclear whether the archbishop intended to present the people around Lisbon as smugglers, but his example did perpetuate the view of the Portuguese as contrabandists. By using a peninsular example to explain Hispaniola's internal dynamics, however, the Archbishop empathized with the challenges of the people of Hispaniola and portrayed local residents as Castilian subjects driven by the same necessity as their peninsular counterparts to find a solution to their economic woes.

THE AUDIENCIA OF SANTO DOMINGO AND VISITADORES AGAINST CONTRABAND TRADE

If the church in Santo Domingo was a reflection of the different opinions, concerns, and interests that circulated throughout society in the city and island, the *Audiencia* was not different (see Figure 2.3). Although the *oidores* of the *Audiencia* were the legitimate representatives of royal authority, they were not seen as mere conduits for the distribution of royal justice for those who sought it. Their actions were often guided by their own self-interest. As historian Tamar Herzog has observed in her study of the *Audiencia* in Quito, the *oidores* were not mere executors of an abstract and codified Justice. Every judicial intervention by an *oidor*, whether self-interested or not, was always interpreted by plaintiffs and onlookers as a sign of friendship or animosity toward each opposing side in a case. At the same time, the merits of a case were not necessarily linked to its outcome. They were heavily influenced by the rank and power in society of the plaintiffs, the relationships they cultivated, and preexisting local rivalries. Thus, the rulings of an *oidor* were one more piece in the complex networks of clientelism and patronage in a city or region.[33]

Even for those governors and *oidores* who embraced the office with a sense of service to the crown and tried to distance themselves

---

[33] Tamar Herzog, *La administración como un fenómeno social: la justicia penal de la ciudad de Quito (1650–1750)* (Madrid: Centro de Estudios Constitucionales, 1995), 131–34; Genaro Rodríguez Morel, *Cartas del Cabildo de la Ciudad de Santo Domingo en el siglo XVI*, 25. For a more general explanation of the particularities of the early modern Spanish judicial system, see Robert C. Schwaller, *Géneros de Gente in Early Colonial México: Defining Racial Difference* (Norman: University of Oklahoma Press, 2016), 50–55.

FIGURE 2.3 Building of the *Audiencia* of Santo Domingo. Photo by the author.

from local rivalries and factions, their decisions were influenced by the pressures of their peers and the realities of living in a small city, in the relative isolation of an imperial borderland, coexisting and attending public events with many of the plaintiffs of the cases they had to oversee. As a consequence, knowing well that their rulings were being constantly interpreted by their neighbors, many *oidores* made strategic use of their power to strengthen their social and economic interests within the island. Referring to the relations between Santo Domingo elites and the *Audiencia*, *Visitador* Francisco Alonso de Villagrá observed in 1594 that "in the *Cabildo* of the city I see much disorder and excess in the election of officers by the *regidores* and *oidores*. The *regidores* offer presents and their votes in the *Cabildo* [to the *oidores*] when they bring cases to the *Audiencia* [in exchange for a favorable sentence], and the *oidores* accept them and ask for them as they do, being judges in those cases and having more influence in them than reason permits." Even though the *visitador* interpreted this as a "disorder," an unnatural and damaging state of affairs in the administration of justice and local governance alike, it was actually nothing out of the ordinary in a patrimonial state like the Spanish Monarchy and reflected the ways in which both local

Smuggling, Sin, and Survival, 1580–1600   77

groups and the members of the *Audiencia* often formed tight patronage networks.[34]

Despite all local connections and pressures, the *Audiencia* did intervene against cases of contraband trade. Prosecuting smuggling cases, however, was not an easy task. Although everyone knew the identity of the most important smugglers and intermediaries and where they operated, locals feigned ignorance when questioned about their identities. The *Audiencia* regularly sent judges to the north to investigate the smuggling cases they heard about, but in many instances, the investigations brought few charges. According to *oidor* Pedro de Arceo, "The proceedings made by this *Audiencia* to send judges every year against them [the residents in the north] are not enough. There are so many stratagems that the judges return without finding out much, because everyone commits perjury and does everything under such secrecy that it is impossible to prove anything."[35]

Governor Lope de Vega Portocarrero (1588–96) also commented on the impossibility of gathering evidence to prosecute the smugglers. "Although we have sent judges to punish it [contraband]," Governor Lope de Vega explained, "nothing could be done, because those who smuggle are blacks under the order of their masters, and when they know that a judge is on his way, they go to the mountains."[36] This stunning admission by the governor reveals the leading role that enslaved peoples of African descent played in the contraband trade and the great degree of involvement of enslaved African laborers in the illicit deals of their enslavers. According to the census that Antonio Osorio gathered in 1606, the island had a population of 1,157 Spanish *vecinos* (heads of household) and 9,648 enslaved Africans, divided between the few sugar

[34] "En el Cabildo de la ciudad veo mucho desorden y exceso en esto de la elección de oficios de parte de regidores y oidores, de los unos en irse a convidar y ofrecer con sus votos, trayendo pleitos en la Audiencia, y de los otros en aceptarlos y pedirlos como lo hacen, siendo jueces en ellos tomando en esto más mano de la que fuera razón." Francisco Alonso de Villagrá to the Council of the Indies. March 22, 1594. AGI, SD. 70, R. 1, n. 28.

[35] "No bastan la diligencia que se hacen por esta Audiencia enviando jueces pesquisidores cada año contra ellos, y hay tales modos y trazas que casi se vienen los jueces sin averiguar nada porque todos se perjuran y hacenlo todo tan secreto que no hay orden de averiguar ni sacar probado." Pedro de Arceo to the Council of the Indies. May 28, 1587. In Incháustegui, *Reales Cedulas*, vol. III, 710.

[36] "Aunque se ha enviado jueces a castigarlo no han podido hacer nada, porque los que rescatan son los negros por orden de sus amos y cuando saben que va juez vanse a la sierra." Governor Lope de Vega Portocarrero to the Council of the Indies. July 12, 1593. AGI, SD. 81, R. 3, 39.

78 *Islanders and Empire*

mills still in operation (800 workers), domestic service (1,556), and those working in rural properties, either farms cattle ranches (remaining 7,292).[37] The free black population was still scarce.[38] As David Wheat has pointed out for Hispaniola and the rest of the Spanish Caribbean, enslaved Africans performed most of the tasks needed for the functioning and maintenance of the colonies. Apart from conducting all kinds of tasks in households and urban centers, as well as feeding the population and producing export commodities such as sugar and ginger in the country-side, enslaved laborers were also crucial for the smuggling economy and culture that appeared in Hispaniola in the second half of the sixteenth century. Entrusting enslaved people with the day-to-day smuggling operation provided cover from the illegality and risks of the smuggling operations to their Spanish masters. It also allowed a modicum of deniability to the Spaniards if their laborers were caught. At the same time, the contraband trade must have permitted a great degree of mobility to those enslaved people entrusted with the transportation of goods from farms and cattle ranches to the points of exchange with foreign merchants.[39]

The role of maroon communities in the contraband trade during these years is unclear. As we saw in the previous chapter, the existence of runaway communities and the impossibility of their eradication by the Spanish colonial powers is well documented on the island. In the last twenty years of the sixteenth century, the Spanish carried out at least four *entradas* or attacks on the runaway communities of the Bahoruco, but they met with limited success.[40] It is possible that maroon communities participated in the contraband trade with foreign merchants or, at least, that they were in communication with enslaved Africans who did engage

---

[37] See Table 4.2.

[38] The census lists twenty-seven free African women heads of household, and eleven male. David Wheat, "*Nharas* and *Morenas Horras*: A Luso-African Model for the Social History of the Spanish Caribbean, c. 1570–1640." *Journal of Early Modern History*, vol. 14 (2010), 132.

[39] Concepción Hernández Tapia, "Despoblaciones de la isla de Santo Domingo en el siglo XVII." *Anuario de Estudios Americanos*, vol. XXVII (1970), 315–20; Roberto Cassá, *Historia social y económica de la República Dominicana* (Santo Domingo: 1983), 96–99; Wheat, *Atlantic Africa*, 186–90, 211. These numbers are only approximations. Since Spanish censuses only specified *vecinos* or heads of household for the number of Spaniards, the challenge for historians has been deciding how large the average Spanish household was, or in other words, what multiplier to use to reach the most accurate estimate of the Spanish population. I have decided to avoid multipliers and leave the numbers of *vecinos* as found in the documentation.

[40] Robert C. Schwaller, "Contested Conquests: African Maroons and the Incomplete Conquest of Hispaniola, 1519–1620." *The Americas*, vol. 75, n. 4 (2018), note 110.

Smuggling, Sin, and Survival, 1580–1600   79

in illicit trade in the name of their enslavers. Governor Lope de Vega's mention of enslaved Africans escaping to the mountains may imply that much. The *escribano de cámara* of the *Audiencia* Jerónimo de Torres wrote how in 1577, Portuguese and French traders always made a stop in the port of Yaquimo, distant only eight leagues by land from the Spanish town of La Yaguana. In Yaquimo (currently, the Haitian town of Jacmel), there was a cattle ranch that belonged to a resident of La Yaguana, but there were no Spaniards residing in it. Torres described that only inhabitants as people of African descent and Indians. Torres did not specify if they were enslaved or not, but he did explain that they acted as informants for the Europeans, letting them know if there was an armada in La Yaguana, or a Spanish ship ready to be plundered. Enslaved or not, African and even the few remaining native peoples possibly benefitted from their relationship with European merchants and raiders. Maroon communities may have also profited from similar arrangements, and in the process, made the prosecution of contraband a lot harder for crown officials.[41]

Smuggling was an open secret in Hispaniola. In the most isolated areas of the island, many local residents of either Spanish or African descent did not have any reservations about admitting that contraband existed or even that they indirectly bought contraband goods. The purchase of smuggled goods was a necessity for those living in the most remote parts of the island without access to legal markets or the coin to spend for those overpriced goods. When asked who their providers were, however, the reply was very different, and according to the *visitador* Rodrigo Ribero, they "generally confessed to everything they smuggle and that they can't live without doing it, but when asked particularly about who the smugglers are: *Fuenteovejuna*." The mention of "Fuenteovejuna" makes reference to the events that occurred in the Castilian village of Fuenteovejuna in 1476, where a commander, a knight of the order of Calatrava, harmed its inhabitants. As retaliation, the villagers came together and killed him.

---

[41] Jerónimo de Torres, in Rodríguez Demorizi, *Relaciones*, vol. II, 131. For more on maroon societies in Hispaniola during these years, see Schwaller, "Contested Conquests"; Carlos Esteban Deive, *Los guerrilleros negros: esclavos fugitivos y cimarrones en Santo Domingo* (Santo Domingo: Fundación Cultural Dominicana, 1989); Roberto Cassá, *Historia social y económica de la República Dominicana*, Vol.1 (Santo Domingo: Editora Alfa y Omega, 1992); Jane G. Landers, "Cimarrón and Citizen: African Ethnicity, Corporate Identity, and the Evolution of Free Black Towns in the Spanish Circum-Caribbean," in Jane Landers and Barry M. Robinson, eds., *Slaves, Subjects, and Subversives: Blacks in Colonial Latin America* (Albuquerque: University of New Mexico Press, 2006), 111–46.

80   *Islanders and Empire*

When a royal official was sent to make inquiries and ask for the identity of
the killer, the villagers' only response to the magistrate's questions was
"Fuenteovejuna." By claiming that the entire village killed the knight, the
villagers defended the actual culprits. By mentioning the Castilian city,
Rodrigo Ribero claimed that Hispaniola residents used a similar strategy
to protect local smugglers.[42]

The secrecy around contraband deals was indeed a significant handicap
for the judges, but not the only one. Another obstacle was the attitudes
and expectations of the judges themselves. They were usually residents of
Santo Domingo, relatives, friends, servants, or clients of the members of
the *Audiencia*, or temporary well-connected visitors on business on the
island. Governors and *oidores* gave the job of contraband judge to people
close to them as a way to favor those within their own patronage network.
These men, in turn, looked upon the job as an opportunity to gain a salary
and enlarge their list of services to their patrons and the crown. This was
also the case for those accompanying the judge, the *escribano* and the
alguacil, who were appointed to put into writing the proceedings and keep
under custody arrested smugglers respectively. For most judges sent to the
north of the island, making arrests was not a priority. What mattered most
was the collection of fines from those accused of smuggling. Since the
salaries of these judges and their teams were extracted from the fines they
collected in their investigation, a successful prosecution was not necessarily measured in terms of arrests, but in how much money a judge was able
to collect as a consequence of his investigations. Already in 1585, the *fiscal*
(prosecutor) of the *Audiencia* Francisco de Aliaga, complaining about the
practices of some of his colleagues within the *Audiencia*, pointed out that
there were royal decrees explicitly limiting how frequently judges could be
sent around the district to investigate cases. Aliaga considered that since
the land was poor, it was better to leave some crimes unpunished and help
the residents of the region than to burden them with judges. In the
previous two years, the judges sent to the north of the island had received
95 *reales* a day for their commission and "have left the land ruined."
Aliaga might have been expressing his own interested opinion as well as
that of his allies on the island. Nevertheless, it seems clear that local

---

[42] "lo confiesan en general todo lo que rescatan y que no pueden vivir sin hacerlo, mas en
particular preguntando quién es, Fuenteovejuna." Rodrigo Ribero to the Council of the
Indies, December 29, 1580. AGI, SD. 70, R. 1, n. 10. The events at Fuenteovejuna would
later inspire the famous Spanish playwright Lope de Vega Carpio to write his
Fuenteovejuna (1619).

Smuggling, Sin, and Survival, 1580–1600   81

residents saw judges, and not smugglers, as the real problem for their livelihoods. Aliaga's observation also hinted at the abuses that his colleagues in the *Audiencia* committed by appointing these judges to enhance their own and their allies' social and political positions on the island.[43]

Aliaga was not the only one to point out the abuses of judges sent to the north. Arriving in 1593, the *visitador* Francisco Alonso de Villagrá also noticed that the levy of heavy fines against smugglers was only secondary. What the judges and their officials did, wrote Villagrá, "is to receive their salaries and once finished their assignment, go back to their houses to eat what they have made and look for another [assignment] without having made any meaningful sentence, and there is no doubt that of all the judges that have gone to fulfill these tasks in the last 14 years, and there have been many, none of them have brought 100,000 *maravedis* to the royal coffers, while they have become very wealthy." Villagrá was not the only one who understood the socioeconomic underpinnings around the prosecution of contraband. Local residents of the northern villages of the island were also aware of these practices, and thus, their responses and interactions with these ad hoc prosecutors need to be understood not only as a defense of their only viable way of life, but also as an attempt to keep outsider intervention at bay. They saw these practices as predatory, and did everything in their power to counter them.[44]

A common strategy to thwart the activities of visiting judges was to use local officials to challenge their authority in the villages they went to investigate. These village officials were themselves among the local notables who defended local interests and undoubtedly benefited from keeping judges away. Governor Gregorio González de Cuenca related how, in late 1580, a judge was sent by the *Audiencia* to La Yaguana, and found three French ships anchored in the town's port trading with the locals. When the judge arrived at La Yaguana, the *alcalde mayor* (regional magistrate)

---

[43] "porque este dicho distrito está tan pobre y necesitado y miserable que hay más necesidad que los vecinos de él sean favorecidos que no molestados y es más servicio de Vuestra Majestad que algunos delitos queden sin castigo que no que se acabe la tierra porque los jueces que de dos años y medio a esta parte han salido con 96 *reales* cada día de salario la tienen arruinada." *Fiscal* Francisco de Aliaga to the Council of the Indies. June 23, 1585. AGI, SD. 51, R. 8, n. 82.

[44] "cobrar sus salarios ellos y sus oficiales y acabada la comisión venirse a sus casas a comer lo que han ganado y pretender otra sin hacer condenación que importe nada y es cosa sin duda que todos los jueces que han salido a esto de catorce años a esta parte, que han sido muchos, no han traído de provecho a la real caja de Vuestra Majestad 100,000 maravedíes y ellos han venido muy ricos." *Visitador* Francisco Alonso de Villagrá to the Council of the Indies. March, 22, 1594. AGI, SD. 70, R. 1, n. 28.

82 *Islanders and Empire*

asked him to go back to Santo Domingo, since prosecuting smuggling cases in the region was his responsibility. The *Audiencia* overruled the *alcalde*'s complaint, but he appealed his case to *Visitador* Rodrigo Ribero, who had recently arrived on the island. The *visitador* fined the members of the *Audiencia*, cancelled the commission of the appointed judge, and gave the papers of the investigation to the *alcalde mayor* so he could continue with the prosecution. Local officials thus used the overlapping layers of the royal bureaucracy and authority to achieve a favorable resolution to jurisdictional conflicts such as this one, while keeping judges away from their own illicit dealings.[45]

The crown was well aware of the abuses of local judges, as well as the widespread problem with smuggling across the circum-Caribbean region. The official appointment of Fernando Varela, a special judge commissioned by the crown in 1594 to investigate contraband cases throughout the Caribbean islands and Tierra Firme, explained how "although my *Audiencias* have named and sent judges for the investigation and punishment of it [contraband], they do not do it, but simply receive their salaries leaving the cases and the crimes in the state they found them." The appointment of Varela as a special prosecutor was an attempt to fix this problem. Instead of leaving the administration of justice in contraband cases to the *Audiencia*, the crown decided to send a trustworthy official from Spain. Because of the enormity of the task Fernando Varela was given, having to inspect Hispaniola as well as Puerto Rico, Cuba, Jamaica, and Cartagena, he was also forced to appoint deputy judges to expedite his mission. These judges may have taken their commissions more seriously than those appointed by the *Audiencia* of Santo Domingo, but local residents resented them equally, or even more, than those motivated by enhancing their salaries with collected fines, possibly because judges with peninsular commissions could not be co-opted as easily as local judges.[46]

The case of Judge Alonso de Orozco, a deputy of Fernando Varela, reveals the level of resistance that local people in Hispaniola mobilized against royal judges sent to prosecute contraband cases by the end of the sixteenth century. Orozco arrived at a farm in the outskirts of the town of Santiago de los Caballeros, in the north of Hispaniola, on September 4,

---

[45] Governor Gregorio González de Cuenca to the Council of the Indies. February 28, 1581. AGI, SD. 51, R. 4, n. 54.

[46] "porque aunque algunas de mis Audiencias han proveído y enviado jueces para la averiguación y castigo de ello, no tratan de hacerlo, sino de cobrar sus salarios dejando los casos y delitos en el estado en que los hallan." Royal decree commissioning Fernando Varela as judge. December 19, 1594. AGI, Escribanía, 17A.

Smuggling, Sin, and Survival, 1580–1600   83

1597. Francisco Varela had sent him from Santo Domingo to apprehend Francisco Jiménez, a very important smuggler in the region. Soon after his arrival at the farm, Orozco learned that close by, two enslaved Africans were leading forty horses loaded with ginger and hides on their way to the coast to trade with foreign merchants, so he headed to Manzanillas Bay, a habitual smuggling enclave, to try to intercept them. He located them in the proximity of the town of Montecristi, where he found out that they had just delivered the cargo to a French ship anchored on the coast. Knowing also that these two enslaved workers were the intermediaries between the foreigners and many *vecinos* from Montecristi, he detained them and with his *alguacil* and *escribano*, he returned to Santiago. On the road he encountered one of the *alcaldes* of Montecristi, who was heading back to the town, and apparently warned the *vecinos* of the detention of the two enslaved men.[47]

Alonso de Orozco spent the night in a farm near Santiago. Early the next morning, an enslaved man showed up at the farm and inspected the place before running away once again. Orozco later believed that he was sent to inspect the size of Orozco's party. Half an hour later, a group of more than seventeen men armed with lances and axes surrounded the hut where Orozco was staying. At the head of the group was Francisco Jiménez himself, the man Orozco had been sent to detain, as well as the *alcalde* he had encountered on the road earlier, a *regidor* of the town of Montecristi, the son of a prebendary of the diocese of La Vega, a man identified as the (possibly free) *mulato* Francisco Santana, and many of their enslaved laborers. Jiménez asked for the identities of the thieves who entered his farm and stole his slaves. Alonso Orozco responded, "the king," to which Jiménez replied that they "do not know the king" and that "in those lands they were king and jury." He added that Orozco and Varela were thieves who only came to those lands to steal. A fight between the parties ensued, in which the prisoners were liberated. Jiménez injured Orozco in his shoulder while he cried: "Thief! I will make you, Varela, and those in his company bleed, and I won't stop until I succeed." After these and other threats to the owner of the farm for harboring Orozco, the party left with the prisoners.[48]

---

[47] Testimony of Alonso de Orozco to judge Fernando Varela. October 27, 1597. AGI, SD. 24, n. 57.

[48] "A esto, Francisco Jiménez respondió que no conocía al rey, y que en aquella tierra ellos eran rey y jurados. Luego llamó a Orozco ladrón, que el licenciado Varela, juez, le envía a robar." Ibid.

84 *Islanders and Empire*

Francisco Jiménez's attitude toward Judge Orozco and Varela exemplifies the fierce resentment that many residents in the north felt about the commission of judges to the region. Residents made no distinctions between judges appointed by the *Audiencia* or those sent by *visitadores* appointed directly by the crown. Many inhabitants of the interior of Hispaniola, whose only contact with royal authority had been through the judges sent by the *Audiencia*, learned to mistrust these officers and anyone sent in the name of the king, especially those who could not be bought. For most northern Hispaniola residents, the monarch was a distant figure whose justice or protection was only experienced by very imperfect proxies, through royal officials who took advantage of their offices to benefit themselves and their clique. When Jiménez exclaimed "they do not know the king" and that "in those lands they were king and jury," it is hard to know for sure the real meaning behind his words. He may not have been necessarily repudiating the monarch himself, but rather impugning the justice that the king represented as embodied by his royal officials on the island. He was responding to Orozco's claim that the king, through the judge's hand, was taking Jiménez's slave. He did not recognize the king's justice in Orozco's commission, which explains his attack on the magistrate and his threat to Judge Varela. Another possibility is that Jiménez meant exactly what he said. That is, in the distant lands of northern Hispaniola, away from the king and his representatives, local residents made their own laws and followed their own rule. Since being the king's vassal did little to improve his life, Jiménez disentangled himself from all European social and political norms and made new ones to fit his present circumstances. Under this interpretation, Jiménez was a man without masters, and those who came to impose their will wanted to take away his livelihood, the only livelihood that allowed him to prosper on the remote shores of Hispaniola.

The events surrounding Orozco's arrest of the two enslaved laborers also gives us a quick glimpse of the individuals who ordinarily participated in the contraband trade. Enslaved people typically performed the most laborious tasks as muleteers and scouts (in the case of the attack against Orozco and possibly at the shores) and were an important presence among the attackers of Orozco's party, which reveals the willingness of Spanish masters to use their enslaved Africans in the attack and for the purpose of intimidating other Spaniards.[49] With them, Jiménez brought several elected officials of the surrounding towns, other villagers, the son

[49] More on the participation of enslaved Africans in Spanish disputes in Chapter 5.

Smuggling, Sin, and Survival, 1580–1600   85

of a high clergyman, and quite possibly, a free black man (Francisco de Santana), proving that smuggling as a socioeconomic activity involved a wide and representative cross section of the population of Hispaniola.

Fernando Varela's commitment to his commission made him especially hated among important sectors of the population. In an anonymous letter signed by the "Unhappy Island of Hispaniola," Varela was accused of having sent to the interior, in nine months, more than one hundred deputies with high salaries, thus leaving the land "as if enemies had sacked it, making uncounted mischief and taking things by force. And doing all this to provide for more than twenty servants and nephews that he brought ... thinking that this island was like another Perú."[50] The letter's anonymity does not necessarily mean that the accusation against Varela was untrue. The desire of the author or authors to keep their name secret may indicate, nonetheless, that the authors were an interested party in the contraband trade. The attempt to create a clear distinction between a wealthy land like Peru and Santo Domingo is more interesting. It hints at the fact that when the land was rich, the use of the judicial mechanisms by royal officials to benefit their patronage networks could be understood and even tolerated. Since Hispaniola was poor, the authors saw such behavior as abusive and immoral. Contraband was perceived by an important sector of the population as a nonnegotiable right, while the attempts of the crown to stop such trade were interpreted as violent impositions that could be answered with violence.

By signing the letter "Unhappy Island of Hispaniola," the author tried to present himself as a spokesperson for a majority of the island residents against the judge and thus legitimize his claims against him. As rhetorical as this move might have been, the arrival of Varela to the island did upset both a great number of local residents and the *Audiencia* alike. Right after the judge's arrival, the *Audiencia* as a body wrote a letter the Council of the Indies complaining of the level of scrutiny that the island had been under in recent years with two general *visitas* to the *Audiencia*. They believed that by constantly having a superior on the island to review and undo the decisions of the *Audiencia*, the court and its members were losing their authority in the district. The *oidor* Simón de Meneses was among those most aggravated by the presence of the new judge. Before Varela's

---

[50] "Y la dejan como si enemigos las saquearan haciendo mil desafueros y tomando las cosas por la fuerza, solo a fin de acomodar y enriquecer más de veinte criados y sobrinos que trajo ..., pensando que esta isla era otro Perú." Letter signed by "La Infeliz Isla Española." October 22, 1595. AGI, SD. 81, R. 5, n. 90.

86   *Islanders and Empire*

arrival and under the auspices of the *Audiencia*, Meneses had led a massive investigation against smuggling that produced a long list of convictions, which effort, he reported, he conducted without any remuneration. When Varela arrived, since the investigation of smuggling cases fell under his jurisdiction, Meneses was forced to hand to the new judge the indictments of the cases he had prosecuted. Meneses did not take this kindly, and he wrote numerous letters complaining about the lack of confidence that the monarch showed in his officials.[51]

In his inquiries, Varela claimed that there was much more than a disinterested service to the crown behind Meneses' investigation. The judge accused the veteran *oidor* of thirty-one counts of smuggling and collaboration with smugglers in exchange for free or heavily discounted enslaved Africans and merchandise, letting high profile members of the local elite involved in contraband trade out of jail, and even naming some of them as judges to prosecute contraband cases in the north of the island. Some of these accusations against Meneses were also echoed in a letter written by Antonio Franco de Ayala, a *vecino* in Santo Domingo and a member of the city elites. Franco de Ayala narrated how Meneses had systematically forgiven and released known smugglers and given them commissions as judges (probably in exchange of merchandise or maybe simply as a move to consolidate his position in local society). Since Meneses arrived at the city, Franco de Ayala said, he had done everything in his power to insult some of the most important members of the elites of the city and usurp their properties. Meneses was likely thinking ahead. Franco de Ayala claimed that the *oidor* knew well the proceedings involved in any *juicio de residencia*.[52] He was aware that the public official being judged could name his enemies within the community he had served to shield himself from any vindictive accusations. Meneses took advantage of the system to enrich himself at the cost of some local residents, knowing that by the time his *residencia* came, he could name them as his enemies and thus be protected from their accusations. Also,

---

[51] The *Audiencia* of Santo Domingo to the Council of the Indies. May 2, 1595. AGI, SD. 51, R. 17, n. 132; investigation of smuggling cases led by Simón de Meneses, 1595. AGI, SD. 51, R. 17, N. 130B; AGI, Escribanía, 17A; *oidor* Simón de Meneses to the Council of the Indies. October 20, 1595. AGI, SD. 51, R. 17, n. 138.

[52] The *juicio de residencia* was an investigation that took place at the end of a royal official's tenure. It was normally conducted by his successor, and its goal was to determine whether a royal official had served appropriately without abusing his post. A positive result in a *residencia* normally ensured a new appointment at a higher level in the royal administration, while a negative result normally resulted in fines, prison, loss of property, and in the most extreme and rarest of cases, the death penalty.

Franco de Ayala reported, Meneses had tried to convince him to write letters against the previous *visitador*, Francisco Alonso de Villagrá, and when Franco de Ayala refused, the *oidor* had proceeded against him for being "troublesome and prone to scandals."[53]

In contrast, Franco de Ayala praised Judge Varela and the work he had done to investigate the crimes occurring on the island, but lamented that the judge had been thrown off the island before he could finish his commission. Franco de Ayala was one of those wealthier residents of the island who might not have participated directly in contraband trade, although he likely benefited from the lower prices of contraband goods indirectly. Franco de Ayala directly felt the consequences of the actions of certain royal officials' involvement in the local culture of smuggling. It is hard to know if what he said about Fernando Varela being expelled from the island by the *Audiencia* is true, but the fact that Varela signed all his final sentences from Puerto Rico after leaving Hispaniola indicates that either he was unable to do so from Santo Domingo because of local pressures or was unwilling to put himself at risk once the sentences were made public. The execution of the sentences was left in the hands of the *Audiencia*, which meant that most of those arrested were released without punishment.[54]

GALLEYS

Foreign merchants did not arrive in Caribbean waters exclusively seeking commercial opportunities. From the 1520s and 1530s, French and English corsairs ravaged the Spanish islands and ships they encountered in the Caribbean Sea. Later, in the second half of the century, when local residents sought commercial exchanges with foreigners, the roles of merchant and privateer became interchangeable depending on the specific circumstances they encountered. Foreign merchants did not hesitate to take any Spanish ship that they encountered in their search for trade with local residents. The few merchants from Seville who did business in Hispaniola and local ship owners were the habitual victims of these attacks. Many of the

---

[53] The complete inquiry into Meneses' wrongdoings, including the crimes he was accused of, can be found in AGI, SD. 51, R. 20, n. 162 and AGI, SD. 70, R. 1, n. 40; Letter of Antonio Franco de Ayala to the Council of the Indies. February 25, 1596. SD. 51, R. 17, N. 142a.

[54] Franco de Ayala to the Council of the Indies. February 25, 1596. AGI, SD. 51, R. 17, N. 142a.

88   *Islanders and Empire*

more prosperous residents of Santo Domingo who relied on these legal trade networks to sell their products often lost their merchandise to the hands of foreign merchants/pirates. These merchants probably traded with other residents of the island and sold them enslaved workers and cloth, which in turn were bought by the same wealthy residents who had lost their products in the first place. This scenario may have been very common. It also shows the multiple contradictory layers of meaning and consequences that the contraband culture had for the residents of Hispaniola.[55]

Royal officials in Madrid and Hispaniola often interpreted contraband trade as a problem that could be solved with more active policing not only from the land with the commission of judges to prosecute smugglers, but also from the sea with armed ships patrolling the coasts of the island. With this in mind, the *Audiencia* wrote to Madrid in 1580 urging the king to send two galleys to defend the island "and stop the French infestation that robs and oppresses the island and in front of our eyes takes the best of its fruits to France."[56] After years of pleas by the *Audiencia* and some members of the *Cabildo* of Santo Domingo, the Council of the Indies approved of the measure, and two galleys arrived in the port of the city in July 1582. The Spanish crown had traditionally used galleys in the Mediterranean Sea, but during the sixteenth century,

---

[55] For a narrative of the depredations that corsairs unleashed in the coasts of Hispaniola in the early sixteenth century, see Deive, *Tangomangos*. Some scholars like Jesse Cromwell and Alan Karras have pointed out that smuggling and piracy are two distinct phenomenons in which the social background of individuals involved and the threat of violence (almost absent in the former, almost ubiquitous in the latter) are different. Their views are probably informed from their research of the eighteenth-century Caribbean, but Hispaniola's archival record for the late sixteenth century tells a muddled story in which both practices coexisted intimately at times. Jamie L. H. Goodall's findings on the British Caribbean in the late seventeenth century coincide with mine. Alan L. Karras, *Smuggling: Contraband and Corruption in World History* (Lanham, MD: Rowman & Littlefield Publishers, inc., 2010), 19–24; Cromwell, *The Smugglers' World*, 18–19; Jamie L. H. Goodall, "Tippling Houses, Rum Shops and Taverns: How Alcohol Fueled Informal Commercial Networks and Knowledge Exchange in the West Indies." *Journal for Maritime Research*, vol. 18, n. 2 (2016), 97. For a sixteenth-century example of contraband trade that turned into piracy, see Kris E. Lane, *Pillaging the Empire: Piracy in the Americas, 1500–1750* (Armonk, N.Y: M.E. Sharpe, 1998), 29.

[56] "con que cese de ser infestada de franceses que la roban y oprimen y casi a vista de ojos llevan la mejor parte de los frutos de ella a Francia." This is both a reference to the ships stolen and the exchanges of foreign traders with local residents, which was also perceived as theft. The *Audiencia* of Santo Domingo to the Council of the Indies. February 17, 1580. AGI, SD. 51, R. 3, n. 49.

Smuggling, Sin, and Survival, 1580–1600

they were also sent to some strategic ports of the Americas.[57] From the moment they arrived, they met with near-impossible challenges in the performance of their duties. The *Cabildo* of Santo Domingo approved a tax to raise 10,000 *ducados* to pay for the salaries of the soldiers, but they took the collection of the money upon themselves and it never actually reached the hands of the soldiers.

As for the supply of food to maintain both the soldiers and the galley rowers (mostly convicts, but also enslaved people), the responsibility was spread among the towns of the island, which from the beginning argued that they were too poor to meet this task. To ensure the implementation of this measure and the payment of the salaries of soldiers, the *Audiencia* named two officers, a *receptor* and a *tenedor de galeras*. According to a witness, "there was great interest among the members of the *Cabildo* about who was going to have these positions, and each of them wanted the job for themselves or one of their clients." However, as soon as the rules and responsibilities of the position were drawn, they lost interest, so the salaries of the positions had to be increased, and a mixture of begging and threats were necessary to fill the offices.[58] In addition to such struggles, the appointed men did nothing to improve the collection of supplies or money for the galleys. As with the judges sent to the north of the island, their own salaries absorbed most of the coin they collected to pay for the crew, and nothing was done to force the towns of the island to supply the foodstuff. In a letter to the Duke of Medina Sidonia in Spain ten months after his arrival, the commander of the galleys Ruy Díaz de Mendoza told how no one in his crew had eaten more than half a ration since they were on the island, and the soldiers still had not received a salary or learned how much they would be paid. As a consequence, the crew was restless, and they

---

[57] For a summary on the Iberian use of galleys in the Mediterranean, see John Francis Guilmartin, Jr., *Gunpowder & Galleys: Changing Technology & Mediterranean Warfare at Sea in the 16th Century* (Annapolis: Naval Institute Press, 2003). See also, David Wheat, "Mediterranean Slavery, New World Transformations: Galley Slaves in the Spanish Caribbean, 1578–1635." *Slavery & Abolition*, vol. 31, n. 3 (2010), 327–44. For a detailed account of the crown's decision to send the galleys to Santo Domingo, see Richard Boulind, "Shipwreck and Mutiny in Spain's Galleys on the Santo Domingo Station, 1583." *Mariner's Mirror*, 58 (1972) 297–330. Special thanks to David Wheat for providing this last reference.

[58] "había grandes pretensiones entre justicia y regimiento sobre quién había de tener estos oficios. Pretendiolos cada uno para si o sus deudos." *Visitador* Rodrigo Ribero to the Council of the Indies. February 10, 1583. AGI, SD. 70 R. 1, n. 20.

90 *Islanders and Empire*

were involved in numerous crimes on land that their commander was unable to prevent.[59]

If the lack of food or pay was not enough of a challenge, when the galleys were patrolling the island, they also had to overcome the serious obstacles created by the collusion of inhabitants with foreign merchants. Ruy Díaz de Mendoza admitted he was able to capture some ships, but the lack of local cooperation had frustrated most of his captures. He wrote that "the French have had better friends than these galleys, because they were warned, and thus the five richest ships that passed to the Indies escaped my hands."[60] These claims of collaborations with foreign smugglers were not exaggerated. Local inhabitants carefully followed the progress of the galleys around the island and sent messengers ahead to warn foreign merchants of their imminent arrival, thus eliminating the surprise factor and giving them ample time to escape or prepare their defenses. Diego de Osorio, the captain of the other galley, wrote to the crown in 1584 requesting authorization to punish those local residents who warned the foreign ships. "Some of the inhabitants of this island," he wrote, "have so much faith in the French that they enthusiastically go to their aid to the detriment of these galleys. And I have never seen any of these men punished because they are country people and they have their own way to avoid falling into the hands of the authorities, even though these officers do little to capture them."[61]

As Osorio pointed out, the authorities in the interior of the island did little to stop the warnings to foreign merchants. When they intervened, it was normally to their own benefit, as in 1583, when the galleys fought against a French ship in front of the town of Bayahá. The foreign ship came to the coast, and some of the enslaved captives that it carried, as well as some members of its crew, escaped

---

[59] Ruy Díaz de Mendoza to the Duke of Medina Sidonia. May 26, 1583. AGI, SD. 80, R. 2 n. 55.

[60] "haber tenido los franceses mejores amigos que estas galeras, pues los avisaban y así me han quitado de las manos cinco navíos, los más ricos que han pasado a Indias." Letter of Ruy Díaz de Mendoza to the Duke of Medina Sidonia. May 26, 1583. AGI, SD. 80, R. 2, n. 56. For some successful histories of the galleys capturing four French ships, see Archivo General de Simancas (AGS), Guerra y Marina (GYM), 142, n. 121 and 151.

[61] "Algunos vecinos de esta isla tienen tanta fe con los franceses que con mucho ánimo acuden a las cosas suyas con gran tibieza a las que tocan estas galeras, y de estos no he visto ninguno castigado porque son gente campesina y tienen sus modos para no venir a manos de justicias y de ellas son poco perseguidos." Letter of *cabo de galeras* Diego Osorio to the Council of the Indies. June 18, 1584. AGI, SD. 80 R. 2, n. 73.

Smuggling, Sin, and Survival, 1580–1600   91

to the interior. They were captured by Bernardino de Ovando, *alcalde mayor* of the town of Bayahá, who claimed them for himself and his men. The *Audiencia* of Santo Domingo backed Ovando's claims, thus depriving the galleys of the prize, its only remaining source of income. Aboard the galleys, the situation became so difficult that in July 1583, violence ensued. Eleven overworked and underfed galley slaves, taking advantage of the fact that the other galley had sunk a few days earlier in a sand bar, managed to take control of the ship, kill the captain Ruy Díaz de Mendoza, and use the galley to rob a few ships on the north coast and Hispaniola. They used the desire of some royal officials to save the galley to negotiate their freedom, and after returning the war ship in exchange for another vessel, they were allowed to sail back to Europe.[62]

In 1587, two new galleys arrived in Santo Domingo, but they faced the same difficulties as their predecessors. The lack of local collaboration, supplies for the galleys in their expeditions, and pay for the soldiers made it impossible for the ships to mount a real challenge against smugglers. Despite the repeated pleas of their new captain Diego de Noguera, the galleys spent most of their time inside the port of Santo Domingo. Many of the convicts serving as galley rowers were liberated by the *Audiencia* because they had served their time, while others died, thus reducing the rowing crew to critically low numbers. After years of inactivity, one of the galleys rotted in the port and was destroyed by Drake's forces in 1586, while the second one was finally sent to Cartagena in 1591. In the years to come, the authorities of the island repeatedly petitioned the crown to send new galleys to patrol the shores of the island, but considering the reports surrounding the lack of local support that the original galleys received, it is not surprising that these requests fell on deaf ears. Even though the galleys had been hailed as the definitive solution for the contraband problems of the island, in practice, their effect was limited by the lack of collaboration of the members of the *Audiencia* and the pervasive local interests in the contraband trade.

---

[62] Ruy Díaz de Mendoza to the Duke of Medina Sidonia, AGI, SD. 80, R. 2 n. 55. For an account of the mutiny, see the confession of Bartolomé López Mellado, one of the mutinied convicts of the galley provided in 1603 after he was captured in Granada (Spain) for a different crime. John Carter Brown Library B603 B330y 1-size; a shorter version of this letter is available in AGI, SD. 80, R. 3, N. 86E. For an English translation of another account by Bartolomé Hemasabel of the mutiny and the negotiations that took place with the mutineers, see Boulin, "Shipwreck and Mutiny," 302–12. The original is in AGI, Indiferente General, 1887.

92   *Islanders and Empire*

SMUGGLING AND RAIDS ON THE SOUTHERN COAST

The absence of galleys could have not come at a worse time for imperial interests. During the mid 1590s, foreign ships became increasingly bold. Following Drake's exploits, many other English ships frequented the Caribbean in search of Spanish ships to board or colonists to trade with, depending on the circumstances. One English captain, known by the name of "Lanton" (James Langton, lieutenant of the Earl of Cumberland), became a common smuggler and pirate in the waters around the port of Santo Domingo between 1593 and 1594. Langton was rumored to have participated in Drake's sack of the city and still to be working for the English knight. The former is possible.[63] The latter was not true, but this rumor indicates how large Drake's shadow loomed over the population of Santo Domingo in the aftermath of the pirate's sack of the city. As early as 1593, Langton's ships had regularly traded in the north of the island with local officials, residents of the city of Bayahá, and contrabandists like Juan Cid and Luis Osorio Justinian, both *alcaldes* of this village. In 1594, Langton positioned his ships near Cape Caucedo (southeast of Santo Domingo), from where he was able to intercept any ship arriving or leaving the port. He stayed for two months, during which time he took at least nine ships. He was not the only one. *Oidor* Simón de Meneses wrote to the crown in October 1595 reporting that the port had been blockaded for the last eight months, and remarking how "an Englishman leaves tired of stealing and another one comes to the port. Now Admiral Langton is there and no ship enters or leaves port without him taking it."[64]

The fact that Langton was singled out and known by name was not accidental. In addition to blocking the maritime traffic to and from the port, his ships terrorized nearby sugar mills and farms, asking for ransom in exchange for not burning their properties to the ground. In 1594, under the auspices of the *visitador* Villagrá, two frigates were sent to try to capture one of Langton's barges that had been seen in Ocoa Bay, only a few miles west of Santo Domingo. Although they managed to capture the

---

[63] Since Langton is not listed among the Drake's officers, Kenneth Andrews believes he might have been a junior officer. Kenneth Andrews, ed., *English Privateering Voyages to the West Indies, 1588–1595* (Cambridge University Press, 1959), 238, note 1.

[64] "Se va un inglés después de harto de robar y se pone otro en el puerto y ahora está el almirante de Lanton y no entra ni sale navío que no le robe." *Oidor* Simón de Meneses to the Council of the Indies. October 20, 1595. AGI, SD. 51, R. 17, n. 138. For the increase of English incursions in the Caribbean, see, Andrews, *The Spanish Caribbean*, 155, 170.

Smuggling, Sin, and Survival, 1580–1600   93

barge, they were surprised soon afterwards by the arrival of one of Langton's larger and well-armed vessels. After a short battle in which one of the frigates was sunk, Juan Montero, the captain of the other one, realized he could not win against the better armed and manned ship, so after a discussion of the terms, he surrendered the ship. Once aboard Langton's ship, the English captain reproached them for the futility of their attempts against him. He claimed that two merchants of the city had warned him that an expedition was getting ready to attack him, giving him enough time to prepare. This testimony was ratified by Pedro Juan Justinian, who was at the time a prisoner on Langton's ship. While the English captain was in Cape Caucedo, Justinian saw different Spanish *vecinos* arrive to trade and bargain with Langton, but he was taken under the deck each time so he would not be able to identify them. Juan Montero's testimony contradicted that of Justinian. The Spanish captain described how Langton, his pilot, and secretary told him in the privacy of the captain's cabin the real version of the events. The two local merchants that Langton had publicly signaled as his source about the attack, under the pretext of paying a ransom for Justinian, had made several visits to the English ship, trying to delay him while captain Montero and his men took Langton's barge in Ocoa. It was Justinian who, in order to gain his freedom, revealed to the English captain the deception and was thus able to arrive in Ocoa on time.[65]

The normalcy of the visits of the merchants to Langton's ship, whether motivated by deception or by trade, point to the ease with which foreign captains exchanged information and traded with local residents even only a few miles from Santo Domingo. These exchanges allowed the English captain to buy, barter, or extort provisions for his crew and continue his blockade of the port for indefinite periods of time. Langton never lacked sources of information about the affairs of the city either. Even though the city had guards posted in Cape Caucedo to avoid land incursions of the pirates, these guards were easily bribed, as was proven when *oidor* Quesada, in an inspection of the house of the guards, found salted codfish, which they could have only obtained from the English smugglers.[66] The fact that some residents of the city were willing to trade with a foreigner

---

[65] The investigation against the two Spanish captains of the expedition against Langton's barge, led by *oidor* Simón de Meneses and dated on February 9, 1594, can be found divided in two different parts in AGI, SD, 15, n. 13 and AGI, SD. 51, R. 17, 131B.

[66] Letter of Juan Quesada Figueroa to the Council of the Indies. April 28, 1596. AGI, SD. 51, R. 17, n. 147.

94   *Islanders and Empire*

who was also blockading the port only heightened the sense of insecurity, which is patent in the letters of some members of the *Audiencia* and city residents to the crown.

Langton's constant threat to the sugar mills near Ocoa Bay forced some sugar mill owners to deal with the English captain in ways that the governor and members of the *Audiencia* perceived as treasonous and even heretical. Gregorio de Ayala, *regidor* of Santo Domingo, was accused of dealing illegally with Langton. According to *visitador* Villagrá, when the English captain attacked and sacked his sugar mill, Ayala knelt in front of Langton and asked him in the name of her Lady the Queen of England not to burn his mill and to let him pay protection money. Langton was allegedly "so moved to see a Catholic kneeling in front of an English captain and swearing by the life of his Lady, that not only did he accept a lot less money in exchange for leaving the mill and properties untouched, but swore to him that not now, nor ever, would he hurt him," and even gave him a letter signed by him so any other English captain who might come to sack his property would recognize it and spare him. The archbishop himself looked into the case, but it does not seem that Ayala was prosecuted for his actions, since according to *visitador* Villagrá, he was very close to the governor.[67] According to Juan Caballero Bazán, owner of another sugar estate near Ocoa and who also had been in trouble for communicating with Langton, Ayala told him that instead of arming men to protect his property, it was easier to prepare boxes with supplies and have them ready for the English when they came, keeping separate a part for Langton, who was the most important of them all. Ayala advised Caballero Bazán to hide all the copper pans (for purging the sugar), and as soon as he saw them coming, to go out and meet them with the boxes and let them know that he does not have anything else because he had already been robbed. This way, he would preserve his property, and the English would take something back too. Langton's exploits and the kind of bargaining that sugar mill owners were forced to adopt are the best examples of the constant state of siege that the city of Santo Domingo experienced during the late 1590s and early years of the seventeenth

---

[67] "pudo tanto con el traidor del inglés ver arrodillado delante de si un católico que le juraba por la vida de la reina su señora, que no solamente le rescató su hacienda e ingenio por mucho menos de lo que él pensó sino que le prometió que ahora ni nunca le haría daño en él, y aunque se sospecha que le dejó algunas cartas de recomendación para otros tales como él que por aquí vinieran." Francisco Alonso de Villagrá to the Council of the Indies. May 7, 1594. AGI, SD. 70, R. 1, n. 29.

century, as well as the ambivalent relationships that some of its residents maintained with foreign traders, and even pirates.[68]

Some royal officials also tried conciliatory measures to end contraband trade. In 1598, Governor Diego Osorio moved away from trying to pressure local residents with judges into compliance, which had proven to be a failure, and tried a new tactic of appeasement and reconciliation. Osorio met with all those accused or suspected of smuggling and tried to strike a deal with them. In exchange for their help in expelling all foreign ships from the island shores and ending the contraband trade, Osorio promised he would get them full pardons for all their crimes. During one year, the agreement bore some fruits. The governor placed these residents in charge of small militias in the ports where contraband activity was most active, and there is ample evidence that they conducted numerous attacks on foreign ships trying to contact local residents to trade. The pact between the governor and these local elites, however, did not last. Governor Osorio died in 1600, and his efforts to lead a transition of local inhabitants from smugglers to enforcers of the law died with him. With the powers they received from the governor, these local groups monopolized contraband trade in the regions they patrolled, thus using their newly gained authority to their own ends. This new local defiance of royal authority did not seem to surprise anyone in Santo Domingo. Contraband, it seemed, was a deeply entrenched cultural and economic practice that would not be uprooted easily.[69]

DESPERATE TIMES

During the second half of the sixteenth century, at the same time that the presence of northern Europeans increased in the circum-Caribbean region, the Spanish Monarchy created the fleet system as the main form of state-sanctioned trade with its American colonies in an attempt to protect its trade and shipments of precious metal for the mainland from European depredation. For Hispaniola this reorganization had profound repercussions. Sidelined from the main route of the fleets, as its commercial connections with the rest of the Spanish empire declined,

---

[68] Ibid; Juan Caballero Bazán to his foreman Antón Ricardo Catalán. December 17, 1593. AGI, SD. 51, R. 17, N. 131B.

[69] Captain Diego de Paredes Carreño to the Council of the Indies. May 6, 1599. AGI, SD. 81, R. 5, n. 125; Antonio de Paredes Carreño to the Council of the Indies. 1600. AGI, SD. 98, R. 1; Juan de Castro Garay to the Council of the Indies. February 27, 1603. AGI, SD. 82, R. 3, n. 30.

96   *Islanders and Empire*

Hispaniola became one of the most important centers of contraband trade of the Caribbean. Ships from the main sailing nations in Europe frequented the island ports and established commercial exchanges and alliances with local people. The inhabitants of Hispaniola embraced the contraband trade as the only possible way to supply themselves with enslaved workers and European goods, due to the diminishing links between the colony and the Spanish trading routes. People from all social classes and backgrounds participated directly or indirectly in the trade and benefitted from it. Remote ports of the island turned into profitable business centers for both locals and foreign merchants. The increased presence of English and French merchants and privateers in Caribbean waters also led to increased raids of vessels, plantations, and even port cities like Santo Domingo. During these years, the reports from political and religious authorities on the island to the court in Madrid became increasingly alarming.

These reports of attacks and incessant trade between locals and foreign merchants transmitted to Spain a sense of both physical and religious vulnerability. Local authorities were not only unable to defend the island from the attacks, but they were also often unwilling to prevent the close relationship that some local residents had forged with foreign merchants, on which they were at times active coconspirators. These interactions were allegedly pillaging the land and its peoples of all its wealth, either by the direct plundering of Hispaniola's resources or via the illegal trade that led to the slaughtering of cattle and the financial benefit of enemies of the Spanish Monarchy. Possibly even more importantly, in the eye of some crown and religious officials, the constant presence of northern European sailors, merchants, and seafarers placed the local population at risk of learning and spreading the heretical beliefs that these traders brought with them. In response to these reports, Madrid stationed galleys in Santo Domingo to patrol the waters around the island in the early 1580s. The efforts of the soldiers in these vessels to suppress smuggling met with constant active and passive resistance from local residents, who thwarted every attempt they made to fulfill their mission.

By the early seventeenth century, Hispaniola residents were represented in the letters arriving in Madrid as a troubled society out of control, acting against their own economic interest, and against their God and king. Just as Calchas and Proteus saw the birth of the monster as a sign of the dark times to come in the Cristóbal de Llerena's play that opened this chapter, the crown interpreted the pervasiveness of contraband culture in Hispaniola and the failures to suppress it as a sign that more extreme measures were needed to preserve the island, both for the Spanish Monarchy and for Christianity. Smuggled goods became the material representations of the relationships that Hispaniola residents established with northern European traders and its most inescapable outcome for Madrid: that is, Protestant contamination of the island and its complete loss for the true Catholic religion. This fear was not metaphorical for the crown, and some residents of Santo Domingo shared some of those fears when they encountered smuggled goods in the market. As we will see in the next chapter, the radical plan that was adopted was suggested by none other than a member of the local elite in Santo Domingo, showing once again the complex politics and diversity of opinions that existed around the smuggling culture of the island.

3

Repressing Smugglers: The Depopulations of Hispaniola, 1604–1606

He managed to escape wearing only his shirt. *Oidor* Pedro Sáenz de Morquecho had been sent to the interior of the island on a special mission from the *Audiencia* of Santo Domingo in 1598 to inspect the land and investigate contraband cases. While he was resting somewhere in the countryside, a group of eighty Frenchmen and twenty local men on horseback ambushed him. His companions were captured, and the documents of the judicial proceedings he had completed during his trip were all burned. In a letter to the Council of the Indies, Sáenz de Morquecho recounted how nineteen foreign ships were loading products on the northern shores of the island, while another eight had already departed, noting: "As I have already informed Your Majesty, the only remedy I can find by land is doing with these peoples of the northern coast what was done with the *moriscos* of the Kingdom of Granada, taking their farms and moving them to other parts, or having galleys and armada by the sea to eliminate those who come to trade, while sending ships from Castile to trade in the ports of the northern coasts."[1]

Sáenz de Morquecho expressed the frustration of some royal officials with the state of the island and its residents. As explained in the previous chapter, galleys had been unable to stop smugglers in Hispaniola, and thus the Council of the Indies ignored Sáenz de

---

[1] "No hallo remedio por tierra como tengo avisado a Vuestra Majestad si no es haciendo a esta gente de la banda del norte lo que se hizo con los moriscos del reino de Granada, quitándoles las haciendas y pasándolos a otra parte, o andando galeras y armada por la mar que quiten estos navíos que vienen a rescatar, y que vayan navíos de Castilla con mercadurías a los puertos de la banda del norte." Dr. Pedro Sáenz de Morquecho to the Council of the Indies. January 5, 1599. AGI, SD. 81, R. 5, N.124.

Morquecho's new request for ships to patrol the island, as well as those made by many subsequent officials. The *oidor*'s comparison of the northern residents of Hispaniola with *moriscos*, however, is much more revealing. On the Iberian Peninsula, *moriscos* were men and women who had converted from Islam to Christianity either voluntarily, or in the case of those living in the Kingdom of Granada after 1492, by force after the royal edict of 1502 compelled all Muslims who wanted to stay in Castilla to convert or leave the kingdom. The mass conversions that ensued raised suspicions among established Christians (who referred to themselves as "old Christians") about the sincerity of these converts, while the Inquisition policed the public and private behavior of these new Christians searching for any hint of heresy. The Second War of the Alpujarras (1568–71), in which *moriscos* rebelled against the suffocating pressures of the crown upon their lives and customs, only exacerbated such fears. *Moriscos* were seen as disloyal and rebellious. By the late sixteenth century, they were sometimes believed to be a fifth column, working secretly for the Ottoman Empire and North African corsairs from inside the Iberian Peninsula.[2]

By the same token, Sáenz de Morquecho believed that the attack he suffered at the hands of a mixed French and Spanish force was proof that the northern residents of Hispaniola were actively working against their king and natural lord, his ministers, and their embodiment of the true Catholic faith. If the crown did not act, the loss of the island to the hands of European heretics and rivals of Spain was only a matter of time. In the words of Captain Diego Paredes Carreño, a local resident, the foreign merchants "brought a great quantity of heretical books to spread their sect in this island, and they give them to everyone who wants them."[3] Sáenz de Morquecho's comparison of the people of Hispaniola with *moriscos* situated them for his contemporary Spanish readers as marginal subjects whose loyalty was questionable and whose behavior demanded a prompt response by the crown to enforce acceptable Christian behavior and to maintain its dominion.

---

[2] Karoline P. Cook, *Forbidden Passages: Muslims and Moriscos in Colonial Spanish America* (Philadelphia: University of Pennsylvania Press, 2014), 2.

[3] "Traían mucha cantidad de libros heréticos para derramar su mala secta en esta isla y los daban graciosamente a quien los quería." Captain Diego Paredes Carreño to the Council of the Indies. May 5, 1599. AGI, SD. 81, R. 5, n. 125.

This chapter analyzes the implementation of the crown's plan, approved in August 1604 to depopulate the northern and western coasts of Hispaniola, a region of roughly 20,000 square miles, by destroying the existing villages and relocating their population to newly erected villages around Santo Domingo. Although the depopulation was carried out by the governor and his officials, different local groups resisted the relocation, defying the governor's authority and even taking up arms against him. In the following two years, the entire island of Hispaniola would be engulfed in a whirlwind of revolts, rumors, and accusations, resulting in population removals, judicial trials, and confrontations between the governor, some *oidores* of the *Audiencia*, members of the local elite, and the former residents of the depopulated lands. I interpret the depopulations of Hispaniola as an attempt by the crown to impose order upon a colony increasingly perceived as a disorderly entrepôt for the contraband trade, as well as socially and religiously noncompliant. I argue that even though smuggling might have been the proximate cause for the increasingly frequent alarms that reached Madrid during these years, the perception of religious and political impropriety, and the risks that these posed to the presumed religious purity and loyalty of Spanish vassals on the island might have been just as important (or arguably even more so) in spurring the Council of the Indies to action. This narrative, however, was fiercely challenged by the Hispaniola elites, who exculpated themselves of all wrongdoing while blaming any and all questionable behavior on landless peasants, whom they accused of leading all the smuggling efforts. Local people resisted the depopulations with their actions in the remote villages, valleys, and bays of the island, as well as with the stories they told and wrote about those events.

The first section of this chapter will briefly situate the Hispaniola depopulations in the long history of population relocations that the Spanish Monarchy had already enacted on different occasions on both sides of the Atlantic. All such relocations were connected to a desire to increase social, economic, and religious control over populations, resources, and land. In the rest of the chapter, I will examine the depopulations from the perspective of different participants and consider the possible motives for such a drastic intervention by the crown by looking at the actions of enforcers of the measures, particularly, Governor Antonio Osorio and the judges of the *Audiencia*, and local actors, working either individually or as a body in their *Cabildos*. Governor Osorio and some of his aides shared the idea that the depopulations were necessary because the northern residents of Hispaniola had abandoned the

Catholic religion (and thus civilization) and had betrayed their king for the economic benefits of trading with heretics and foreigners. As for the reaction of the people of Hispaniola to the depopulations, it ranged from collaboration with the governor in some cases, to acquiescence, passive resistance, or open defiance of the orders. Whatever their response, local people demonstrated a fierce independence and desire to continue their lives unconstrained by royal mandates and prohibitions. Even though the crown succeeded in destroying the northern and western villages of the island, the results of the depopulations were far from the royal victory that ministers of the crown had desired. In the last section, I will explain how the local elites rejected the official explanation for the depopulations and how they reframed the story both for themselves, as well as for the new governor of Hispaniola.

The depopulation of the northern and western coast of Hispaniola in 1605 holds a very contentious place in the modern historiography of the Dominican Republic.[4] The depopulations are viewed with such disdain and dread that the Dominican historiography calls this event *las devastaciones* or the devastations. "Devastation" in this context is a historically and politically loaded term, so I opted to use the term depopulation, which conveys the intent and purpose of the plan without the controversial nationalistic undertones. Moving away from the term "devastation" is not intended to sanitize a process that was undoubtedly violent and controversial. Rather, I use the term depopulation to place the events in Hispaniola from 1604 to 1606 in a long tradition of forced population removals the Spanish Empire conducted during the sixteenth century.

---

[4] Along with the dictatorship of Rafael Leónidas Trujillo (1930–61) and the long history of anti-Haitianism in the country, the depopulations are one of the most revisited topics in the historical literature of the island. The depopulations signaled the beginning of what has been traditionally viewed as a long century of Spanish neglect of its oldest and once-prosperous colony. In the course of the last century, Dominican historians have not only seen the depopulations as the origin of the economic plight that would befall Hispaniola, but also as the reason behind its poverty, the surge of foreign settlements, the French control of the western third of Hispaniola, and finally, the political duality (Haiti and the Dominican Republic) that exists on the island today. The depopulations are often seen as the key traumatic event in the nation's foundational myth. Such dramatic interpretation has also had a profoundly negative impact on the development of modern scholarship about Hispaniola during the seventeenth century. For more on the depopulations and their presence in Dominican historiography, see Juan José Ponce-Vázquez, "Casting Traitors and Villains: The Historiographical Memory of the 1605 Depopulations of Hispaniola," in Marina Llorente, Marcella Salvi, and Aida Diaz de León, eds., *Sites of Memory in Spain and Latin America* (Lanham: Lexington Press, 2015), 151–66.

POPULATION REMOVALS IN THE HISPANIC WORLD

By the seventeenth century, the Spanish Monarchy had conducted numerous forced population relocations of peoples across its vast and growing empire. The crown made ample use of such policies in order to consolidate control over recently conquered territories or in the aftermath of local uprisings. In the decades preceding the depopulation of northern and western Hispaniola, the Spanish crown had ordered the removal and relocation of numerous communities across the empire. An examination of these processes allows for a better understanding of the context in which the Spanish crown used forced relocation as a tool to extend its rule over land, resources, and more importantly, people. Even though social and political control were crucial in the removal and relocation of various groups, religious reasons also played an important part in the justifications behind these resettlements. The forced relocation of entire communities was often used as a mechanism for their Christianization. Bringing these communities into the orthodoxy of the Catholic church went hand in hand with the Spanish desire to civilize, by which they meant living in urban spaces like Spaniards and adopting Spanish social, cultural, and religious norms.[5]

One of the first instances of these evangelizing relocations took place during the early years of Spanish settlement in Hispaniola. Soon after their arrival in 1516 and in their joint role as governors of Santo Domingo, the Jeronymite friars cancelled the *encomiendas* given to absentee courtiers because they were perceived as abusive. Instead, in 1519, they initiated the construction of towns in which Indian communities would be settled. The friars' original instructions, however, had been much more radical. Under the influence of Bartolomé de Las Casas, they had been instructed to end all the *encomiendas* of the island and relocate the entire Indian population into towns of 300 Indians, far from the supervision of any *encomendero*.[6] The friars moved cautiously throughout their time in Hispaniola. Fearing that the application of such a plan might lead to an open rebellion among the Spanish population, the Jeronymite friars deemed such a scheme impossible to implement and opted instead to relocate only the indigenous

---

[5] Richard L. Kagan, and Fernando Marías, *Urban Images of the Hispanic World, 1493–1793* (New Haven, CT: Yale University Press, 2000), 19–44.

[6] Las Casas' influence in the instructions was so strong that he included them in his own *Historia de las Indias*, finished in 1559. Bartolomé de Las Casas, *Historia de las Indias*, Book III, Chapter LXXXVIII (Santo Domingo: Sociedad Dominicana de Bibliófilos, 1987), 121–30.

people taken from absentee *encomenderos*. A few villages, known as *pueblos tutelados*, were built in the Cibao and Macoris regions to provide accommodation for a little over 3,000 Indians, or about 9 percent of the remaining native population of Hispaniola. Local *caciques* were appointed as community leaders in each town. The natives still had to mine for gold for eight months a year, but most of the benefit of their labor reverted to their communities. The money was used to buy food as well as clothing, since Spaniards thought that nakedness was a sign of barbarism. Their earnings were also used to pay the salary of the priest in charge of educating them in Christianity and Spanish culture.[7]

The Jeronymite friars tried to expand this system; thus in 1519, thirty towns were built to accommodate the surviving native population and eliminate all *encomiendas*. Unfortunately, by then an epidemic of small-pox had decimated the remaining native population. In addition, local political infighting and the death of their protector Cardinal Cisneros in Spain led to important changes in the government of Hispaniola, putting an end to the rule of the Jeronymite friars on the island and any future creation of more *pueblos tutelados*.[8] While this relocation and resettle-ment may have been intended to ameliorate the living and working con-ditions of the native people, the measures also ensured a more effective Christianization and continued to subject Indians to labor requirements.

These same objectives would be applied years later in the lands of the Inca Empire. In the Andes between the late 1560s and the early 1580s, viceroy Francisco de Toledo engaged in an aggressive policy of resettle-ment of the Andean population into new towns, known as *reducciones*. The kingdom of Peru had entered into a period of progressive crises: a steep indigenous population decline had reduced the number of members paying tribute; there were conflicts among Spanish settlers, Spaniards, and the Church; silver production was decreasing in the mines; and there was an active Inka rebellion against the Spanish. Toledo believed that the resettlement of the native population would solve many of these problems. In the territories of the *Audiencia* of Charcas and Lima, Toledo created over 800 new settlements in which he relocated approximately 1.4 million Andeans. Following his example, successive resettlements of native

---

[7] Erin Woodruff Stone, "Indian Harvest: The Rise of the Indigenous Slave Trade and Diaspora from Española to the Circum-Caribbean, 1492–1542" (Ph.D. dissertation, Vanderbilt University, 2014), 138–39.

[8] Frank Moya Pons, *Después de Colón: Trabajo, sociedad y política en la economía del oro* (Madrid: Alianza Editorial 1987), 161–62.

populations were ordered in the 1570s and 1580s in the territories of the *Audiencias* of Quito and Santa Fe. Public officials, priests, and Indian *kurakas* benefitted from the existence of *reducciones*, which allowed for easier access to laborers, souls, and a tribute-paying population. Although their existence was hotly contested and many natives refused to live exclusively in these towns or even fled from them, many *reducciones* survived. This was in part because membership in these newly created communities provided natives with rights to land and a modicum of self-government, as well as representing a link to their traditional cultural communal values. The success of *reducciones* as stable settlements depended on a complex balancing act between local interests, the Spanish Empire's taxation, and religious impositions on the local Andean population.[9] Royal officials and local residents in Hispaniola often referred to the Hispaniola depopulations as *reducciones*, thus recognizing that, while the populations were different, the goals that the crown sought to accomplish (population control, civilization through Christian instruction, and the vigilance of both religious and secular authorities) were similar.[10]

In the Iberian Peninsula, the Spanish crown conducted a mass forced relocation of the *moriscos* of the Kingdom of Granada in the aftermath of the Second War of the Alpujarras (1568–71). The Kingdom of Castilla had granted very generous terms to the inhabitants of the Kingdom of Granada for its surrender, which took place in January 1492. Those earlier terms included the protection of property and tolerance of Islam as well as other social, economic, and religious institutions. These early manifestations of goodwill soon gave way to an increasingly aggressive policy against Muslims, which in turn led to the First War of the Alpujarras in 1500. In its aftermath, all Muslims were forced to choose

---

[9] As Susan Ramírez has pointed out, Toledo's *reducciones* might be the most famous in the Andes, but they were not the first; *reducciones* there started as early as the 1530s. Susan Elizabeth Ramírez, *The World Upside Down: Cross-Cultural Contact and Conflict in Sixteenth-Century Peru* (Stanford: Stanford University Press, 1996), 30, 176 (note 52). For a recent analysis of Toledo's *reducciones* in the Andes, see Jeremy Ravi Mumford, *Vertical Empire: The General Resettlement of Indians in the Colonial Andes* (Durham, NC: Duke University Press, 2012) 76, 120; and Steven A. Wernke, *Negotiated Settlements: Andean Communities and Landscapes under Inka and Spanish Colonialism* (Gainesville: University Press of Florida, 2013) 10, 214. Special thanks to Karen Graubart for her historiographical guidance and for allowing me to read a draft of two chapters from her upcoming book titled tentatively *Republics of Difference: Racial and Religious Self-Governance in the Iberian Atlantic* (Oxford University Press, forthcoming).

[10] For an example of calling the depopulation *reducciones*, see AGI. 52, R. 6, n. 73.

Repressing Smugglers 105

between conversion to Christianity or exile. Most of them converted, becoming *moriscos*.[11]

There were *moriscos* in other parts of the Iberian Peninsula, with many of them converted to Christianity several generations earlier. They did not speak Arabic and were relatively well integrated into Castilian society. The *moriscos* from Granada, however, were recent converts whose embrace of Christianity was more strategic than sincere. They spoke Arabic and wrote and read texts in *aljamiado* (Arabic script used to write Spanish and Portuguese). Cultural practices such as the use of veil for women (*almalafa*), amulets, and henna persisted despite being perceived by Christian onlookers as foreign and dangerous.[12] The increasing suppression of *morisco* culture and forced acculturation of *moriscos* to Christian customs led to the Second War of the Alpujarras. Castilian authorities saw expulsion as the only solution to put an end to the rebellion, as well as to isolate those groups that refused to put down their arms. During and after the rebellion, at least 80,000 individuals were removed from their homes throughout the Kingdom of Granada and relocated all across western Andalucía and other parts of Castilla, taking them as far as Valladolid, Palencia, or Salamanca. They traveled under extreme weather conditions with very little assistance, which led to a high number of deaths. Some historians have calculated that around 30 percent of these forced migrants died en route.[13]

The expulsion of the *moriscos* was far from the end of the crown's real or imagined problems. In the years that followed, the crown received numerous denunciations concerning the spread of *moriscos* throughout the peninsula. There was a fear that they might be more mobile and thus able to enter treasonous alliances not only with the Ottoman Empire but also with the Protestant enemies of the crown. The increasing anxiety

---

[11] Antonio Domínguez Ortiz and Bernard Vincent, *Historia de los moriscos: vida y tragedia de una minoría* (Madrid: Revista de Occidente, 1978), 17–19. For the extreme complexity of the term *morisco*, see L. P. Harvey, *Muslims in Spain, 1500–1614* (Chicago: University of Chicago Press, 2005), 2–6.

[12] Cook, *Forbidden Passages*, 15–24.

[13] Domínguez Ortiz and Vincent, 50–56. For a close-to-the-ground account of the transformation of Granada in 1492, see David Coleman, *Creating Christian Granada: Society and Religious Culture in an Old-World Frontier City, 1492–1600* (Ithaca: Cornell University Press, 2003). For a gripping study on the enslavement of *morisco* children in the aftermath of the War of the Alpujarras, see Stephanie M. Cavanaugh. "Litigating for Liberty: Enslaved Morisco Children in Sixteenth-Century Valladolid." *Renaissance Quarterly* 70, 4 (2017): 1282–320.

106   *Islanders and Empire*

about their allegiance led to the eventual expulsion of all *moriscos* from all the Iberian territories of the Spanish Monarchy between 1609 and 1614.[14]

Although the scale of relocations varied dramatically between the Andean *reducciones* and the relocation of the *moriscos*, it is evident that by the late sixteenth century, the forced movement of people had become an important instrument in the Spanish imperial repertoire. It allowed the crown to consolidate power, maximize economic resources, evangelize communities, and deal with perceived social, military, and religious threats to the integrity of its territories on both sides of the Atlantic. The population on the northern coast of Hispaniola, as the previous chapter illustrated, was defying the imperial commercial monopoly by trading with foreign merchants who were often enemies of Spain. According to the mercantilist economic notions of the time, such alliances emboldened and strengthened those kingdoms to make war against Spain, to the detriment of the Spanish Monarchy's economy and military preparedness. Most significantly, the levels of what was perceived as religious contamination on the island had become a serious concern for colonial officials in Hispaniola – as evidenced, for instance, by *oidor* Sáenz de Morquecho's comparison of Hispaniola inhabitants with *moriscos* – and indicated the need to relocate Hispaniola's residents away from the remote northern shores of the island and recivilize them in newly established towns that would be under the gaze of Spanish secular and religious institutions. It is in this context that the Council of the Indies first heard the proposal of a Santo Domingo resident, one who appeared before the court at a low point in his personal and professional career.

THE DEPOPULATION PLAN

When Baltasar López de Castro arrived in Santo Domingo on August 11, 1604, he probably could not believe that he had left in disgrace only a few years earlier. As news spread that he was in town, he was received with

---

[14] Domínguez Ortiz and Vincent, 57–59. Some *moriscos* were exempt from the expulsion edict, and others managed to return covertly later. For a fascinating account of the lives of the *moriscos* (and especially *moriscas*) from their removal from Granada to their expulsion from the Iberian Peninsula, see Mary Elizabeth Perry, *The Handless Maiden: Moriscos and the Politics of Religion in Early Modern Spain* (Princeton: Princeton University Press, 2005). For a detailed study on *moriscos* who managed to stay in Granada after the expulsion, see Enrique Soria Mesa, *Los últimos moriscos: pervivencias de la población de origen islámico en el reino de Granada (siglos XVII–XVIII)* (Valencia: Universidad de Valencia, 2014). Thanks to Joaquín Rivaya-Martínez for this reference.

cheers from his friends, neighbors, and relatives, happy for his return from Spain. López de Castro was born in Santo Domingo to an important family of the city, and his marriage to Sabina de Sandoval, granddaughter of the chronicler Gonzalo Fernández de Oviedo, confirmed his social preeminence in the city.[15] While still a young man, Baltasar inherited the position of *escribano de cámara* of the *Audiencia* of Santo Domingo after the death of his father Nicolás López in 1569. According to the royal concession granting him the post, he was given the right to name substitutes until he was of an age to fill the position himself, but diverse bureaucratic complications and the desires of other members of the island's elite to occupy the post prevented him from doing so until 1580, when he was finally sworn in. As one of the two officials in charge of crafting the paperwork of all the litigation that went before the judges of the *Audiencia*, he was a man of great power and influence on the island. During Drake's attack on Santo Domingo in 1586, he was one of the few men who rode to oppose the English forces. In 1592, he was sworn in as *alférez real* of the *Cabildo* of Santo Domingo, which entitled him to a vote in the decisions of that institution and confirmed him as a member of the city's notables. His two official posts provided him a bridge between the interests of the royal judges of the *Audiencia* and the local elites in the *Cabildo*.[16]

The world that López de Castro had crafted for himself came to an end in 1597 when he was banished from his office of *escribano mayor*, forced to pay a penalty of 500 *ducados*, and exiled from Santo Domingo and twenty leagues around the city for four years. This stiff punishment came after he used intemperate words against some members of the *Audiencia*.[17] Forced to leave his home, López de Castro decided to go to court to plead his case in person to the Council of the Indies.[18] From the time of his arrival in Spain that same year, López de Castro penned different *memoriales* or treatises to the Council, writing each in the hopes of gaining enough political favor to have his sentence revoked.

[15] Hugo Eduardo Polanco Brito, *Los escribanos en el Santo Domingo colonial* (Santo Domingo: Academia Dominicana de la Historia, 1989), 141.

[16] E. Rodríguez Demorizi, *Relaciones Históricas de Santo Domingo*, vol. II (Ciudad Trujillo: Ed. Montalvo, 1945), 161–63.

[17] If this is the real reason for his banishment, the punishment seems to be excessive for the crime. Cipriano de Utrera, "Sor Leonor de Ovando." *Boletín del Archivo General de la Nación*, 68 (1951): 122.

[18] *Memorial* from Baltasar López de Castro to the Council of the Indies. May 20, 1596. AGI, SD. 70, R. 1, n. 40.

108   *Islanders and Empire*

On November 20, 1598, he wrote two accounts detailing the natural wealth of Hispaniola and its current poverty due to the inhabitants' practice of trading with foreigners. He argued that this unlawful trade was siphoning away the riches of the island to the crown's enemies and that the contacts with these foreigners posed serious risks of religious contamination for Catholic residents. In the first letter, he listed the numerous measures taken, though to no avail, by both the crown and the *Audiencia*, to curb contraband, such as the galleys sent to patrol the shores or the judges assigned to prosecute smuggling. López de Castro suggested different remedies, including more control of cattle owners, forcing them to count and regulate their herds and ensure that the animals were brought back to the areas around Santo Domingo before they could be taken north and sold to smugglers. In his second *memorial*, López de Castro went a step further. Since the villages in the north were small and sparsely populated, the best solution, he believed, would be to relocate the villagers and their herds to lands nearer the capital. This measure, he claimed, would bring numerous benefits. First, it would solve Santo Domingo's ongoing meat supply problem. Secondly, it would also provide enough manpower to defend the city in case of a new attack. Most importantly, smugglers would be under the close supervision of the authorities in Santo Domingo.[19]

Initially, the Council of the Indies ignored López de Castro. After all, he was hardly the first person to suggest some form of depopulation of the northern settlements. Sáenz de Morquecho's suggestion, coming that same year, followed the same lines when he asked the crown to treat Hispaniola residents like the *moriscos*. Back in 1568, the *oidor* Juan de Echagoian, responding to a suggestion to allow Portuguese ships to trade in Santo Domingo, replied: "It would be better for His Majesty to depopulate the land than allow foreigners to come to it."[20] A few years later, in 1573, the crown issued a royal decree ordering the relocation of the coastal towns in the north and west of the island to the interior to avoid contraband trade. The *Audiencia*, however, completely ignored the decree, and the Council of the Indies did not pursue it any further.[21] In 1580, the village of Montecristi, in the northwest, and the region around

---

[19] Both *memoriales* are included in Rodríguez Demorizi, *Relaciones*, vol. II, 161–87.
[20] "mejor le está a Su Majestad despoblar la tierra que no que estén en ella extranjeros." Rodríguez Demorizi, E. *Relaciones*, vol. I, 144.
[21] Rodríguez Demorizi, *Relaciones*, vol. II, 142, note 10. Rodríguez Morel, *Cartas del Cabildo de Santo Domingo en el siglo XVII* (Santo Domingo: Archivo General de la Nación, 2007), 11–12. The decree is in AGI, SD. 868, Libro III, 3v–4r.

Repressing Smugglers 109

the former town of Puerto Real were depopulated, and its peoples were concentrated to the newly created town of Bayahá. The experiment did not last for long and, except for a few people, the settlers returned to their former lands after a few months.

After López de Castro wrote his *memoriales*, letters and reports detailing how deep the contraband culture was entrenched in Hispaniola's society continued to arrive to the Council of the Indies. The death of Felipe II in 1598 and the accession of Felipe III to the throne brought changes within the Council of the Indies, perhaps leaving new councilors more open than their predecessors to López de Castro's ideas. In February 1602, mentioning López de Castro as the inspiration behind the measure, the Council approved the measure to depopulate the northern and western villages of the island and concentrate the population in the lands surrounding the city of Santo Domingo. López de Castro still had to pay the fine of 500 *ducados* as previously established, but after four years the crown lifted his banishment and allowed him to return to his post as *escribano de cámara*. In addition, as the author of the plan, he was entrusted to deliver the orders to the royal authorities in Santo Domingo.[22]

PRELIMINARIES TO THE DEPOPULATIONS

Upon his arrival to the city on August 11, 1604, López de Castro wasted no time in heading to the building of the *Audiencia*, where he met the new governor, Antonio Osorio, and the members of the *Audiencia*, giving them the depopulation orders and instructions. Osorio was a knight of the Order of Santiago and was possibly appointed to the post due to his merits as a soldier and military leader, given that all governors placed on the island in the aftermath of Drake's attack were governors *de capa y espada*.[23] Osorio had spent his life as a soldier for the Spanish Monarchy, with postings in the Mediterranean and in northern Europe. He fought in the battle of Lepanto in 1571, was stationed for a time in Italy, and had fought aboard the royal galleys until 1579. He then crossed Europe to fight in Flanders for fifteen years, where he was promoted from common

---

[22] Petition by Baltasar López de Castro to the Council of the Indies. June 9, 1603. AGI, SD. 1, n. 51.

[23] Ministers *de capa y espada* (with cape and sword) were those with a military background and possibly some tie to the nobility, as opposed to *togados* (robed), ministers who had risen through the royal administration due to their university background and often lacked any ties to the nobility.

110   *Islanders and Empire*

soldier to *alférez* and captain, and might have been part of the troops that the Duke of Parma had assembled in Dunkirk for the failed invasion of England. His years in Flanders ended when he was sent to Cádiz with 1,000 men to rebuild its defenses after the 1596 English sack of the city. He was then appointed *corregidor* of the town of Jerez de la Frontera, near Cádiz, where he was serving when he was named the new governor of Santo Domingo. This latest commission came with the news of the death of his brother Diego, who had been captain of the galleys of Santo Domingo and was later appointed governor there.[24] Antonio arrived in the city sometime in 1602.

Three days after López de Castro's arrival, Governor Osorio gathered the *Audiencia* to initiate the depopulation of the towns of Puerto Plata, Bayahá, Montecristi, and La Yaguana. Three of the four judges of the *Audiencia*, led by the *oidor* Francisco Manso de Contreras, opposed the mandate. Manso de Contreras, along with his close ally the *oidor* Francisco Mejías de Villalobos and *fiscal* Pedro Arévalo Sedeño, argued that the orders could not be executed legitimately since Archbishop Dávila y Padilla, who had been appointed coexecutor of the commission, had died on June 26, only a few days before the arrival of the orders. They proposed writing back to Spain to inform the crown of the death of the archbishop and to wait for new orders. Within the *Audiencia*, only the *oidor* Marcos Nuñez de Toledo supported the governor in his intention to initiate the depopulation plans. López de Castro, in his function as *secretario de cámara* and as an appointed aide to the governor, lobbied in favor of the plan's execution, arguing that by the time the orders came back, the smugglers would have squandered even more of the island's riches, mentioning as well the spiritual peril threatening the smugglers' souls in their exposure to foreign pirates. Although the opponents of depopulation won the ensuing vote, Governor Osorio, as the person in charge of the depopulations, decided to carry out the orders.[25] These included a full pardon to everyone who had been engaged in any way in contraband trade to date. The pardon was contingent upon local residents' willingness to relocate to the new towns that would be created in the proximity of Santo Domingo. Anyone caught smuggling after the proclamation of depopulation orders would be condemned to death and would lose all of their property.[26]

Oidor Manso de Contreras' opposition to the plan was rooted in more than a defect of form. Manso grew up on the island of Margarita, off the

[24] AGI, SD. 1, n. 56.
[25] Rodríguez Demorizi, *Relaciones,* vol. II, 218.
[26] Ibid., 202–04.

coast of Venezuela, where his father was governor. He aided his father and occupied different positions in the local government, such as *regidor* and *alcalde ordinario*, even becoming the island's representative in Spain. Later, he was appointed governor of Santa Marta and Riohacha; as a reward for his defense of this post, he was promoted as *fiscal* of the *Audiencia* of Santo Domingo and later to the rank of *oidor*. He continued to have strong family ties in Margarita, where his wife resided, as well as in Puerto Rico and in Santo Domingo, where he was related to the prominent Bardeci family.[27]

Although these connections weighed heavily in his opposition to the depopulations, his decision might have gone beyond traditional family loyalty. Before becoming *oidor* in Santo Domingo, he had also held the

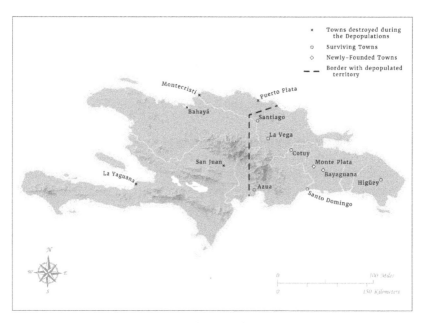

FIGURE 3.1 Main towns and villages of Hispaniola after the 1604–6 Depopulations (Alexander Fries, University of Alabama Cartographic Research Laboratory).

---

[27] For a full study of the wide family relations that Manso de Contreras had in Hispaniola and across the Spanish Caribbean, see Luis Rafael Burset Flores, *El ejercicio del poder a dos manos: el capital social del licenciado Francisco Manso de Contreras* (Bayamo: Ediciones Bayamo, 2018).

Islanders and Empire

post of Governor of Cartagena and *procurador general* of Margarita, while maintaining important economic interests in both cities. While in Spain from 1601 to 1602, he was named *fiscal* of the *Audiencia* of Santo Domingo, but never took up this office. He remained in Spain, and, in 1603, the new President of the Council of the Indies, the Count of Lemos, asked Manso's opinion about López de Castro's depopulation plan. Manso responded favorably, believing he would be entrusted with the commission. Indeed, he had won the trust of the Count of Lemos, was promoted to *oidor*, and then quickly ordered to depart for Santo Domingo to be there when the depopulation orders arrived. This likely fueled his belief that he would personally undertake the mission.[28] Once in his post, Francisco Manso tried to become an ally of the governor and even informed him of the crown's plans to depopulate the north of the island. His friendliness toward Osorio did not last, and as soon as López de Castro arrived in August with the official orders – in which Manso appeared merely as an assistant to the governor – his attitude toward Osorio and the depopulations swiftly changed. He may have felt insulted that his responsibilities had been reduced to those of López de Castro, a mere *secretario de cámara*. So Manso did everything in his power to incite and support local unrest with the help of his friend, the *oidor* Gonzalo Mejías de Villalobos.[29]

As soon as the depopulation orders were made public, a torrent of protests, criticism, and anger washed over Santo Domingo, with much of it directed against López de Castro, who received the harshest criticisms for having penned the idea in the first place.[30] Groups gathered on street corners and in homes to discuss the news of the depopulations, writing letters amongst themselves or to the Council of the Indies and exchanging what information they had heard about the official plans. One man was arrested for spreading rumors and trying to convince others to resist the royal orders. The most serious of those rumors was the circulation of a letter, written by an unknown "important official" of the Council of the

---

[28] Manso left Spain hurriedly in April 1603, but he wouldn't arrive in Santo Domingo until April 1604, after spending almost a year in Margarita, where he had his wife and business to attend to. Frank Peña Pérez, *Antonio Osorio, monopolio, contrabando y despoblación* (Santiago, República Dominicana: UCMM, 1980), 119; Cipriano de Utrera, *Sor Leonor*, 129–30.

[29] Testimony of *fiscal* Pedro Arévalo Sedeño. In AGI, SD. 17, n. 12.

[30] Many of those who received López de Castro warmly after his return started to turn against him. On many occasions, he confessed, he felt his life and that of his family threatened by his support of the depopulations. Despite the threats, López de Castro continued supporting the plan and became the governor's closest collaborator.

Indies, warning the island's residents that new papers had arrived in the Council of the Indies contradicting López de Castro's assessments. It advised residents to stall the depopulation process for as long as possible. In the next few months, the content of this letter, whose authorship was later attributed to the *oidor* Manso, would circulate throughout the island and was undoubtedly used by the residents in the northern villages as a reason to hinder the governor's actions. For his part, Osorio tried to react quickly to silence any such unfounded reports. To this end, on August 20, 1604, he issued an edict prohibiting any gathering – either in public or in secret – or the writing of letters or papers regarding the depopulations, under the penalty of death and loss of property. Such a prohibition might have helped stop talk in public spaces, but it was impossible to police the privacy of people's homes, so the edict might have produced the opposite of its intended effect. Rumors continued to spread throughout the island, and they had important consequences for the implementation of the governor's commission.[31]

A day before that edict was issued, the governor received the first official local response to the depopulations. In a long letter signed on August 19, 1604, the *Cabildo* of Santo Domingo bargained for an alternative solution. It pointed out the impossibility of removing all the cattle from the north, which were the most suitable lands for these animals; the great chance of losing them during the move to the new settlements – to the benefit of those with no property, who would keep the cattle and stay in the depopulated areas; the risk of enslaved Africans running away, taking advantage of the confusion; and the possibility of foreigners establishing themselves in the ports to trade. They also argued that the tithe collected in those lands would be lost to the detriment of the ecclesiastical institutions of the islands, such as the cathedral, the hospitals, and the convents. This was true, with an important caveat: in Hispaniola, only ranchers with corralled cattle paid tithe to the church. For decades cattle ranchers avoided such payments by grazing their herds freely in the mountains, only culling them when their meat and hides were necessary.[32]

---

[31] The edict is published in Rodríguez Demorizi, *Relaciones*, vol. II, 221–23.

[32] Oral communication with Genaro Rodríguez Morel, September 7, 2017. This tax-dodging measure, during the course of the depopulations, proved fatal. Most residents of the north complained that they could not remove the cattle from the mountains, and that, as a consequence, most of their wealth had been left behind. Undoubtedly, many cattle were left in the mountains. It is, however, impossible to know the precise numbers: news of the depopulations triggered a sharp increase in residents' slaughtering cattle to sell their hides to foreign traders, to the horror of governor Osorio and his aides, for whom these acts

114 *Islanders and Empire*

As a solution to these potential problems, the *Cabildo* suggested a partial depopulation, in which towns like Montecristi, populated by small ranchers, would be dismantled and relocated in Puerto Plata.[33]

The members of the *Cabildo* of Santo Domingo also asked for harsher punishments, such as exile or execution, of all those convicted of smuggling. The *Cabildo* pointed out that most of the people who resided in the north were "common folk and *mestizos*, *mulatos*, and blacks," people who have little or no property to lose. They were the people blamed for most of the theft, destruction, and contraband in the north. They owned less than 200 head of cattle, maybe one or two enslaved Africans, and they lived off their cattle and the land. These people would also keep the property of those "more honest *vecinos*," a minority, who would be unable to retrieve it if they were forcefully removed from their land. With the depopulation, these thieves would deepen their relationship with "Lutheran" smugglers, without the vigilance of the local officials or royal ministers who were currently residing in the northern towns and who provided a modicum of royal justice in the region, as well as a good religious example.[34] The *Cabildo*'s letter reveals a common thread in the way local elites presented the problems derived from smuggling to the crown and its officials. The initial reaction of the elites in the city of Santo Domingo was an effort to protect the interests of larger land and cattle owners, at the expense of *mestizo*, *mulato*, black smallholders and landless peasants, whom they indirectly accused of being the real culprits behind the contraband trade. These elites presented themselves as a civilizing example to the people of color residing on cattle ranches in the vast Hispaniola countryside. Without them, it was argued, the mixed-raced population would be reduced to barbarism and theft to survive.

Governor Osorio seemed to ignore the *Cabildo*'s complaints, and a few weeks later, on September 2, 1604, he took the next step. He issued a royal pardon to anyone who had engaged in contraband: all offenses up to that point would be forgiven if transgressors agreed to relocate themselves, their families, and property. During that month, however, repeated reports confirmed that contraband trade had continued as usual and

represented yet another defiance of Hispaniola residents to the royal orders, as well as a squandering of the island's riches.

[33] Memorial of the *Cabildo* of Santo Domingo. August 19, 1604. AGI, Escribanía de Cámara de Justicia (Escribanía), 11B, R. 1, p. 192r. It was also published in Rodríguez Demorizi, *Relaciones*, vol. II, 253–73.

[34] "La mayor parte de los vecinos y habitantes en la isla por aquellas partes es gente común y mestizos, mulatos y negros, unos que no tienen hacienda ni que perder." Ibid., 260.

over fifty foreign ships, some of them with several small sloops, were seen trading on the northern shores of the island. In late August, Osorio had sent letters to the *Cabildos* of the northern towns informing them of the depopulation plans. The first reply, authored by the *Cabildo* of Montecristi, did not arrive in Santo Domingo until November. In that letter, the *Cabildo* insisted on the poverty of the residents and the impossibility of moving without catastrophic losses. The members of the *Cabildo* suggested in turn gathering the residents of Bayahá with those of Montecristi and stationing galleys in the town. In another letter, sent also in November, the *Cabildo* of Montecristi requested a six-month grace period for the residents to gather their possessions. Governor Osorio was unmoved, noting that they had had time to organize themselves since August and knowing that smuggling continued in the area. With that in mind, he warned them to be ready to leave by early January.[35]

By December 1604, it must have been clear to Osorio that the depopulations would be an extremely complex process whose ultimate success was far from assured. The northern residents also knew that all was not lost and stalled at every opportunity. The representatives of the towns of Bayahá and Montecristi arrived in Santo Domingo, as requested by Governor Osorio, but instead of receiving instructions from their respective *Cabildos* to take possession of the lands for their new towns, they were instructed to contradict the depopulations. Osorio, his patience exhausted, jailed and fined them. While the representatives were imprisoned, *oidor* Manso de Contreras visited and encouraged them to appeal their sentences and not give up in their opposition to the depopulations.[36]

Letters full of rumors surrounding the depopulations continued to circulate throughout the island. In a letter to the Council of the Indies, the *fiscal* of the *Audiencia*, explained how the residents were writing letters against those who hindered them and praising those who favored them. He then added: "I beg Your Majesty to be informed that these are the designs of evil men who have no other way of living than the exercise of that evil smuggling, which sustains them, and they have turned it into an art that they execute with shrewdness."[37] As the depopulations progressed and new difficulties arose, expressing dissatisfaction with local

---

[35] Rodríguez Demorizi, *Relaciones*, vol. II, 225, 227–28. Letter from Antonio Osorio to the *Cabildo* of Montecristi, December 9, 1604. AGI, SD. 52, R. 5, 19A.

[36] Osorio to the Council of the Indies. January 24, 1605. AGI, SD. 52, R. 4, n. 19. For Manso de Contreras's support of the envoys from Montecristi, see AGI, SD. 17, n. 12.

[37] "Suplico a Vuestra Majestad esté informado que estos son trazos de hombre malditos que no tienen otro modo de vivir sino el uso y ejercicio de esto malditos rescates de que se

Islanders and Empire

attitudes and behaviors became a way for public officials to show their support for the plan, thus signaling their loyalty to the king and the governor, while distancing themselves from those who resisted the depopulations. Even the *oidor* Mejías de Villalobos, one of Manso de Contreras' main allies, who continued in his efforts to thwart the process, showed a similar opinion in his letters to Spain. In official communications, he continued his support for the depopulations. In one letter, referring to local residents and the difficulty of removing them from the northern coasts, he explained his view using a metaphor: just as there were two types of cattle on the island, one tamed in corrals, and another wild in the mountains, the inhabitants of Hispaniola were also of two types. People with property were like tame cattle. People without property, however, were like wild cattle, indomitable "like wild hogs in Spain," who would be hard to remove and would stay behind trading with foreigners with the help of those in Santo Domingo.[38] Mejías de Villalobos' metaphor echoes the opinion of the *Cabildo* of Santo Domingo in August 1604. By singling out the rural (and mostly mixed-race) poor as the real obstacle to the depopulations, Mejías de Villalobos was in fact exculpating the elites, his relatives, and peers, from any wrongdoing. Also like the *Cabildo* of Santo Domingo, his comparison implicitly positioned white Spaniards as civilized, while people of color were seen as savage and unruly.

In the meantime, Osorio continued with his preparations, and, during December 1604, he commissioned two men to go to La Yaguana and Puerto Plata with orders to punish any ongoing smuggling. While the depopulation of Puerto Plata took place without trouble thanks to the cooperation of local residents, complications arose in La Yaguana. Governor Osorio, perhaps in an attempt to build bridges with Manso de Contreras, gave the commission to depopulate La Yaguana to Manso's cousin, Captain Jerónimo Agüero Bardeci. While in the village, Agüero took advantage of his position to go to nearby ports and engage in contraband trade himself, while spreading the rumor that the village would not be depopulated. In exchange for money, he offered himself to the residents as an envoy to Spain and claimed he would petition the crown to reverse its decision. While in La Yaguana, a Dutch fleet of four ships anchored

---

sustentan y tienen de ello hecho arte, la cual ejercitan con tanta sagacidad." Pedro de Arévalo Sedeño to the Council of the Indies. December 20, 1604. AGI, SD. 52, R. 4, n. 18.

[38] "como en España los jabalíes." Gonzalo Mejías de Villalobos to the Council of the Indies. December 30, 1604. AGI, SD. 82, R. 2, n. 51.

near the village. A few of the Dutch sailors approached the village in a boat with a white flag and were led by a known smuggler in the region who happened also to be an acquaintance of Agüero Bardeci. The Dutch proceeded to read a letter denouncing the brutalities of the king of Spain for depopulating those lands and offered the villagers the chance to defect and become Dutch subjects, with a promise that their properties would be respected and defended against Spanish attacks. The letter was copied and circulated through the island. Some witnesses even saw Agüero Bardeci himself reading the letter in a private gathering.[39] Even though no action was taken to accept the Dutch offer, rumors of the encounter did not pass unnoticed by many other residents of the island.

The news of the main Dutch fleet anchored in the Bay of Guanahibes (see Figure 2.2) trading freely with the locals, and supplying themselves with everything they needed, reached the governor by late January 1605. By mid February, Osorio had heard what had transpired in La Yaguana and departed Santo Domingo with forty soldiers to expel the Dutch, but they had left before Osorio arrived, so he proceeded to Bayahá to start the depopulations. This task had been originally entrusted to the *oidor* Manso de Contreras, but his resistance to the depopulation process made the governor mistrust him, so Osorio went in person. He reached Bayahá and Montecristi in March, 1605, and proceeded to burn the *bohíos* and houses. He also gathered some of the cattle that were spread through the mountains. Some of the residents left for the new settlements immediately while the rest were given twenty-five days to depart with their cattle and property. He did the same in the village of La Yaguana, where he collected information from witnesses and started a judicial process against Agüero Bardeci for the part he had played in the Dutch visit to the village. In May, he joined López de Castro in Monte Plata, one of the new towns, to encourage the displaced locals to settle.

Two new villages – named San Antonio de Monte Plata and San Juan Bautista de Bayaguana – were created in the proximity of Santo Domingo. The names of these new villages not only combined the names of their new residents' towns of origin (Montecristi and Puerto Plata, Bayahá and La Yaguana) but also proclaimed political and religious allegiance: inclusion of saints' names in newly created towns was a common occurrence in the Spanish world, and the dedication of one of the towns to San Antonio (Osorio's patron saint), included a good measure of flattery for the governor. In this

---

[39] AGI, SD. 52, R. 5, N. 19A; AGI, Escribanía, 3A.

case, however, the names of saints might have also been intended to signal a return to proper Christian life for the town's new inhabitants. In the eyes of both Osorio and López de Castro, life in the frontier had taken a toll on the new residents. López de Castro reported how the governor had brought a baker from Santo Domingo so they could have the fresh bread they had never enjoyed in the north. Osorio also opened two stores in the new towns, invited many to eat with him and begged them to go to Santo Domingo, so the men and their wives "got accustomed to good clothing, food and good language, and saw the stores of the city, where they would find everything they bought from the heretics." These were not the only attempts to accommodate the newcomers. Osorio tried to reintroduce the residents to what he interpreted as civilized behavior, including clothing, and food appropriate for good Christians.[40] The depopulation was as much a civilizing mission as it was an attempt to eliminate contraband. Diego López de Brenes, the chaplain and *comendador* of the hospital of San Nicolás in Santo Domingo, testified that some of the residents of the new villages had told him that "having been taken from the old towns to the new ones, they felt as if they had been taken from hell or from the road to it."[41] López de Brenes' testimony implied that at least a few of the northern residents viewed their lives in their old towns as dangerous from a moral and religious standpoint. The chaplain's testimony could also be interpreted as relief on the part of some local people to go back to the comforts of a civilized urban lifestyle, which was considered to be inextricably connected to a Christian life.

On the other hand, local resistance to the depopulations reflected not only a local desire to continue living their lives as they saw fit, but also a rejection of the civilizing narrative that the Spanish authorities were trying to impose. The northern residents of Hispaniola resisted a monolithic interpretation of what it meant to be civilized and resented the social, political, economic, and religious normativity that the Spanish Monarchy, through its ministers, was trying to enforce.

---

[40] "para que ellos y sus mujeres se aficionasen al traje, comidas y buen lenguaje, y para que viesen tiendas de mercaderías a do hallarían todo lo que les vendían los herejes." Baltasar López de Castro, *Relación de la Ejecución del Arbitrio para el remedio de los rescates en la isla Española y comprobación de ella*, 1605. John Carter Brown Library, B606 L863r 1-Size.

[41] "en haberlos quitado de los sitios antiguos y traídos al nuevo ha sido sacarlos del infierno o del camino a él." Proceedings against those who impeded the Depopulations, August 21, 1605. AGI, SD. 52, R. 5, n. 44.

THE NORTH RESISTS

The residents of Bayahá departed the ruins of their village in March 1605 at the behest of Governor Osorio, who was the last one to leave. He informed them that he would meet them in the new towns to get them settled. Once the governor passed them on the road, most of them returned to Bayahá and then proceeded to gather with some residents from Montecristi in the valley of Guaba. Naming themselves "the Assembled" (*"los Congregados"*), they armed themselves with weapons acquired from the Dutch fleet that had been trading in the area, gathered all their property, and prepared to resist the governor's plans to remove them. As their leader, they chose Hernando Montoro, a free man of color identified as a *mulato*, who was the owner of a ranch in the Guaba valley. Governor Osorio considered the residents' actions a personal treason and wrote to the crown about the new developments in unequivocal terms. The people in Guaba argued that they were not given enough time to remove their property and move to the new towns (they had had six months, and they requested six more). They were also fearful of punishment for having continued to trade with foreigners. Osorio suspected, nonetheless, that since they had been granted six months to move and they had not made any attempts to gather their belongings, they really did not have any intention to leave.[42]

Osorio also received news that the people at Guaba were killing their cattle at an increased rate, which could only mean that they were selling the hides to foreign traders.[43] This was confirmed by two enslaved Africans captured as they left Guaba. Juan Bran testified, using a child as an interpreter, saying he had been sold by a group of French merchants to Spaniard Lázaro Hernández for ten horses loaded with hides. When asked how much cattle his master had, he said none, since he had killed his entire stock to sell the hides to smugglers in exchange for clothing. Antonio Bañón was the other enslaved African captured. The sources describe him as a *ladino*, and he told how Portuguese merchants had sold him to a local Spaniard Antonio Laudin, Sr., who gifted him to Antonio Laudin, Jr. when the younger man married Bibiana de Acosta. Laudín Jr. had recently died, so Bañón had become property of Acosta, his widow. Antonio informed his captors that his mistress had recently

---

[42] Osorio to the Council of the Indies. October 20, 1605. AGI, SD. 52, R. 5. n. 51; AGI, SD. 17, N.12.

[43] AGI, SD. 17, N.12.

120   *Islanders and Empire*

ordered all her cattle killed and then exchanged their hides for some clothes and two young enslaved African girls, for whom she paid 60 and 50 hides, respectively.[44] This is an extraordinary narrative of how Hispaniola residents in rural areas acquired enslaved people and how African captives became part of dowries. This testimony also illustrates how the northern residents of the island had chosen to convert their bovine property into a much more easily transferable property, namely clothing and the enslaved Africans who would in turn be tasked with the work of producing more hides and selling them to foreign merchants.

Governor Osorio sent a group of forty men led by Captain Lope de Villegas to Guaba in June 1605, intent on making an impression on the residents. He gave Lope de Villegas documents promising the villagers that if they agreed to relocate, they would be fully pardoned. The conversations of Lope de Villegas and his men with the leaders in Guaba did not produce any results. Hernando Montoro insisted on his demand of six months to gather cattle and properties, a request which Villegas considered to be "impertinent." The fact that Montoro was a man of color and the leader of the rebellion may have played a part in Villegas' assessment of his request. Informing the governor of these developments, Lope de Villegas next sent a Dominican friar with documents, offering immunity once again to all the people in Guaba if they relocated. The friar posted the documents in different parts of the valley. The offer seemed to have elicited the interest of a few families in the valley, but they feared for their lives if they revealed their desire to leave. When a young Spanish man walked out of the valley, and Lope de Villegas asked him why he was leaving, he responded that he was tired of being ordered to keep watch. The young man informed him that in Guaba there were at least 140 armed men out of a population of over 600, including women and children, as well as enslaved and free people of African descent. The young man also explained that they were ready to fight to the death to stay.[45]

Despite having retired to a remote valley in the north of the island, Montoro and his people were not isolated from the events occurring elsewhere on the island and beyond. Lope de Villegas met again with Montoro in July 1605, during his second visit to the Guaba valley.

[44] AGI, Escribanía, 11A, R. 2, August 4, 1605.
[45] AGI, SD. 17, N.12; Safe conduct entrusted to Fray Jacinto de Soria for "The Assembled," June 10, 1605. AGI, SD. 83, R. 1; Testimony of Lope de Villegas, August 2, 1605. AGI, Escribanía, 11A, R. 2; the total population estimate for the Guaba rebels is taken from a letter from Bartolomé Hernández to the Guaba rebels, November 2, 1605. AGI, SD. 17, n. 14.

Montoro and his men remained waiting in ambush and armed with their muskets ready and their matches lit.[46] When Lope de Villegas tried to convince him to desist, Montoro told him that he was expecting a messenger with a letter from Santo Domingo with information about whether Osorio's pardon was reliable. He also told him that any day he was expecting a royal pardon granted in honor of the birth of the king's heir (the future Felipe IV of Spain was born in April 1605), and in less than two weeks, they would all be walking together in the streets of Santo Domingo.[47] In reality, no pardon ever reached Hispaniola. There is little doubt that Montoro was well informed of the events taking place beyond the island shores, so he might have mentioned this pardon as a way to gain some extra time. It is also possible that in Santo Domingo, people like Manso de Contreras or other residents were giving him false information in order to keep up the spirits of those gathered in Guaba, and thwart the depopulation process altogether. However, not all the information that the people in Guaba received was incorrect. They knew of the imminent arrival of another expedition led by Osorio even before Villegas and his men. Two days before the governor's arrival, Montoro's group encircled Villegas' encampment and stole most of his horses.[48]

At the same time that Osorio commissioned Villegas to talk to the people in Guaba in June 1605, he was also preparing for a possible failure of the negotiations, asking the *Audiencia* to gather 100 men. There were many problems with raising the men among the island residents, many of whom were opposed to the depopulations. The *Cabildo* of Santo Domingo, possibly in an effort to improve its relationship with the governor, offered 1,000 *ducados* to help in the efforts. Finally, only sixty very uncooperative men were gathered of the requested 100. According to Osorio, these men orchestrated "one thousand treasons, mixing the orders I gave them, disobeying them, taking me through unused trails and creating so many impediments that a thousand times I wished I were alone."[49] Despite the obstacles, Osorio arrived at Lope de Villegas'

---

[46] Montoro and his men bought the weapons from the Dutch ships that were visiting the island ports around that time. They paid six cattle hides per musket and sixteen hides for a barrel of powder. AGI, Escribanía, 11A, R. 2.

[47] Testimony of Lope de Villegas, August 2, 1605. AGI, Escribanía, 11A, R. 2.

[48] Testimony of Lope de Villegas, August 2, 1605. AGI, SD. 83, R. 1.

[49] "los que iban conmigo me hicieron mil traiciones trastocándome las órdenes que daba y no guardando ninguna, llevándome por caminos inusitados, haciéndome tantos estorbos y embarazos que mil veces deseé verme sólo." Ibid.; Correspondence between Osorio and the *Cabildo* of Santo Domingo. May 6 and 11, 1605. AGI, SD. 83, R. 1.

122   *Islanders and Empire*

encampment in late July 1605 and led his men to the interior of the valley, where he found an empty campsite. The governor guessed that the people in Guaba had left for Guanahibes Bay, so he proceeded with his troops to the shore. To his amazement, the people of Guaba were boarding a fleet of fourteen Dutch ships. A group of forty Spanish men and their Dutch allies landed and readied themselves to face the governor's forces. An exchange of fire between both parties ensued with some deaths, until finally the Dutch and their local allies withdrew and went aboard their ships. Unable to capture them, Osorio returned to Guaba, where, with the testimonies of the captains who accompanied him, he began a written judicial process against the people who had gathered there. A sentence was issued on October 10, 1605, and it declared the former residents of Bayahá and Montecrsiti who escaped to Guaba guilty of high treason. They were condemned to death *in absentia* as rebels, their property was to be expropriated, and they were to be punished by death if found. Osorio then proceeded to gather as much cattle as he could find in the valley, amounting to 3,000 heads, which reportedly was only a small fraction of the cattle that had existed before the earlier massive slaughter to sell their hides. In the depopulated lands, Osorio's men captured one of the rebels, who was unceremoniously hanged according to the sentence lately issued. They then returned with the cattle to the new towns.[50]

In the meantime, those in Santo Domingo who opposed the depopulations observed with great frustration how the governor continued to press forward. They had tried to aid the rebels in Guaba, encouraging them to resist with promises of pardons and new orders arriving from Spain, but in reality the crown did not appear to have any intention of stopping the depopulations. Indeed, after the violent resistance in Guaba, any talk against the depopulation could be easily construed as treason. On October 22, 1605, a little over two weeks after Osorio declared the residents of Guaba traitors, someone (or more likely a group) crafted a letter in which the island of Hispaniola addressed the king in the first person. In the letter, its author(s) sought to establish the island's legitimacy as the first territory in the Americas in which the Catholic faith was introduced, the colony from which all the others followed, as well as being the recipient of the benefits from the beloved Catholic kings and their successors – all of which were proof of the very civilized nature of the island's inhabitants among all of the crown's possessions. The letter then complained about being forgotten and treated "with the greatest rigor and

---

[50] Antonio Osorio to the Council of the Indies. October 20, 1605. AGI, SD. 52, R. 5, n. 51.

Repressing Smugglers 123

roughness by the ministers of Your Majesty." The document went on to describe how the territories so carefully populated in the past were being destroyed by the royal ministers, "with the temples violated and set ablaze, destroying the cattle ... with the greatest strength and violence ever seen or expected among Christians." The author(s) used the letter to explain how residents were fearful of speaking up about these injustices and how the governor was only acting for his own benefit, and then begged for the king to send a witness to the state of affairs on the island who would provide him with an objective account.[51] The writer(s) of the letter depicted the island's loyal Christian subjects as facing excessive and inappropriate force from fellow Christians, with the implication being that such levels of violence might be legitimate when used against non-Christians, but certainly not against loyal Catholic subjects of the king. Despite its attempt to smear the governor's actions, the letter seems to have caused little effect among the ministers of the Council of the Indies, possibly because it arrived during October, a month in which Osorio had written six letters to the council detailing every step he took and the opposition he encountered, so the anonymous letter was possibly construed as artifice.[52] Nevertheless, the elites of Hispaniola who were behind the letter undoubtedly believed that they deserved better treatment than the forcible removal from their own lands. In that way, this letter can be understood as a plea for respect for the stature of Hispaniola and its residents as the oldest Spanish settlement in the Indies and for royal justice in the face of bad government at the hands of overzealous ministers.

Despite such complaints, Osorio seemed to prioritize the success of the depopulations over his own personal feelings against the "rebels" of "the Assembled" because the encounter in Guanahibes Bay was not the end of his diplomatic efforts to lure in those who were disobeying his orders. In early October, 1605, having been informed that the *alcalde mayor* of the city of Santiago and militia captain Bartolomé Hernández knew many of the people in Guaba, Governor Osorio commissioned him to go the valley

---

[51] "Y me veo tratar con el mayor rigor y aspereza de los ministros de Vuestra Majestad que jamás no se ha visto en provincial alguna" and "despojada y destruida por los ministros de Vuestra Majestad, violando y abrasándome los templos, destruyéndome y asolándome los ganados ... con la mayor fuerza y violencia que se vio ni es para ver entre cristianos." Anonymous letter of "the island Hispaniola" to the Council of the Indies. October 22, 1605. AGI, SD. 83, R. 1.

[52] The Council of the Indies acknowledged the receipt of Osorio's letters and agreed with the governor's actions. Council of the Indies to Antonio Osorio. May 5, 1606. In Incháustegui Cabral, *Reales Cédulas*, tomo III (Madrid, 1958), 831–34.

124   *Islanders and Empire*

to convince as many people as possible to move to the new settlements.[53] Hernández came recommended by Diego de Villafañe, who was *alcalde ordinario* of Puerto Plata, a village depopulated earlier that year. Despite being one of its richest residents and the owner of a sugar mill, which he lost during the depopulation of the town (he put his total losses at around 12,000 ducados), Villafañe closely collaborated with Osorio. The reasons behind Hernández's faithful collaboration are not clear. In later years, Hernández presented official documentation proving that he had not ever been accused of contraband trade, so he might have seen the depopulation as an opportunity for social advancement. Both men appeared to have viewed the determination of the governor to carry out the depopulation orders as a point of no return and might have tried to make the best out of the situation. In the case of Villafañe, he owed the Dominican convent in Puerto Plata a *censo* of 300 gold *pesos*, which was cancelled by the destruction of the convent itself.[54]

Captain Hernández arrived in November 1605 with documents permitting him to explain to the people of Guaba that their lives and properties would be spared if they decided to relocate before December 1. In his address, he mentioned that troops were on their way and that this might be their last chance to leave peacefully. He then appealed to their religiosity, telling them to return to good Christian practices and to stop leading dissolute lives. That same day, eight former residents of Bayahá came forward to accept the pardon, and by the end of the month, twenty-nine heads of households and their families had accepted the pardon. Hernández's message seems to have struck a chord among the people in Guaba. At the same time, it also seems plausible that the difficult living conditions and the growing sense that they would lose this struggle played an equally large role in their change of heart. Hernández's success convinced Osorio to extend the deadline to January 1, 1606, and during this time at least another thirty residents

---

[53] Letter from Antonio Osorio to Bartolomé Hernández, October 6, 1605. AGI, SD. 17, n. 14, 4r.

[54] In early modern Spain and its American colonies, an individual offered to place a *censo* (also known as *censo al quitar*) on a piece of his or her property in favor of an ecclesiastical institution, such a convent or monastery. In exchange for a loan from the convent, this individual agreed to pay a percentage of the principal in perpetuity or until it was repaid in full. For more on *censos*, see John Charles Chasteen and James A. Wood, eds., *Problems in Modern Latin American History: Sources and Interpretations* (Lanham: Rowman & Littlefield, 2004), 9; Diego de Villafañe's *censo* is listed among those owed to the Dominican convent in Puerto Plata in AGI, SD. 17, n. 6.

and their families decided to leave the valley, thus completing the depopulations there without military intervention.[55]

Governor Osorio and his representatives continued to crisscross the island in an effort to shepherd cattle and settlers from their old villages in the north to the newly created settlements near Santo Domingo. In the town of La Yaguana, Osorio's men also met the resistance of residents unwilling to relocate. In April 1605, at approximately at the same time that Osorio was destroying the village of Bayahá, Captain Diego de Rebolledo was commissioned to depopulate La Yaguana, where he had been the *alcalde ordinario*. His men burned fields and houses in the process, angering the local clergy, particularly the head of the Franciscan convent, who harangued neighbors to raise arms against the governor's men for trying to destroy the order's building. The local parish priest also resisted the relocation and resided in the ruins of his town for a few months.[56] He was not the only one – many other residents stayed behind, continuing to kill their cattle and trade with foreign smugglers. According to the testimonies of two soldiers sent by Osorio to control the contraband trade, the residents accelerated the rate at which they killed their cattle with the help of their enslaved laborers and continued trading with thirty foreign schooners that frequented every port near the village. While they did this, they warned the soldiers that if they did anything to intervene, they would kill them, and they made a point of reminding them of this every day. In some cases, the soldiers ignored the warnings and tried to arrest some residents trading in some of the ports, but as soon as they were spotted, the residents boarded the ships of the foreign smugglers, "where they were well received."[57]

On one occasion, the soldiers managed to capture a young enslaved African man named Pedro de Lara, who was carrying a few hides on his back to the coast. As they took him prisoner, they encountered Lara's owner, Juan de Guzmán, the sight of whom must have made quite an impression on the soldiers. Guzmán was on horseback and completely covered in bovine blood while holding a spear in his hands, blocking the road. He ordered the soldiers to release the prisoner, and after what was possibly a very tense moment, the soldiers told Guzmán to go with God,

---

[55] AGI, SD. 17, n. 14.

[56] Carlos Esteban Deive, "Las Devastaciones de 1605 y 1606," in Raymundo González de Peña, coord., *Historia general del pueblo dominicano*, tomo II (Santo Domingo: Academia Dominicana de la Historia, 2018), 67–68.

[57] "donde eran bien favorecidos." Testimony of Juan Moreno, July 1605. AGI, Escribanía, 11B, Ramo 2, 612r.

126   *Islanders and Empire*

and he finally acquiesced and left the scene without violence and without his enslaved laborer.[58] What the soldiers might have thought about the sight of a man on horseback covered in blood is open to speculation. The fact remains that they mentioned this encounter in their testimony, indicating the shock Guzmán's ghastly appearance caused. Such a description possibly confirmed fears that the frontier residents of Hispaniola were behaving in ways that no proper civilized Christians should and thus justified the crown's intervention.

The people of La Yaguana, however, explained their behavior in a different way. They claimed to fear the governor's retaliation for their past actions. Local residents of La Yaguana told the same two soldiers who encountered Guzmán that they were certain of being killed if they ever left their lands. Overwhelmed by their inability to stop the trade and the threats of local residents, the soldiers returned to the village of San Juan, which was also being depopulated, and warned their superiors. In the meantime, a group of sixty families (approximately 400 people, including enslaved Africans), which amounted to almost the entire town of La Yaguana, boarded the ship of local resident Hernando Guerra, as well as other foreign ships, and left Hispaniola for the region of Bayamo and Santiago, in eastern Cuba, which was also famous for their abundant contraband trade.[59]

The arrival of 150 soldiers from Puerto Rico by late 1605 greatly improved the governor's policing capacity. These soldiers equipped him with a group of officials, without ties to the island population, whom he could trust with his orders. He ordered two groups of fifty men to sweep the island, one from Puerto Plata throughout the northern shores all the way to the west toward Guaba, and the other from the region around the village of San Juan to the former town of La Yaguana and then north to meet their colleagues in Guaba.[60] These patrols became customary for the rest of Osorio's governorship, and resulted in the capture of a great number of men who were still in the depopulated regions, including runaway slaves, free people of color, white ranchers and foreigners, many of whom received death sentences for their infractions. In March 1607, the governor reported that his men had captured a total of 150 runaway

[58] Ibid.   [59] Ibid.
[60] Court proceedings against the Guaba Valley rebels. AGI, SD. 83, R. 1. By the end of 1605, Governor Osorio reported that the man in charge of the troops heading to Puerto Plata died on the way to the north and suspected he had been killed because he obeyed his orders. It is not clear that this was the case. Osorio to the Council of the Indies, December 4, 1605. AGI, SD. 52, R. 5, n. 55.

slaves and more than thirty men had been hanged, some of them known smugglers.[61] In the following months, new reports would arrive of many others residing in the depopulated areas, such as a group formed by a man from Galicia, a French man, twenty-seven African men, and nineteen African women, although the soldiers only managed to capture a few of them.[62] The sources are not very specific about the number of enslaved Africans who took advantage of the chaos of the depopulations to escape. At the same time, many smugglers often wanted to exchange their cattle hides for enslaved Africans, so it is likely that many of them ran away from their new masters, too. The number of African men and women mentioned in the sources likely represents only a small sample of the number of enslaved African people who achieved or maintained their freedom in Hispaniola in the aftermath of the depopulations.

Despite the fact that Osorio had not trusted *oidor* Manso de Contreras to carry out the depopulations as expressed in the royal orders – in part due to Manso's overt opposition to the plan – and perhaps also to stop him from interfering, the governor commissioned the *oidor* to go to Cuba to bring back the residents of La Yaguana. Manso accepted the appointment in November 1605, but delayed his departure until February 1606. He left on a ship to Havana via Cartagena, where he attended to personal business for over a month. Once in Cuba, Manso ignored his commission and declared himself competent to judge contraband cases in Cuba with the collaboration of the governor. He traveled through the interior of the island making arrests and boasting of his abilities to catch smugglers. Eventually, however, he made the case to the governor that all of these smugglers should be pardoned because otherwise, the interior of Cuba would be completely depopulated. On this trip, Manso fell sick with gout and fatigue, so he returned to Havana.[63] Meanwhile, the former residents of La Yaguana had communicated with Governor Osorio and requested either to stay in Bayamo or to be allowed to return to Hispaniola without being punished. In October 1606, Governor Osorio forgave them as he had done with those in Guaba and commissioned a ship, a crew, and some soldiers to escort them back to Santo Domingo, meaning that when Manso finally made it to Bayamo, he could not find them.[64]

---

[61] Antonio Osorio to the Council of the Indies, March 23, 1607, AGI, SD. 52, R. 7, n. 88.

[62] Antonio Osorio to the Council of the Indies, December 1607, AGI, SD. 52, R. 7, n. 100.

[63] AGI, SD. 17, n. 12. For a detailed account of Manso de Contreras' stay in Cuba, see Irene A. Wright, "Rescates: With Special Reference to Cuba, 1599–1610." *Hispanic American Historical Review* (1920): 333–61.

[64] Antonio Osorio to the Council of the Indies. October 12, 1606. AGI, SD. 52, R. 6, n. 73.

128   *Islanders and Empire*

As early as April 1605, at the request of the crown, Osorio began gathering testimonies regarding the behavior of Manso de Contreras and his colleague the *oidor* Gonzalo Mejías de Villalobos. The numerous testimonies gathered corroborated the accusations: Manso de Contreras helped many of his relatives, abused his power, accepted bribes, and was repeatedly accused of abusing women regardless of status or condition, including married women or even nuns. Such behavior earned him a great number of enemies.[65] Mejías de Villalobos, for his part and possibly under pressure from the evidence mounting against him, joined forces with the governor against his former ally. By the time Manso finally returned from Cuba in early 1608, he found that he had lost most of his influence in the city, so he resorted to writing letters to the king complaining of the abuses of the governor and the tyrannical rule he had imposed in the island. Surprisingly – despite all the evidence against him – Manso was not punished for his actions. Instead, he was promoted to the *Audiencia* of Panamá, where he arrived in 1609 and served for ten years. He was then promoted as *alcalde del crimen* of the *Audiencia* of Mexico, but he had little time to enjoy his promotion, as he died soon after his arrival.[66]

AFTERMATH: RETELLING THE HISTORY OF THE DEPOPULATIONS

In July 1608, with the arrival of the new president/governor Diego Gómez de Sandoval, it was Osorio's turn to find himself questioned over his actions in his *juicio de residencia*.[67] Many groups on the island had

---

[65] For these testimonies, see AGI, SD. 17, n. 12. Juana Gil-Bermejo postulated that years later, the stories of Manso de Contreras's chain of sexual improprieties might have inspired playwright Tirso de Molina, who resided in Santo Domingo from 1616 to 1618, when he gave literary life to the first incarnation of Don Juan Tenorio in his play *El burlador de Sevilla y convidado de piedra*. See Juana Gil-Bermejo García, "El Burlador de Sevilla (Posible origen histórico en Las Antillas)." *Archivo Hispalense*, 60 (1977): 173–84. For a study of the abuses of his partner in crime, *oidor* Gonzalo Mejías de Villalobos, see Marc Eagle, "Portraits of Bad Officials: Malfeasance in Visita Sentences from Seventeenth-Century Santo Domingo," in Christoph Rossenmüller, ed., *Corruption in the Iberian Empires: Greed, Custom, and Colonial Networks* (Albuquerque: University of New Mexico Press, 2017), 90–92.

[66] For an example of letters that Manso de Contreras wrote complaining about the governor's abuses, see March 21 and May 15, 1608. AGI, SD. 83, R. 2. For news of his death, see AGI, Mexico 73, R.11, n. 136.

[67] Governors of Santo Domingo were also Presidents of the *Audiencia*. Their role was mostly ceremonial in the proceedings of the High Court except in case of a tie when voting for a case.

Repressing Smugglers 129

grievances against Osorio, especially those among "the Assembled" in Guaba. The leaders of the accusations against Osorio in his *residencia* were the former resident of Bayahá Bartolomé Cepero, a known smuggler who received amnesty in an earlier smuggling investigation, and Gaspar de Juara, a resident of Jamaica who was also Manso de Contreras' servant. As everyone possibly knew, Manso was the real author of the accusations, and these were accompanied by a long list of witnesses that included members of the *Cabildo* of Santo Domingo as well as former residents of the depopulated villages in the north of the island. Many people on the island felt wronged by Osorio's dogged implementation of the royal orders. It is, however, difficult to determine to what extent some of the most personal accusations, those that could cause the most damage to the former governor's reputation, were real or fabrications. For instance, one recurring charge against Governor Osorio was that he sexually abused free and enslaved women of color. There are several testimonies in which different women denounced a pattern of abuses that are all remarkably similar. If these accusations were actually written by Manso de Contreras, it makes sense that he chose to charge the governor with the crime with which he himself was most commonly accused. Although it is impossible to ascertain the backstory for these accusations from the available sources, the testimonies do appear to come from the women themselves rather than from Osorio's political enemies. In any case, the fact that both Manso de Contreras and Osorio were accused of sexually predatory behavior and the charges were completely ignored do signal a pattern in which elite Spanish men ordinarily raped and abused both free and enslaved women, and sometimes white women, with complete impunity.[68]

The arrival of the new governor marked a fresh start in the local attempt to take control of the narrative of the depopulations. Even though the elites of Santo Domingo had lost the battle to nullify the relocation orders coming from Spain or to interrupt the depopulations, they engaged in a discursive battle to win the new governor of the island to their cause and, perhaps in doing so, to rectify some of the injustices of the process. Only a few days after the arrival of Governor Diego Gómez de Sandoval, the *Cabildo* of Santo Domingo wrote two documents in which its members tirelessly argued for an alternative narrative of the depopulations. In their version, the only smugglers had been a few "vagabond people that walk around in the new communities and their fields, without property or

---

[68] For a list of the accusations against Osorio, see AGI, Escribanía, 11C.

130 *Islanders and Empire*

desire to serve a master."[69] Members of the Santo Domingo elite also denounced in a second *memorial* a few people (probably referring to Osorio and López de Castro without mentioning them) who had maliciously informed the king that Hispaniola and the city of Santo Domingo had been found guilty of heresy. They refuted such claims and requested that the new governor inform the king that "in all the island, there has not been such an offense in many years" while exhorting the zeal with which the residents of the island had defended the crown. They also denounced, without giving names, how certain people had written lies to the crown. In these supposed fabrications, the residents of the northern towns had risen against the king and chosen a new one, whom they followed to battle, and where they were defeated by the forces of the governor without any help from the residents of Santo Domingo. They justified the "absence" of the people who congregated in Guaba, and those who left to go to Cuba, on the grounds that they had been accused of participating in contraband deals, of which they were innocent and for which were afraid of being punished. The members of the *Cabildo* of Santo Domingo insisted on the loyalty of the city and the island to the king and begged the new governor to relay such information to defuse any misunderstanding that such lies might have created.[70]

The depopulations had been driven by a narrative characterized by the purported need to subject Hispaniola residents to a closer scrutiny from civil and religious institutions, due to their lack of proper civilized Christian behavior, in order to preserve the island for the king and the true Catholic faith. By contrast, these letters of the *Cabildo* of Santo Domingo to the new governor represented the attempts of the city's elite to provide an alternate narrative of the depopulations in which the inhabitants of the island, and especially those in Santo Domingo, had always remained loyal to the crown's policies. In this version, those guilty of contraband, and therefore uncivilized Christian behavior, had been but a misguided few. These smugglers were people without lands, properties, or the desire to serve their superiors. They represented the fringe of Hispaniola society, and as such they had to be carefully watched and

[69] "*gente vagabunda que anda en los pueblos nuevos y en el campo de ellos, que no tienen hacienda alguna y no quieren servir.*" Memorial of the *Cabildo* of Santo Domingo to Governor Gómez de Sandoval, July 28, 1608, in Rodríguez Demorizi, *Relaciones*, vol. II, 269–71.

[70] "*que en toda esta isla no hay ni ha habido de muchos años a esta parte quien en semejante delito haya incurrido.*" Memorial of the *Cabildo* of Santo Domingo to governor Gómez de Sandoval, August 1, 1608, in Rodríguez Demorizi, *Relaciones*, vol. II, 271–73.

expelled from the island. Already in 1606, the city of Santiago de los Caballeros – the only northern town that was not depopulated – issued an edict ordering anyone not included on a list of *vecinos* or property owners in town to leave and never come back under penalty of death. The members of the *Cabildo* argued that since contraband had been carried out by men without professions who had acted as intermediaries between foreigners and the rest of society, such men posed a threat to the survival of the town, causing law-abiding residents to appear guilty by association. In this case, the residents of Santiago did not try to hide the fact that people from all sectors of society were involved. Rather, they were trying to protect the town from the influence of those landless intermediaries at a time when the depopulations were not yet completed and when they were fearing for the future of their town.[71]

By accusing the poor of the ills of the island, the elites of Santo Domingo embraced a similar argument to that of the *vecinos* of Santiago in that they also exculpated themselves of any wrongdoing. This was a clear reversal of their position earlier in 1605, when they had maintained that the biggest obstacle to the depopulations was for land-owners to gather the cattle from their ranches and take them to the new lands. According to this new narrative, the rest of the island's population had never engaged in such deals, but they had been nonetheless unjustly treated by Governor Osorio. The residents of Hispaniola had been, and still were, loyal Catholic servants of the king, as the glorious history of the island had repeatedly proven, and they would willingly give up their property and life in his defense. The writings by the local elites during these years represent a rejection of the civilizing narrative that the crown, through its governor on the island, had imposed on them. This rejection became even more forceful in the aftermath of the depopulations as the local elites tried to reclaim their own account of the events. In their telling, it was the *mestizos* and *mulatos* from the lowest levels of society, the smugglers and barbarians, who had abandoned the true Christian faith for profit. At the same time, the missives sent to the Council of the Indies followed a distinct pattern. They presented exaggerated versions of the events that occurred on the island during the depopulations, such as the idea that the people in the north chose their own king. The denial of such an apocryphal version of the events provided the *Cabildo* of Santo Domingo the discursive space it needed to distance itself from the actual

---

[71] Edict by the *Cabildo* of Santiago de los Caballeros. February 16, 1606. AGI, SD. 52, R. 6, n. 73.

132 *Islanders and Empire*

events and thus deny the justification of the depopulations altogether. According to this alternative account, the reasons why the residents in the north decided to congregate in the Guaba Valley or leave for Cuba was because they had been falsely accused of smuggling.

These attempts to reframe the narrative had no effect on the views of the crown, but they did manage to fulfill their purpose within the island. This revised narrative made clear to the new governor the terms on which the local elites wanted to be approached regarding the depopulated territories and provided both the elites and the governor a clean slate to begin their relationship. Other people (namely, López de Castro, former Governor Osorio, and the landless black peasants) would be to blame for the island's misfortunes. The letters carry an implicit desire to look beyond the depopulations and reset relationships with the new governor of the island. Local groups also sought the reversal of some of the depopulation measures, such as the destruction of the new towns – thus returning the lands where these were built to their previous owners – and the repopulation of some of the cattle ranches in the north and west of the island.[72]

Those who opposed the depopulation were extremely divided in their reasons why. People in the north opposed Osorio because they would otherwise lose their lands and livelihoods. They were at times manipulated by the elites in Santo Domingo and by men like Manso de Contreras to continue the struggle even after it was clear that the governor was determined to carry out his orders until the end. However, for the members of the *Cabildo* of Santo Domingo, their opposition to the depopulations was rooted in the benefits many of them obtained from the contraband trade, but their properties and lives were never really at risk. In the end, they were able to comfortably distance themselves from the northern residents they had previously supported. Through their letters, they transformed the narrative of the events that had transpired on the island in the previous years and went on to establish a productive relationship with the new governor of the island.

The concentration of the population in the area surrounding the capital altered the social and economic patterns of the island. It ended, at least temporarily, widespread contraband, and it destroyed the settlements that had benefitted directly from such trade, as well as the livelihoods of those who lived in the area. As the island was deprived of its main market for the local production of ginger, sugar, and hides and of its main supply of

---

[72] Rodríguez Demorizi, *Relaciones*, vol. II, 273.

textiles, the island export economy slowly sank. On a larger scale, it could be argued that the resettlement of the people of Hispaniola needs to be viewed as the final moment of a long process that started at least in the 1570s with the progressive commercial isolation of the island and its residents' search for alternative commercial partners beyond the limited economic opportunities offered within the Spain's commercial sphere.

The important commercial interests rising in the north and west of Hispaniola were a direct challenge to the centrality of Santo Domingo as the crown's only social, political, and economic center on the island. The depopulations marked a strong corrective to Hispaniola's natural evolution over the sixteenth century, one that forcefully prioritized royal institutions in the capital and their power of surveillance of the population over local interests that favored a much more transnational approach to Hispaniola's commercial woes. With Santo Domingo's primacy reaffirmed, local groups were forced to find ways to operate within the bounds of the island's institutions of power and thus benefit from their influence within the Caribbean and the Spanish Monarchy.

4

Tools of Colonial Power: Officeholders, Violence, and Exploitation of Enslaved Africans in Santo Domingo's *Cabildo*

The *Cabildo* of Santo Domingo was scheduled to appear together as a body in an official celebration taking place in the monastery of San Francisco one morning in 1637 (see Figure 4.1). The night before, however, a group of enslaved Africans removed the stands where the *Cabildo* was supposed to sit and hid them in an undisclosed location. The following day, the resulting scandal led the *Audiencia* of Santo Domingo to open an investigation in which two young *regidores*, Rodrigo Pimentel and his friend Francisco Fernández de Torrequemada, were accused of ordering their slaves to hide the stands. It seemed that Rodrigo de la Bastida Peñalosa, who was the head of an important family in the city, had invited the *Cabildo* of Santo Domingo to attend in the name of the Franciscan order, but some members of the *Cabildo* thought that he was overstepping his authority. Both Pimentel and Fernández de Torrequemada argued that the invitation had been extended exclusively to the *alcalde ordinario* Luis Garabito Aguilar, and not to the *Cabildo* as a whole, and even if it were, the *Cabildo* should have voted about whether or not to attend. It seems that the complaints by Pimentel and Fernández de Torrequemada went nowhere, so they decided to take matters in their own hands and used their enslaved people to sabotage the event. They knew that without the stands to seat the members of the *Cabildo* prominently in a privileged spot among the attendees, many of its members (including themselves) would refuse to participate. Their earlier protests made them obvious suspects for the mischief. They must have also known that their attempt to sabotage the assistance of the *Cabildo* would be interpreted as a personal insult by both Bastida Peñalosa and Garabito Aguilar, but either they did not care about the consequences, or this was precisely what they intended.

134

FIGURE 4.1 Ruins of the monastery of San Francisco in Santo Domingo. Photo by the author.

During the investigation, both Pimentel and Fernández de Torrequemada denied any implication in the disappearance of the stands and denounced the *alcalde ordinario*, Garabito Aguilar, as "suspicious and hateful."[1] It is impossible to know if this was the first instance in which these families opposed each other, but the enmity between the Garabito and Bastida families against Pimentel would continue throughout their lives.

Although this dispute may appear to be a petty prank between the faction of Rodrigo Pimentel and that of the Bastida within the *Cabildo* of Santo Domingo, it is connected to more meaningful disputes about social, political, and economic resources. As Frances Ramos has shown in her important work about the local elites in Puebla, disputes among the members of the local *Cabildo* are much more than pointless Baroque quarrels over preeminence. They reveal the constant struggle for recognition which these local networks had to win in order to ensure their access to very real, tangible, and, in the case of Santo Domingo, scarce resources.[2] Rivalries

---

[1] "odioso y sospechoso." AGI, Escribanía de Cámara de Justicia, 23B, 285r.
[2] Frances L. Ramos, *Identity, Ritual, and Power in Colonial Puebla* (Tucson: University of Arizona Press, 2012), 133–39.

136 *Islanders and Empire*

between the powerful families in Santo Domingo, organized in strong local networks of patronage, had existed since the early days of the colony. These rivalries became an important avenue to receive preferential treatment in the allocation of indigenous labor, access to credit, and other favors from royal officials at a time in which the colonial project in Hispaniola was at a crossroads. In the aftermath of the depopulation, with the destruction of the northern villages, the smuggling networks that had become an important economic lifeline for the island population were destroyed, and new forms of sociopolitical and economic cooperation, as well as rivalries, appeared around the city of Santo Domingo.

In this chapter, I will explore two complementary dimensions of the acquisition and display of power by local elites in Santo Domingo. The first one is political and institutional. In the early seventeenth century, the sale of offices became a standard practice in the Spanish Monarchy that allowed local elites across the empire to buy seats of *regidores* in local *Cabildos* in perpetuity, thus gaining control of their own local governments. A seat on the *Cabildo* of Santo Domingo became a prized possession for these elites as a way to reaffirm their position in the island social hierarchy. It also enabled its members access to important economic opportunities that triggered rivalries among its members like the ones just discussed. The second display of power is also political, but it is more narrowly focused on racial politics – on the role of these elite men as slaveholders and the way they used their enslaved laborers in their personal and political rivalries. Pimentel and Fernández de Torrequemada's behavior and mobilization of their enslaved people proves Sherwin Bryant's profound insight that slavery as an institution went beyond supplying the colonial needs for labor: it was "a fundamental aspect of colonial practice, sovereignty, and governance."[3] The elites of Santo Domingo proudly manifested their power and tried to impose it upon their peers through their use of their enslaved people, whose obedience (particularly when deployed in opposition to others) gave true meaning to the institutional and class power these elite men had acquired. Political institutions and slavery became technologies of colonial power that supported each other and granted those who occupied these spaces as *Cabildo* members and slaveholders (often at the same time) the tools to perpetuate their elite status.

---

[3] Sherwin K. Bryant, *Rivers of Gold, Lives of Bondage: Governing Through Slavery in Colonial Quito* (Chapel Hill: The University of North Carolina Press, 2014), 3.

Tools of Colonial Power   137

In the following pages, I do not intend to explain the rise of an elite through membership in local institutions such as the *Cabildo*. Rather, I trace the transformation of the relationship between a group of Santo Domingo residents, who were already the most privileged sector of society by birth and wealth, with the *Cabildo* of the city, the most important institution of local power. These men used their membership in the city council to acquire new economic opportunities through their management of the city resources. With this in mind, I will open the chapter in the aftermath of the depopulations, tracking local residents who abandoned their newly erected villages or those in the interior to move to Santo Domingo. Next, I will explore the phenomenon of the sale of offices, its implementation by the Spanish Monarchy, and its effects in Santo Domingo. Local elites made ample use of their control over enslaved people to steer political disagreements with their peers to their advantage. I end the chapter addressing the ways in which Santo Domingo's local elites involved enslaved Africans involved in their own personal and political quarrels. Local magnate Rodrigo Pimentel, whose life and exploits will be the subject of Chapter 5, often resorted to this practice, even when it led to assassination attempts of political rivals, but he was not the only one. Attacks by enslaved people became a way for slaveholders to protect themselves from the repercussions of these actions while achieving a double humiliation of their victim: the attack itself and the attack against a high member of society at the hands of its lowest member, an enslaved African. These attacks presented numerous challenges and life-changing moments for enslaved Africans forced to act on behalf of their slavers.

RELOCATING TO THE NEW TOWNS AND SANTO DOMINGO

In the years following the depopulations, foreign trade ships continued to arrive at the northern coasts of the island, but they did not receive the welcome of previous years. Although some of these merchants might have managed to trade with locals, in most cases, their trade prospects often ended in skirmishes with groups of soldiers who patrolled the island's depopulated shores. By the end of 1610, Governor Gómez de Sandoval informed the Council of the Indies that Diego Martínez, one of the captains in the Guaba rebellion, had been captured. He had been sailing the northern coasts of Hispaniola in foreign ships while enticing residents of the island to trade with them. Martínez was hung for his crimes. In 1611, a group of soldiers faced fifty Englishmen who had disembarked

138   *Islanders and Empire*

near the site of the old town of La Yaguana, thirty-five of whom were either killed in combat or hung. Swift justice was applied equally to foreigners and local residents who were caught participating in the illegal trade. The harsh punishment and its quick execution without the possibility of appeal became a powerful deterrent to engaging in contraband. Since living in the countryside no longer brought the benefits of the contraband trade, many residents turned to the city of Santo Domingo as a place to seek new economic opportunities.[4]

As the complaints and denunciations of the island residents made against the depopulations made abundantly clear, the concentration of the former residents of the depopulated towns into the newly created settlements of Monte Plata and Bayaguana was an extremely unpopular measure. Despite the assurances by Baltasar López de Castro and former governor Antonio Osorio that the locations for the new towns were excellent for habitation, the new settlers complained bitterly of the unhealthiness of the land. As early as November 1608, a group of settlers had written to Gómez de Sandoval, the new governor and president of the *Audiencia*, that "not only he [Osorio] took away our lands, lives, and honor, but he forced us to rebuild our towns in the most infertile, unhealthiest place with the worst constellation in the entire island."[5] Osorio's successor, Governor Gómez de Sandoval, continued receiving reports of residents of the new populations contracting diseases and even dying from their afflictions. Many of these residents petitioned the governor to allow them to move to Santo Domingo. The reasons argued for the relocation were normally the abundance of diseases and the inappropriateness of the new villages for human habitation. Although these reasons cannot be dismissed, they were part of a larger movement in which residents from old villages like Cotuy and Santiago also petitioned the Governor for permission to relocate to Santo Domingo. These residents had likely benefitted directly or indirectly from the contraband trade, and after the depopulations, either they had been deprived of their lands, or they had lost the economic opportunities associated with living near the northern shores and, therefore, sought new economic opportunities in the capital. In the years following the depopulations, many residents

---

[4] Gómez de Sandoval to the Council of the Indies, November 1, 1610. AGI, SD. 54, R. 1, N.38. Testimony of Sergeant Flores, September 9, 1611. AGI, SD. 54, R. 2, n. 75.

[5] "No se ha contentado [Osorio] con quitarnos las haciendas y a muchos las vidas y honras, pero obligándonos que reedificásemos los pueblos en los sitios más estériles, enfermos y de peor constelación que hay en toda esta isla." A group of *vecinos* to Governor Gómez de Sandoval, November 1608. AGI, SD. 83, R. 4.

Tools of Colonial Power

continued the denunciations against Governor Osorio and the injustice done to them for what they saw as the sins of a few and requested their relocation as a matter of justice. Even more than before, Santo Domingo became the center of the social, political, and religious life of the island, and it was around these concentric circles of power that access to desirable consumer goods became possible. Even if these men and women had lands in the interior, establishing their main residence in Santo Domingo made possible their participation in the social and political life of the capital, and thus they were able to encounter new economic opportunities.

Other events also contributed to the desire to relocate to the capital. In March 1609, a fire spread through the town of Bayaguana destroying eighteen houses, the provisional church, and the pillars of the new church that was being built. The causes of the fire seemed to have been accidental, but village residents preferred to relocate instead of rebuilding. The governor said as much in his letter to the Council of the Indies, deeming it "convenient for the service to Your Majesty that the *vecinos* of that town and those from the new villages are persuaded that under no circumstance they will move from their current residence nor they will go back to the old one." With that in mind, the governor issued an edict ordering them to rebuild their houses and the church within fifty days.[6] Three years later, in June 1611, a new fire spread over Bayaguana, destroying thirty-six houses.[7] As the living conditions in the new settlements worsened, the desire of many of the settlers to live in Santo Domingo increased.

Although the governor seemed to have maintained the policy of not allowing the inhabitants of the new towns to move to Santo Domingo, he also had reasons to support newcomers into the city. In a letter to the Council of the Indies, he pointed out that, during his visit to the new towns, he observed the failures of cattle to reproduce, crops to grow, and people to thrive due to diseases. He reassured the Council that encouraging those who wanted to move to Santo Domingo could have two positive effects. First, voicing a similar opinion to that of his predecessor

---

[6] "por convenir al servicio de Vuestra Majestad que los vecinos de aquella ciudad y los demás de las nuevas poblaciones se acaben de persuadir a que por ningún caso han de mudar de sitio ni volver al antiguo." Diego Gómez de Sandoval to the Council of the Indies, April 20, 1609. AGI, SD. 53, R. 1, N.2. Gómez de Sandoval issued a similar order one month later when another accident caused a fire in the town of Azua, burning twenty houses and the church. Gómez de Sandoval to the Council of the Indies, April 20, 1609. AGI, SD. 53, R. 1, n. 4.

[7] AGI, SD. 84, R. 1. The fire took place on March 12, 1609. References to the 1611 fire can be found in AGI, SD. 54, R. 2, n. 62.

140 *Islanders and Empire*

Antonio Osorio, Governor Gómez de Sandoval believed that living in society and surrounded by political and religious institutions would improve the moral character of men and women accustomed to living in isolated parts of the island. For peninsular authorities on the island, these men and women had lived for too long removed from what crown officials perceived was the civilizing influence of government, religious mentorship, and urban society. Allowing them to relocate to Santo Domingo would, in the mind of the governor, make them once again fully functioning members of Spanish society on the island.[8]

Second, an increase in the population of the city of Santo Domingo, the governor argued, would provide an important number of able men for its defense at a time where the threat of enemies in the Caribbean waters was only expanding. The great majority of the city walls remained unfinished, and the small garrison of approximately 140 soldiers and fifty sailors was insufficient to protect the city and its inhabitants from a land attack.[9] The white residents of the city, organized as a militia, as well as the small but increasing free population of color, were still the most important line of defense against foreign invaders. Although officially the orders to keep the population of the island from moving to Santo Domingo were enforced, those with influence and capital found ways to relocate. Those residents of other villages who had property in Santo Domingo and/or dependents were easily able to argue for their relocation. Others, as we saw earlier, tried to support their claim with the fact that their parents and grandparents had not resided in their current village, so they argued that they should be able to relocate. Juan Lebrón de Quiñones provides an excellent example of how those with a certain wealth or status on the island were able to make Santo Domingo their primary residence. Lebrón was a former resident of La Yaguana and relocated to the village of Bayaguana. He requested permission from the governor to move to Santo Domingo, arguing that he was also a *vecino* in Santo Domingo.[10]

Complaints and requests to relocate to Santo Domingo seem to disappear from the existing documentary sources after 1610, despite the fires

---

[8] Letter of Governor Gómez de Sandoval to the Council of the Indies. September 30, 1610. AGI, SD. 54, R. 1, n. 23.

[9] Ibid. Most of the western perimeter of the city walls would remain unfinished until the late 1680s, and it would not be completely finished until well into the eighteenth century. The garrison numbers are included in this letter of Diego de Ibarra, *contador*, to the Council of the Indies. August 9, 1608. AGI, SD. 83, R. 4.

[10] Letter of Governor Gómez de Sandoval to the Council of the Indies. May 18, 1610. AGI, SD. 54, R. 1, N.16.

Tools of Colonial Power 141

that consumed the town of Bayaguana a year later. This striking absence of documentation may be the result of the great archival gaps we have for Hispaniola during these years. But it is also possible that the governor did not report these petitions to the Council of the Indies or that local residents found subtler ways to relocate. By the 1610s and 1620s, quite a few people from the depopulated villages of Montecristi or Puerto Plata appear in correspondence as residents in Santo Domingo. The villages of Monte Plata and Bayaguana, and to a certain extent other northern villages like Cotuy and Santiago, saw their population decrease, but all these settlements survived. Santiago remained as the northernmost Spanish settlement on the island until the early eighteenth century, when Puerto Plata was refounded.

Even though the historical record is thin when it comes to the island's rural life during the seventeenth century, it is reasonable to assume that the exodus of Spanish residents to Santo Domingo also had important repercussions in the lives of those who remained in the countryside.[11] As David Wheat has pointed out, the Spanish Caribbean colonies survived because of African labor, and most of that labor resided on the farms and ranches outside cities. Conducted after the depopulations, Governor Osorio's 1606 census reveals 9,648 enslaved Africans throughout the island.[12] Most African captives brought to the Caribbean before the 1590s had been taken from the Upper Guinea region and came to the Spanish Caribbean either directly or via the Cape Verde islands. These captives were identified with ethnonyms such as "Biafara," "Bran," and "Zape." As the Portuguese colonization of West Central Africa gained momentum in the last decades of the sixteenth century, the origin of most African captives destined for the Spanish Caribbean shifted south to the port of Luanda, founded by the Portuguese in 1574. By the early seventeenth century, most of the enslaved Africans brought to Santo Domingo were given (or took themselves) the ethnonym "Angola."[13] At the same time, the enslaved population of African descent born on the island likely

[11] For some glimpses of Hispaniola rural life during the seventeenth century, see Juana Gil-Bermejo, *La Española: anotaciones históricas, 1600–1650* (Sevilla: Escuela de Estudios Hispanoamericanos, C.S.I.C, 1983), 97–124. For a more recent study on this topic, but mostly centered on the eighteenth century, see Raymundo González, *De esclavos a campesinos: vida rural en Santo Domingo colonial* (Santo Domingo: Archivo General de la Nación, 2011).

[12] David Wheat, *Atlantic Africa and the Spanish Caribbean, 1570–1640* (Williamsburg: Omohundro Institute of Early American History and Culture; Chapel Hill: University of North Carolina Press, 2016), 186.

[13] Ibid., 23, 25–26, 70–79.

142 *Islanders and Empire*

increased. The baptismal records of the cathedral for Afrodescendants in the year 1636 (the first year available) provides a brief snapshot of the changes within the African population on the island. Out of seventeen recorded baptisms, in six of them at least one of the parents used the ethnonym of "Angola" (no other ethnonym is present), while in another six one of the parents is described as *mulato* (three of these were also free men or women).[14] These numbers indicate that by 1630s, "Angola" was the predominant ethnonym of African captives in Santo Domingo, but locally born enslaved Africans were just as numerous. Many of the latter were the result of interracial relations.

Osorio's 1606 census (see Table 4.1 and 4.2) also reveals the types of work enslaved Africans performed on rural properties in Hispaniola. Out of the 9,648 enslaved Africans listed on the census, 800 labored in the twelve remaining sugar mills on the island. Even though they are listed as mills, only a select few were the traditional water-powered mills; most of them were likely *trapiches*, smaller mills powered by oxen or horses. An additional 88 Africans were listed as domestic slaves in these plantations, 550 enslaved cowboys worked in the 189 cattle ranches throughout the island (cattle, sheep, and some pig farms), and the remaining 6,742 Africans worked in 430 farms in the countryside, planting subsistence crops such as cassava, corn, and yuca, as well as export products like ginger and some tobacco.[15] Even though Spaniards removing to Santo Domingo may have taken some enslaved Africans with them for domestic service, the majority must have stayed behind, caring for the property, crops, and cattle under the supervision of overseers. These overseers might have been enslaved African themselves, as was the case on the ranch owned by Luis Juvel in 1641, where his black overseer, Melchor Luis, is described as a *criollo*, meaning that he was born on the island.[16] The departure of many Spaniards to Santo Domingo may have provided enslaved Africans in some of these rural properties with more freedom of movement, as well as relatively more flexible work

---

[14] José Luis Sáez, *Libro de bautismos de esclavos (1636–1670)* (Santo Domingo: Archivo General de la Nación, 2008), 29–33.

[15] The census can be found at E. Rodríguez Demorizi, *Relaciones históricas de Santo Domingo*, vol. II (Santo Domingo: Montalvo, 1945), 375–421; Wheat, *Atlantic Africa*, 186–90; Roberto Cassá, *Historia social y económica de la República Dominicana*, tomo I (Santo Domingo: Alfa y Omega, 2000), 96–98. For different analysis on the census, see Gil-Bermejo, *La Española*, 81–96; Concepción Hernández Tapia, "Despoblaciones de la isla de Santo Domingo en el siglo XVII." *Anuario de Estudios Americanos XXVII* (1970): 281–320.

[16] AGI, SD. 56, R. 3, n. 17.

Tools of Colonial Power 143

TABLE 4.1. *Rural properties in Hispaniola divided by type, 1606 (Osorio's census)*

Sugar mills	Cattle, sheep, and pig ranches	Farms
12	189	430

TABLE 4.2. *Distribution of enslaved African laborers by occupation in Hispaniola, 1606 (Osorio's census)*

Domestic work	Work on sugar estates	Domestic work in sugar estates	On ranches	On farms	TOTAL
1468	800	88	550	6,742	9,648

regimes. Further research on the rural life of Hispaniola's enslaved and free population of African descent is certainly needed.

THE SALE OF MUNICIPAL OFFICES

For a select few Spanish residents able to relocate to Santo Domingo, membership in the *Cabildo* became a natural aspiration of their status, the most effective avenue to access the intangible but very real social prerogatives that set them apart from the rest of society. In Hispaniola, the salaries that the ten *regidores* of the *Cabildo* received for fulfilling their responsibilities were never an incentive to purchase the office. According to Governor Gómez de Sandoval, the villages of Hispaniola were too poor to be able to afford a salary for their councilmen. Santo Domingo was the exception, and even there the amounts were merely symbolic. Since 1541, the ten *regidores* in the *Cabildo* of Santo Domingo had received twelve *fanegas* of salt (priced at ten *reales* each) and 2,000 *maravedis* (little more than five *ducados*) every year. The *alférez mayor* received twice this amount. With such meager wages, the members of the *Cabildo* could not sustain themselves, so they were all supposed to have additional financial resources.[17]

---

[17] Gómez de Sandoval to the Council of the Indies. May 20, 1610. AGI, SD. 54, R. 1, n. 18. Constantino Bayle mentions that Santo Domingo had ten *regidores*. I have not been able to find any other document that specifies a different amount of *regidores* in Santo

144   *Islanders and Empire*

A seat in the *Cabildo* of the city, however, did open the door to important social, political, and economic opportunities. Apart from the honors related to the positions – including a preeminent place reserved in festivities, processions, ceremonies, and religious services – the *Cabildo* regulated the markets of the city, watched over weights and measures, administered and raised local taxes (with previous royal consent) for maintenance of city property, and at certain point during the seventeenth century, also collected royal taxes like the *alcabala*. Some of these funds undoubtedly and unavoidably found their way to the pockets of the members of the *Cabildo*. They also benefited from their control of local markets, or rather, from their disregard of the obligation to impose such control. In 1653, the interim governor complained about the long-established practice of the city's ruling class to turn a blind eye to the state of local markets and shops. Referring to the members of the *Cabildo*, he pointed out that they and their relatives were the main producers of food for the sustenance of the city, which they sold in their own houses or often had their enslaved laborers sell in the streets, instead of establishing appropriately regulated markets. This allowed them to unilaterally increase prices to the detriment of the poor and those dependent on such products.[18]

When in session, the *Cabildo* allowed its members to air their grievances, promulgate local legislation, and come to an agreement on the approach to take against a belligerent governor or member of the *Audiencia*. For the local elites, the *Cabildo* was a select club where friendships were established, profitable deals were struck, but also where members could become life-long enemies. The roots of those enmities could have multiple origins: perceived slights, disagreements within the deliberations of the *Cabildo*, or long-held family disputes. Belonging to a different powerful local network could also be a reason for profound disagreements and competition. Most *regidores*, however, would probably agree that it was preferable to be part of the *Cabildo* alongside their powerful enemies rather than not to be part of the sessions at all. In a city like Santo Domingo, where local institutions like the *Cabildo* coexisted with royal institutions like the *Audiencia* and the governorship,

---

Domingo. Although in the seventeenth century, the king increased the number of *regidores* in many *Cabildos* in Latin America to benefit from the sale of these offices, there is no evidence of such an increase for Santo Domingo. Constantino Bayle. *Los Cabildos Seculares de la América Española* (Madrid: Sapientia, 1953), 101.

[18] Francisco de Montemayor y Cuenca to the Council of the Indies. November 20, 1653. AGI, SD. 88, R. 1.

Tools of Colonial Power

membership to the *Cabildo* also provided entry to productive relationships with officials of these other institutions. Local residents with ambition, connections, and a certain wealth sought to associate themselves with *oidores* and governors. These royal officials had influence on the expenditure of royal funds, and, at least in the early seventeenth century, they also granted appointments to vacant posts in the district of the *Audiencia*. For the local elites, associating with them could lead to beneficial outcomes in the case of legal proceedings for them, their patrons, their relatives, and their entire patronage network.

Becoming a *regidor* thus constituted the most effective method of gaining access to the inner circle of the governor and members of the *Audiencia*. *Regidores* exercised a high degree of influence that turned residents into very desirable allies for peninsular officials, who often arrived in Santo Domingo deeply in debt, without a home to live in, and with many other personal needs to fulfill before they could even start doing their jobs. *Cabildo* members were naturally situated to become local facilitators, gaining power and influence in the affairs of the *Audiencia*. Santo Domingo thus became an unusual place in the Spanish Caribbean, marginal to the interests of the crown in all aspects except for the fact that it was still the site of the *Audiencia*, and therefore a vital node within the Spanish administrative network. Local residents were amply aware of the power and influence that resided in the *Cabildo*, and they competed among themselves for a post in this institution, since it allowed them to coexist in close proximity with the powerful magistrates of the *Audiencia* to their advantage and that of their allies.

During most of the sixteenth century, with some exceptions, access to the *Cabildos* in Spanish America had been limited to those directly appointed by the king as a reward for their services to the crown. Like many other Spanish urban centers in the Americas, before the 1590s the *Cabildo* of Santo Domingo had *regidores perpetuos*, men who had been given their offices of councilmen for life and with the possibility to transfer to their male descendants in perpetuity. The inheritance of these offices allowed a few families in cities across Spanish America to consolidate their hold on the local institutions of government. The influence that these urban oligarchies had in the life of the cities was considerable. During his *visita* or royal inspection of Santo Domingo in the early 1580s, Rodrigo Ribero suspended six *regidores perpetuos* for abuses they had alledgedly committed. In his opinion and that of the *Audiencia*, it was preferable to have the *regidores* chosen yearly, because *regidores perpetuos* created too many problems. In other words, Ribero and the

146　　　　　　　　　*Islanders and Empire*

Audiencia were aware of the influence that these local officeholders had in the life of the city (to the detriment of the *oidores*) and deemed it appropriate for the king to switch to a system where *regidores* would change every year.[19] As legal scholar Francisco Tomás y Valiente pointed out, however, the crown disliked elective positions in *Cabildo*s because they might foster the appearance of a local center of resistance that would be very hard to control, particularly in the Americas.[20] By giving the office of *regidor* as a reward for services to the king, the crown might have believed that it maintained a certain degree of royal influence in local affairs.

Regidores *perpetuos* continued to exist at least until the 1640s, but by the early 1590s, the crown ceased this form of appointment.[21] Always in search of new sources of revenue, the crown ordered all the available offices in the American *Cabildo*s to be sold to those deemed appropriate to occupy them in November 1591, including the offices of *regidor*, *alguacil mayor*, and that of *alférez mayor*.[22] The buyers would then be able to hold their office for the rest of their lives. Following previous decrees, the sale would take the form of a public auction, with the *fiscal* of the *Audiencia* leading the sale and the *oficiales reales*, who were in charge of the royal treasury, in attendance. All buyers were given three years to acquire a confirmation of the sale from the crown, which gave royal officials in Spain the chance to ensure that the candidate, the price paid for the office, and the conditions in which the sale had taken place met their expectations. If they did not comply, after three years, the sale would be nullified, and the crown could sell the office again.[23]

---

[19] Francisco Tomás y Valiente, *La venta de oficios en Indias (1492–1606)* (Madrid: Instituto de Estudios Administrativos, 1972), 49; Letter of Licentiate Castillo to the Council of the Indies, May 5, 1583. AGI, SD. 51, R. 6, n. 67.

[20] Tomás y Valiente, 92.

[21] I have not found any evidence that yearly elected *regidores* existed in Santo Domingo by the 1590s. They might have only existed in the early years of the colony, but might have soon been replaced by *regidores perpetuos*.

[22] The *alférez mayor* of a city or town, like a *regidor*, had a vote in the decisions of the *Cabildo*, but he also enjoyed the privilege of carrying the royal banner in official gatherings and celebrations, and therefore occupied a prominent position in such public events.

[23] For the full text of the royal decree, see Tomás y Valiente, *La venta de oficios en Indias*, 159–61. The sale of offices for Spanish America as a whole has been dissected from the perspective of law history in two classic studies: J. H. Parry, *The Sale of Public Offices in Spanish under the Hapsburgs* (Berkeley: University of California Press, 1953), and the above-mentioned work by Tomás y Valiente. See also Fernando Muro Romero, "El beneficio de oficios públicos con jurisdicción en Indias. Notas sobre sus orígenes." *Anuario de Estudios Americanos*, XXXV, Sevilla (1978), 21. Some regional studies on the sale of offices have also appeared, paying particular attention to the sale of treasury

Tools of Colonial Power

Until the 1591 royal decree, membership to the *Cabildo* had been a prerogative of those residents who had received their post for services to the king, which at times also meant that they had important connections in the Iberian Peninsula to promote their interests in court. After 1591, the doors of the *Cabildo* were open to those with enough respectability to be deemed eligible for the post and enough wealth to purchase it. With the introduction of the new legislation, in the following ten years at least ten individuals became *regidores* of Santo Domingo through the purchase of the office, and at least another nine did in the island's other villages. It is very possible that many of these men used their profits from the contraband trade to legitimize their position in local society through their purchase of a public office. More likely, they bought their office to practice their livelihood with a certain degree of impunity. Such might have been the case of men such as Diego Carrasco Barrionuevo and Hernando Guerra, who purchased their seat in the *Cabildo* of Santo Domingo and La Yaguana, respectively, in 1593, or Juan Cid, who became *regidor* in Bayahá through purchase in 1595.[24]

The depopulations coincided with the proclamation of a new royal decree, given in Madrid on December 14, 1606, that would introduce relevant changes in the transfer of local administrative offices in Spanish

---

offices during the seventeenth century and the negative effects that such sales had on the capacity of the crown to collect revenue. See, for instance, Kenneth J. Andrien, "The Sale of Fiscal Offices and the Decline of Royal Authority in the Viceroyalty of Peru, 1633–1700." *The Hispanic American Historical Review*, vol. 62, n. 1 (1982), 49–72; Michel Bertrand, "En torno a una problemática de la administración colonial: La Real Hacienda de Nueva España (1680–1770)." *Anuario de Estudios Americanos*, XLVI, Sevilla (1989), 195–217; Angel Sanz Tapia, "La venta de oficios de hacienda en la Audiencia de Quito (1650–1700)." *Revista de Indias*, vol. 63, n. 229 (2003): 633–48. For regional studies focused on the sale of municipal offices across Spanish America, see Julián Ruíz Ribera and Angel Sanz Tapia, eds., *La venta de cargos y el ejercicio del poder en Indias* (León: Universidad de León, 2007), 199–221; Maria Luisa Pazos Pazos, *El ayuntamiento de la ciudad de México: continuidad institucional y cambio social* (Sevilla: Diputación de Sevilla, 1999); Pilar Ponce Leiva, *Certezas ante la incertidumbre: élite y cabildo de Quito en el siglo XVII* (Quito: Abya-Yala, 1998); Peter Marzahl, *Town in the Empire: Government, City and Society in Seventeenth-Century Popayán* (Austin: Institute of Latin American Studies, University of Texas at Austin, 1978); Jorge Daniel Gelman, "Cabildo y élite local: el caso de Buenos Aires en el siglo XVII." *Revista Latinoamericana de Historia Económica y Social*, 6 (1985): 3–20; Darío G. Barriera, *Abrir las puertas a tierra: microanálisis de la construcción de un espacio político* (Rosario: Museo Provincial Histórico de Santa Fe, 2013), 292–325.

[24] For more about the smuggling activities of Diego Carrasco Barrionuevo and Juan Cid, see Chapter 2. Hernando Guerra is mentioned in Chapter 3. The information available on these sales are in: Diego Carrasco, November 9, 1593, AGI, SD. 29, n. 62; Juan Cid, May 4, 1593, AGI, SD. 29, n. 72; Hernando Guerra, March 15, 1595, AGI, SD. 29, n. 63.

148   *Islanders and Empire*

America. Previously, only the post of *escribano*, once purchased, was transferable to another person. This transfer had to occur thirty days before the death of the office-holder, and the beneficiary had to pay to the royal treasury a third of the value of the office. The new decree allowed unlimited transfers of an office and changed the payment model: for the first transfer of a publicly auctioned post of *escribano*, the beneficiary had to pay half the current value of the office, as estimated by the *Audiencia* of Santo Domingo. For any subsequent transfers, the beneficiary would pay a third of its price. The new decree also established hard time limits to the transfer of offices. The owner of the office had to name his successor and stay alive for the following twenty days, which prevented the transfer of titles on the deathbed of the owners. From the moment the successor had been named, the owner of the office would have sixty days to relinquish his office to the nearest Viceroy or *Audiencia*.[25]

The most important change that the new 1606 royal decree introduced was to extend such regulations to all the local administration in Spanish America. In other words, if previously the sale of offices of the *Cabildo* had been limited to the life of the buyer, the royal decree of December 14, 1606, allowed the unlimited transfer of offices in the *Cabildo*, within the time restrictions and transfer fees established by the decree. From then on, the benefits associated with an office were not limited to the social, political, and economic payoffs during the lifetime of its owner. The possibility of transferring the title to another person turned the office into a commodity, a family heirloom. The new decree created a new market in which all offices in the local administration could be privately bought, sold, and transferred to relatives, clients, or the highest bidder. Clearly, membership in the *Cabildo* presented to its members a great array of social, political, and economic opportunities. With the introduction of the royal decree of November 1, 1591, and particularly the one in December 1606, the sale and purchase of offices in Hispaniola became another common tool in the hands of the local elites to transfer wealth, power, and privileges to relatives, clients, and allies.

BECOMING A REGIDOR

For Santo Domingo's elites, the competition for material and economic contacts, opportunities, and resources must have been fierce, whenever

---

[25] For the full text of the royal decree, see Tomás y Valiente, *La venta de oficios en Indias*, 173–77.

Tools of Colonial Power

they could be found. Osorio's census for 1606 counted 648 *vecinos* for the city of Santo Domingo, including 38 free men and women of color (some of them slaveowners). To these numbers we must add approximately 1,468 enslaved Africans working in the city and an unspecified number of African enslaved workers laboring in the nearby farms and sugar plantations. With an estimated total of 1,151 *vecinos* and 9,658 enslaved Africans across the island, Hispaniola was sparsely populated.[26] The increasing privateering activity of northern European countries during these years, especially the Dutch West India Company, meant that few merchant ships arrived in the port of Santo Domingo, either because they were captured or because Spanish merchants refused to take the risk of embarking for the port.[27] This was calamitous for Hispaniola landowners, whose agricultural product rotted on the docks. In 1628, the *Audiencia* reported that the island had produced 30,000 *quintales* of ginger, 40,000 hides, 15,000 *quintales* of sugar, as well as an abundance of cassia fistula, tobacco, and other products. The island needed ships with a combined cargo space of 4,000 tons to carry the product to Spain. But that year, of all the ships that came with the fleet of New Spain, only one sailed into Santo Domingo, and had a cargo space of only 200 tons.[28] Complaints of produce rotting in the ports without a ship to carry them to Spain and requests for more ships were common throughout the first three decades of the seventeenth century.[29] Alternatives to this very minimal legal trade were limited. Some wealthy landowners might have been able to take small vessels to Havana, Cartagena, or other Caribbean ports, but they were a minority, and the chances of being captured by enemies were high. Contraband was limited or practically non-existent except perhaps for those well connected. In this context, acquiring,

---

[26] The very limited immigration to the island and numerous diseases that affected the island in the second half of the century might have maintained the population at its 1606 levels or less. The census can be found at E. Rodríguez Demorizi, *Relaciones históricas*, vol. II (Santo Domingo: Montalvo, 1945), 375–421.

[27] For the increased activity of the Dutch West India Company during these years, see Wim Klooster, *The Dutch Moment: War, Trade and Settlement in the Seventeenth-Century Atlantic World* (Ithaca: Cornell University Press, 2016), 43–48.

[28] The *Audiencia* to the Council of the Indies, September 20, 1648. AGI, SD. 55, R. 8, n. 55, doc. 4.

[29] See for instance, *procurador* de Santo Domingo Luis de Narváez Valdelomar to the Council of the Indies. March 6, 1619. AGI, SD. 26; The city of Santo Domingo requests preference to load local cargo over any other individual. September 2, 1623. AGI, SD. 27A.

150 *Islanders and Empire*

maintaining, and accumulating wealth became a real challenge for local residents of all social backgrounds.

At the same time, family rivalries ran deep, spanned decades, and in many ways shaped the political landscape in the city. These elite families often grouped themselves in factions that sought to influence royal officials and events to the advantage of friends and relatives and to the detriment of their neighbors and rivals. *Regidores* of the *Cabildo* were often the heads of these patronage networks, which included other *regidores*, royal officers, and residents from all walks of life. The heads of these nodes of patronage frequently faced the opposition of other formidable local networks. Social and political life in Santo Domingo and the rest of Spanish America thus mirrored the articulation of the Spanish Monarchy itself. This is what Alejandro Cañeque has aptly named the "economy of favor," a web of personal relationships in which every member of society, with the king at its hub, was an interwoven thread in these concentric circles of patronage. Individuals worked at the service of their betters (and were rewarded for it), while acting as patrons themselves and rewarding those who worked under their protection.[30] In Santo Domingo, like everywhere in the Spanish Atlantic, these competing patronage networks were in a constant tug-of-war for power and privilege that their protagonists hoped would lead to wealth and fortune for them and their families.

This competition between patronage networks were not always reflected in the prices of the post of *regidor* of the *Cabildo* of Santo Domingo, which oscillated wildly throughout the early seventeenth century due to both social and political reasons. The post was originally priced at 300 *ducados* in 1592, but Governor Antonio Osorio believed that prices were too low and unilaterally increased all the prices of municipal offices across the island.[31] In 1604, he set the price for the first office he sold at 750 *ducados* and the next one he sold at 1,500 *ducados*, a price that he thought to be appropriate for the office from then on. The buyer was a former servant of Diego Osorio, his brother and predecessor in the office of Governor and President of the *Audiencia* of Santo Domingo. This person had amassed a certain

---

[30] Alejandro Cañeque, *The King's Living Image: The Culture and Politics of Viceregal Power in Colonial Mexico* (New York: Routledge, 2004), 174.

[31] Prices of *Cabildo* offices were listed in silver *ducados* in the late sixteenth and early seventeenth century, and starting in the 1650s, they start to be listed in silver pesos. In order to streamline the narrative and make comparisons possible, I have listed all the prices in silver *ducados*.

Tools of Colonial Power

wealth on the island, so it is likely that Osorio, knowing the importance of establishing a precedent, sought this man's collaboration. Such a high and unprecedented price ignited protests among local residents, and the *Cabildo* resented the price increase. According to Osorio, they were "used to having them [the offices] for free and believed the increase is extremely prejudicial."[32]

The crown seemed to agree with Osorio's price increase. The *fiscal* of the Council of the Indies agreed with Osorio's reasoning, counseled the monarch to grant confirmation of the sale for 1,500 *ducados*, and also believed that no office should be sold under 250 *ducados* because it gave access to institutions of power to people from the lower ranks of society, who were unprepared to take on such responsibilities.[33] It is thus not surprising that during Antonio Osorio's tenure (1603–8), no other office of *regidor* was sold in Santo Domingo. Gómez de Sandoval, Osorio's successor as Governor and President of the *Audiencia* of Santo Domingo, did not maintain such a harsh price structure, but prices nonetheless stayed at or over 1,000 *ducados* throughout the 1620s. Approximately half of these sales were made at auction, which showed a healthy demand (and possibly, competition) among people of wealth to gain a seat among the city's ruling elite.

For those who received the position as a transfer from relatives, since they only paid either half or a third of the estimated value of the office, they were rarely inconvenienced. Almost half of the people who became *regidores* during the 1620s received the position from a relative or a patron. Starting in the 1630s, the value of the office started to plummet until prices stabilized during the decade of 1670s at around 200 *ducados*. Santo Domingo shared this downward tendency in the price of municipal offices with other cities in Spanish America. Despite similarities with cities such as Cartagena, there were also some important differences. In Santo Domingo, this tendency started at least ten years before Quito and twenty years before Cartagena. Quito, on the other hand, experienced an increase in the last decades of the seventeenth century, which shows that despite general trends, every city showed distinct local dynamics at play.[34] It is not a coincidence that after 1630, at the same time that prices started their

---

[32] "porque los unos y los otros estaban hechos a tenerlos y comprarlos de balde y así les parece que es fuerte cosa haberlos puesto en este punto." Antonio Osorio to the Council of the Indies, January 5, 1608. AGI, SD. 52, R. 8, n. 103.

[33] Ibid.

[34] Ruiz Ribera and Sanz Tapia *La venta de cargos*, 199–221; Ponce Leiva, *Certezas ante la incertidumbre*, 171, 175.

152   *Islanders and Empire*

dramatic decline, the great majority of the local residents who became *regidores* received their office as a transfer from a relative, a patron, or an ally. This might signal a change of strategy by elites, who likely realized that auctions unnecessarily inflated the price of the office for the sole benefit of the crown. Renouncing to the office while still alive, however, not only provided an economic benefit to those buying (having to pay only half or a third of its value), but opened the door to the exchange of money or favors between buyer and seller, or instead, allowed the passing of the office to someone within one's family of patronage network. Except in the isolated cases where auctions still took place, establishing the price of the office of *regidor* became the job of the *Audiencia*, and this was a process that local elites could also heavily influence to their benefit.

When a resident requested an office to be transferred to his name, the *fiscal* of the *Audiencia* interviewed different members of the local elites, and they would offer an opinion of the post's estimated value. The archival evidence does not reveal the criteria to choose these men, other than that they were all upstanding individuals in the community – men of a certain wealth and position in society, in most cases members of the *Cabildo* themselves, whose word and expertise could therefore be trusted. It seems evident, however, that if a person requested to transfer an office and was well connected in the city, he would try to place his friends and allies among the witnesses to influence the price. If this person also knew the *fiscal* or someone else inside the *Audiencia*, his chances to influence the price increased considerably.

The case of Francisco de Castro Rivera illustrates the extent of local influence when setting the price of a seat in the *Cabildo* of Santo Domingo. He was the owner of a sugar mill in the outskirts of Santo Domingo, and in April 1635, received a transfer of the seat of *regidor* from Captain Andrés de Ollo, another sugar mill owner, who, in 1620, bought the office by auction for 1,750 *ducados*, the highest price ever paid for the office during the seventeenth century. The *Audiencia* then interviewed a few local elites such as the *alcalde ordinario* Lope de las Marinas and *regidor* Gómez Dávila Benavides to establish the current value of the office. They all agreed that, due to the state of the land and recent transfers of other seats of *regidores*, the value of the office was 600 *ducados*. The fiscal approved this assessment and, after Francisco de Castro payed half of the value of the office, the *Audiencia* issued the title of the office.

Once the request of confirmation of the transfer arrived in Spain, however, the *fiscal* of the Council of the Indies rejected the sale. He argued that there was a huge difference between the selling price and the amount his predecessor paid only fifteen years before, while presenting a list with the value of the office of *regidor* from 1621 to 1634. Francisco de Castro argued that at least one other Santo Domingo resident had received his confirmation even though this seat was also valued at 600 *ducados* and added that, in fifteen years, everything in the land had lost value. The Council was not completely satisfied with such reasoning but agreed to issue the confirmation of the office provided Francisco de Castro paid another 100 *ducados* in Madrid. Despite his protests about the decision and his claims of being unable to pay, Francisco de Castro complied.[35] Francisco de Castro Rivera thus became the first of three generations of Castro Riveras who served in the *Cabildo* of Santo Domingo during the seventeenth century. Francisco's son, Gaspar Castro Rivera, succeeded his father in 1645. This time, the seat of *regidor* was valued at 400 *ducados*, of which he paid a third. Gaspar's son, Gonzalo Castro Rivera, occupied the office in 1678, when it was valued at 202 *ducados*, of which he also paid a third. In each of these occasions, when setting the price, the *Audiencia* of Santo Domingo convened a panel of local experts from the elites to find out the current price of the office and followed their recommendation.[36]

The case of the Castro Rivera family illustrates the capacity of local elites to influence and push down the monetary value of municipal offices in Santo Domingo. Although they invariably argued that the poverty of the land was the reason for such a decrease, it was their direct participation in a highly politicized process to establish the value of the office that ultimately drove prices down. The only feasible reason for those already part of the *Cabildo* to admit that the value of their own offices had decreased was to give friends and allies access to the institution. Santo Domingo was a small community where the pool of expert witnesses was limited. That increased the possibility for the elite to seek the assistance of neighbors and friends during the interview process. At a time when the great majority of municipal offices were transferred within families, competition was not an issue, and it was in the best interests of these men to reduce the price that they paid to become members of the *Cabildo*. In their eyes, the monetary value of the office was unimportant. What mattered was the membership to the *Cabildo* (and by extension, access to the

---

[35] Documentation regarding the transfer of office of *regidor* to Francisco de Castro Rivera. Initial date, April 26, 1635. AGI, SD. 85, R. 5.

[36] Transfer of office of *regidor* to Gaspar Castro Rivera. September 2, 1645. AGI, SD. 38, n. 21. Transfer of office of *regidor* to Gonzalo Castro Rivera. September 19, 1678. AGI, SD. 38, N.25.

154 *Islanders and Empire*

Audiencia), which allowed these men to control the political processes in the city while enjoying the honors of the post.

The alliance between at least some members of the *Audiencia* and local elite interests proved at times crucial to overcome any opposition to the progressive decrease in value of the municipal offices in Santo Domingo. This happened in 1638 when the *fiscal* of the *Audiencia* complained about the price of 500 *ducados* that witnesses insisted that a seat of *regidor* was worth, even though its previous owner had paid 1,000 *ducados*. Despite the *fiscal's* opposition, an *oidor* moved to approve this low value.[37] The intervention of the *oidor* in the case and his dismissal of the *fiscal's* argument in favor of the local residents highlights once again the importance of these connections between local elites and peninsular crown officials in the transfer of municipal power and in the decreasing prices of public offices. Lacking support within the *Audiencia*, or worse, having some enemies within its walls, could be costly to aspiring *regidores,* like José Castellanos de Losada in 1674. In his case, all witnesses declared that the price of the office was 200 *ducados*. The *fiscal* asked the treasury officials to compare this estimation with recent sales, and they confirmed it, but the *fiscal*, nonetheless, fixed the price at 364 *ducados*, disregarding both local residents' and the petitioner's request to reconsider his position.[38] It seems clear that at the very least, José Castellanos lacked the support he needed from within the *Audiencia* to back up local claims about the price of his *regidor* seat. He was the last *regidor* to pay such a relatively high price. That same year, a much better-connected Diego Nieto Laguna bought his *regidor* seat at auction for 200 *ducados*, setting a new low price for the office.[39]

Prices continued to decrease until they reached their lowest point in the 1670s and 1680s; between 160 and 250 *ducados*. When asked about the reasons for such low prices in 1677, local residents argued that it was due to "the poverty of the land and the lack of money of the neighbors of the city," as well as the fact that there were three vacant posts of *regidor* that no one wanted.[40] The earthquake of 1673 and the epidemics of dysentery and plague that spread throughout the city during the 1670s, taking the

---

[37] Transfer of office of *regidor* to Juan de Luaces Otañez. Initial date, August 23, 1638. AGI, SD. 34, n. 17.

[38] The *fiscal's* price in the original is 500 *pesos*. Transfer of office of *regidor* to Juan Castellanos de Losada. Initial date, August 20, 1674. AGI, SD. 38, n. 9.

[39] The case of Diego Nieto Laguna is in AGI, SD. 63, R. 1, n. 8.

[40] Transfer of office of *regidor* to Antonio Solano de Tovar. June 11, 1677. AGI, SD. 38, n. 21.

lives of many island residents, might have also hindered any desire for a long-term investment, such as public office, at a time when life was especially precarious. Lack of liquidity played a part in the unwillingness of some eligible candidates from the privileged sections of society to become *regidores*. The intermarriage of the few elite families of Santo Domingo might have also made the purchase of the office unnecessary for many elite groups who were already in the *Cabildo*. It seems clear, nonetheless, that the consolidation of the offices of the *Cabildo* in the hands of a few individuals, along with the steady efforts of these elites to lower the prices they paid throughout the seventeenth century, did undoubtedly play an important part in the continued decrease of the value of these offices.

SLAVERY, COERCION, AND THE PURSUIT OF POLITICAL POWER

With a proportionally growing population of African descent, a stagnant and even declining white population, and the extremely active bureaucratic apparatus surrounding the *Audiencia*, the governor, the *Cabildo* of the city, the prebendaries of the cathedral, and the archbishop, Santo Domingo was a site of intense elite competition for political advantage, economic opportunities, and social status. These rivalries went beyond the competition for institutional power and had a great influence in shaping the relationship that slaveholders had with enslaved people.

The labor of enslaved Africans and their descendants continued to be a central pillar in sustaining the economic aspiration of Spaniards and their descendants in Santo Domingo and the rest of the Spanish Caribbean, as well in the preserving those territories for the Spanish crown. But beyond the labor needs of the colony, the ownership of enslaved Africans also served an important symbolic function for Spanish society. The streets of Santo Domingo were a stage on which families and individuals showcased their wealth and competed for social and political preeminence. This is what *visitador* Rodrigo Ribero observed when he arrived on the island in 1580. In a letter to his superiors in Spain, he expressed his shock at the elaborate sumptuary expenses incurred by the island's elites and the number of slaves that surrounded them at all times. He described how "even loading themselves with debt ... [local residents] always have in their household six or eight negroes and as many negresses to keep them company, and just like the men go out with their negroes, so do women with their negresses, either on horse or by foot ... and there are women

156 *Islanders and Empire*

who have in their house thirty negresses only to keep them company and provide them service."[41] He pointed out how such a growth in sumptuary expenses had happened in the previous few years as a result of a spike in the demand for local products (hides and ginger mostly), but these trends also coincided with the decline of sugar as the main staple of the local economy, which allowed slaveowners to use some of their slaves to boost their social capital among their peers in Santo Domingo.[42] Similarly, in 1606, Governor Antonio Osorio asked the crown to limit the number of enslaved laborers that slaveholders kept in their houses, alleging that this custom led to excess because "those who do not have any more wealth than twenty-five slaves keep half of them or more for their own service despite being superfluous and expensive ... when in Spain this work can be done by one or two servants."[43] The implication of Osorio's statement were twofold: first, local slaveowners were wasting precious resources while living dissolute lives surrounded by their enslaved laborers; second, enslaved people were indolent and did not work nearly hard enough to justify their residence in their owners' main house.

Peninsular officials like Ribero and Osorio did not understand the complex nature of the relationship that slaveholders maintained with many of the enslaved with whom they had grown up, or the symbolic capital these enslaved people represented when dressed in sumptuous clothes while walking with their owners through the city, in what Tamara Walker aptly calls the "aesthetic of mastery."[44] Ribero saw Hispaniola as a slave society where slaveholders had fallen prey to their passions and had forgotten that

---

[41] "que aunque sea cargándose de deudas ... no deja de tener en su casa seis u ocho negros y otras tantas negras por lo menos para su acompañamiento, que como el hombre sale con sus negros asimismo la mujer sale con negras en cuerpo, ora vaya a pie o a caballo ... que hay mujer que tiene en su casa treinta negras para solo su acompañamiento y servicio." Rodrigo Ribero to the Council of the Indies, December 29, 1580. AGI, SD. 70, R.1, n. 10.

[42] By social capital, I am referring to what Pierre Bourdieu defined as the sum of resources that an individual possesses as a result of his membership in a group, which provides each member of the said group "the backing of the collectively-owned capital, a 'credential' which entitles them to credit, in the various senses of the world." Pierre Bourdieu, "The Forms of Capital," in John G. Richardson, ed., *Handbook of Theory and Research for the Sociology of Education* (New York: Greenwood Press, 1986), 248–49.

[43] "que los que no tienen más caudal que veinticinco esclavos ocupan la mitad de ellos y a veces más era en el servicio de ellas siendo cosa tan superflua y tan costosa ... en lo que en España se hace con una o dos criadas." Antonio Osorio to the Council of the Indies, October 12, 1606. AGI, SD. 52, R. 6, n. 74.

[44] Tamara J. Walker, *Exquisite Slaves: Race, Clothing, and Status in Colonial Lima* (Cambridge University Press, 2017), 21, 25–42. See also Herman L. Bennett, *Africans in Colonial Mexico: Absolutism, Christianity, and Afro-Creole Consciousness, 1570–1640* (Bloomington: Indiana University Press. 2003), 30–31.

Tools of Colonial Power

their wealth was rooted in the productivity of their slaves. He saw the relationship between slaveholders and the enslaved as one-dimensional, pertaining exclusively to the extraction of raw labor, thus failing to understand the complexity of the relationship between slaveholders and the enslaved Africans forced to serve in their homes.[45] These displays of wealth showed the dominion that the slaveowning class enjoyed over enslaved bodies and luxury goods. This was particularly important in a society like Hispaniola in the 1580s, where the plantation agriculture was in clear decline and large numbers of slaves were no longer needed in the fields. Many enslaved African laborers were sold in Havana, while others were brought to Santo Domingo, where they served their slaveholders and grew up alongside them.[46]

Despite the island's increasing economic troubles by the end of the sixteenth century, the lavish display of enslaved bodies continued to be a crucial marker of status, nobility, and influence over the institutions of the colony, as it was in many other cities across Spanish America throughout the colonial period. Upon visiting Mexico City in 1625, the English traveler Thomas Gage observed how "the gentlemen have their train of blackamoor slaves, some a dozen, some half a dozen, waiting on them, in brave and gallant liveries, heavy with gold and silver lace, with silk stockings on their black legs and roses on their feet, and swords by their sides. The ladies also carry their train by their coach's side of such jet-like damsels."[47] The parallels between this scene in Mexico City and the one described by Ribero in 1580 Santo Domingo reveal that the pageantry of enslaved laborers in the households of Santo Domingo was similar to practices in other parts of Spanish America decades later. We do not have any testimonies of sumptuous displays of slaves in the early seventeenth century, but that does not necessarily mean that they stopped. It is likely that those who could afford the display continued the practice as a

---

[45] Walker, 32; Bennett, 5.

[46] Alejandro de la Fuente has noted that in the late sixteenth century, one of the main imports from Santo Domingo into Havana were slaves. Many of them might have been smuggled into Hispaniola by foreign traders, but others were probably sold by local slaveholders who did not need them anymore. Alejandro de la Fuente (in collaboration with César del Pino García and Bernardo Delgado Iglesias), *Havana and the Atlantic in the Sixteenth Century* (Chapel Hill: University of North Carolina Press, 2008), 39.

[47] Quoted in Bennett, *Africans in Colonial Mexico*, 18–19. Tamara J. Walker exposes similar behaviors in colonial Lima. Walker, *Exquisite Slaves*, 25–31; see also Tamara J. Walker, "'He outfitted his family in notable decency': Slavery, Honour and Dress in Eighteenth-Century Lima, Peru." *Slavery and Abolition*, vol. 30, no. 3 (September 2009), 383–402.

158   *Islanders and Empire*

way to signal to their neighbors and rivals their own status. Additionally, those who saw them did not consider them unusual or excessive, but a completely normalized commodification of enslaved black bodies in the Spanish colonial world.

Still writing in 1580, Rodrigo Ribero also spoke of the intimate bonds between slaveowners and enslaved people. He expressed his contempt for slaves who were born or grew up on the island and accused them of being lazy, given to pleasures, and without a profession or trade. He believed that this was because "the negress sits with her mistress and has her like her sister, because they have grown up together since they were children in such friendship and sibling equality. And it is almost the same among men and therefore, there is need to remedy this."[48] Apart from the traditional disdain that many *peninsulares* had for colonial society, the perceived infectious indolence of enslaved people in general, and domestic slaves in particular, Ribero was already hinting at the transformation of the relationship between masters and at least a few of their enslaved laborers within the household. The local elites surrounded themselves with the company of domestic slaves from a very early age, many of them born on the island, and engaged enslaved children as playmates when growing up.

As Debra Blumenthal has shown in Valencia during the 1500s, an enslaved worker's value in an urban setting went beyond the economic value of her/his labor. Enslaved servants were closely associated with notions of household respectability. Owning slaves was a sign of prestige and honor, and often slaveowners displayed paternalistic behavior toward their enslaved workers as a refined form of domination.[49] Santo Domingo seems to have experienced a similar transformation. In this case, the almost complete disappearance of plantation agriculture meant that many slaves were transferred to their owners' households to elevate the social capital of the households. In 1659, Rodrigo Pimentel himself had at least nine domestic enslaved workers in his household. In 1643, Luis Juvel, also a *regidor*, had seventeen slaves in his household, most of them

---

[48] "la negra se sienta con su ama y la tiene como su hermana porque se han criado desde niños juntos en aquella amistad en igualdad de hermanos. Lo mismo casi en los hombres y ansí hay necesidad de remedio." Ribero to the Council of the Indies, December 29, 1580. AGI, SD. 70, R.1, n. 10.

[49] Debra Blumenthal, "'Defending Their Masters' Honor': Slaves as Violent Offenders in Fifteenth-Century Valencia," in Mark D. Meyerson, Daniel Thiery, and Oren Falk, eds., *"A Great Effusion of Blood"? Interpreting Medieval Violence* (Toronto: University of Toronto Press, 2004), 38; Debra Blumenthal, *Enemies and Familiars: Slavery and Mastery in Fifteenth-Century Valencia* (Ithaca: Cornell University Press, 2009), chapters 4 and 5.

Tools of Colonial Power 159

children.[50] The paternalism that slaveholders deployed toward their slaves, incorporating them into their households in very intimate ways from birth, might have been a tool to strengthen their control. It could also be understood as an attempt by slaveowners to limit the mobility of the enslaved during those early formative years, thus restricting their knowledge of other spaces and curbing (probably unsuccessfully) the desire of enslaved children to create their own spaces of resistance, or what Stephanie M. H. Camp has called "rival geography."[51]

Regarding the perspective of the enslaved and how their lives were impacted by the intimacy of these interactions, the available sources are much more difficult to interpret. These forms of intimate socialization that slaveowners encouraged might have led, in some cases, to strengthening the personal bonds between slaveholders and enslaved Africans continuing into adulthood, sanding the edges of the verticality in master–slave relationships without necessarily destroying its profound inequalities. We cannot assume, on the other hand, that enslaved peoples mostly collaborated with their masters out of a sense of loyalty born from such paternalistic behavior. It is likely that many slaves obeyed for a combination of reasons such as avoiding punishment, carving out their own autonomous spaces after a task was completed, or improving their social and material circumstances as part of a calculated move. As new captives from Africa arrived in decreasing numbers during the seventeenth century, the enslaved population of Hispaniola was mostly born locally, which played an important part in establishing a new set of conditions for the interracial interaction that took place on the island during the seventeenth century.

The case surrounding the death of Silvestre Cuello in 1641 provides a telling example of the possible synchronicity between the actions of enslaved people and slaveholders, which could have been masked as obedience of the enslaved to the slaveowner. Cuello was employed as an *estanciero* in a ranch owned by *regidor* Luis Juvel. Cuello supervised sixteen enslaved men and women who, according to the testimony of several enslaved people, deeply resented him for making them work too hard. A Portuguese named Rodrigo Landrobe was also a witness. He reported rumors among the enslaved laborers about a romantic relationship between Cuello and Isabel del Castillo, the owner's wife, who was also in the *hacienda*, but he dismissed

---

[50] AGI, Escribanía, 22A, 329r; AGI, SD. 56, R. 3, n. 17. It is unclear what the duties of these children were, where they slept, or whether they remained in the house once they grew up.

[51] Stephanie M. H. Camp, *Closer to Freedom: Enslaved Women and Everyday Resistance in the Plantation South* (Chapel Hill: University of North Carolina Press, 2004), 7, 18.

160 *Islanders and Empire*

these as gossip.[52] After Landrobe's visit of almost two weeks at the *hacienda*, Isabel del Castillo had called Landrobe to her quarters and said to him: "It seems, Rodrigo, that my virtue is lost among these negroes."[53] At that same moment, a fight broke out in the main kitchen where Silvestre Cuello slept. An enslaved man called Pedro and the black overseer Melchor Luis (also enslaved) entered the kitchen armed with spears, and with cries of "death to the villain" attacked Cuello, who fell to the ground mortally wounded.

When Isabel del Castillo and Landrobe asked Pedro and Melchor Luis to explain their actions, they responded that they had acted under orders of their master Luis Juvel. Melchor Luis asked four other slaves to dig a hole for the dying Cuello, who begged for confession. Once placed in the hole, Cuello asked Pedro to give a message to Luis Juvel, but Pedro did not allow him to finish his sentence. After responding that "Don Luis was not his *señor* anymore," Pedro stabbed Cuello multiple times, and finally, an old enslaved man approached Cuello with a machete and slit his throat. The next morning, Isabel and Landrobe departed for Santo Domingo, where they met Don Luis Juvel. When Landrobe told Juvel everything that had happened, the ranch owner responded: "If I had been there, I would not only have killed him [Cuello]. I would have dismembered him."[54]

Melchor Luis and the other enslaved people in Luis Juvel's ranch appeared to have deeply resented Silvestre Cuello's attitude and his imposition of discipline to make them work harder than they were accustomed. That much is clear in the testimony of the slave Melchor Luis.[55] As a soldier who had served in Brazil before arriving in Santo Domingo, Silvestre Cuello likely observed the brutal working conditions of enslaved Africans in the sugar plantations. Had he attempted to reproduce that discipline in Luis Juvel's ranch, he would have shocked Juvel's slaves.[56] At the same time, the social position of Silvestre Cuello, who was Portuguese

---

[52] That was also the impression of the opinion of Juan Quijada, a *mulato* and tailor who was also visiting the hacienda at the time. The entire case can be found at AGI, SD. 56, R. 3, n. 17.

[53] "Parece Rodrigo, que mi honra está perdida entre negros." Ibid.

[54] "si yo fuera allá no solo lo mataba sino que lo hacía picadillo." Ibid.

[55] Melchor Luis told the story of how one night when asked by Cuello where he was going, he replied that he was going to walk to his [*sic*] house to check on his mistress because she was without his master and he feared that maroons might come down from the mountains to hurt her. As a reply, Cuello told him that he was a "shameless dog" (in the original, "perro desvergonzado"). Ibid.

[56] Cuello is described in the opening of the case as "a soldier of the first ones that arrived from Brazil" ("soldado de los primeros que vinieron de Brasil"). Ibid.

Tools of Colonial Power 161

and thus an outsider without relevant social and political ties to the white elite of the island, might have made him an easy target. It is far from clear whether Cuello was really having an affair with the mistress of the household, Isabel de Castillo. Melchor Luis claimed that the rumor had been circulating for a while, but he never saw anything improper between them. A more likely scenario is that some slaves created the rumor, attributed it to Cuello, and made sure it reached the ears of Luis Juvel, thus providing them with a perfect means of revenge against the Portuguese overseer. If Luis Juvel actually gave the order to kill Silvestre Cuello, this would indicate an unusual degree of complicity between Juvel and his own enslaved laborers to carry out the killing of a white resident of the island. The *fiscal* of the *Audiencia* described it as "an act punishable with even more rigor for having committed a crime so enormous and contrary to nobility. And even though Silvestre Cuello lacked such nobility, because he was a poor Portuguese and his [Juvel's] servant, the atrocity of such a crime and its circumstances clamor for its punishment."[57]

But it is also possible that Luis Juvel did not give the order to murder Cuello, and Melchor Luis and the other slaves decided to rid themselves of the overseer. The highly ritualistic nature of the killing, with the oldest member of the group performing the mortal throat-cutting wound, would seem to indicate that Melchor Luis and his companions applied considerable care in his execution. But why declare in front of Juvel's wife and the other guests in the ranch that they were doing it under orders of their master? The slaves may have believed that to some degree, their actions would be sanctioned by their master and that by placing their actions under his authority, they would avoid punishment. Whichever way we interpret it, the murder of Silvestre Cuello seems to have been the result of a peculiarly cooperative relation between Luis Juvel and his enslaved field laborers. This cooperation did not result solely from slave acquiescence to the slaveholder's wishes. Instead, it seems that Juvel's enslaved people had their own reasons to attack and kill the overseer. According to the testimony of another slave of the ranch, Pedro said that he killed Cuello "for his own pleasure and because his master had ordered him to do it."[58] Luis Juvel's injured honor provided Pedro and Melchor Luis with the cover

---

[57] "castigado con más rigor por haber cometido un delito tan enorme y ajeno de la nobleza. Y que aunque esta faltase al dicho Silvestre Cuello, por ser un pobre portugués criado suyo, la atrocidad del mismo delito y circunstancias de él piden a voces su castigo." Ibid.

[58] "[Pedro] lo había hecho por su gusto y porque su amo se lo había mandado." Testimony of Gracia, slave of Luis Juvel. Ibid.

162   *Islanders and Empire*

they needed to act against Cuello for their own motives. It was a convenient convergence of the wills of a master and his enslaved laborers.

Juvel's case is not the only one in which slaveholders deployed enslaved Africans against other white colonists. Juvel's case is unique not necessarily because of the violence, but because such violence was directed against an outsider, a person without strong connections within the local society. In Santo Domingo, privileged families not only exhibited their enslaved laborers, but they also used them in their own political machinations against their peers for power and influence in the city. The example that opens this chapter, in which Rodrigo Pimentel and his friend Francisco Fernández de Torrequemada ordered their enslaved laborers to remove and hide the stands of the *Cabildo*, reflects the ways in which local Spaniards metaphorically hid behind those they held in bondage while using them to do their deeds. The fact that they were not physically involved in these acts meant that they could claim complete deniability (as Pimentel and Fernández de Torrequemada did) when accused of committing them. In the meantime, enslaved people found themselves caught in between the repercussions of disobeying their owners' wishes and the backlash if they were caught by the authorities obeying them.

This is exactly what happened to Simón in 1582. Simón was an enslaved man owned by the canon of the cathedral of Santo Domingo Luis de Morales. One day in December he was interrogated in connection with the abuses that both the *oidores* of the *Audiencia* of Santo Domingo and some local residents had committed against the governor. He denied any involvement, so he was placed on the rack and tortured with water, after which he confessed, which speaks of his attempt to protect his owner as well as himself, since he probably anticipated the terrible consequences of revealing Luis de Morales' involvement in the harassment of the governor. Simón explained how, following his owner's orders, he and an enslaved *mulato* man owned by another resident posted libelous writings about the governor in different parts of town. He also told how his slaveholder, Morales, had asked him to go with the same enslaved man to the cemetery and take some skulls and bring them to him. After they collected six or seven skulls, Morales wrote some words on them (Simón said he did not know what they were) and asked the slaves to place them in some specific street corners of the city.[59] It is unclear what this macabre display of human remains throughout the city might have meant, but it seems to have been an intimidation campaign aimed at the governor and

[59] Ribero to the Council of the Indies, December 1582. AGI, SD. 51, R. 6, n. 65.

Tools of Colonial Power

his allies. If we add the fact that one of the *oidores* of the *Audiencia* at the time, and one of the main governor's enemies, was named Alonso de las Cabezas (literally, "of the heads") the whole incident might have been intended as a gory reminder to the governor of the power of his enemies.

At times, the involvement of enslaved people in the fights between Santo Domingo local elites went well beyond the public political arena into realm of the private and familial sphere. In 1675, Lope de Morla invited his father-in-law, Diego Franco de Quero, to his house. Their relationship had been tense for quite a long time. Franco was a knight of the Order of Santiago, and the head of an important family on the island. His wife had died many years before, and, in 1675, Franco de Quero had been elected as *alcalde ordinario* (municipal judge) of Santo Domingo, where he had been an influential power player for many years. Lope de Morla had married Diego Franco's daughter, Elena Enríquez, without the father's consent and against his wishes, creating a scandal in the city and a rift between father and daughter. Initially, Franco de Quero disinherited his daughter, but later he claimed that he gave Elena her deceased mother's dowry in order to maintain an amicable relation with the couple. The old knight was received cordially in his son-in-law's house. They started talking and at some point during the conversation, Lope de Morla asked Franco de Quero to confirm the rumors he had heard that he intended to marry again. When Franco de Quero confirmed the rumors, Lope de Morla became very agitated, rose from his chair, shouted at his father-in-law, and pushed him to the floor. At that point, a group of enslaved men described as black and *mulato* came out of hiding, removed Franco de Quero's sword and his cape with the emblem of the order of Santiago, which they proceeded to cut to pieces while they insulted him. Diego Franco de Quero filed a lawsuit in the *Audiencia* against Lope de Morla, but the case never moved forward because Lope de Morla had important allies within the *Cabildo* of Santo Domingo and the *Audiencia*, so his actions were not punished.[60]

The fact that his male enslaved laborers were waiting to participate in the confrontation seems to indicate that Lope did not just lose his temper; rather, he had carefully orchestrated the whole scene. Lope invited his father-in-law and deliberately inquired about his intention to marry again. If Franco did so, a new wife and possibly more children would destroy the chances of Lope's wife to inherit a good part of her father's patrimony.

---

[60] Diego Franco de Quero to the Council of the Indies. May 4, 1675. AGI, SD. 284; Lawsuit among the heirs of Diego Franco de Quero. October 22, 1678. AGI, Escribanía, 8B.

164 *Islanders and Empire*

The removal of the sword and the cape that signaled his status as a knight or *hidalgo* seemed a premeditated move by Lope's slaves (either at the behest of their master, or perhaps something they decided to do by themselves) and one intended to dishonor Diego Franco. The fact that such acts were performed by enslaved people added insult to the humiliation. Local slaveowners did not hesitate to use their enslaved laborers in the most personal confrontations and rivalries with their elite peers – and enslaved people seem to have participated in these quarrels (whether forced, with a certain level of complicity, or simply as a calculated move) with the (quite realistic) expectation that their slaveowners would protect them from the legal consequences.

MURDER BY ENSLAVED PROXY

Throughout the seventeenth century, Rodrigo Pimentel, the protagonist of this chapter's opening vignette (and Chapter 5) arguably became one of the most infamous political actors of his time precisely for using this tactic of hiding behind his slaves both in private and public political disputes. In the mid 1630s, Pimentel was one of the two local officials in charge of collecting the *alcabala,* or sales tax, among the local residents.[61] His colleague, Juan López de Luaces Otañez, was a peninsular who had married into the local elite. López took his responsibilities as tax collector seriously and did not show any hesitation in confiscating enslaved Africans and other material properties from local residents who had not paid their share of the *alcabala,* including Pimentel's own relatives and allies. These actions angered Pimentel. In a social gathering in a common friend's house where Juan López was present, Pimentel walked in and asked aloud: "I would love to know who is the loathsome cuckold who took part in the seizing of a slave of a relative of mine, because I would have him beat to death."[62] Even though he did not name names, all the present knew he was talking about Juan López, who apparently pretended not

---

[61] Starting in 1602, the crown granted the city of Santo Domingo the privilege of paying the *alcabala* as a lump sum of 2,000 *ducados* divided among its *vecinos.* This process was called *encabezamiento.* This concession was renewed every few years, and both the *Audiencia* and the *Cabildo* of Santo Domingo continued to request further exemptions with mixed results. For the 1602 tax concession, see AGI, SD. 1, n. 312.

[62] "holgárame saber quién era el cornudo infame que fue parte para que prendiesen a una esclava de una parienta mía que lo había de hacer matar a palos."AGI, Escribanía, 23B, 36v.

Tools of Colonial Power

to hear him. This act of temporary deafness surprised all the people present more than Pimentel's thinly veiled insults and threats, and they might have taken López's avoidance of conflict as an act of cowardice, which probably did not help López in the long run vis-à-vis his peers. This interaction also reveals the social and economic importance of enslaved people to their owners in this urban setting. The loss of an enslaved laborer due to tax debt triggered the mobilization of the slaveholders' social network, as well as a public confrontation of this magnitude, which de-escalated only because of the unwillingness of one of the participants. Also worth noting is the fact that Pimentel did not threaten to kill him personally, but said that he would have him killed. This detail would become important to Pimentel's subsequent actions and reputation.

In revenge, Pimentel mobilized his friends and relatives in the *Cabildo* and gathered them to sign a document deposing Juan López from his post as collector of the *alcabala* and naming in his stead Juan Fernández de Torrequemada, Pimentel's friend and accomplice in the hiding of the *Cabildo* stands that same year.[63] This move likely gave Pimentel complete control of the funds that he collected to engage in his own businesses and allowed him to target whomever he wished for collection while forgiving the taxes of his friends and relatives, thus strengthening his own position as the head of his own patronage network in Santo Domingo. Juan López continued denouncing these practices, which eventually led to Rodrigo Pimentel's confinement in jail for three months. He was only released when his allies in the *Cabildo* of Santo Domingo pleaded with the governor that they would ensure that the *alcabala* accounts would be clarified.[64]

In 1638, Juan López received from his brother-in-law the office of *regidor* of the *Cabildo* of Santo Domingo. Pimentel must have considered this news as threatening to his position of preeminence in the *Cabildo*, or maybe he despised the man too much to share the room with him on a regular basis. He decided to act and placed his revenge-taking in the hands of an enslaved man he owned named Alonso Pimentel. He is described as a *mulato*, and the fact that they shared the last name, although common in

---

[63] Juan Fernández de Torrequemada volunteered to become collector that year. August 28, 1637. AGI, SD. 55, R. 18, n. 95; Letter of Juan López de Luaces Otañez to the Council of the Indies. November 25, 1639. AGI, SD. 86, R. 3.

[64] The *Cabildo* of Santo Domingo to Governor Juan Bitrián. November 18, 1638. AGI, SD. 55, R. 18, n. 96.

166   *Islanders and Empire*

Spanish colonial households, might even indicate that they were brothers or that Alonso was his illegitimate son.[65] Soon after the news of the cession of the office of *regidor* to Juan López was made public, Alonso Pimentel ambushed Juan López in front of his house and attacked him with a knife, possibly in an attempt to cut his throat. Juan López received some serious injuries to his face and head, but the wounds were not fatal. Numerous witnesses testified in the ensuing investigation that throughout the night, Alonso Pimentel had been looking for Juan López in different parts of the city.[66] Rodrigo Pimentel was immediately considered a suspect and held first under house arrest and later in different prisons in the city. The *Audiencia* described the crime as "perfidious, infamous, and vile, for which military and aristocratic privileges must be lost so that crimes so damaging to the Republic can be punished adequately."[67] Rodrigo Pimentel's arrest in the aftermath of the attack proves that the judges of the *Audiencia* believed that this use of a slave surrogate to attack another members of the local elites was completely plausible, and they also believed Pimentel capable of making his enslaved laborers do his bidding. In order to prove this point, the *oidor* in charge of the case included the fact that back in June 5, 1631, during the inspection carried out by a *visitador*, Rodrigo Pimentel made Alonso smear dirt and horse manure on the door of the house where the *visitador* was staying. The *visitador* imprisoned Rodrigo Pimentel for six months for this attack and Alonso was captured and imprisoned in the *visitador*'s house. He managed to escape, and except for the time that Pimentel stayed in jail, the crime remained unpunished.[68]

If the Spanish peninsular officials of the *Audiencia* pointed out the gravity of the crime, other members of the local elites tried to exculpate Pimentel, claiming that it was impossible for a man of his rank to act in such despicable manner. *Regidor* Juan de Aliaga, as a witness of the defense, affirmed that the accusations against Pimentel were "a devilish rumor, just as it happened in the death of Our Lord Jesus Christ, and if

---

[65] Unfortunately, there is not sufficient evidence to clarify whether or not Alonso and Rodrigo were connected through blood ties, but I believe it's worth contemplating this as a possibility.

[66] The complete investigation can be found in AGI, Escribanía, 23B.

[67] "Por ser el crimen alevoso, infame y vil, por el cual se pierde el privilegio de la nobleza y el militar, para que con toda quietud y conformidad se castiguen semejantes delitos tan dañosos en la República." Ibid., fol. 60v.

[68] Ibid., fol. 170r; Francisco Pimentel Enríquez to the Council of the Indies. January 20, 1632. AGI, SD. 97, R. 4, n. 80.

Tools of Colonial Power

Don Rodrigo was indeed offended, he would have sought satisfaction by taking personally the said Juan López Otañez to the countryside, because this is what men with duties such as captain Don Rodrigo do."[69] In other words, Aliaga's defense of Pimentel was that men of his rank and position did not attack or kill people through the hand of their enslaved laborers. There is, however, evidence of similar attacks later in seventeenth-century Hispaniola, like the one by Lope de Morla against his father-in-law, thus providing repeated examples that not only did these attacks occur, but that in the bitter battle for social and political prestige among local elites in Santo Domingo, enslaved peoples often became the slaveowners' weapon of choice against their rivals.[70] From the perspective of the enslaved, participating in such acts might prove a valuable means to ingratiate themselves with their masters, improve their daily living conditions, and may, perhaps, help them to gain their own freedom. Since they were in the hands of powerful elite members of Hispaniola society, they might have even believed they would not be punished, an assumption that seems often to have been correct.

An attack at the hands of an enslaved person was not only convenient to limit the involvement of the slaveowners, but it also had a special meaning. Pimentel's witness, Juan de Aliaga, conceded as much when he affirmed in jest that López "was affronted because he received his injuries from the hands of a *mulato*, but it might have been worse had he received them from the hands of a pretty lady."[71] A successful attack by an enslaved person was only marginally more damaging to one's reputation than one committed by a woman, and in both cases, it was a stain on a white man's honor and manhood. It is therefore possible that the attack was not intended to kill López, but to humiliate him.[72] Attacking someone indirectly using enslaved people meant that they were not social equals

---

[69] "voz del diablo como sucedió en la muerte de Cristo Señor Nuestro y que demás de lo dicho no se persuade a que Don Rodrigo estuviese agraviado, se dejara de desagraviar por sus manos sacando al dicho Juan López Otañez al campo, que es lo que se practica en los hombres que tienen obligación como tiene el dicho capitán Don Rodrigo." AGI, Escribanía, 23B, fol. 526v.

[70] For other cases, see Juan José Ponce-Vázquez, "Unequal Partners In Crime: Masters, Slaves and Free People of Color in Santo Domingo, c.1600–1650." *Slavery and Abolition*, vol. 37, no. 4 (2016), 704–23.

[71] "que se le hizo agravio [a López] en darle las dichas heridas no solo siendo de mano de mulato, más lo fuera muy grande de mano de una linda dama." AGI, Escribanía, 23B, fol. 526v.

[72] Blumenthal, "Defending Their Masters' Honor," 40.

168   *Islanders and Empire*

worthy of a face-to-face confrontation. Everyone in Santo Domingo would likely have understood the meaning behind the attack.

Alonso disappeared from the city immediately after the attack, and despite multiple rewards issued for anyone who could bring him to justice or provide information about his whereabouts, or threats of punishments of anyone who helped him, he could not be found. He was sentenced to death in absentia. After leaving the city, Alonso Pimentel went to live to the valley of Guaba, in the north of the island. In 1644, six years after the attack on López, he came back to Santo Domingo and surrendered himself to justice. He declared himself innocent of all wrongdoing and testified that he ran away because he was scared when he heard he was being accused of the crime. Even though some members of the *Audiencia* wanted to torture him to find out the truth, Rodrigo Pimentel's lawyers argued it was unnecessary since Juan López had already died from causes unrelated to the attack, and his family did not want to continue Alonso's prosecution. In October 1644, Alonso Pimentel was freed, thus nullifying the previous death sentence, and returned to the service of his master in Santo Domingo.[73] Once again, Alonso Pimentel's return to the city, and his master's use of his political contacts in Alonso's defense, seems to indicate that both remained in contact while Alonso was away. The timing of Alonso's return (Juan López had died sometime between 1642 and 1644) hardly seems coincidental and might also signal that Pimentel instructed his slave to return once he believed that his connections could get him an acquittal from the previous sentence. According to a witness, Pimentel asked Alonso to return once he, Pimentel, was able to establish a friendly relationship with the new governor to get Alonso acquitted.[74]

The circumstances surrounding Alonso Pimentel's return seem to indicate that the relationship between the two men was unusually intimate. For male and female enslaved peoples, intimacy with their masters was also affected by a powerful gender divide. Masters might ask male enslaved workers to participate in these attacks against their peers, while women were subject to other unwanted intimacies within and outside the household. Masters routinely coerced enslaved women to extract sexual access to their bodies. As Marisa Fuentes has pointed out, enslaved women "sometimes survived in ways not typically heroic" and sometimes

---

[73] AGI, Escribanía, 23B, fol. 853v–889r.
[74] Testimony of Daniel del Castillo Vaca. AGI, Escribanía, 22A, 49v.

Tools of Colonial Power 169

"succumbed to the violence inflicted on them."[75] Whether or not Alonso was Rodrigo's son or brother, he was described as a *mulato* slave, which illustrates the increasing frequency with which, during the seventeenth century, the white male population of Hispaniola entered into sexual activity with enslaved and free women of color. Even when these women participated strategically, they did so within the constraints of extremely unequal power relations.

This is not the only instance in which Pimentel used his enslaved laborers against other Spaniards who presented a threat to him in some way. An *oidor* described how everyone knew that Rodrigo Pimentel was in a long-term relationship with Isabel de Ledesma, a married woman upon whom he lavished presents and attention and whose husband he had banished from the island many years before. On one occasion, Juan Agustín, the owner and captain of a frigate, celebrated and flirted with Ledesma, and Pimentel ordered five of his slaves to ambush and attack Agustín and his companion in the streets of Santo Domingo. Thanks to the intercession of some nearby residents who heard the noise in the street and came out to defend Agustín and his colleague, they managed to escape with their lives, although they did receive serious injuries in the confrontation.[76]

In isolation, the attack against Juan Agustín might seem like an act of passion and Pimentel's quest for revenge against an outsider who had insulted him and committed the indiscretion of courting his partner. But placing this attack in the context of the one against Juan López, as well as previous interventions by Alonso Pimentel against the *visitador*, it becomes clear that the use of enslaved people of African descent to settle personal and political disputes of all kind was a common occurrence in Santo Domingo during the seventeenth century. Rodrigo Pimentel is the best recorded member of the local elite to adopt these tactics, but as the examples of Lope de Morla and Luis Juvel demonstrate, he was far from the only one deploying his own slaves to defend his own social, political, and economic interests.

THE RISE OF LOCAL ELITES

In the dawn of the seventeenth century, local people of Hispaniola of certain economic means took advantage of changes in the system to

---

[75] Marisa J. Fuentes, *Dispossessed Lives: Enslaved Women, Violence, and the Archive* (Philadelphia: University of Pennsylvania Press, 2016), 3.
[76] Bernardo Trigo de Figueroa, June 24, 1657. AGI, Escribanía, 22A.

acquire posts in the local administration within the Spanish monarchy to secure for themselves and their descendants positions of power in their hometown and villages. This change of policy coincided with the aftermath of the depopulations, which almost completely eliminated contraband as a viable economic activity on the island for a time. Even though the purchase of local offices happened across the island, in Santo Domingo, the purchase of a local office became an investment in access to a sphere of power and influence from which buyers hoped to benefit socially and economically. These local men sought to perpetuate their families' fortunes into the upper echelons of the island's public life despite the economic uncertainties the island suffered.

As Santo Domingo became central to the social, political, and economic aspirations of the local elites, the fights between their members represent singular attempts to assert individual claims within heavily contested local institutions. To aid their efforts, slaveholders did not hesitate to use enslaved Africans and Afrodescendants in their disputes with their peers. These disputes went from participation of enslaved people in campaigns of intimidation to involving them in political assassinations and campaigns of terror against other elite rivals. In Santo Domingo, slave ownership went well beyond the reproduction of either economic or symbolic power, although these both certainly were crucial for the survival of the colony and the aspirations of the slaveholding class. The forced involvement of enslaved laborers into their owners' political rivalries provided elites with alibis to avoid the legal and personal risks associated with their direct involvement. By removing themselves from these attacks upon their peers and entrusting them to enslaved workers, slaveholders sought to humiliate other white men. For added effect, this demeaning attack could happen in public, and, likely, every witness or person who heard of it would be aware of the symbolism behind such a violent act. At the same time, the participation of enslaved Africans in these attacks placed them in difficult personal situations, forced to choose between obeying their slaveowners and committing an illegal and heavily punishable act, or defying them and facing daily retribution. It is possible to imagine that in participating in these plots, some enslaved Africans might have thought they could extract concessions from their masters or improve their living conditions, especially when some of these enslaved men or women had blood ties with their slaveholders. The power imbalance in their relationship, however, likely made these expectations aspirational rather than contractual.

Rodrigo Pimentel has been the protagonist of some of the central events of this chapter. He provides a clear and particularly successful example of the power and influence that members of the *Cabildo* of Santo Domingo acquired, although rarely to the level that Pimentel did. Control of the city also meant control of its markets, its port, and the goods that came through its doors with or without the complicity of the royal authorities. Under the influence and protection of Pimentel, contraband went through a second renaissance centered not in far away beaches in the north, but in Santo Domingo itself. It is time for Rodrigo Pimentel to take center stage.

5

"Prime Mover of All Machinations": Rodrigo Pimentel, Smuggling, and the Artifice of Power

Someone vandalized the outer walls of the palace of the *Audiencia* of Santo Domingo in the late 1650s. The culprit possibly did it under the cover of darkness that enveloped every early modern city after dusk. As evidence, this person left a couple of verses written in red ochre paint. The graffiti read: "There is no other law or king than Don Rodrigo Pimentel."[1] It is unclear whether the inscription was meant as a compliment or as a complaint against the powerful local leader (possibly the former, since it included the title of Don), but it did capture perfectly the social and political climate in the city of Santo Domingo at the time. Perhaps not as succinctly as this graffiti, the *oidor* Pedro Luis de Salazar summarized the power that Rodrigo Pimentel had accumulated during those years in a letter to the Council of the Indies in 1651 with the following words:

He is the master of the president of the *Audiencia*, the city and ecclesiastic *Cabildo*, arbiter of *residencias*, shield of all commerce and of ministers, advocate behind all the cases in the district, smuggler of all merchandise, chief price-gouger among price-gougers, accountant behind all accounts, the city budget, special taxes, and sales taxes; prosecutor of good ministers and defender of bad ones, with many relatives. He dictates the contents of the letters the city sends, and those the president now writes to Your Worship. And in conclusion, he is the prime mover of all machinations.[2]

---

[1] "No hay más ley, ni más rey, que Don Rodrigo Pimentel." List of charges against President/governor D. Felix de Zúñiga y Avellaneda, August 28, 1658. AGI, SD. 2, n. 70.

[2] "porque él es dueño del presidente de la Audiencia Real, del Cabildo de la ciudad y del eclesiástico, árbitro de las residencias, coraza de los comercios, de los ministros, procurador general de los pleitos de todo el distrito, único atravesador de las mercadurías, estanco de los estancos, contador general de todas las cuentas, bolsa de la ciudad, de la

"Prime Mover of All Machinations" 173

This description of Rodrigo Pimentel as "the prime mover of all machinations," (in the original, "el primer móvil de todas las máquinas") is particularly illuminating. "Prime mover" is a term with origins in Aristotelian physics and was commonly used in seventeenth-century astronomy to refer to the creator and cause of all celestial movement in the universe. In the context of seventeenth-century natural philosophy, it referred to the artifice or design that underlay all natural things, with the world conceived as a complex machinery or *machina mundi*.[3] In this metaphor, Salazar presents Rodrigo Pimentel as an all-powerful and twisted demiurge, an unmovable mover in charge of every facet of life in the Hispaniola of his time.

At first glance, Salazar's statement seems to be an exaggeration. In Spanish America, it was not uncommon for one man to accumulate considerable authority over a municipal body, while at the same time, exert some influence in adjacent institutions for a few years. Yet, the case of Rodrigo Pimentel goes well beyond mere influence. During his long political life (from the 1630s to his death in the early 1680s), Pimentel, at times, held an unparalleled control of most, if not all, corporate bodies of Santo Domingo, including the city's *Cabildo*, the secular church, part of the regular church, and the *Audiencia*. In this chapter, I delve into the public life of Rodrigo Pimentel, a member of the local elites who rose over his peers in wealth and influence to become a master manipulator of local institutions, as well as the head of a renowned smuggling operation with contacts across the Caribbean. I will focus on Pimentel's unwavering influence over both the *Audiencia* and the office of president/governor, his use of these institutions' resources to conduct his own smuggling business, as well as to strengthen his social and political standing and influence in Hispaniola and the Greater Caribbean.

Rodrigo Pimentel's political life provides an illuminating example of the particularities of Santo Domingo's institutional life; but, on a larger

---

sisa y de la alcabala; perseguidor de los buenos ministros y defensor de los malos, para todo muy emparentado, y él es quien dicta las cartas de la ciudad y las que ahora el presidente escribe a vuestra merced, y en conclusion, él es el primer móvil de todas las máquinas." Pedro Luis de Salazar contra Rodrigo Pimentel, March 2, 1651. AGI, Escribanía, 23C.

[3] For a description of the *Machina Mundi* in the astrological sense, see Jürgen Mittelstrass, "Nature and Science in the Rennaissance," in R. S. Woolhouse, ed., *Metaphysics and Philosophy of Science in Seventeenth and Eighteenth Centuries. Essays in Honor of Gerd Buchdahl* (Boston: Kluver Academic Publishers, 1988), 17–43. Special thanks to Francesca Bregoli, Gregory Cushman, and Erik Peterson for their help with interpreting this particular passage.

174 *Islanders and Empire*

scale, it also reveals the profound limitations of the Spanish Monarchy's bureaucratic apparatus to govern its own Caribbean territories and, by extension, most of its colonial dominions beyond Mexico City and Lima. In the "loose archipelago of power" that was the Spanish empire under the Habsburgs, colonial centers of royal authority, embodied in institutions such as the *Audiencias*, often fell into the sphere of influence of local individuals and groups who redirected the power and reach of these institutions for their own personal benefit.[4] *Audiencias* and governors frequently became extensions of the communities that hosted ministers and royal officials, and not anchors of royal power in remote Spanish possessions, as the crown initially intended. In their daily dealings with the high courts, these local groups of power both made and unmade the Spanish empire: they limited the influence of Madrid, but by using royal institutions for their own ends, they shaped the edges of the empire according to their own interests.

Rodrigo Pimentel was the most powerful local man in Santo Domingo during the seventeenth century, even arguably the most powerful man in the history of Hispaniola during the entire colonial period. A man who by the end of his life managed to accumulate a personal fortune of more than 300,000 *pesos*, an amount that, according to D. A. Brading, would have made Pimentel one of the great magnates of wealthier regions of Spanish America such as Central Mexico.[5] In a poor colony like Hispaniola, Pimentel's increasing fortune allowed him to exert an even greater influence on local society and government. His actions benefited his relatives and allies through his ability to sway governors, ministers of the *Audiencia*, and local elites across the Caribbean in mutually beneficial partnerships that earned him copious amounts of wealth and influence over the institutions and people of the island. Pimentel's exploits did not go unnoticed by his rivals and neighbors. They wrote incessantly to the crown about what they perceived as Pimentel's abuses and monopoly of the resources of the city. At times, Pimentel's rivals managed to gain the upper hand in the local political scene, but considering the complaints that reached the Council of the Indies from the 1630s to Pimentel's

---

[4] The expression "loose archipelago of power" is especially appropriate for the Spanish Caribbean. Martin Austin Nesvig, *Promiscuous Power: An Unorthodox History of New Spain* (Austin: University of Texas Press, 2018), 3.

[5] D. A. Brading. "Government and Elite in Late Colonial Mexico." *The Hispanic American Historical Review*, vol. 53, n. 3 (August, 1973): 392.

"Prime Mover of All Machinations" 175

death in the early 1680s, all the evidence seems to indicate that Pimentel maintained control over island's affairs for much of this time.

Previous studies on the *Audiencia* of Santo Domingo have focused on its place within the institutional apparatus of the Spanish Monarchy, its functions as a court itself, the relationships among the *oidores*, the president/governor, and local institutions, always with *Audiencia* members at the center of the narrative and looking outward.[6] Here, I recenter the narrative around local people and their relationships with members of the *Audiencia*. Using Pimentel as an example, I analyze how these local residents, mostly members of local elites, exploited their privileged relationship with the institution and its members for their own social, political, and economic benefit. The abundance of documentation around Rodrigo Pimentel's life is scattered through a myriad of documents, observations, and complaints. From the 1630s until his death in 1683, Pimentel was at the center of Hispaniola's social, political, and economic decision-making processes. This makes him ideal for understanding how residents of Hispaniola tried to take advantage of their proximity to royal institutions for the advancement of their own social, political, and economic goals, which often diverged from official royal policy in the Spanish Caribbean. Controlling the *Audiencia*, or at least influencing the decisions emanating from the court and its members, became paramount for the socioeconomic aspirations of the elite networks in Santo Domingo. These networks not only encompassed people on the island but, because of the reach of the *Audiencia*'s district well beyond the island's shores, it also involved associates and partners all across the southern Spanish Caribbean, including the coast of New Granada as well as the Spanish mainland.

Exerting influence over the governor of Santo Domingo became one of the most important goals of these local groups. Even though the powers of the *Audiencia* members remained fairly stable from the late sixteenth century and throughout the seventeenth century, governors saw their prerogatives and ability to accumulate power, wealth, and influence

---

[6] Marc Eagle's work is particularly relevant: Marc Eagle, "The Audiencia of Santo Domingo in the Seventeenth Century" (Ph.D. diss., Tulane University, 2005); Marc Eagle, "Beard-Pulling and Furniture Rearranging: Conflict Within the Seventeenth-Century Audiencia of Santo Domingo." *The Americas*, vol. 68, n. 4 (2012): 467–93; and Marc Eagle, "Portraits of Bad Officials: Malfeasance in Visita Sentences from Seventeenth-Century Santo Domingo," in Christoph Rosenmüller, ed., *Corruption in the Iberian Empires: Greed, Custom, and Colonial Networks* (Albuquerque: University of New Mexico Press, 2017), 87–110.

176   *Islanders and Empire*

over local affairs increase notably in the seventeenth century. For this reason, I first address these subtle but important changes in the office of governor of Santo Domingo. I then provide a biographical sketch of Pimentel and illustrate the ways that local people managed to influence royal ministers and attract them to their patronage networks. The accumulation of political capital also translated to economic capital, and the following two sections address the ways in which Pimentel monetized his influence over the *Audiencia* and the governors, used their collaboration to run a massive contraband network, and took advantage of the royal treasury to fund his business. The final sections of this chapter cover some of the challenges that Pimentel faced in running his illicit operations and how he managed to overcome them, the peak of Pimentel's power in Santo Domingo, the circumstances around his arrest and transfer to Spain, and his vengeful return to Hispaniola.

THE GOVERNORS OF SANTO DOMINGO

Throughout the late sixteenth and early years of the seventeenth century, through an accumulation of events triggered in part by Drake's attack on Santo Domingo and by the depopulations, the office of governor of Santo Domingo, who was also the president of the *Audiencia*, went through some important transformations. First, the inability of the president/governor and the other members of the *Audiencia* to organize the defense of Santo Domingo against Drake's attack forced the crown to reassess the profile of individuals who would fill the governorship. In 1588, the appointment of Lope de Vega Portocarrero as new governor marked a clear departure in policy. Where previous governors had been "robed" ministers, that is, individuals with a university education, Vega Portocarrero was instead a man with military experience and was possibly more capable of implementing the executive and military duties of his post. All the governors who followed Vega Portocarrero throughout the seventeenth century were "cape and sword" ministers, individuals without a university education but with a military background, better suited to the challenges that Santo Domingo faced in the seventeenth century, a Spanish port city in an increasingly hostile Caribbean world.[7]

Despite the appointment of military men to the governorship of the island, the reality of political life in Hispaniola was that the *Audiencia* often found ways to sidestep and ignore governors. In theory, as an

---

[7] From the original Spanish, *ministros togados* and *ministros de capa y espada*, respectively.

"*Prime Mover of All Machinations*" 177

appellate court, the *Audiencia* of Santo Domingo had mainly judicial responsibilities. As president of the *Audiencia*, the governor would participate in the judicial proceedings in case of a tie, but would not otherwise have the power to interfere in the decisions of the court. Even though technically the governor was in charge of all the daily executive decisions in his jurisdiction, in practice, things could be very different. In Hispaniola there was a long tradition of executive power held in the hands of the members of the *Audiencia* during the early sixteenth century, so the alliance of the *oidores* with the local elites often rendered the governor almost completely powerless within the political organization of the island if he did not have support from colleagues or locals.

The difficulty of imposing his rule and the ability of the *Audiencia* to circumvent and erode the governor's influence were at the root of the numerous conflicts between the *Audiencia* and the governors in the 1580s and 1590s. In order to alter the balance of power in Hispaniola, the crown had to provide the governor with some means of enforcement. This change took place in the aftermath of the depopulations. A garrison of 100 soldiers was sent to the island to help Osorio depopulate the northern and western shores of the island. In 1614, the crown officially approved stationing the garrison permanently in Santo Domingo to protect the city and the island from pirate raids, as well as to prevent any contact between the local population and foreign merchants. The island garrison became a powerful instrument in the hands of governors to enforce both the crown's policies, and often, the governor's own personal agenda. The presence of soldiers in the city and their need for food, drink, housing, and other services must have had a very positive effect on the economy of Santo Domingo. As the needs for defense increased throughout the seventeenth century, so did the number of soldiers in the garrison. By 1635, the garrison already had 300 soldiers divided into two companies, each of them led by a captain, with the governor of Santo Domingo as their *capitán general*.[8] The presence of this group of professional soldiers at his disposal reinforced the position of the governor, whose orders were not simply sanctioned by his title, but also by the soldiers he commanded.

More soldiers meant more salaries to pay at a time in which Santo Domingo's treasury had no means to sustain itself. The depopulations eradicated most of the contraband trade, but also undermined the

---

[8] AGI, SD. 294. During the seventeenth century, the number of troops stationed in Hispaniola reached its peak in the aftermath of the failed English invasion of Santo Domingo in April 1655, with over 700 soldiers, but its numbers oscillated wildly.

178 *Islanders and Empire*

Audiencia's ability to fund itself through the fines raised from prosecuting smugglers. Even though some local residents sentenced by the *Audiencia* of Santo Domingo found ways to avoid paying their fines, many others were forced to pay. According to the *oficiales reales*, who were in charge of the treasury, these funds constituted the most important infusion of capital into the royal coffers and made possible the payment of the salaries of the *oficiales reales* themselves as well as the members of the *Audiencia* and the governor.[9]

Starting in 1608, Santo Domingo became one of the Spanish Caribbean ports that received an annual injection of capital called *situado*. This subsidy became standard operational procedure for the crown to fund the defense and local bureaucracy of different port cities in the Greater Caribbean region that did not have a self-sustaining source of revenue. Despite the unsuccessful efforts by the Spanish crown throughout the sixteenth century to pressure local residents to pay for their own defense, the escalation of French, English, and Dutch attacks throughout the sixteenth and early seventeenth centuries, as well as the need to protect Spanish coastal settlements, forced the crown's hand. In 1570, Florida's settlement in San Agustín became the first of many to receive a *situado* to host a permanent garrison for its defense. Soon afterwards, other ports cities such as San Juan of Puerto Rico, San Juan de Ulúa, Havana, Nombre de Dios, and Santo Domingo received *situados* for their defense and administrative expenses.[10] In the case of Santo Domingo, this injection of capital came every one or two years from the treasury in Veracruz. By 1639, after numerous complaints by Santo Domingo officials that the money they received from Veracruz was subject to various delays and was less than promised, the crown transferred the *situado* of Santo Domingo to the city of Cartagena or Panamá, where it stayed until it was transferred back to Veracruz in the 1670s.[11]

---

[9] Letter of the *Oficiales Reales* of Santo Domingo Diego de Ibarra and Juan de Rivamartín to the Council of the Indies. June 18, 1607. AGI, SD, 52, R. 7, n. 94.

[10] Paul E. Hoffman, *The Spanish Crown and the Defense of the Caribbean, 1535–1585: Precedent, Patrimonialism, and Royal Parsimony* (Baton Rouge: Louisiana State University Press, 1980), 146–48; Rafal Reichert, *Sobre las olas de un mar plateado: a política defensiva española y el financiamiento militar novohispano en la región del gran Caribe, 1598–1700* (Universidad Nacional Autónoma de México, 2013), 42–45.

[11] By the late 1670s, the *situado* would be moved back to Veracruz, and by the 1680s, the Spanish Caribbean fleet or *Armada de Barlovento* would be in charge of taking the *situado* from Veracruz to Havana, where it would be picked up by an envoy from Santo Domingo. The delays were often due to the mishandling of part of the funds and resistance from treasurers to handing in the money to the envoys of Santo Domingo,

"Prime Mover of All Machinations" 179

The *situado* gave governors the capacity to influence and attract the local elites to their side. Even though the *oficiales reales* were the only ones entrusted with the custody of the royal funds and the payment of salaries, the governors often used their position to intimidate and manipulate the *oficiales reales* in order to make use of the funds to line their own pockets or those of their retinue, local allies, and clients. The ability of governors of Santo Domingo to access these funds had profound effects in the way they were regarded by the members of the *Audiencia* and the local elites. From an official with little or no leverage in Santo Domingo's political arena in the late sixteenth century despite his rank, in the seventeenth century these changes made the governor of Santo Domingo one of the most important political figures of the island's political life.

CREATING TIES THAT BIND: INFLUENCING ROYAL OFFICIALS

Born around 1609, Rodrigo Pimentel came into the world only a few years after the depopulations and at the same time that these changes to the office of the governor were occurring. Although in later years his enemies would repeat the fact that he began life poor and unaccomplished, Pimentel's family held considerable influence in Santo Domingo's political landscape. His father, Francisco Pimentel Enríquez, was a *regidor perpetuo* and, in addition, was chosen to be *alcalde ordinario* more than ten times, and Rodrigo, possibly stewarded by his father, followed in his footsteps by being elected to the post of *alcalde ordinario* at the tender age of eighteen years old in 1627. Membership to the *Cabildo* was a long-established family affair, and Rodrigo's grandfathers and his uncle on his father's side, Álvaro Caballero Pimentel, were also *regidores*. When his uncle Álvaro died in 1629, he left Rodrigo an inheritance of several cattle

arguing they did not bring the appropriate paperwork, etc. Governor Juan Bitrián (1636–45) suggested Cartagena as the new port of origin for the *situado* of Santo Domingo (coming now from Peru instead), but it is unclear as to why Cartagena was chosen by the crown. The Royal Decree of the transfer of the *situado* from Veracruz to Cartagena is dated September 22, 1639. AGI, SD. 60, R. 2, n. 15, document 6. For a yearly list of the funds sent to Santo Domingo from Veracruz from 1608 to 1639, see Rafal Reichert, "El situado novohispano para la manutención de los presidios españoles en la region del golfo de Mexico y el Caribe durante el siglo XVII." *Estudios de Historia Novohispana*, 46 (2012): 76–78. For a list of the funds gathered in the Royal Treasury of Cartagena bound to Santo Domingo from 1645 to 1672, see José Manuel Serrano, *Ejército y fiscalidad en Cartagena de Indias. Auge y declive en la segunda mitad del siglo XVII* (Bogotá: Áncora Editores, 2006), 120–21. See also, Rafal Reichert, "Gastos militares que sufragó la Nueva España para mantener los presidios en la región del Circuncaribe durante el reinado de Carlos II, 1665–1700." *Jahrbuch für Geschichte Lateinamerikas*, 49 (2012): 58–81.

180   *Islanders and Empire*

ranches, and before he died he passed on the office of *regidor* of Santo Domingo, which Rodrigo officially occupied in 1630. The leverage that Pimentel's father exerted over the *Audiencia* was also evidenced by the fact that, when the value of the office of *regidor* was assessed, the *Audiencia* determined that it was only worth 600 *pesos*, which was an extraordinarily low price for the time. That same year, possibly aided by the close relationship that the Pimentel family had with Governor Gabriel de Chaves Osorio (1628–34), Rodrigo was also named captain of the local militia. These two appointments extended the importance of the Pimentel family in local affairs one more generation, while positioning Rodrigo to become an influential man in Santo Domingo's politics.

Despite their renovated importance in Santo Domingo's political landscape, governors, just like any other members of the royal bureaucracy, also sought the support of local residents of the island. Governors often became important allies of powerful local patronage networks. It is in this context that the Pimentel family sought the patronage and influence associated with establishing amicable relationships with the island governors. During the early 1630s, the first years of Rodrigo Pimentel as *regidor* of the *Cabildo* of Santo Domingo, the Pimentel family managed to maintain and even expand their influence on the island, but these years were not exempt from difficulties for them. In 1630, *visitador* Alonso de Hurtado arrived on the island, sent by the Council of the Indies to investigate the reports of wrongdoings by Governor Chaves Osorio. The Pimentel family, who had benefitted from their close relationship with the governor, was greatly affected by Hurtado's arrival.

During those years, the *regidor* and at times *alcalde mayor* of Santo Domingo Francisco Rodríguez Franco was the most powerful local man in Santo Domingo. In 1632, the *visitador* Alonso de Hurtado wrote to the Council of the Indies describing how Rodríguez Franco, as the richest man in the city, regularly covered the expenses and debts of governors and *oidores*, thus gaining their trust and becoming himself a powerful influence in the executive and judicial government of the island and the Caribbean region. Hurtado also accused Rodríguez Franco of fraud against the treasury and orchestrating an active contraband network in collaboration with the members of the *Audiencia* and local merchants.[12] The testimony of the *visitador* shows that Rodrigo Pimentel's rise to a position of considerable power and influence over individuals and institutions in Hispaniola was not an exception. Before him, other men like

[12] AGI, SD. 27A

"Prime Mover of All Machinations" 181

Francisco Rodríguez Franco had occupied a similar role in Hispaniola society, and it is not unlikely that Pimentel's first steps as an active member of the local elite were guided by the example of or complicity with Rodríguez Franco.[13] During these first years, Pimentel cultivated the friendship of his peers, as well as the former allies of his uncle and father, while forging his own social network.

The events following the failed assassination of Juan López de Luaces Otañez in 1638 described in Chapter 4, reveal the ample network of allies that Pimentel had managed to secure in the nine years he had been serving as *regidor*. In March 21, 1639, only a few months after the conclusion of the trial against Pimentel for the attempted assassination of Juan López, the political and religious elites of the city gathered for a banquet to celebrate the day of San Benito. Among those attending were the Archbishop Fray Facundo de Torres, Rodrigo Pimentel, the *oidores* of the *Audiencia* Juan Melgarejo and Juan de Retuerta, and the *fiscal* Francisco de Alarcón, as well as a number of *regidores*, prebendaries, and members of the religious orders, who took advantage of these gatherings to get closer to royal officials.[14] In the eyes of the Council of the Indies (whom the governor informed) the participation of members of the *Audiencia* in these kinds of social acts went beyond what could be interpreted as an acceptable interaction of a member of this High Court with local residents of its jurisdiction, many of whom had or would likely have cases reviewed in the court in the future. Upon receiving news about Pimentel's trial for his mishandling of the *alcabalas* and these kinds of gatherings between the *Audiencia* and the local elites, the Council wrote to the *Audiencia* of Santo Domingo in 1641 and, in unequivocal terms, reprimanded its members for frequenting Pimentel's company, and for favoring him in the cases before the court.[15] Despite the admonishments of the Council, these kinds of close interactions were common and reveal the ways in which patronage networks were formed and maintained. They were a normal part of the social and political life of Santo Domingo and

---

[13] And Rodríguez Franco was preceded by others. In December 1608, a poem appeared plastered in the walls near Santo Domingo's main plaza. It mocked Governor Gómez de Sandoval and accused him of running the city aided by "bellacos [rogues] y olivos [olive trees]." The latter was an allusion to the fact that one of his main local allies was the *regidor* Rodrigo de los Olivos. AGI, Escribanía, 3B.

[14] Juan Bitrián to the Council of the Indies. June 30, 1640. AGI, SD. 55, R. 20, N.123, doc. 1. Sworn statement by Diego Méndez, *escribano* of the *Audiencia*. April 2, 1640. AGI, SD. 55, R. 20, n. 123, doc. 4.

[15] Royal Decree, March 8, 1641. AGI, SD. 57, R. 3, n. 41, doc. 3.

182   *Islanders and Empire*

many other Spanish American cities, and they became an important avenue both for royal ministers to secure local support, as well as for local people to protect and advance their social and economic interests.

Indeed, the decade of 1640 saw Rodrigo Pimentel and his network of allies come to directly control the local institutions of power, including the secular church. In 1640, the Archbishop Fray Facundo de Torres died in Santo Domingo. Named to the post in 1632, he had been a close friend of the Pimentel family. Ironically, his death created an opportunity for Rodrigo Pimentel to increase his influence on the archdiocese's institutional apparatus. No other archbishop would arrive in Santo Domingo until 1650, so in his absence, the Ecclesiastical *Cabildo*, with the Dean of the Church at its head, oversaw the religious affairs of the island, including the appointment of new priests, the collection and division of the tithe, etc. In 1644, the Dean died too, and the Council of the Indies elected Rodrigo's brother as his successor, the Archdeacon Pedro Serrano Pimentel, thus placing the decisions of the island's ecclesiastical institution in the hands of the Pimentel family. This was also the opinion of a resident of the island who, in a letter to the Council of the Indies, wrote that Pedro Serrano "has a brother [Rodrigo], a *regidor* of great cunning in his proceedings; he comfortably negotiates in his favor ... so it is feared, Sir, that if said Archdeacon became Dean, the ecclesiastics would be governed by the secular powers, which would result in very serious complications."[16]

Pedro Serrano's election, which was likely recommended by numerous letters of support to the Council, indicates the influence of the Pimentels over the ecclesiastical institutions of the island was already considerable. In fact, the secular church was not the only religious sphere in which Rodrigo Pimentel amassed considerable influence. Both his grandfather and father were patrons of the convent of Santa Clara, and Pimentel was also its *mayordomo*, or secular person in charge of the financial accounts of the convent. Since the convent of Santa Clara was connected to the Franciscan order, it also seems clear that he also had important connections with the monastery of San Francisco.

---

[16] "[Pedro Serrano] tiene un hermano regidor de mucho artificio en su proceder con lo cual negocia a su comodidad ... con lo cual se teme mucho Señor que si el dicho arcediano ascendiese a deán, los eclesiásticos serían gobernados por lo secular de donde resultarían gravísimos inconvenientes." Bartolomé Sánchez to the Council of the Indies. May 6, 1644. AGI, SD. 87, R. 2.

"Prime Mover of All Machinations" 183

Rodrigo Pimentel's rise to power as the head of powerful patronage network and his control of the local political scene probably made him arbiter of numerous conflicts between local people, conflicts that stayed beyond the radar of the *Audiencia* of Santo Domingo, and allowed him to become a grand *pater familias* in the city's affairs and the surrounding countryside. Forty miles outside Santo Domingo, in the village of Monte Plata, a widow called María Nieto owned a cattle ranch and some farmland in 1646.[17] According to the *Cabildo* of the village, María's farmland extended over the village's communal lands, so a village resident named Alonso Parra, with the support of one of the *alcaldes* of the village, Alonso del Castillo, tried to cultivate part of the lands despite the widow's protests. In July 1646, Pimentel wrote a letter to Alonso del Castillo. In the letter, Pimentel explained that there had been a previous attempt to usurp the widow's lands, and as a result, he had already written to the other *alcalde* of the village warning him about the possible repercussions of such actions. Faced by this new attempt to take María Nieto's land, Rodrigo declared that he was "indeed very puzzled, since you, Sir, could not have ignored what I wrote to your colleague, which should suffice to excuse any unpleasantness. If you believe that because she [María Nieto] is lonely and a widow, she would not have anyone to defend her household, you are gravely mistaken." After informing the *alcalde* that attached with the letter there was a provision signed by the *Audiencia* to stop the expropriation of the widow's land, he urged the *alcalde* to obey it, because otherwise, "it will cost [you] much more than the value of the land, and I will make sure that you do not get access to it. I understand that you did not see my previous letter, because you needed a new one."[18] This letter, written by Pimentel himself, is one of the few existing documents in which Rodrigo fully embodies his role as head of a powerful local network of clients. María Nieto placed herself under Rodrigo's protection, and his response to the *alcalde* of Monte Plata conveys a mocking yet self-assured tone that leaves no room to question

---

[17] It is unclear (although possible) that María Nieto was a relative of Pedro Nieto Laguna, who became *regidor* in Santo Domingo under Pimentel's tutelage.

[18] "Y cierto que lo he extrañado mucho que no pudo ignorar vuestra merced lo que yo había escrito a su compañero, que bastara para excusarse de ocasionar disgustos, pues si les ha parecido que por ser viuda y sola no tendrá quién defienda a su casa se engañan mucho." ... "pues costará más de lo que valen las tierras y estimaré no se de lugar a ella, que bien entiendo no debió vuestra merced de ver mi carta pues ha sido menester esta." Rodrigo Pimentel to Alonso del Castillo, July 8, 1646. AGI, Escribanía, 23C, fol. 173v.

184 *Islanders and Empire*

his authority, matched with a subtle yet quite explicit threat of violence that he likely would have carried out by relying on his enslaved laborers.

Being at the center of such an extensive local patronage network offered Rodrigo a perfect platform to influence the *Audiencia*. Pimentel's efforts to ingratiate himself with some of its members bore fruit at several moments throughout his political life. At times, his ability to secure provisions signed by the *Audiencia* according to his desires shows a man in almost complete control of the daily functions of the court. In 1646, the *oidor* Juan Melgarejo Ponce de León, complained to the president of the Council of the Indies about the influence that Pimentel held over his partner, *oidor* Juan de Retuerta. Melgarejo pointed out that, out of the four votes of the members of the *Audiencia*, Pimentel held three in his hands and that

it is extremely prejudicial that there is a person with such a hand to disturb the peace of the Republic, to trouble the *Audiencia*, and to dare go against the orders of its head, encouraging disobedience. And if someone tries to oppose them, he and his allies start writing letters against the ministers of His Majesty, trying to discredit their actions on the island.[19]

Beyond showing Pimentel's grip over the *Audiencia*, Melgarejo's missive showed that local people understood the importance of crafting and controlling an adequate narrative about the reality on the ground in Santo Domingo, and they regularly engaged in letter-writing campaigns to provide the authorities in Spain with the stories that solidified their own position within the island's sociopolitical landscape.

With the sudden death of governor Nicolás de Velasco in December 1648, Juan Melgarejo, as the senior *oidor,* became interim governor. In a surprising turn, Melgarejo and Pimentel became close allies, which is proven by the fact that Melgarejo made him lieutenant captain general (*teniente de capitán general*) a few days after Melgarejo was appointed interim governor.[20] This appointment made Pimentel second in command (after Melgarejo himself as interim governor) in all military affairs on the

---

[19] "Es cosa gravemente perjudicial que haya persona que tenga semejante mano para turbar la paz de una República e inquietar una Audiencia y atreverse a ir contra las órdenes de su cabeza, siéndola de bando de inobediencias, inquiriendo hacer alguna demostración e irles a la mano la toma con sus aliados para escribir contra los ministros de Su Majestad procurando sino desacreditar sus acciones en la isla." Juan Melgarejo Ponce de León to the Count of Castrillo, President of the Council of the Indies. July 18, 1646. AGI, Escribanía, 23C, 2r.

[20] The title is dated in January 19, 1649. AGI, Escribanía, 23C, 347v. This position did not officially exist on the island until the end of the seventeenth century, when the military

island and district. Even though the Council of the Indies did not allow the appointment of lieutenant captain general at this time, by the time Madrid disavowed the appointment, Pimentel had made good use of it for many months. This commission may have been the way for Melgarejo to ingratiate himself with Pimentel to seek his friendship and support. Juan Melgarejo's behavior was not an exception but yet another example of royal ministers who early in their careers on the island opposed Pimentel and later ended up as one of his associates. Governor Juan Bitrián de Viamonte (1636–45) is another example. During his tenure, Pimentel and Bitrián maintained a tense relationship. By the end of his time on the island, however, fearing a negative result in his *juicio de residencia*, Bitrián sought Pimentel's help to escape unscathed, and he even gave Pimentel power of attorney to mediate on his behalf in court.[21]

Governor Bitrián was not the only one to seek Pimentel's assistance to deal with his legal problems. According to the scribes of the *Audiencia*, before 1652, Pimentel received at least fifty-seven powers of attorney from people residing in every part of the district of the *Audiencia* of Santo Domingo asking for his intercession.[22] One of these people was Ruy Fernández de Fuenmayor, resident of Santo Domingo, member of one of the oldest and most important families on the island, and interim governor of Venezuela from 1637 to 1644. When his tenure ended, he gave his power of attorney to Pimentel to defend him in his *residencia*. About Pimentel's ability to influence the court, Governor Nicolás de Velasco (1645–8) wrote:

In the *Audiencia* (and this is a pity) [Pimentel] has such a hold [over its members] because of his close friendship with the [*oidor* of the *Audiencia*] Licenciate Juan de Retuerta, who without any dissimulation comes in and out of his [Pimentel's] house day and night, and with [*oidor*] Don Francisco de Pantoja, also a close associate. [Pimentel] has the powers of attorney of the richest and most powerful people in the district, from whom he receives requests, shipments of gifts, and presents. I hear constantly that whoever is on Pimentel's side, they always obtain their justice.[23]

---

conflicts with the French settlers in Western Hispaniola made necessary a person exclusively dedicated to military affairs.

[21] AGI, Escribanía, 22A, fol. 998v; Request by Rodrigo Pimentel during the *Cabildo* of Santo Domingo to defend Juan Bitrián. February 21, 1646. AGI, SD. 87, R 3.

[22] AGI, Escribanía, 23C.

[23] "En la Audiencia (aquí es la lástima) tiene tanta mano por la estrecha parcialidad que con el licenciado Juan de Retuerta tiene que a mis ojos de día y de noche sale de su casa [de Pimentel], y el licenciado don Francisco de Pantoja, que sigue esta parcialidad, con que tiene los poderes de las personas más ricas y poderosas del distrito (quéjanseme de que

186   *Islanders and Empire*

Rodrigo Pimentel's influence over the *Audiencia* was well known across the Spanish Caribbean, and he exploited such influence to acquire social and economic capital (see Table 5.1). Since many of these regions were active contraband centers with English, French, and Dutch merchants, fostering partnerships with these local residents became important in expanding Pimentel's cross-Caribbean smuggling network. It is especially relevant that more than half of all powers of attorney that Pimentel received came from Venezuela, a region with important links to transimperial smuggling.[24] Many of the presents that Pimentel received as payment for his mediation with the *Audiencia* were likely smuggled goods. In many ways, active and enduring communication between people across the northern coast of South America, part of Central America, the Spanish Caribbean islands, and Hispaniola tells us that the formation of what Ernesto Bassi has described as the "transimperial Greater Caribbean" during the late eighteenth century and early nineteenth century was well under way already in the mid seventeenth century, if not earlier.[25]

The authority that Pimentel exerted over the *Audiencia* was not only based on his friendship with the high-ranking officials of the court. He was well aware of the influence of low-level officials like *escribanos* and the *relatores*, and they were also part of the network of associates that Pimentel had inside the *Audiencia*.[26] According to the *oidor* Pedro Luis

---

siendo la parte que defiende don Rodrigo Pimentel tiene justicia) de que se origina el envío de las agencias, regalos y dineros." Juan de Retuerta was *oidor* of the *Audiencia* of Santo Domingo from 1636 to 1647. Francisco Pantoja de Ayala was also *oidor*, from 1644 to 1652. Nicolás de Velasco Altamirano to the Council of the Indies (undated). AGI, Escribanía, 23C.

[24] For more of the history of Venezuela's historical links to smuggling during this period, see Jesse Cromwell, *The Smugglers' World: Illicit Trade and Atlantic Communities in Eighteenth-Century Venezuela* (Willilamsburg: Omohundro Institute of Early American History and Culture; Chapel Hill: University of North Carolina Press, 2018), 52–58.

[25] Ernesto Bassi, *An Aqueous Territory: Sailor Geographies and New Granada's Transimperial greater Caribbean World* (Durham: Duke University Press, 2016).

[26] *Relatores* were secretaries appointed by the court in charge of writing the briefs of the cases coming to court and reading them to the *oidores*. Historian Tamar Herzog has pointed out the importance of this low-level official in the functioning of the *Audiencia*s. Also, as the officers in charge of crafting the summary of the cases that the *oidores* would read before they agreed on a sentence, the narratives they created had the power to change the course of the cases reviewed by the court. Paraphrasing Angel Rama, these officers of the court had the power of manipulating the memory of events through their craft. Tamar Herzog, *La administración como un fenómeno social: la justicia penal de la ciudad de Quito (1650–1750)* (Madrid: Centro de Estudios Constitucionales, 1995), 37–38; Angel Rama, *The Lettered City* (Durham: Duke University Press, 1996), 24.

TABLE 5.1 *Provenance of* Audiencia *cases received in Santo Domingo with powers of attorney addressed to Rodrigo Pimentel before 1652, by city of origin.*

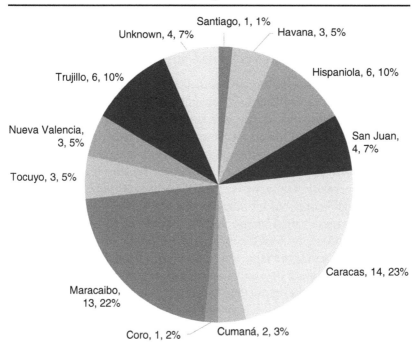

Source: AGI, Escribanía, 23 C.

de Salazar, Pimentel paid these officials for their help, but on other occasions, "they considered themselves paid by just pleasing him," which probably meant that doing a favor for a man like Pimentel was always a good investment in social and political capital. Salazar also reported how at times both sides of the same case came to Pimentel with presents trying to gain his influence for their side. His power in the district was so great that "whoever is not working for him or under his protection is therefore lost and disgraced. Every ship arriving in this port brings more letters, documents, money, and presents for him than for the entire city altogether."[27] Pimentel's influence over the *Audiencia* proceedings might have

---

[27] "y quedan muy bien pagados con solo haberle dado gusto ... el que no corre por su cuenta y se le encomienda se tiene por perdido y desgraciado y así todos los bajeles que vienen a este puerto entran para él solo más cartas, papeles, dineros, y regalos que para todo el lugar

188   *Islanders and Empire*

varied depending on the ministers in the court and the governor, but his continued impact over the outcome of cases it is undeniable, whether directly or indirectly through his network of allies working at all levels of the *Audiencia* of Santo Domingo.

PIMENTEL THE SMUGGLER

Although the accumulation of political capital was one of the main activities that occupied Rodrigo Pimentel during his first two decades of public life (1630s–40s), it was not the only one. His control of local institutions like the *Cabildo* of Santo Domingo and royal institutions like the *Audiencia* went hand in hand with more intense participation in economic activities that produced important benefits for him and his patronage network. On many occasions, it was precisely his leading role in the smuggling of goods into the city that allowed him to gain the favor of his colleagues in the *Cabildo* and the *Audiencia*. In other words, his economic success gave him the material wealth that he needed to attract political allies, and at the same time, his political influence allowed him to expand his smuggling operation. As one side of the equation grew, the other one developed even further. Governor Nicolás de Velasco claimed that "in the city [Pimentel] has gained most of the votes of his faction by selling them on credit merchandise and wines that he smuggles, with great prejudice to this Republic. As a result of this, in the *Cabildo* he accomplishes everything he undertakes, whether just or unjust."[28]

It was precisely after Velasco's death in 1648 and after Pimentel's appointment as lieutenant captain general by interim Governor Juan Melgarejo Ponce de León that the references to Pimentel's participation in contraband activities increased, possibly due to the fact that, as second in command of the military on the island, he was able to introduce merchandise through Santo Domingo without any opposition from the soldiers guarding the port. Pedro de Pujadas, the *alcaide* or keeper of the fortress of Santo Domingo, wrote to the crown how, ever since Juan Melgarejo became interim governor, "he [Melgarejo] has assembled many associates, in particular a confidant of his, a great merchant who

---

junto." Pedro Luis de Salazar to the Council of the Indies. March 2, 1651. AGI, Escribanía, 23C.

[28] "En la ciudad tiene la mayor parte de los votos de su bando granjeados con fiarles mercadurías que atraviesa y vinos en perjuicio de esta República con que el *Cabildo* sale con todo lo que intenta, justo o injusto." Nicolás de Velasco Altamirano to the Council of the Indies (undated). AGI, Escribanía, 23C.

smuggles everything that arrives in port during the night without paying any levies to Your Majesty. His name is Don Rodrigo Pimentel. [Melgarejo] has made him lieutenant ... so he can easily navigate the night-sentries and the guards at the gates and the city walls without being bothered."[29] Despite Pujadas' attempts to undermine Pimentel's freedom of movement in and out of the city, the smuggler's relationship with the new interim governor prevailed over the military concerns and personal antipathies of the old veteran.

The *fiscal* of the *Audiencia* Francisco de Alarcón also complained about the smuggling activities in Santo Domingo under Pimentel's direction. He related how many ships arrived in port under the pretense of needing to sell some merchandise to repair the vessel, a typical excuse captains of all nations used to enter Caribbean ports. Some of them brought correspondence to residents of the island from Spain, which proved that their stop in Santo Domingo was far from fortuitous. The *fiscal* narrated how on May 7, 1649, a well-armed ship of 400 tons arrived at the mouth of the port of Santo Domingo but did not enter. Two hours later, the first mate and the pilot of the ship went to see Governor Melgarejo and explained that were

FIGURE 5.1a *Puerta de Atarazanas* (Shipyard Gate). This was one of the gates facing the city's river docks that smugglers likely used. Photo by the author.
b *Puerta del Río* (River Gate). This was the other city gate facing the city's river docks, and the one closer to the governor's residence in the building of the *Audiencia*. Photo by the author.

[29] "[Melgarejo] ha entrado haciendo muchas hechuras y en particular a un confidente suyo grande mercader de lo que llega a este puerto, que lo atraviesa todo y lo saca de noche sin que se pague derechos a Su Majestad. Llámase don Rodrigo Pimentel. A este ha hecho teniente general ..., mas el designio y la intención es para que este tal teniente general tenga con más libertad y comodidad para que las postas y las guardias que están en las puertas y muralla no le hagan embarazo ni molestia." Pedro de Pujadas to the Council of the Indies. February 26, 1649. AGI, SD. 87, R. 5.

190   *Islanders and Empire*

on their way to Campeche via Cumaná and Margarita but were short of water and provisions.[30] The following night, a small boat owned by the king and manned by soldiers traveled to and from the ship unloading merchandise under Rodrigo Pimentel's close supervision. These trips continued during the next two nights while the *alcaide* of the fortress Pedro Pujadas observed, unable to do anything about it. Alarcón reported that Pimentel was himself on board of the ship and bought the merchandise that he wanted at the price that he desired, and only when he was finished were other residents allowed to trade. Pimentel acquired good-quality fabrics from England and France, as well as Italian silks, all highly desired commodities. After eight days selling goods, the ship left the port with over 30,000 *pesos*, leaving three men in the city to sell the remaining merchandise. These men embarked for Seville as soon as they finished their business in the city.[31] As the high number of witnesses of these dealings seems to indicate, contraband trade in Santo Domingo did not involve a great degree of secrecy around the deals, which were known by the population at large. Despite the public nature of the contraband trade, not everyone could freely participate. Smuggling in the port city took place under the exclusive control of certain individuals: governors, members of the *Audiencia*, and local men like Pimentel acted as gatekeepers.

The tenure of Governor Juan Bitrián (1636–45) provides evidence of a large smuggling operation orchestrated from the highest level of the royal administration and involving close collaboration of local people, although it is likely that similar schemes existed in earlier administrations. In this case, it appears that Governor Bitrián was the one in charge of the entire strategy and not the local traders. Bitrián controlled a complex system in which he used the funds of the treasury and a network of local collaborators. These deals were subject to conditions established by Bitrián himself. When a new merchant ship arrived in port, the *maestre* or shipmaster was informed that they could only trade with certain people in the city. Meanwhile, small local producers and everyone else outside Bitrián's network were forced to sell their products at low prices to those local landowners and merchants who were allowed to trade. These products were then used as payment for the fabrics, garments, and other items they bought from the merchants.

---

[30] Both Cumaná and Margarita were common smuggling locations at the time. These regions were also on and off the coast of Venezuela, respectively. This was a region where Pimentel had abundant contacts, so it is likely that this ship was taking advantage to trade illicitly in those ports and that its stop in Santo Domingo was far from accidental.

[31] Francisco de Alarcón Coronado to the Council of the Indies. May 17, 1649. AGI, SD. 57, R. 1 n. 16.

"Prime Mover of All Machinations"

In addition to making use of ginger, hides, some sugar, and other local products, the governor also used money from the treasury illicitly. In theory, governors did not have the authority to handle the treasury. In Santo Domingo, as in most Spanish cities where a royal treasury existed, the *oficiales reales* (*contador* and *tesorero*, and in bigger port cities a *factor* as well), were the only people authorized to handle the king's money, pay salaries of ministers and soldiers, account for any expenses, and protect the crown's finances interest. Although these men were appointed by the authorities in Spain, they were Santo Domingo residents and *vecinos*, and as such, they were immersed in the same local networks as their peers. They either became powerful instruments in the hands of more powerful patrons, or they were coerced to give up control of the treasury. In 1645, the *Audiencia* wrote a letter to the Council of the Indies in Madrid complaining how, during the governorship of Juan Bitrián, the *oficiales reales* acted as the governor's "cashiers" instead of protecting the royal interest.[32]

Bitrián made sure not to touch any part of the money from the treasury destined to his own salary or that of the *oidores* of the *Audiencia*, but he made ample use of the funds meant to pay the troops stationed on the island. Under the pretense that the soldiers of the garrison were naked and without appropriate clothing, he would pay their overdue salaries in fabrics at inflated prices, thus increasing his own profit margins. The remaining clothes were sold throughout Santo Domingo and the island through Bitrián's allies, local merchants, both white and black, at inflated prices. In order to cover the use of the funds of the treasury in the accounting books, Bitrián and his allies falsely claimed that salaries to soldiers were paid in currency as the regulations ordered. Part of the benefits from the trade with outside merchants was channeled to Bitrián's local allies. This coin was justified as the repayment of fictitious loans that these local elites and merchants had theoretically made to the treasury to help paying *socorros* to soldiers and royal ministers in times of shortfall.[33]

Governor Bitrián maintained strict control over this system, from which only certain members of the local elites benefitted. It is possible that, despite their differences, Pimentel was part of Bitrián's network due to his stature in local governance. There is not any doubt, however, that he

---

[32] In the original, "cajeros." The *Audiencia* of Santo Domingo to the Council of the Indies. August 12, 1645. AGI, SD. 56, R. 6, n. 40, Document 3.

[33] *Socorros* were small sums of money paid weekly to soldiers and royal ministers to cover their most basic necessities when there was not enough money to pay complete salaries. The balance was normally paid with the arrival of the new *situado*, although in the case of soldiers, delays could go on for years, and many actually died without receiving full pay.

192   *Islanders and Empire*

was aware of its existence and learned of the ways the governor used the money from the treasury to conduct his private deals. *Oidor* Juan Melgarejo was also well aware of these practices and did not hesitate to use them once he became interim governor. During his short tenure (1648–50), he sent a group of soldiers and local militia to the mountains to try to destroy a *maniel* or village of runaway enslaved Africans. When the expedition returned, Governor Melgarejo paid the members of the party in clothes that he valued at inflated prices, while asking them to sign documents in which they testified that they had actually been paid in coin. He also regularly paid the soldiers with clothes.[34]

Both Pimentel and Melgarejo took advantage of each other's position to advance their own agendas. For Melgarejo, like Bitrián before him, acquiring wealth and securing allies for his *residencia* were important goals. For Pimentel, when Melgarejo appointed him lieutenant governor in 1649, his control of the port allowed him to acquire exclusive control of the illicit commerce arriving in the city. However, since the ships arriving in Santo Domingo were few, far between, and unpredictable, Pimentel understood that in order to procure a stable supply of contraband goods, he would need to obtain them in other ports. His influence over the governor and other crown officials allowed him to do so, like Bitrián before him, using the *situado*.

SITUADOS: SMUGGLING WITH THE KING'S COIN

Starting in 1608, an annual shipment of coin called *situado* was used to pay for the royal bureaucracy and the military personnel stationed on the island. Every year, the governor of Santo Domingo was in charge of naming a *maestre de la plata* who, in exchange for a salary, would be entrusted with the task of bringing the *situado* from the Caribbean port where the payment was made: from Veracruz, Cartagena, or even Portobelo via Panamá to Santo Domingo. This system was full of complications. The *situado* roughly equated the sum of money needed to pay the salary of bureaucrats and soldiers in Santo Domingo. Deducting the transportation costs from the *situado*

---

[34] The Council of the Indies absolved Melgarejo of this and other charges, including trading and demanding merchandise and enslaved Africans at advantageous prices or in exchange of favors. Being absolved, of course, did not necessarily imply innocence, and even if the charges were spurious, they do hint at common practices among high bureaucrats in Santo Domingo. Appeal to the Council of the Indies of the *residencia* of Juan Melgarejo Ponce de León, 1652. AGI, SD. 7, N. 115E.

"Prime Mover of All Machinations" 193

meant that there was never enough money to pay all the salaries, even if the full amount made it to Santo Domingo. The *oficiales reales* of the ports where the *situado* was paid had little incentive to relinquish the funds, and it is likely that many of them found ways to discount important sums from the total owed. Also, the navigation from Cartagena or Veracruz to Santo Domingo involved numerous perils. Encounters with pirates and other opportunists eager to get their hands on a *situado* were common, and more than a few shipments of coined silver were lost in these naval encounters.

Even though the governor of Santo Domingo named the *maestre de la plata*, this was not a direct appointment. The *maestre* had to be chosen through an auction in which the candidates offered to bring the *situado* at the lowest cost possible for the treasury. This system allowed Santo Domingo residents of upstanding reputation, social status, and wealth to accumulate merits in the service of the crown while earning a considerable salary. Since the trip was risky, the person chosen for *maestre* needed to have financial backers willing to pledge a significant amount of coin as protection against any loss or mishandling of the *situado*. For this reason, it was essential for any candidate for *maestre de la plata* to enjoy a vast network of wealthy allies, relatives, and partners. Santo Domingo governors played a role in the election of the *maestre de la plata* far beyond their official responsibilities. Already in 1612, the *fiscal* Jerónimo de Herrera complained that Governor Alonso Gómez de Sandoval had handpicked one of his servants to collect the *situado*, and in another year, when a person close to governor Sandoval brought the *situado*, he also brought 6,000 *ducados* worth of flour, Chinese silks, and other merchandise bought illegally with the money of the *situado*. When the *contador* of the treasury realized this, he informed Governor Gómez de Sandoval, who ordered him not to meddle in other people's affairs.[35]

Not all governors were as involved in the election of the *maestre de la plata* as Gómez de Sandoval. In the following decades, other powerful groups in the city positioned their relatives and allies to achieve the post. In 1626, Governor Diego de Acuña reported how many friends, relatives, and dependents of the archbishop, the *oidores*, and the *fiscal* of the *Audiencia* bid for the office, while other more qualified candidates refrained from doing so for fear of possible reprisals.[36] In this instance,

---

[35] Jerónimo de Herrera to the Council of the Indies. May 23, 1612. AGI, SD. 54, R. 3, n. 88.
[36] Diego de Acuña to the Council of the Indies. March 28, 1626. AGI, SD. 55, R. 6, n. 41.

194 *Islanders and Empire*

Governor Acuña's role as a mere observer of this political tug of war, according to his own testimony, was extremely unusual, and it is unlikely that the governor did not have a favorite candidate in this bidding war. The networks surrounding high-ranking public officials and religious figures always had a stake in the election of the *maestre*, but their intervention was normally conditioned by the desires of the governor. That was the case during the tenure of Governor Gabriel Chaves Osorio (1628–34). According to Alonso de Hurtado, who arrived on the island as *visitador* to investigate Chaves Osorio's behavior, the governor had such an interest in introducing contraband Chinese fabrics on the island that without an auction, he appointed his ally the *contador* of the treasury as *maestre de la plata*, paid him 1,000 *ducados* from the *situado* for his services, and also paid him his salary of *contador* for the time he was away.[37]

It was, once again, Governor Juan Bitrián who elevated the manipulations of the *situado* to an art form. During his governorship, the payment of the *situado* suffered constant delays, to the point that the *situados* from the years 1636, 1637, and 1638 were not paid until 1639, and according to Bitrián himself, they were short over 60,000 *pesos*.[38] During those years, the treasury was likely exhausted, and it was extraordinarily difficult to pay even *socorros* to royal ministers, officials, and soldiers. Since Governor Bitrián could not count on the *situados* those years to feed the treasury coffers and his own ambitions, he was forced to look for money anywhere he could find it. Through extortion, threats, and jail sentences against local residents, the governor and his allies were able to gather important amounts of coin. In 1640 alone, Bitrián and his men extorted 40,000 *pesos* from the Santo Domingo residents. It is possible that high-ranking ministers like the *oidores* received a small part of this money as *socorros*, but the soldiers of the garrison, most of them lacking any leverage against the governor, received little help from their superior, and by governor Bitrián's own admission, by 1640 their salaries were two years delayed.[39] Already in 1638, the absence of salaries for soldiers was so dire that numerous soldiers were found walking barefoot through the fortress. Many

---

[37] Alonso de Hurtado to the Council of the Indies. October 11, 1632. AGI, SD. 27A.

[38] Juan Bitrián to the Council of the Indies. June 29, 1640. AGI, SD. 55, R. 20, n. 120.

[39] Ibid.; Pedro Luis de Salazar to the Council of the Indies. July 15, 1642. AGI, SD. 56, R. 2, n. 10. The letter contains a detailed list with the names of the local residents whom the governor pressured to pay and the methods used to force them to pay.

"Prime Mover of All Machinations" 195

bought their scarce clothes on credit, which undoubtedly led to abuses by the local merchants in Santo Domingo. In the meantime, governor Bitrián sent his nephew, whom he had appointed as captain in the city fortress, as *maestre de la plata*. To pay for expenses and salary, Bitrián's nephew allegedly received the small fortune of 15,000 *pesos*, while bringing 20,000 *pesos* of the *situado* in merchandise from China, which was placed for sale at high prices in the shops of local merchants allied with the governor.[40]

This kind of behavior continued throughout Bitrián's administration. In 1642, with more than 240,000 *pesos* of the *situado* delayed, the governor sent Simón de Suazo as *maestre de la plata*. According to the *fiscal* Francisco de Alarcón, Simón worked at the service of merchant Ricardo Suazo, who that same year had brought to port a ship called *Ulises* with 20,000 *pesos* in merchandise. Suazo sold these goods in exchange for 40,000 *pesos* worth of local produce, which he would have been able to sell in Cádiz for at least 80,000 *pesos*. Many residents desired the post of *maestre de la plata* but did not dare to voice their aspiration so as not to anger the mercurial governor, who had dealings with Suazo. One of those local residents, an officer of the *Audiencia*, was apparently willing to go without a salary under the condition that he was paid the 20,000 *pesos* in loans he was owed.[41] Even though the governor often upheld all the ordinary proceedings surrounding the election of the *maestre de la plata*, he also pressured possible candidates behind the scenes in order to ensure that his candidate won the auction for the post. At the same time that the auction was publicly announced throughout the city by the town crier, Bitrián also spread a warning. No one but Suazo would go for the *situado*. As a result, no one bid for the post. Suazo's salary was set at 3,000 *pesos*, despite protests by the *fiscal* of the *Audiencia* who pointed out that only a little over a year before a local resident was paid 1,200 *pesos* for the same job. Suazo was required to leave bonds worth only 40,000 *pesos*, even though this only amounted to 25 percent of the money he was bringing. Governor Bitrián also named Suazo *alcaide* of the fortress of San Jerónimo, in the words of the *fiscal* of the *Audiencia* Francisco de Alarcón, "with the only purpose of using those men [his allies] for his own ends and because it is appropriate for his dealings." *Fiscal* Alarcón believed that Suazo was being paid to bring the governor's property,

---

[40] Ibid.
[41] Francisco de Alarcón to the Council of the Indies. August 4, 1643. AGI, SD. 56, R. 3, n. 21.

which they had "swindled from these poor soldiers in exchange of rags, and then shipped in galleons to Seville where he [the governor] keeps [the wealth] he has gathered here, which is plenty."[42]

These cases reveal the high stakes behind the appointment of the *maestre de la plata* for the *vecinos* of Santo Domingo, high-ranking ministers, and officials of the *Audiencia*. As the only steady and more-or-less regular injection of coin to the island, the *situado* became a very important avenue to acquire wealth for a few, especially those close to the governor, and always with his complicity. The incorporation of Santo Domingo into the network of Caribbean towns receiving money to pay for administration and defense radically transformed local politics. The governor of the island became, at least in theory, the most influential man of the island. His power derived from his control of the military, the treasury, and the regular arrival of the *situado*. In turn, local elites competed among themselves for the friendship and patronage of the governor to gain access to some of the money from the transportation and handling of the *situado*. Rodrigo Pimentel's success (as well as others before and after him) derived from his ability to attract government officials to his side through presents, goods, credit, and/or legal assistance at the end of their terms. This relationship often led to a reversal of roles in which Pimentel became the mastermind and center of the operation, while governors and royal ministers benefitted and aided Pimentel from their official posts.

In 1649, only a few months before Juan Melgarejo was appointed interim governor, Rodrigo Pimentel managed to appoint Antonio de Ledesma, a man in his trust, as *maestre de la plata*. The instructions that Pimentel wrote to Ledesma, which have been preserved, offer an intimate portrait of the dealings of a smuggler with his associate. Pimentel handed these instructions to Ledesma for his trip to Cartagena, and in them, Pimentel detailed the amount of merchandise Ledesma had to buy with the money from the *situado* and how much he should spend (initially 10,000 *pesos*, although later he increased it to 20,000). Pimentel also mentioned the names of the contacts Ledesma would find in towns like Riohacha, Maracaibo, or Coro

---

[42] "siendo su fin solamente valerse de tales hombres para hacer por mano de ellos su negocio y ser a propósito para sus contrataciones"; "estafada a estos pobres soldados a trueco de trapos, y remitirla en estos galeones a Sevilla donde tiene toda [el gobernador] la [riqueza] que aquí ha granjeado, que es mucha." Ibid.

"Prime Mover of All Machinations" 197

who would help him on his trip by land from Cartagena to Caracas. These contacts were high-ranking military officers, royal officials, and members of the local *Cabildos*. They would assist Ledesma with the logistics of the trip and would inform him of the prices of different products throughout the region and what products were needed in Cartagena. In Pimentel's words, "if it is possible to conduct some business with safe, local individuals in Cartagena, you will do so, and everywhere else you visit, you will conduct any business that the situation allows."[43] The instructions that Pimentel wrote to Ledesma reveal yet another way that Pimentel found to benefit from the vast network of associates he had accumulated throughout the Greater Caribbean via his control of the proceedings of the *Audiencia*, and it shows the multiple avenues that Pimentel found to turn his political influence in Hispaniola into sound economic profit in other locales. Hispaniola elites thus established mutually beneficial partnerships with local elites and crown officials throughout the Spanish Caribbean world. Men like Pimentel used these social and commercial networks to exchange goods, information, and political influence, which allowed them to maintain a position of privilege in their respective communities.

Despite the almost exclusive use of the *situado* Pimentel enjoyed, his letters to Ledesma also show that it was in his own interest that most of the transported money made it safely to Santo Domingo. Both the economy of the island and his own wealth depended on the arrival of the *situado* to the island, so soldiers, local residents, and royal officials could pay back the debts incurred during the periods between payments. In many cases, he, his friends, and his allies were the beneficiaries of those debts. After Ledesma's departure from Santo Domingo, Pimentel sent him some enslaved Africans with instruction about how to sell them and for how much. He also added: "Sir, bring the coins upfront, so we can use them, for the *situado* has been so short that we have lost many *reales* from the treasury, and many people who owe me will not be able to pay me back."[44] Pimentel depended on the *situado* for his economic well-being

---

[43] "Si en Cartagena se pudiere hacer algún negocio con personas seguras de la plaza con algunas ganancia cierta se dispondrá con toda seguridad y en las demás partes por donde vuestra merced pasare se hará el despacho que dieren las ocasiones." AGI, Escribanía, 22B.

[44] "Traiga vuestra merced los reales por delante porque nos valgamos de ellos que con la poca cobranza del situado se nos han desvanecido muchos reales de la caja pues no tendrán pagamento los que me los deben." Ibid.

198   *Islanders and Empire*

as much as (or even more than) any other Santo Domingo resident. When local people like Pimentel controlled the *situado*, and not peninsular governors, the island population benefitted in greater measure, since most of the coin made it to the hands of local people in one way or another, while peninsular governors like Bitrián syphoned those riches out of the island to enjoy them back in Spain.

In his letters to Ledesma, Pimentel also gave him instructions about how he was supposed to handle the merchandise he had bought once he arrived in Santo Domingo. As lieutenant governor, Pimentel commissioned a small merchant ship with soldiers and artillery to bring the *situado* to the island. He ordered Ledesma to "have all the clothes unencumbered, so that once the ship anchors, it can be transported in a couple of sloops that I will have waiting for your arrival to port at dusk." Pimentel arranged things like this so the *fiscal* Pedro de Alarcón, one of the few members of the *Audiencia* whom he had been unable to persuade to his side, could not interfere. Apparently, on the occasion that Simón de Suazo went for the *situado*, Alarcón, suspecting there was contraband in the ship arriving with the *situado*, entered the ship and slept in it to prevent anyone unloading goods during the night. For that reason, Pimentel stressed to Ledesma the secrecy of the operation: "Sir, don't tell anyone what you are bringing either before or after your arrival."[45]

Ledesma's arrival to Santo Domingo took place exactly as Pimentel anticipated. The ship arrived too late to be admitted into port, so it anchored right outside the city. That same night, a few soldiers from the garrison transported the merchandise to the houses of Rodrigo Pimentel and Diego de Mosquera, a merchant who regularly collaborated with Pimentel to sell his smuggled goods. Despite all these arrangements, *fiscal* Francisco de Alarcón heard about the operation. He declared that when the *contador* entered the ship the next morning, he only found 4,000 *pesos*, even though he was expecting to find at least 24,000. The city gates regularly closed at nine every night and the keys were given to the governor, but Pimentel had ensured that the gates stayed open so his men (likely assisted by enslaved Africans) could bring the goods into the city. Alarcón believed this was further proof of the complicity between Governor Melgarejo and Pimentel in the mishandling of the *situado*. The clothes and goods that Pimentel introduced in the city were sold in

---

[45] "que toda la ropa venga zafa de manera que en dado fondo se pueda sacar en un par de chalupas que tendré prevenidas disponiendo la llegada al puerto al anochecer"; "a nadie comunique vuestra merced lo que trae antes ni después de llegado." Ibid.

"Prime Mover of All Machinations" 199

the streets and in the shops of his relatives and allies. He brought so much of it that he arranged for people expecting payments from the *situado* to be paid in textiles.[46] Just like governor Juan Bitrián had managed to do during his tenure, Pimentel found ways to pay the salaries of the infantry with fabrics. His alliance with governor Melgarejo and the appointment of his brother, *regidor* Álvaro Pimentel, as interim *contador* of the treasury gave him an almost unlimited access to the royal coffers and the *situado* from the end of 1648 to 1651.

Apart from paying soldiers with textiles instead of coin, new and unexpected opportunities arose at times to seize the part of the *situado* used to pay the salaries of soldiers. In 1650, the *Audiencia* of Santo Domingo sent a report to Spain reporting that, in the aftermath of the rebellion of Portugal in 1640, there were concerns about possible seditious behavior by Portuguese residents in the Spanish colonies. After a debate in the *Audiencia* about what to do with the Portuguese living on the island, interim governor Melgarejo discharged all the Portuguese soldiers in residence and shipped the unmarried men to Spain.[47] Local merchants, and particularly Pimentel, turned the expulsion of the Portuguese soldiers into a business opportunity. Most of these soldiers were owed a great part of their salaries that the treasury had been unable to pay. Many of them, having to leave the island without any payment, were forced to seek the assistance of local merchants. Pimentel and their associates, in exchange of signed consent to receive payment of their delayed salaries, gave the soldiers clothes and other merchandise at inflated prices, thus ensuring a great profit margin. The expulsion of the Portuguese soldiers may have earned local merchants benefits near 8,000 *pesos* in total.[48]

The arrival of the newly appointed governor Luis Fernández de Córdoba, and the beginning of the proceedings of the *residencia* against Juan Melgarejo, gave *fiscal* Alarcón an opportunity to expose the illicit affairs that took place during Melgarejo's tenure. Pimentel, in an effort to defend both himself and Melgarejo, mobilized significant witnesses from his circle of allies to prove that Alarcón's accusations were the machinations of a desperate man. Captain Juan Sánchez Aragonés, a resident of

[46] Complaint filed by *fiscal* Francisco de Alarcón Coronado in the *juicio de residencia* of Juan Melgarejo Ponce de León. 1650. AGI, Escribanía, 12A.

[47] The *Audiencia* to the Council of the Indies. March 14, 1650. AGI, SD. 57, R. 2, n. 23.

[48] Francisco de Alarcón Coronado to the Council of the Indies. May 27, 1652. AGI, Escribanía, 23C.

200   *Islanders and Empire*

the village of Cotuy and member of the local militia, was one of those who
Pimentel tried to make testify for the defense. Sánchez received a message
from Pimentel's brother Álvaro asking him to come to Santo Domingo
and go to his house so he could be instructed in how to answer the
prosecutors of the case. Sánchez, however, disregarded Pimentel's instructions and testified freely against Melgarejo. The day after the proceedings
were made public, a free servant of Rodrigo Pimentel identified as a
Portuguese mulatto, attacked Juan Sánchez in a street of Santo
Domingo. Sánchez received very serious injuries but survived the attack.
Despite the testimony of the victim and the witnesses, the investigation
was never finalized, showing to all Santo Domingo residents once again
that Pimentel was not afraid of using violent tactics to shame, intimidate,
or seek vengeance against his enemies, regardless of their social station.[49]

   In the midst of the trial against Melgarejo, the new governor Luis
Fernández de Córdoba, apparently oblivious to (and surprised by) the
tense conflict within the *Audiencia*, described to his superiors in Spain
how badly the *fiscal* and other *oidores* treated Melgarejo and how they
regularly gathered in the house of one of the discharged Portuguese soldiers,
plotting to find witnesses to testify against the former interim governor. The
narration of Fernández de Córdoba is accompanied by testimonies by
Pimentel and many of his allies and clients inside the city's *Cabildo* and
the *Audiencia*, which shows that Pimentel used the situation to get closer to
the new governor.[50] Melgarejo's trial also became a proxy war in which
Pimentel's enemies were able to complain against him. Bernabé de Mesa
was one of these witnesses, backed by Damián del Castillo Vaca and
Baltasar de Figueroa y Castilla, both important members of the local elites.
Mesa went on to narrate how Melgarejo had accepted bribes in exchange
for favorable sentences. In Melgarejo's own sentence, however, the former
governor was found innocent of this and many other charges, while
Bernabé de Mesa was charged with some undetermined crimes, possibly
as payback, and received the exorbitant sentence of 200 lashes, ten years in
the galleys, and 2,000 *pesos*. This punishment was later reduced to four
years in exile from the island and a fine of 1,000 *pesos*, which Bernabé's

---

[49] Letter of the *oidor* Pedro Luis de Salazar to the Council of the Indies. March 2, 1651. AGI,
   Escribanía, 23C. The judge of this case was Juan Francisco de Montemayor y Cuenca, a
   young *oidor* who arrived in the city in early 1651. His connections to Pimentel might have
   been tenuous back then, but the notary in charge of the case, Francisco Facundo de
   Carvajal, was deeply connected with Pimentel's network.
[50] Report by governor Luis Fernández de Córdoba about the behavior of the members of the
   Audiencia. September 1, 1650. AGI, SD, 57, R. 3, n. 41, doc. 3.

"Prime Mover of All Machinations"   201

friends Damián del Castillo Vaca and Baltasar de Figueroa y Castilla were forced to pay in his stead. Pimentel won his little proxy war, but as a consequence of this sentence against Bernabé de Mesa, Damián del Castillo Vaca became one of Pimentel's fiercest enemies.[51]

In mid 1651, a plague struck the city, claiming among its victims the governor Luis Fernández de Córdoba and his successor as the most senior *oidor*, Pedro Luis de Salazar. Francisco Pantoja became interim governor and appointed *regidor* Álvaro Pimentel, Rodrigo's brother, as interim *contador*, since the previous one had also died in the epidemic. The *alcaide* of the fortress also died and was replaced in the interim by the *regidor* Juan de la Vega Torralba, brother-in-law of Pimentel. According to Damian del Castillo Vaca, this situation was again used by Pimentel to seize the *situado* and pay the soldiers in clothes and goods and, at the same time, to humiliate his enemies. He sent Luis Garabito Villalobos, an eighty-year-old man, to Azua escorted by soldiers armed with muskets lit and ready to fire, which according to Damián del Castillo Vaca, equated him with being a criminal, or worse, a traitor. Juan Sánchez Aragonés, possibly still recovering from his wounds, was jailed for four months without being given a reason and twenty days after being released, was again imprisoned for another month.[52]

By occupying new positions in the administration and acting against their enemies, the Pimentel family consolidated near total control of local religious, secular, and military institutions of the island, including the *Audiencia*, and thus the *situado*, developed pan-Caribbean smuggling networks, and channeled a great part of the inbound trade arriving to the island for their own benefit and those allied with them. During the period between mid 1645 and mid 1651, despite the opposition from some members of the *Audiencia* and rival local networks, Rodrigo Pimentel seized and used to his advantage most colonial institutions in Hispaniola and was able to conduct his business freely and without significant obstacles.

---

[51] Request of appeal of the *juicio de residencia* against Juan Melgarejo Ponce de León, 1652. AGI, SD. 7, N. 115E. The enmity between Baltasar de Figueroa y Castilla and Pimentel was older and had a much more personal origin. When Baltasar's mother died, his father, also named Baltasar de Figueroa, married Isabel de Pimentel, Rodrigo Pimentel's sister. After the death of Figueroa senior, Rodrigo Pimentel won a lawsuit for his sister and nephews' right to the Figueroa's inheritance and house, thus depriving Baltasar de Figueroa of the right to his father's estate. AGI, Escribanía, 22A.

[52] Damián del Castillo Vaca to the Council of the Indies. October 30, 1651. AGI, SD. 7, R. 115C.

CHALLENGES TO PIMENTEL'S POWER

The arrival of the new governor Andrés Pérez Franco (1652–3) signaled an important reversal in the fortunes of the Pimentel family. Unlike Juan Melgarejo, who was willing to negotiate with Pimentel despite their initial disagreements, the new governor was an old veteran with long experience as a colonial bureaucrat, and he was unwilling to yield or even share power he considered his own. Also, he seemed to have been a difficult man to deal with, with little or no patience for establishing fruitful reciprocal contacts with the members of the *Audiencia* or with local residents. This attitude clearly showed in one of his first decisions as governor. Despite having arrived with a company of seventy-eight soldiers levied in New Spain to fill the garrison of Santo Domingo, Andrés Pérez Franco decided to re-enlist the thirty-one Portuguese soldiers that still resided on the island, in a clear confrontation with those *oidores* and members of the local elites, who had promoted their discharge during the interim governorship of Juan Melgarejo.[53] He also showed a strong tendency to interfere in the cases being reviewed by the *Audiencia*, to the frustration of the *oidores*, who saw their authority trampled. He did so by appealing to his authority as *capitán general*. Every time he wanted to intervene in a case, he would call the city to arms under the excuse of a possible imminent attack, which gave him the authority to stop all the cases being judged in the *Audiencia* and place them under military jurisdiction for as long as the supposed threat lasted. He also prosecuted the members of the *Audiencia* for different causes ranging from their immoral lifestyles to the ways in which they carried out their duties, in what mainly seems to have been a way to keep these ministers on a short leash. By the end of 1653, the Council of the Indies had received a steady stream of letters from the *Audiencia* complaining of the governor's behavior.[54]

---

[53] The source is hardly impartial (Pimentel's brother), but the information does reveal the damage that the new governor was doing to the control that the Pimentel family had over the institutions. Álvaro Silvestro Pimentel to the Council of the Indies. May 12, 1652. AGI, SD. 75, R. 3.

[54] Francisco Pantoja de Ayala and Juan Francisco de Montemayor y Cuenca to the Council of the Indies. August 22, 1652. AGI, SD. 57, R. 4, n. 61. For details about governor Pérez Franco's prosecution of *oidor* Juan Francisco de Montemayor y Cuenca for "scandalous lifestyle," see AGI, SD. 58, R. 3, n. 14. For the governor's prosecution of *oidor* Francisco Pantoja de Ayala, see AGI, SD. 57, R. 5, n. 73. For a summary of the accusations against Andrés Pérez Franco that the Council of the Indies collected from the *Audiencia* by September 1653, see AGI, SD. 57, R. 5, n. 74.

"Prime Mover of All Machinations" 203

In this new climate of direct intervention by the governor in all aspects of the administration of the island, Rodrigo Pimentel also became a victim of the governor's hands-on approach to government. The governor deposed Álvaro Pimentel from his job of interim *contador* of the treasury, thus eliminating his direct access to the *situado*. Access to the port of the city for smuggling became virtually impossible for Pimentel, who was no longer lieutenant governor. The governor, who probably enjoyed ample support among the newly recruited soldiers he had brought from New Spain, and the Portuguese he had re-enlisted, controlled the entry of goods to the island and did not hesitate to seize ships that arrived without proper documentation and to pocket a third of the confiscated goods, as he himself admitted to the Council of the Indies. He made for himself a small fortune of at least 70,000 *pesos* in about a year.[55] This would indicate that in the years 1652–3, the governor seized smuggled property valued in 210,000 *pesos*. Assuming that the governor followed the letter of the law in those seizures (and this is questionable), such high volume of smuggled goods entering the port of Santo Domingo seems to indicate that merchants and people across the Caribbean and the Atlantic had become accustomed to selling goods without a license in Hispaniola and knew that royal officials would not question them.[56]

In the middle of this prosecution of illicit activities, Rodrigo Pimentel also became the focus of the governor's attention. The perfect excuse was provided by Pimentel's former associate, Antonio de Ledesma, who had been *maestre de la plata* in 1649 under the auspices of Pimentel and conducted business for him with the money of the *situado*. In a strange turn of events, Ledesma denounced his former boss for having kept all the merchandise he brought on his trip without giving him 50 percent of the benefits as they had agreed. Governor Pérez Franco sent a group of soldiers to Ledesma's house, where they confiscated a desk containing personal correspondence between Ledesma and Pimentel during the trip.

[55] The practice of keeping a third of the confiscated cargo was common among many governors in Santo Domingo throughout the seventeenth century, but rarely accepted by the crown, especially after 1620s. This case was not an exception to this tendency, and after Pérez Franco's death, the crown still tried to recover the money that he had kept for himself by seizing any property he might have left. Letter of Andres Pérez Franco to the Council of the Indies. January 14, 1653. AGI, SD. 75, R. 3. Royal Decree. September 3, 1654. AGI, SD. 75, R. 3.

[56] Andrés Pérez Franco offers a few examples of ships that came to Santo Domingo loaded in the Canary Islands with smuggled goods. At least one of them was owned by a *vecino* of Campeche. Andrés Pérez Franco to the Council of the Indies. January 14, 1653. AGI, SD. 75, R. 3.

204 *Islanders and Empire*

Ledesma avoided incriminating himself and maintained that the merchandise in question had been purchased with the order of payments he had in the name of Rodrigo Pimentel, which he settled once he received the *situado*. In his defense, Pimentel maintained the same story, even though the payments order in his name during that trip was under 3,000 *pesos*, and not 20,000 as Ledesma ended up spending in his name. He also argued that he never had an agreement with Ledesma. Pimentel was sent to jail and later placed under house arrest. Governor Pérez Franco left the case in the hands of *oidor* Diego de Orozco, who declared Pimentel innocent of all charges, to the governor's surprise (but possibly not to Pimentel's). Only a few days later, the governor annulled Orozco's sentence for being against royal law, declared Pimentel guilty, condemned him to pay 10,000 *pesos*, removed him for life from the office of *regidor*, and exiled him from the island for six years.[57]

Orozco did not take the governor's interference in his case lightly. He does not seem to have been part of Pimentel's circle, but he defended the legality of his verdict. He also reported that, before arriving at a sentence in the case, he consulted the notary of the *Audiencia* Diego Méndez "because *relatores* and *escribanos de cámara* usually had good opinions about the cases." Méndez told him that he did not find any reason to sentence Pimentel.[58] Diego Méndez was a member of the local elite and an associate of Pimentel. His intervention in this case shows how members of the local elite could exercise considerable influence in the decisions of the *Audiencia*, without necessarily having the *oidores* in their side, but through the lower members of the institution.[59]

Pimentel was only allowed to appeal the court decision once he had paid the 10,000 *pesos*. He was then placed in a frigate and sent to Spain to serve his exile. A few days after his departure from Santo Domingo, Pimentel arrived in San Juan, where the ship docked to resupply before the transatlantic voyage. In September 1653, while still in Puerto Rico, an ailing Pimentel received the news that governor Pérez Franco had suddenly died. Pimentel took immediate advantage of this lucky break and boarded a ship back to Santo Domingo, where a much more amenable *Audiencia*, in December 1653, reversed the governor's sentence and

[57] The whole case is held in AGI, Escribanía, 23B, *pieza* 5.

[58] Ibid.

[59] For a wonderful analysis of the importance of understanding the world in which notaries reside, the powers they mediated, and how these shaped the documents historians read, see Kathryn Burns, *Into the Archive: Writing and Power in Colonial Peru* (Durham: Duke University Press, 2010); for the influence of notaries over the overall functioning of the *Audiencia* system, see Herzog, *La administración como un fenómeno social*, 45.

returned his 10,000 *pesos*.[60] Pimentel went back to being one of the biggest social, political, and economic forces in the city, and Antonio de Ledesma, as he confessed later, spent years hidden in the convent of Santo Domingo afraid of a retaliatory attack from Pimentel.[61] As this episode reveals, even though Pimentel's influence was always subject to changes depending on the governor, his network of clients and associates both within the *Audiencia* and on the island remained strong, which became the key to his long-lasting success. Governors and *oidores* came and went, but most of the new arrivals needed and sought to establish relationships with powerful local leaders, and local residents took advantage of those bonds for their own benefit.

The importance of a strong patronage network as the root of all social and political success in Hispaniola became evident in the events that followed the death of Governor Pérez Franco. The governor's mistrust of the other *oidores* of the *Audiencia* and, in particular, of his successor as interim governor, *oidor* Juan Francisco de Montemayor y Cuenca, led him to make an unprecedented decision. Before his death, he wrote a political will in which he gave his political attributions to the *alcaldes ordinarios* of the *Cabildo* of Santo Domingo and his military powers to the *sargento mayor* of the fortress, thus depriving Montemayor, as the most senior officer in the *Audiencia*, of his powers by the laws of succession.[62] When Governor Pérez Franco died, according to custom, the *Cabildo* of Santo Domingo celebrated a plenary session to receive Juan Francisco de Montemayor as new interim governor. Right before the new governor arrived, the senior *alcalde ordinario* Baltasar Fernández de Castro tried to take advantage of Pérez Franco's political will and possibly of the fact that he believed that Rodrigo Pimentel was on his way to Spain to begin his exile. He started the session and asked the notary to read Pérez Franco's document. The response that he received, however, was far from what he desired. His partner and junior *alcalde ordinario* Baltasar de Figueroa responded that the royal decrees clearly stipulated that the most senior *oidor* would be the interim governor. Others, like *regidor* Gaspar de Castro Rivera, were less diplomatic and clearly stated that the document was complete nonsense and that

---

[60] AGI, Escribanía, 22B; *Oidor* Gaspar Vélez Mantilla to the Council of the Indies. July 28, 1656. AGI, SD. 58, R. 3, n. 45.

[61] Testimony by Antonio de Ledesma. 1659. AGI, Escribanía, 22A, 298r.

[62] Andrés Pérez Franco to the Council of the Indies. August 12, 1653. AGI, SD. 57, R. 5, n. 75, doc. 4.

206   *Islanders and Empire*

Pérez Franco could not pass his office to whomever he desired. The *alcalde* insisted that "he knew that there are laws that state that many royal decrees must be obeyed but not carried out," to which Juan Esteban Páez Maldonado responded by warning him to watch what he said. Finally, despite the insistence of the *alcalde*, everyone reaffirmed their conviction that tradition should be followed and proceeded out of the room to receive the new interim governor, who by then had arrived at the doors of the *Cabildo*.[63]

As feeble and unorthodox as Baltasar Fernández de Castro's attempt to seize power in Santo Domingo was, it sheds light on the relative power vacuum on the island in Pimentel's absence. With a powerful governor like Pérez Franco dead, and the unofficial political and economic leader of the island (Pimentel) on his way to Spain, the *alcalde ordinario* of Santo Domingo deemed the existing circumstances appropriate to his bid for power. Fernández de Castro did not fail because the governor's orders to hand power to the *alcaldes ordinarios* were against tradition or against the crown's policy. Fernández de Castro's plans failed because he overestimated his social and political status and did not secure enough local support among his peers. Without a powerful patronage network, local elites interpreted Fernández de Castro's bid as merely eccentric, and they therefore dismissed it. Pimentel's attacks against his peers, his handling of the *situado*, and his influence over royal ministers and institutions were also unorthodox and illegal, but his actions were backed by a powerful patronage network willing to support his interests and its own.

"NO MORE LAW OR MORE KING THAN RODRIGO PIMENTEL"

The English attack on Santo Domingo in 1655 brought a sudden change to the rhythm of the island politics and the conflicts between its elites.[64] As with any event on the island, the English attack became an opportunity for

---

[63] "él sabía que hay leyes que disponen muchas cédulas del Rey se deben obedecer pero no cumplir." Notarized narration of the events. August 19, 1653. AGI, SD. 57, R. 5, n. 75, doc. 2. This narration was written by the notary of the *Cabildo* at the request of some of the *regidores* who attended the meeting. It was later sent to the Council of the Indies by Francisco de Montemayor y Cuenca, the *oidor* who became interim governor after the death of Andrés Perez Franco. This seems to indicate that at least one of the *regidores* informed the new governor of the meeting that took place right before his arrival, possibly in an attempt to be in his good graces.

[64] For a recent account of the battle from an English perspective, see Carla Gardina Pestana, *The English Conquest of Jamaica: Oliver Cromwell's Bid for Power* (Cambridge: Harvard University Press, 2017), 65–92. See also Bernardo Vega, *La*

"Prime Mover of All Machinations"

those members of the elites better suited for military service to prove their worth, serve next to the governor in times of need, and gain honors for themselves and their families. This was the case of the Garabito brothers, members of a military dynasty spanning at least three generations on the island and Pimentel's enemies; or Damián del Castillo Vaca, also an adversary of Pimentel, whose direct participation in the battle brought him a promotion to *maestre de campo* and numerous recommendations to the king.[65] Although Rodrigo Pimentel was a captain of the Santo Domingo militia, none of the descriptions of the English attack place him in the field. A man of great wealth by this time, Pimentel seems to have served close to the governor, providing enslaved laborers for the war effort and transportation of supplies for the army fighting outside the perimeter of the city, rather than leading troops in the field. These and other services prompted the Count of Peñalba, governor during the English invasion, to write two letters of recommendation asking the king for a knighthood for Pimentel.[66] Although Pimentel's economic and logistic contributions to the campaign were great, as was to be expected from someone of his social standing, the recommendation might have also been one of the many steps that the governor took to distribute honor and bring unity among the elites at a time in which cooperation was key to repel the English attackers.[67]

---

derrota de Penn y Venables en Santo Domingo, 1655 (Santo Domingo: Academia Dominicana de la Historia, 2013).

[65] In areas where there was not an active war (*guerra viva*), the *maestre de campo* ranked only second to the *capitán general*, which was the military rank of governors. For a full explanation of this military rank, see *Diccionario enciclopédico hispano-americano de literatura, ciencias y artes: Edición profusamente ilustrada con miles de pequeños graba- dos intercalados en el texto y tirados aparte, que reproducen las diferentes especies de los reinos animal, vegetal y mineral*, vol. 12 (Barcelona: Montaner y Simón Editores, 1893), 91. Thanks to Juan Andrés Suárez for this reference.

[66] The letters are dated in April 20 and July 30, 1656. AGI, SD. 58, R. 3, n. 60.

[67] In the aftermath of the battle, the Count of Peñalba sent the Council of the Indies numerous letters detailing the individual contributions of many of Hispaniola's residents and public officials to the defense of the city. Some examples of these recommendations are in AGI, SD. 58, R. 3, n. 19, 22, and 23. In some of the narratives of the battle, he even wrote about the assistance of some individuals, though he later bitterly protested their actions during the English attack. This was not so much a change of heart toward those individuals, but rather a strategic assessment of their actions at a time when their help was greatly needed. For instance, he wrote about the assistance of *oidor* and former interim governor Juan Francisco de Montemayor y Cuenca and the *sargento mayor* Lucas de Berroa in his *Relación de la victoria que han tenido las armas de Su Majestad (Dios le guarde) en la ciudad de Santo Domingo, isla Española, contra la Armada Inglesa de Guillermo Pen, enviada por el señor don Bernardino de Meneses Bracamonte, conde de Peñalba, presidente de la Real Audiencia de aquella ciudad, gobernador y capitan general*

208 *Islanders and Empire*

Despite his personal success in the defense of the island, or perhaps precisely because of it, the governorship of the Count of Peñalba was very short (1655–6). He was quickly promoted to the governorship of the *Audiencia* of Charcas, for which he departed soon after the arrival of his successor, Felix de Zúñiga Avellaneda, Count of the Sacred Empire, on May 1, 1656. Zúñiga was afflicted by an advanced stage of gout, which left him unable to fulfill his functions as governor for long periods. He also displayed a stormy and unfettered temper, which alienated everyone around him. His lack of self-control made him instantly unpopular among most members of the elite and the *oidores* of the *Audiencia*, whom he constantly mistreated both inside and outside the courtroom. Even former *oidor* and interim governor Juan Francisco de Montemayor, who owed Zúñiga a debt for his satisfactory end to his quarrels with the Count of Peñalba, had few good things to say about the new governor. In a letter to a Secretary of the Council of the Indies, he detailed the new governor's ill temper and lack of competency, pointing out that "today, everyone would change their present state for the one they had during the presidency of Andrés Pérez Franco," also famous for his fits of anger.[68]

Zúñiga's behavior isolated him from everyone around him except Rodrigo Pimentel. Always the eager opportunist who knew how to take advantage of influential ministers, Rodrigo Pimentel became the only person able to approach the new governor. Francisco de Montemayor explained how the new governor's temper

forces his subjects to run away from his house and proximity, so ordinarily he is alone without visitors except for don Rodrigo Pimentel, who has become the owner of his will, thus leaving the land very afflicted because of the command that this *vecino* has on the government and everyone else for his own convenience. Because he is rich, everything gravitates towards him, and it seems that this quality is not disagreeable to the president, who is looking to accommodate himself.[69]

---

de la isla (Sevilla, 1655). A year later, however, he sharply complained of their roles in the defense of the city. AGI, SD. 58, R. 3, n. 14 and 19.

[68] "hoy trocarén todos el estado presente por el que tenían en tiempo de don Andrés Pérez Franco." Juan Francisco de Montemayor y Cuenca to Gregorio de Leguía, Secretary of the Council of the Indies for New Spain. July 29, 1656. AGI, SD. 88, R. 4.

[69] "Este humor obliga a los súbditos a huir de su casa y comunicación, con que ordinariamente se está solo sin que nadie le vea sino don Rodrigo Pimentel, que se ha hecho dueño de su voluntad, dejando con esto afligidísimo a este lugar, por la mayoría y mando que este vecino afecta tener siempre y generalmente en los demás y en el gobierno para sus conveniencias. Que como es rico, todo lo atrae. Y esta calidad, según se entiende, no es desagradable al presidente, que desea acomodarse." Ibid.

"Prime Mover of All Machinations" 209

In fact, the contacts between Zúñiga and Pimentel might have been initiated by the new president, who had already heard of the eminent smuggler. According to the *oidor* Andrés Martínez de Amileta, who received Zúñiga, as soon as the new president disembarked in the port of Santo Domingo, he asked him about Pimentel, for "he wished to meet him for the news and recommendations he had heard of him."[70] The fact that a complete stranger to the world of the Greater Caribbean had already heard of Pimentel is evidence of the enormous influence and fame he had managed to amass at this stage in his life and to what extent Caribbean and transatlantic commercial networks and personalities were discussed among candidates for administrative positions in the region.

During the governorship of Felix de Zúñiga, (1656–9), Rodrigo Pimentel extended his control to every single aspect of the colonial administration to a level arguably unparalleled in any other Spanish American colony of his time. Through his friendship and influence with the governor, Pimentel held complete command over most affairs of the city and extended his influence throughout the island and beyond. With the help of the governor, his ally *oidor* Andrés Caballero, and the pressure he exerted on the other ministers, Pimentel managed every judicial decision coming out of the *Audiencia*, controlled judges, witnesses, and the totality of the bureaucratic machinery of the tribunal. Any person living in the district of the *Audiencia* of Santo Domingo seeking a positive outcome in their trial had to seek his patronage.

In order to control the treasury, Pimentel dismissed the officials in charge and appointed Alonso de Jáquez Carvajal, a *Cabildo* member and his brother-in-law, as well as Alonso's half-brother, the notary Francisco Facundo Carvajal, as officers of the treasury. Facundo Carvajal, who was described as a *mulato,* had been imprisoned by the Count of Peñalba for falsifying official documentation but was released by governor Zúñiga, possibly through Pimentel's intervention.[71] Pimentel also had plans to dismiss the *tesorero* Diego de Soria Pardo, but as soon as Soria found out, his wife, either sent by her husband or by her own free will, went in front of Pimentel himself, and pleaded on her knees for her husband's job. This display of submission prevented

---

[70] "que deseaba conocerle por las noticias que traía de su persona y recomendación." AGI, Escribanía, 22A, 32v.

[71] According to many witnesses, Francisco Facundo was the illegitimate son of Alonso de Carvajal and a free *mulata* called Ana de Tiedra, a family servant. AGI, Escribanía 24A.

210   *Islanders and Empire*

Soria from losing his job and ensured that he would be malleable to Pimentel's wishes.[72]

With the treasury under his control, he arranged the election of the *maestre de la plata*, the person who would go to pick up the *situado*, and made clear to everyone in the city that no one but those he appointed were allowed to bid in the open auction. Despite these veiled threats, other *vecinos* sought the post. In the 1656 election, Pimentel's candidate was Diego de Mosquera, who asked for a salary of 3,000 *pesos* and offered 20,000 *pesos* in securities. There were an other three bids in the auction. Two of them asked for smaller salaries and one of them even asked to go for the *situado* without pay "for the good of the Republic." In the end, the officials of the treasury (all of them Pimentel's clients and relatives) chose Diego de Mosquera because, they claimed, he offered better securities than the other candidates. The *fiscal* of the *Audiencia*, Bernardo Trigo de Figueroa, opposed this decision, arguing that the smallest bid had to be chosen and that the securities had to be doubled because that year the *situado* was not 50,000 *pesos* but 130,000. His complaints were ignored. *Oidor* Gaspar Vélez Mantilla also objected to the election of Diego de Mosquera. His protest gained him public scorn and insults from governor Zúñiga and Pimentel, who publicly declared that "he would strip him from his ministerial robes." In the years 1657 and 1658, Pimentel's brother Álvaro would be chosen as *maestre de la plata*.[73]

The military also became a target for Pimentel's ambition. As the center of a large patronage network, the ability to grant these posts to his clients and relatives gave Pimentel a position of power and a salary from the treasury. But most importantly, the control of the military outposts of the city granted him free reign to smuggle merchandise. For these ends, he placed a soldier of his confidence as second in command of the city fortress, and his long-term ally Diego de Mosquera as *alcaide* of another fortification of the city. These men seemed to have paid very little attention to military issues or to the situation of the soldiers stationed on the island. The lack of a steady salary (a problem which probably only worsened once Pimentel took charge of the treasury) spurred the rate of desertions among soldiers. The lack of an effective and respected chain of command able to maintain morale and discipline in the fortress might have also contributed to the high number of desertions. In 1656, in the

---

[72] Testimony of Captain Gaspar Cataño de la Paz. AGI, Escribanía, 22A, 49v, 221r.
[73] AGI, Escribanía, 23C, fol. 38v. AGI, Escribanía, 22A, fols. 16r, 1480v.

"Prime Mover of All Machinations" 211

aftermath of the English attempted invasion, near 900 soldiers were stationed in Santo Domingo. By 1658, there were fewer than 300 left.[74]

Pimentel's control of the military transformed Santo Domingo into a virtual free-trade port. Ships from all nationalities were welcome for business, despite the complaints of other members of the *Audiencia* and some neighbors of the city, for whom the English attack was all too recent. They feared the risks of having foreigners roaming the streets and inspecting the city's defenses. Although there are no records of the traffic that reached Santo Domingo during the governorship of Felix de Zúñiga, it must have been significant compared to previous years. Many different witnesses mentioned the presence of foreign ships, especially Dutch vessels, buying and selling merchandise freely in the port and markets of the city. The charges levied against governor Zúñiga at the end of his term mentioned the arrival of twenty-two Dutch, French, and English ships to Santo Domingo and other ports of the district, like Puerto Rico. At least three of those ships entered the port of Santo Domingo, although there were possibly more. One of those ships was a 700-ton Dutch ship. For an island like Hispaniola, starved for European manufactured goods, the arrival of just one or two well-supplied ships must have marked a sharp departure from the limited access to those goods that the island had suffered during the better part of the century.[75]

Reexportation of many of these goods must have been a common avenue to circulate them and benefit from this increased trade. When these ships were not enough to supply Pimentel with the products he desired, such as wine, wheat, or enslaved laborers, he procured permits for his merchant allies to go to the Canary Islands, Maracaibo, or Curaçao, where they likely had local contacts. Instead of unloading many of these products and slaves in the city ports, he would do so in Ocoa Bay, near the village of Azua and not far from his own lands. In the long run, the extortions that Pimentel exerted over Spanish vessels to sell him products (and probably slaves) at the prices that he demanded might have alienated the few Spanish merchants still willing to take the risk to sail to Santo Domingo and bring business in the city, but at the same time,

[74] Testimony of Colonel Juan Chacón. September 17, 1658. AGI, SD. 2, n. 74; Juan Balboa Mogrovejo to the Council of the Indies. November 26, 1658. AGI, SD. 58, R. 5, n. 77. Lack of punctual pay and desertions will continue throughout the century. For desertions in the 1680s, see Antonio Espino López, "Sobre la creación de fronteras. El caso de la Española y las guerras del reinado de Carlos II, 1673–1697," *Anuario de Estudios Americanos*, vol. 75, n. 1 (2018): 167.

[75] Charges against Félix de Zúñiga. August 28, 1658. AGI, SD. 2, n. 70.

the rumors that Santo Domingo was operating like a free port might have also spread throughout the Caribbean, and other nations might have felt encouraged to trade in the port city.

While the city was open for business, the city markets remained completely unregulated because Pimentel ensured that the *Cabildo* did not look carefully at the way merchants sold their merchandise. Apart from fixing prices, merchants sold their goods directly in their houses, a practice that was clearly illegal but that no one did anything to stop. Pimentel's merchant allies cut across race and gender lines throughout the city. One of these local allies was a free black woman ("negra libre") named Luisa Osorio, who sold meat that Pimentel brought from his lands without proper weights and measures. In the city slaughterhouse, a resident could buy an entire cow for two or three *pesos*, but since the *Cabildo* did nothing ensure a steady supply of meat, the slaughterhouse ran out of meat, and it was left to individual merchants to sell it in their own houses. Pimentel himself sold meat in his house, charging up to eighteen *pesos* per cow.[76]

Through his alliance with Félix de Zúñiga, Rodrigo Pimentel took complete control over the governorship, the *Audiencia*, the treasury, the military, the port, the arrival of food staples, and merchandise of all kinds. Also, his clients and relatives held tight control of the *Cabildo* of the city and (despite his disagreements with the archbishop) the ecclesiastic *Cabildo*. Pimentel's influence went well beyond Hispaniola's shores. Describing Pimentel during these years, a future governor wrote that people from all over the district of the *Audiencia* of Santo Domingo contacted Pimentel to intercede on their behalf to get posts, knighthoods, and other benefits. "A monster rose," he claimed, "to disturb the laws and government with absolute power and tyranny, not only in it [Hispaniola], but in the entire jurisdiction of Tierra Firme, where his rulings were observed like laws."[77] As Juan Francisco de Montemayor pointed out, everyone on the island felt Pimentel's grip, to the extent that soon everyone started referring to the governor as "Don Felix, punishment from heaven." It was during these years that the famous graffiti that read

[76] Testimony of Bernardo Trigo de Figuero., November 1659. AGI, Escribanía, 22A, 15r.

[77] "Se levantó este monstruo a perturbar las leyes y su gobernación con tal absoluto poder y tiranía no solamente en ella [Hispaniola] sino en toda su jurisdicción de Tierra Firme, que sus dictámenes eran leyes en la observancia." Juan Balboa Mogrovejo to the Council of the Indies. February 8, 1661. AGI, SD. 58, R. 8, n. 92. Thanks to Marc Eagle, who encouraged me to give a more careful look at this document.

"Prime Mover of All Machinations" 213

"there is no other law or king than Rodrigo Pimentel" appeared on the walls of the building of the *Audiencia*.[78]

PIMENTEL'S FALL AND NEW RISE

Santo Domingo vecinos and royal officials had been writing letters complaining about Pimentel for decades, but they seem to have intensified almost immediately after governor Zúñiga's arrival in the city. The previous governor, the Count of Peñalba, relayed to the Council of the Indies many of the grievances that he heard while in Cartagena, on route to his new post in Quito.[79] The letters by the former governor of Santo Domingo, however, were likely seen by the members of the Council of the Indies as self-flattery, the attempts of an officer to polish his résumé at the expense of his successor and events happening after his departure. The Council disregarded letters from prominent members of the island elite such as Damián del Castillo Vaca on the grounds that he belonged to the faction close to the Count of Peñalba and thus had a lot to lose from the arrival of a new governor.[80] Even though Governor Zúñiga established rigorous censorship of the outgoing mail from the island, opening and confiscating as many letters as he could find containing complaints about his administration, many of them made it to Madrid, making it impossible for the Council to ignore the situation.[81]

In 1658, the Council interviewed some of the passengers of a ship loaded with products from the island. They brought some letters from residents of Santo Domingo hidden in sugar crates to avoid detection by Governor Zúñiga and his men. The passengers' testimonies and the letters forced the Council to reflect on the news arriving from Santo Domingo. These concerns, added to the proximity of Jamaica, now in English hands, and the fears of another English attack on Hispaniola, likely raised the alarms of the king's ministers. The Council of the Indies sprang into action and named a new governor as well as a *visitador* to conduct an

---

[78] In Spanish, these two quotes are "Don Felix, castigo del cielo" and "No hay más ley ni más rey que don Rodrigo Pimentel." Charges against governor Félix de Zúñiga Avellaneda in his *juicio de residencia*. August 28, 1658. AGI, SD. 2, n. 70.

[79] The Count of Peñalba to the Council of the Indies. July 28, 1656. AGI. SD. 58, R. 3, n. 42.

[80] Damián del Castillo Vaca to the Council of the Indies. February 4, 1657. AGI, SD. 2, n. 66.

[81] The confiscation of mail is explained in the summary of charges against Félix de Zúñiga. August 28, October 15, and November 23, 1658. AGI, SD. 2, n. 70–72.

214   *Islanders and Empire*

investigation on Zúñiga, Pimentel, *oidor* Andrés Caballero, and sixteen other *vecinos* of Santo Domingo. Possibly due to the high rank of governor Zúñiga in court, Felipe IV himself decided that instead of deposing him from his post, he should be summoned back to court. Rodrigo Pimentel was also summoned to court, but for different reasons. After almost thirty years of letters complaining about him, it seemed that, finally, the crown was ready to deal directly with the old smuggler. In a summary of all the accusations against him, the *fiscal* of the Council of the Treasury asked that Pimentel be stripped of any office he held, honorific or otherwise, suffer perpetual exile from the island, and return all the money that he had usurped.[82]

The new governor of the island, Juan de Balboa Mogrovejo, and *visitador* Sancho de Ubilla embarked together from Spain for their trip to Santo Domingo. On the long transatlantic trip, they became good friends. Since Ubilla's role was to clarify Zúñiga and Pimentel's abuses, the support of the new governor became crucial to his endeavor. In his favor, he also had all those who had written against Pimentel and Zúñiga and who became witnesses of the proceedings and at times close allies of the new powers-to-be in the city. In other words, if their commission to make Pimentel accountable was to succeed, the new governor and the *visitador* needed Pimentel's enemies to build their case as well as to provide social and political support.[83]

As soon as the *visitador* arrived in Santo Domingo, he jailed Rodrigo Pimentel in one of the fortresses of the city and confiscated his property. During the year that Pimentel remained in prison, Governor Balboa observed that despite being in jail, Pimentel enjoyed the visits of clients and dependents, who were still extremely faithful to him and informed him of any new developments in the city. From his cell, he gave speeches to his followers, telling them that "he would come back victorious and more powerful than he was before, recalling the times in which his wit and good

---

[82] Summary of accusations against Rodrigo Pimentel, elaborated from the letters received from 1656 by Dr. Diego González Bonilla, *fiscal* of the Council of the Treasury. AGI, Escribanía 22A.

[83] The evidence of the close friendship between Juan de Balboa and Sancho de Ubilla is overwhelming. It is worth pointing out, however, that the accusers of Balboa and Ubilla, later on, became allies of Balboa's successor, Pedro de Carvajal, and the new archbishop Francisco de la Cueva, who were also friends, as well as Pimentel's associates. The *Cabildo* of Santo Domingo to the Council of the Indies. May 28, 1662; Pedro de Carvajal y Cobos to the Council of the Indies. May 30, 1662; Francisco de la Cueva Maldonado to the Council of the Indies. September 12, 1663. These letters can all be found in governor Juan Balboa's *juicio of residencia*. AGI, Escribanía, 12A.

"*Prime Mover of All Machinations*" 215

fortune had vanquished the power of magistrates, adding (with great insolence) that he would get a full pardon for all the wrongdoings that the *visitador* proved against him, for that was the reason he had acquired so much money." Governor Balboa reported the incident, and possibly took Pimentel's words as an empty threat.[84]

Pimentel denied all the charges and denounced the most relevant witnesses in the case that *visitador* Ubilla was building against him as vengeful relatives and friends of a rival factions in the city. Since the *visitador* arrived in Santo Domingo, he pointed out that it was common to see Damián del Castillo Vaca, the Garabito brothers, the Camarena family, Juan de Mieses Ponce de León, and Baltasar de Figueroa among others walking the streets together, lobbying everyone, and trying to convince them to testify against Pimentel.[85] Indeed, the arrival of the *visitador* amalgamated all of Pimentel's enemies into one cohesive group. They made it their common cause to destroy the person who had dominated the island's political and economic life for more than twenty years and often humiliated them in the process. On his behalf, however, Pimentel also mobilized his extended patronage network throughout the island for his defense. His list of witnesses was as long as that of his accusers, thus showing the extreme polarization of the elites of the island. By amassing such a long and illustrious list of witnesses, Pimentel undoubtedly tried to cast some shadow over the legitimacy of the procedure and the *visitador*, therefore planting some doubts in those who would have to read the proceedings back in Spain. Despite his best attempts to derail and delegitimate the trial, he was unable to stop it, and for the second time in his life in early 1661, Pimentel was placed against his will on a boat bound to Spain. Unable to escape from prison, on this occasion he was forced into exile on the Iberian Peninsula.

In Pimentel's absence, his relatives and friends seemed to have maintained a relatively low profile when it came to participating in contraband trade, but others stepped in to take advantage of the abundant possibilities for selling contraband goods on the island. Governor Balboa and the

---

[84] "que había de volver triunfante y poderoso, mucho más de lo que antes era, trayéndoles a la memoria las veces que su maña y buena fortuna había vencido al poder de los magistrados, diciéndoles (con desvergüenza insolente) que las demandas que le probare el visitador las satisfara [*sic.*] con un indulto, pues para eso había adquirido dineros." Juan Balboa Mogrovejo to the Council of the Indies. February 8, 1661. AGI, SD. 58, R. 8, n. 92.

[85] Most of Sancho de Ubilla's case against Rodrigo Pimentel can be found in AGI, Escribanía, 22A. His testimony starts in fol. 381r.

216 *Islanders and Empire*

visitador Sancho de Ubilla established friendships with two local residents: a merchant called Pedro de los Reyes and his father-in-law Francisco Mateos. Pedro de los Reyes was captured by the English when his ship was carrying cocoa from Santo Domingo to Veracruz. He was taken to England, where he arranged to lead an English ship loaded with textiles to Santo Domingo. On the Canary Islands he secured the appropriate documentation that falsely claimed that his ship carried wine exclusively, and once the alibi for the trip had been secured, he headed to Santo Domingo, where he entered the port with the governor's permission. Over a period of ten nights, the textiles were introduced in the city through a small gate in the city walls and into the cellar of Francisco Mateos, who also accommodated the English captain of the vessel. Some witnesses testified that on one of those nights, they saw six men coming into the governor's residence bringing bags of silver worth 6,000 *ducados*, which he shared with the officers in charge of the treasury and the *fiscal* of the *Audiencia*.[86]

The deals that Pedro de los Reyes struck with English merchants, as well as the governor of Santo Domingo and the *visitador,* show that although Pimentel's political and economic arrangements in Santo Domingo benefitted from an impressive transimperial Greater Caribbean smuggling network, his behavior was in no way exceptional. If given the chance (such as that created by Pimentel's arrest), local residents in Santo Domingo adapted to the opportunities that Santo Domingo offered to engage in similar contraband trade by establishing business arrangements with willing and viable partners, regardless of origin, religion, or nation. The ability of Pedro de los Reyes to transform his captivity in England into a successful commercial enterprise speaks of the capacity of Hispaniola residents to reinvent their isolation from Spanish legal commercial circuits into economic opportunity. At the same time, the complicity that Governor Balboa and *visitador* Ubilla had with Pedro de los Reyes, despite their efforts to substantiate the case against Pimentel, reveals that they had no real moral qualms about the practice of smuggling, but they instead jumped at the opportunity of benefitting themselves from such deals if the conditions were propitious.

The archival trail reveals very little of Pimentel's time in Spain. Once in Sevilla, he was taken to the prison, but he was soon transferred to Madrid where he was allowed access to the city. What the sources reveal is that on

---

[86] Case against Pedro de los Reyes. It also includes parts of the *juicio de residencia* against Governor Juan Balboa. 1669. AGI, Escribanía, 7B.

"Prime Mover of All Machinations" 217

September 10, 1661, after only a few months in Spain, the Council of the Indies gave Rodrigo Pimentel a full pardon for all his crimes. The Council took into consideration the ten months he spent imprisoned in Santo Domingo, the honors and merits he had accumulated over thirty years, including the letters of recommendation that different governors had written for him, and even the post of lieutenant governors he occupied under interim governor Melgarejo in the late 1640s. The pardon also mentioned the situation of need in which his family had been left in his absence, and more importantly, it details how Pimentel gave the crown 7,000 *pesos* in silver as a service to the crown. The language of the document implies that this money was a donation and not a purchase of his pardon, but it seems clear that one could have never happened without the other.[87]

Even before acquiring his pardon, Pimentel did not waste any time planning his return to Santo Domingo. While in Madrid, he had himself ordained in minor orders within the Catholic church, thus placing himself under ecclesiastical jurisdiction and protecting himself from any future prosecution in a royal court.[88] He also had the chance to meet and gain the trust of the newly minted governor to Santo Domingo, Pedro de Carvajal, as well as the new archbishop Francisco de la Cueva Maldonado, and it seems that he helped fund their transatlantic trip. He arrived in Santo Domingo in December 1661, only three months after the new governor and archbishop, and was received "with great applause." He then retired to his lands near the river Jayna to fulfill a four-month exile that the Council of the Indies had imposed onto him.[89]

During his exile, he was visited by many, including the new governor and archbishop, who stayed with him for three days, thus proving once again the close relationship existing between them. It is clear that both former governor Balboa and *visitador* Ubilla saw themselves threatened by Pimentel's new friends, so they started their own epistolary campaign against Pimentel and the new arrivals. Balboa pointed out to royal ministers how "in the house of the archbishop, there is not a door

---

[87] Pimentel's pardon is in AGI, SD. 88, R. 3, and also in AGI, Escribanía, 23C, *pieza* 8.

[88] Back in Santo Domingo, he even bought himself a chaplaincy worth 6,000 *pesos*, which he occupied in July 1662. AGI, Escribanía, 23C.

[89] This exile is not specified in the pardon I found, which was probably a draft. The exile might have been added to the final version as a measure to ensure that Pimentel would not retaliate against former Governor Balboa and *visitador* Ubilla, who were in the process of leaving the island.

218   *Islanders and Empire*

opened for those who do not follow Rodrigo Pimentel's flag" and that everything was perceived in terms of factions: the Balboa faction and the Pimentel faction.[90] Meanwhile, the archbishop defended himself and the new governor accusing both Balboa and Ubilla of lying:

> Everything that Don Juan de Balboa and Don Sancho de Ubilla write and do is false and those lies and everything they accomplish are schemes so that their wrong-doings are not known and the truth remains hidden to Your Majesty. Two demons could not have gathered forces and be more opposed to the service of God and Your Majesty ... Don Rodrigo Pimentel does not have more influence over this president [Carvajal] than any other *vecino* in this city. Of that I am witness.[91]

These testimonies reveal the extreme polarization of the city's population into these two rival groups. All newcomers, including governors and archbishops, were forced to take sides and join a faction, at the very least as an act of self-preservation, and, quite possibly, as a path for wealth and promotion out of the island.

While in his lands, Pimentel also started preparing to take his revenge. He asked the *visitador* Ubilla, who was still on the island, for a copy of the proceedings against him so he could have a complete list of the people who testified against him, and upon Ubilla's negative response, he procured the copy through his contacts in the *Audiencia*. Once in possession of the proceedings, he started a campaign of lawsuits, which enjoyed considerable success as a consequence of his influence over the *Audiencia*. Some of his enemies, especially those in the middle and lower ranks of the island elite like Salvador de Caceda or Diego de Salazar, spent more than four years in prison or under house arrest. He also used intimidation as a tool against his rivals. The physician Pedro de Sandoval, who also testified against Pimentel, received so many threats that he left the island and went to live in Campeche. Pimentel also filed lawsuits against his most powerful enemies such as Damian del Castillo Vaca, the Garabito brothers, and those

---

[90] "No hay puerta abierta en casa del arzobispo para los que no siguen la bandera de don Rodrigo Pimentel." Juan de Balboa to the Council of the Indies. September 16, 1662. AGI, SD. 62, R. 2, n. 20. It is of note that while Balboa named the faction he belonged to as his faction, he named his enemy faction after Pimentel, not after the new governor of the archbishop.

[91] "Todo lo que escriben y actúan don Juan de Balboa y don Sancho de Ubilla es falso y ese embuste y todo cuanto obran es cavilaciones para que sus malos procedimientos (si consiguen confusión) no se conozcan como son y se oculte la verdad a Vuestra Majestad. Dos demonios no pudieron hacernos aquí mayor batería ni oponerse más al servicio de Dios y de Vuestra Majestad. Todo lo que hemos escrito a Vuestra Majestad es verdad y lo juro por mis órdenes ... don Rodrigo Pimentel no tiene más entrada con el presidente de la que tiene otro cualquiera vecino de esta ciudad, de que soy buen testigo." Archbishop Francisco de la Cueva Maldonado to the Council of the Indies. September 12, 1663. AGI, Escribanía, 12A.

"*Prime Mover of All Machinations*" 219

who spearheaded the efforts to condemn him. The *fiscal* of the *Audiencia,* however, pointed out to Governor Carvajal the state of disarray that the island might fall into if those lawsuits prospered, so it seems that at least those lawsuits were rejected by the *Audiencia.*[92]

Many Santo Domingo residents wrote letters to Madrid complaining of Pimentel's attacks, but, as in most previous cases, it took the Council of the Indies several years to react. In 1668, the crown sent Rodrigo Navarro to Santo Domingo as a judge to investigate other abuses committed by Pimentel and Governor Carvajal, to execute the *residencia* of Juan Balboa, and to finish some of the cases that *visitador* Ubilla left pending after his death in 1665. Navarro applied himself with surgical efficiency, and in three months completed his assigned tasks. He confirmed the authenticity of the letters sent from the island and asserted the veracity of most of their claims about Pimentel's attacks, his control over the political institutions, the legal and illegal trade of the island, and the polarized climate existing amongst the elites of Santo Domingo.[93]

Nevertheless, it does not seem that Navarro's findings had any effect in sparking a response by the crown. This lack of a reaction might have been due to Pimentel's new status as a clergymen. This is what archbishop Francisco de la Cueva made clear in a letter to the Council, pointing out that Navarro's proceedings went against the ecclesiastical jurisdiction that Pimentel was subject to as a member of the clergy.[94] In any case, Rodrigo Pimentel remained undisturbed in Santo Domingo as a very wealthy man until his death in 1683.[95] In his last two decades of life, he continued taking advantage of opportunities to engage in smuggling activities and influence the *Audiencia* to his benefit. It also seems that concerns about the afterlife and the salvation of his soul might have led him to become a generous patron of the convent of Santa Clara, where he served as a *mayordomo* for a great part of his life. Near the end of his life, he restored the church and arranged for it to be his final resting place. Pimentel placed a plaque in the floor near the altar and included a self-aggrandizing, but probably false, family coat of arms in memory of his contribution. He also added an unusual inscription: "*Timeti Diem Ludicis,*" which translates literally as "fear the day of the judge." During his lifetime, there was not a judge that Pimentel could not buy

[92] AGI, Escribanía, 23C.

[93] Navarro's proceedings are in AGI, Escribanía, 12A, 12B, and 12C.

[94] Letter of archbishop Francisco de la Cueva Maldonado to the Council of the Indies. July 19, 1667. AGI, Escribanía, 12C.

[95] His death certificate can be found in the Archivo General de la Archidiócesis de Santo Domingo, Libro de Entierros 1666–1701, 124v.

FIGURE 5.2 Rodrigo Pimentel's self-aggrandizing plaque. Convent of Santa Clara, Santo Domingo. Photo by the author.

or avoid. At the end of his life, he seemed to be preparing to meet the only judge whose ruling he would not be able to evade (see Figure 5.2).[96]

After his death, his testament revealed that he had left money for every church on the island and paid for a new altarpiece for the cathedral. Many convents in Santo Domingo received donations, especially the convent of Santa Clara to which he bequeathed 20,000 *pesos*, forgave a similar amount that the congregation owed him in past loans, and left twelve dowries for nuns of 1,000 *pesos* each. One year after his death, in a letter to the Council of the Indies, the archbishop of Santo Domingo Fray Domingo de Navarrete said of him:

He was always, my Lord, a father of his native land and a great server of Your Majesty, and to your treasury loaned over 55,000 *pesos* without interests. Today everyone misses him. He did good to everyone, especially his followers, of whom he did not lack. I wish Your Majesty had many don Rodrigos here and everywhere. His talents and gifts were the biggest in the world.[97]

Pimentel's wealth and influence did have a considerable impact in his great network of relatives, clients, and dependents, which included people

---

[96] Many thanks to Kelly Shannon-Henderson for her help with this translation.
[97] "Fue siempre, Señor, padre de la patria y gran servidor de Vuestra Majestad, en cuyas reales casas llego a tener de 55,000 *pesos* arriba prestados sin intereses alguno. Hoy le echan todos de menos. A sus mismos émulos, que no le faltaban, hacía bien. Ojalá tuviera Vuestra Majestad aquí y en todas partes muchos Don Rodrigos. El talento y capacidad, la mayor del mundo."

"Prime Mover of All Machinations" 221

of all condition and rank. Since Pimentel never married or had a known legitimate heir, he probably divided part of his wealth among his relatives. Governor Andrés de Robles, writing in 1684 about the poverty that the island experienced, noted that the needs he observed in the population

> were not experienced until recent years (or so I am informed), and its origin is not the death of the Archbishop (although he is missed for other purposes) but the death ... of Rodrigo Pimentel, whose wealth and piety covered all miseries ... because there was not a secular or religious public work that Rodrigo Pimentel did not manage. And now that his wealth has been divided among many after his death, it is useless and fruitless for everyone.[98]

Pimentel's vast wealth, accumulated throughout decades of deals with countless ministers, foreign and national merchants, and residents from all the corners of the Greater Caribbean, and the Atlantic, vanished along with the man who amassed it.

A PATRONAGE-BASED ECONOMY

During the seventeenth century, local groups in Santo Domingo had to find ways to combat the commercial isolation that the island experienced from Spanish legal circles. Rodrigo Pimentel's life and exploits are representative of some of the strategies that Spanish Caribbean residents developed in order to maintain and increase their position of preeminence in society. In the process, they heavily influenced the daily functions of royal institutions and bent them to their will and interests. Although the degree of success that Pimentel experienced in his dealings with governors, *oidores*, and merchants was greater than any other local resident in Santo Domingo, and maybe in most of the Spanish Caribbean, his strategies to cultivate the friendship of local officials were not different from those used by his rivals. More than ever before, local networks redoubled their efforts in attracting the friendship and influence of crown officials, particularly the governor of Santo Domingo and the members of the *Audiencia*.

Archbishop Fray Domingo de Navarrete to the Council of the Indies. June 28, 1684. AGI, SD. 93, R. 6, n. 260.

[98] "Es cierto que este género de necesidades no se han experimentado hasta estos años (según estoy informado) y no procede tanto de la falta del arzobispo (si bien la hace muy grande para otros fines) sino de haber muerto ... Rodrigo Pimentel, cuyo caudal y piedad cubría todas estas miserias ... pues apenas hay obra pública y sagrada o profana que no la haya hecho D. Rodrigo Pimentel, cuyo caudal dividido entre muchos con su muerte ha quedado inútil y sin fruto para todos." Governor Andrés de Robles to the Council of the Indies. April 24, 1688. AGI, SD. 65, R. 4, n. 121.

222 *Islanders and Empire*

Pimentel's close ties to these officials allowed him to influence the decisions of the court in cases pertaining to the entire Caribbean region, which in turn, provided him with the coin and contacts that he used for his own commercial operations. Pimentel struck deals with different governors who allowed him exclusively to introduce contraband goods within the city of Santo Domingo and to control the markets in the city. For long periods of time, his operations also had the blessings of the *Cabildo* of Santo Domingo, controlled by his relatives and allies, and the Ecclesiastical hierarchy, influenced by his brother the Dean of the local church and other close friends. Closeness to the governor allowed him access to the *situado*, which he used to finance many of his commercial ventures.

The isolation of Santo Domingo from the rest of the Spanish territories and the relatively negligible importance of Hispaniola in the minds of crown officials in Spain allowed its residents to operate with almost complete impunity. As we saw, however, the actions of these local elites had a ripple effect on events beyond the island shores, in the rest of the Caribbean, and throughout the Atlantic. This relative marginality of Hispaniola, at least in the mind of colonial administrators in Madrid, became the main vehicle for political and economic ascension for those fortunate few who could rely on a strong network of relatives and associates on the island. The collaboration of the island officials, and specifically the governor as the most powerful individual of the colony, varied according to the individual in command. With every new governor or *oidor,* new negotiations were required from the local machinery to incorporate the governor into its network. In many ways, during this period, Santo Domingo became a patronage-based economy, in which residents competed for the social and political affection of a very limited pool of crown officials.

Ironically, the presence in Santo Domingo of royal institutions of power, such as the governor and the *Audiencia* in no way deterred the rise of powerful contraband networks; the presence of these institutions was precisely the reason why these networks became so powerful. The close interaction between the local and royal institutional spheres reveal that a study of *Audiencias* across Spanish America must be done in parallel with the local society where these high courts resided. Local patronage networks routinely infiltrated these institutions and incorporated their members into their own cliques, thus redirecting the influence and power of these institutions to serve local interests. Pimentel's life and exploits show that the *Audiencia* continued serving the interest of the Spanish Monarchy, but only insofar as those did not clash with local interests or those of the *Audiencia*'sa members.

6

Neighbors, Rivals, and Partners: Non-Spaniards and the Rise of Saint-Domingue

The residents of the Spanish town of Santiago de los Caballeros were hardly surprised when, in 1690, a French force of 900 men was seen entering the northern region of Hispaniola and heading in the direction of their small city. When the Spanish lookout stationed near Santiago saw the advancing French, they informed the commander of Hispaniola's northern forces Antonio Pichardo de Vinuesa, who raised the city in arms. He called for reinforcements from nearby Spanish towns and readied the defenses. Once on the outskirts of town, the French soldiers sent a message to the Spanish troops: no harm would befall the townspeople of Santiago as long as they swore loyalty to the king of France. If they refused, they would suffer a merciless attack. Pichardo quickly assembled a force of 600 men, many of them likely of African descent. Then the commander evacuated the city, gathered all the captains in a military council and ordered them to surround the town and let the enemy enter without opposition, thus allowing the French to wreak havoc and destroy a great number of houses. The commander clearly intended to avoid a direct confrontation with the French, as well as the bloodshed and death of Santiago's small population.[1]

Two captains, however, requested to go out and ambush the enemy as they approached Santiago, and they were allowed to do so. The Spanish offensive was very successful, killing over eighty French soldiers. In its aftermath, it was rumored that as the Spanish forces attacked, some

---

[1] Governor Ignacio Pérez Caro to the Council of the Indies. August 6, 1690. AGI, SD. 65, R. 6, n. 215; *Oidor* Fernando de Araujo Rivera to the Council of the Indies. April 24, 1691. AGI, SD. 65, R. 7, n. 229.

224 *Islanders and Empire*

French soldiers had shouted "Treason! Treason!" in a clear reference that there had been a pact between the invading force and some local residents. Another rumor held that the attack had resulted from the debts that Pedro Morel de Santa Cruz, Antonio Pichardo's nephew, along with Morel's business associates, had incurred in their dealings with French merchants.[2]

Pedro Morel, who had been absent from Santiago, returned there from Santo Domingo the same afternoon as the attack. He had just been promoted to the military rank of *maestre de campo* by the governor in the capital. According to the information received later in Santo Domingo, everyone expected that Morel would convince his uncle Pichardo to organize a force to pursue the French and attack them as they withdrew, "thus eradicating the reputation he had accumulated during the period of peace in that city [Santiago] and this one [Santo Domingo] of a great merchant with the French."[3] Instead, his first act was to gather all the captains to inform them of his new rank and ensure their obedience. Next, he chastised the men who participated in the ambush against the French troops and did everything he could to tarnish their performance in the field. In addition to this, Morel secured a letter signed by the *Cabildo* of Santiago that requested the removal of the town of Santiago to another part of the island due to its proximity to French territory. Such a petition was interpreted by the governor and the members of the *Audiencia* of Santo Domingo in the capital as scandalous, an abhorrent and clear capitulation of the territory to French settlers. The two captains responsible for the attacks against the French, however, claimed that "they wanted to live there, they would, and they would defend their land to the death."[4]

The response of the military leaders of Santiago to the French attack baffled Ignacio Pérez Caro, the governor of Santo Domingo. He dispatched to Santiago a canon of the cathedral of Santo Domingo, a close friend of Pedro Morel, to convince the residents to rebuild their houses and resettle. It was also rumored that the canon received much of the merchandise that Morel bought from the French merchants and went on to sell (possibly through enslaved Africans and other allies) in Santo

---

[2] Ibid.
[3] "desvaneciendo por este medio el crédito que en tiempo de paces tenía de gran comerciante con dichos franceses así en aquella ciudad [Santiago] como en esta [Santo Domingo]." *Oidor* Fernando de Araujo Rivera to the Council of the Indies. April 24, 1691. AGI, SD. 55, R. 20, n. 126.
[4] "que allí querían y habían de vivir y defender el lugar hasta morir." Ibid.

Domingo. Eventually, the governor himself traveled in person to Santiago to investigate the attack and its aftermath. Pedro Morel and the *Cabildo* of Santiago apologized for writing the letter, and Antonio Pichardo was removed from his post as general of the Spanish forces in the north of the island.[5]

The actions of the local military leadership in Santiago and the events that surrounded the 1690 French attack of the city of Santiago raise numerous questions regarding the relationship of French and Spanish residents of Hispaniola during the last decades of the seventeenth century and the role Spanish residents played in the implementation of Spanish imperial policy in Hispaniola during these years, which proved to be crucial for the future of the island as well as the Caribbean region as a whole. The behavior of Pedro Morel and the captains who participated in the ambush against the French troops represents two extremes in Spanish attitudes toward the French in Hispaniola throughout the last two decades of the seventeenth century. In this chapter, I argue that, during the final decades of the 1600s, French and Spanish residents in Hispaniola had developed a deeply ambivalent yet fluid relationship that ranged from open violence to collaboration in their daily dealings. By the end of the century, however, Spanish residents on the island, especially in the north, came to rely on French merchants and settlers, who provided Hispaniola residents with a modicum of economic prosperity that legal (and illegal) Spanish traders operating in Santo Domingo could only provide at much higher prices and in limited quantities. I also argue that the rise of the intercolonial trade between both sides of the island happened as the efforts of the Spanish crown to eliminate French settlements from Hispaniola also increased. The participation of Spanish local residents in the war effort allowed them to manipulate the Spanish offensive and foil the imperial objective of consolidating Spanish control over all of Hispaniola. Residents of Hispaniola played a direct role in ruining Spanish imperial plans for the island, thus choosing the commercial benefits of accommodation to the neighboring French presence, despite the risks, instead of a safe reunification under Spanish control that would once again commercially isolate them.

In order to explain the relationship between Hispaniola residents with non-Spaniards in the frontier regions, this chapter first examines their relationship with those foreigners who lived among them. Non-Spaniards who tried, or managed, to establish residency in the city of Santo Domingo

---

[5] Ibid.

226   *Islanders and Empire*

appear to have aroused the mistrust of some royal authorities and neighbors. Despite such suspicions, many peoples not born in Spanish territories called Hispaniola their home. They participated in the life of the colony and its defense, and for the most part, their birthplace was rarely held against them by their neighbors, which hints at a higher degree of tolerance and even acceptance of foreigners than many official documents might indicate. If, as Stuart B. Schwartz has pointed out, certain religious tolerance existed in daily practice in Iberian societies and colonies across the globe, a certain level of social and cultural tolerance was certainly possible, and even desirable, in the Spanish Caribbean borderlands.[6] The horizontal ties – that is, the relations that these individuals developed with their neighbors (as opposed to the vertical ties individuals established with royal officials and institutions) – were a much more significant factor in their inclusion in local communities than their birthplace. Decisions of inclusion or exclusion were based on an individual's case, and under certain conditions, a person's belonging to a given community could be called into question. An individual's relations in the community played a crucial role in determining his or her worth to the local society. As Tamar Herzog has shown in her work on the construction of local communities in the early Spanish world, "categories of belonging were not embodied in legal definitions or in acts of authority. Instead, they were generated by the ability to use rights or to be forced to comply with duties." Under such conditions, the lack of protests among local or royal authorities about the rights of certain individuals enjoying local rights and their willingness to perform their duties implied consent. Circumstances might change, however, and the general agreement about someone's status could be questioned subsequently.[7] In Hispaniola, when such inquiries about a longtime resident arose, it was not due to local doubts about the person's belonging to the community, but rather to personal disputes in which this person's origin was used as a weapon. On other occasions, royal officials, imbued with a legalistic sense of their role in relation to the local community, tried to enforce royal policy, even though the community at large remained silent, and therefore unprovoked by the individual's place of origin before becoming a resident.

---

[6] Stuart B. Schwartz, *All Can Be Saved: Religious Tolerance and Salvation in the Iberian Atlantic World* (New Haven: Yale University Press, 2008).

[7] Tamar Herzog, *Defining Nations. Immigrants and Citizens in Early Modern Spain and Spanish America* (New Haven: Yale University Press, 2003), 4.

Neighbors, Rivals, and Partners

In the western borderlands, the dynamic with European newcomers followed a different pattern. During the second half of the seventeenth century, as foreigners settled the unpopulated western parts of the island and moved east, both royal officials and residents were united in their fear of what these encroachments on Spanish lands might mean for the stability and safety of Hispaniola's residents. These settlements, occupied mostly by free and indentured French people, as well as an increasing number of enslaved Africans, appeared throughout the western coasts of Hispaniola at a time when natural disasters and disease prevented the population growth of the Spanish colony, which heightened the sense of the settlement's fragility among Spanish officials. Despite the risks, some local inhabitants were willing to deal with the French when pressing needs arose. The periods of peace between the Spanish and French monarchies also reverberated across every corner of Hispaniola and led to a more harmonious coexistence between French and Spanish peoples, with increasing commercial exchange. The Spanish residents in the northern city of Santiago sold cattle and hides to French residents and merchants, and in exchange, they received clothing as well as other much-needed supplies, and quite possibly, enslaved Africans.

Although crown officials on the island struggled to keep foreign incursions at bay and to limit the interactions of Hispaniola residents with foreigners, they also associated with non-Spaniards constantly, thus blurring the line between what constituted legally and socially acceptable behavior. In some isolated cases, such as the Irish, royal officials allowed certain associations on the grounds that the island was in dire need of military personnel, and these foreigners were Catholic, making them brothers in faith seeking refuge from Protestant oppression. In the second half of the seventeenth century, a radical realignment in the European alliances allowed royal officials in Santo Domingo to justify expanded contacts and diplomatic relations with certain English and Dutch officials and merchants based on the fact that their countries of origin were at peace with the Spanish monarchy. Officially, royal representatives did not allow the residents of Hispaniola to have contact with any foreigners, friend or foe. The reality, however, was very different. The presence of these foreigners in Santo Domingo and other parts of the island only increased the willingness of local residents to do business with them. For Hispaniola locals who were mostly concerned about their own social and economic survival and well-being, doctrinal criteria for who was an appropriate trading partner proved to be irrelevant, particularly as European alliances shifted and the economic circumstances in Hispaniola worsened in the second half of the century.

228   *Islanders and Empire*

PORTUGUESE RESIDENTS IN SANTO DOMINGO

Throughout Santo Domingo's early history, people considered to be foreigners had always been present as permanent residents of the city. Local residents were used to having non-Spaniards as neighbors and partners in their daily lives. Portuguese people had resided in Santo Domingo even before the union of the crowns under Felipe II in 1580.[8] Some of them were direct descendants of the Portuguese immigrants and merchants who settled in Hispaniola during the sixteenth century, and Santo Domingo was the only home they had ever known. Other members of the Portuguese nation continued traveling the Atlantic looking for economic opportunities and arrived in Santo Domingo during the seventeenth century seeking jobs as soldiers in the garrison, overseers, or merchants.[9] The Portuguese rebellion in 1640s limited the free movement that Portuguese peoples had enjoyed throughout the Spanish American colonies, but it in no way completely eliminated it. Starting in 1641 in Santo Domingo, as everywhere else in the Spanish Indies, it became crown policy that Portuguese ships were no longer welcome, and any Portuguese person who could not prove long-time residence (*naturaleza*) was forced to leave the island. Writing as a body, the *Audiencia* of Santo Domingo reported that people of Portuguese descent were informed of the new laws, while those without properties or ties to the community either left the island or joined the garrison as soldiers, thus limiting their mobility and placing them under the close supervision. The High Court added that in the city, a young Portuguese boy was caught praising the Portuguese uprising, and was therefore punished with 100 lashes in what it was likely intended as an exemplary punishment for all the other Portuguese residents to see.[10]

---

[8] See Chapter 2.

[9] For more on Portuguese merchants and settlers in Santo Domingo and the role they played, see Chapter 1. On the role of the Portuguese nation in the early modern Atlantic economy and in the Spanish world, see Daviken Studnicki-Gizbert, *A Nation Upon the Ocean Sea: Portugal's Atlantic Diaspora and the Crisis of the Spanish Empire, 1492–1640* (New York: Oxford University Press, 2007). Also, see David Wheat, *Atlantic Africa and the Spanish Caribbean* (Chapel Hill: University of North Carolina Press, 2016), 105–18.

[10] It is unclear who actually condemned and punished the boy. The most likely candidate is the *Audiencia*, but local judges (the *alcaldes ordinarios*) might have also been behind it. The *Audiencia* of Santo Domingo to the Council of the Indies. July 19, 1642. AGI, SD. 56, R. 11.

Neighbors, Rivals, and Partners

Even though this new legislation did not affect long-time Portuguese residents directly, their lives became subject to scrutiny by the members of the *Audiencia* concerned about the connections that these residents might have with other Portuguese outside Hispaniola and the possibility of a locally supported invasion. One of those residents who aroused the concern of royal officials was Antonio Cuello, who was born on the Portuguese island of Madeira and who arrived in Santo Domingo in 1617 as a soldier of the garrison. That same year, he managed to get himself discharged by finding a substitute to replace him. He became a merchant and soon had a sizable estate (estimated at near 40,000 *ducados*), married a local woman, Sabina Jiménez, and had three sons and three daughters. In 1643, *oidor* Pedro Luis de Salazar started an investigation against Cuello, who in 1637 had been granted a royal license to gather construction materials to encourage the building of ships in Hispaniola. The fact that he was able to procure such a permit speaks of Cuello's connection to the island's important merchant network.[11] Cuello had built a 300-ton vessel, the *San José y la Inmaculada Concepción*, which was ready to depart for Sevilla by the time that *oidor* Salazar started his inquiry. The *oidor* was concerned that Cuello had hidden the fact he was Portuguese to acquire the permit. Also, he protested that the sailors of Cuello's ship were all Portuguese and Dutch passing for Irish. Inspections of the ship ensued, but all the merchandise of the ship happened to be in order, the sailors were deemed to be actual Irish Catholics, the eight Portuguese sailors (out of a crew of forty-two) on board had royal grants, and the only two other foreigners were a sailor from Nice and another from Ghent. Cuello seemed to have survived this scrutiny.[12]

Salazar then continued to make inquiries about Cuello's origins in Madeira and claimed that, despite being a powerful man, Cuello had held low jobs such as tavern-keeper and shopkeeper (*pulpero*). The pettiness of these accusations, as well as the surviving documentation of the case, shows that Salazar might have been unofficially representing the interests of prominent residents of the island who opposed Cuello's pursuits and possibly resented his success. It seemed that Cuello's quest for

---

[11] For a diagram showing Santo Domingo as part of a vast network of Portuguese merchants crisscrossing Spanish America and Europe in 1630s, see Studnicki-Gizbert, *A Nation Upon the Ocean Sea*, 103.

[12] Complaints of *oidor* Pedro Luis de Salazar about Antonio Cuello. November 10, 1643. AGI, SD. 22, n. 19.

230 *Islanders and Empire*

quality woods for his ships brought him in direct conflict with some landholders, among them, the *regidor* Francisco de Castro Rivera, who owned lands and a sugar mill on the outskirts of the city. It is possible that these residents convinced Salazar to spearhead the accusations against Cuello using his Portuguese birth and his alleged low status to cast aspersions on his loyalty and his business dealings. It is even more likely that Salazar had his own reasons for harassing Cuello. According to many witnesses in Cuello's defense, the *oidor* owed about 200 *pesos* to Cuello's son-in-law, Captain Baltasar de Alfaro, who presented a lawsuit against him to the *alcalde ordinario*.[13] Salazar may have resented this move, which aired his pecuniary woes in public, and, possibly as a reprisal, accused Cuello of wrongdoing.

Further evidence of Cuello's good relations with a number of local residents was the fact that many of them testified on his behalf, claiming that he was a great contributor to the economic well-being of the city, including his donations to its religious institutions. One such witness was Andrés Tilman, quite possibly an Englishman, who apparently did not fear reprisal for testifying in favor of Cuello. According to the *fiscal* of the *Audiencia* Francisco de Alarcón y Coronado, Cuello should have been rewarded for his entrepreneurial spirit, and he wished that for his trade in local products, "we had ... in the city half a dozen of Portuguese Cuellos like him. This way, trade in the city would flourish, its citizens would be richer, and Your Majesty better served and honored."[14] Given the shortage of vessels arriving in Santo Domingo, merchants like Cuello, regardless of their origin, were a lifeline for many local landholders who wanted to ship their products to Spain, many of whom were happy to have him as a neighbor. In this case, as in many others, Cuello's Portuguese ancestry had nothing to do with the accusations brought against him. Instead, political, economic, and personal relations took center stage. Formal accusations brought to the authorities based on foreign ancestry were generally rooted on personal differences and used to exploit both real and imagined fears of sedition and invasion.

In 1650, as rumors surfaced in Santo Domingo of a Portuguese attack on Buenos Aires (which never happened), and of the expulsion of all the Portuguese serving in the military in Mexico, some members

---

[13] Ibid.

[14] "ojalá, Señor, tuviéramos para esto en esta ciudad media docena de Cuellos portugueses como él, que con eso estuviera su comercio más tratable, sus vecinos más ricos, y Su Majestad más interesado y servido." Ibid.

of the *Audiencia* of Santo Domingo contemplated the possibility of doing the same in Hispaniola, as well as removing the Portuguese citizens of Santo Domingo to the interior to avoid any possible contact with outsiders. The *Audiencia*, however, was divided on the issue. Some judges believed that some of the Portuguese residents had lived peacefully on the island for a long time, held properties and family, and had never behaved in a way that made them suspect of seditious acts. Instead of removing them to the interior, these judges believed that keeping them in the city and treating them well was the best way to secure their loyalty. Although a final decision was postponed until the Council of the Indies delivered its opinion, as we saw in the previous chapter, Juan Melgarejo, acting as interim governor, discharged all the Portuguese soldiers who were serving in the garrison of Santo Domingo.[15] Two years later, with the arrival of a new governor, the same thirty-one Portuguese soldiers who were discharged were reinstated in their posts, possibly due to the lack of men to replace them, but also because they were deemed to pose no risk to the security of the city.[16] The internal debates within the *Audiencia* reveal that for some royal officials, even during times of war, an individual's place of origin did not dictate his loyalties. In most cases, the decisions against foreigners by local officials were part of the belief that being inflexible would gain them credit in the eyes of the crown. That is precisely what Juan Melgarejo did when in 1652 he petitioned to be given a post of *oidor* in Castilla, and among his merits, highlighted the fact that he had "purged the island of Portuguese and foreigners."[17]

The legislation banning new arrivals to Spanish ports reduced the arrival of new Portuguese immigrants to Santo Domingo, but in no way eliminated it. People of Portuguese descent continued crossing the Atlantic as sailors in Spanish and other European vessels, and many of them jumped ship in Spanish Caribbean ports like Santo Domingo, where they sought economic opportunities, married local women, and put down roots.

---

[15] The *Audiencia* of Santo Domingo to the Council of the Indies. March 14, 1650. AGI, SD. 57, R. 2, n. 23.

[16] Alvaro Pimentel to the Council of the Indies. May 12, 1652. AGI, SD. 75, R. 3.

[17] "Purgado la isla de Portugueses y extranjeros." Juan Melgarejo Ponce de León to the Council of the Indies. 1652. AGI, SD. 7, n. 115.

232 *Islanders and Empire*

OTHER NON-SPANISH RESIDENTS

Foreigners arrived in Hispaniola in a multitude of ways. During the early stages of the English expansion in the Caribbean, many Irish people criss-crossed the region either looking to escape the abusive conditions they experienced in the English colonies or simply hoping to improve their fortunes.[18] Some of them settled in Santo Domingo and became long-time residents of the city. This was the case of Juan Morfo, whose original name might have been John Murphy. Morfo was originally a settler on the island of Tortuga in the northwest of Hispaniola (see Figure 6.1), a colony settled by a motley crew of mostly English and French people in the 1620s. Morfo later told the story of how he escaped Tortuga after the English apparently killed his cousin for being a Catholic priest. It is impossible to know if Morfo's story about the death of his cousin is true. The narrative included an ardent defense by Morfo's cousin of the rights of the king of Spain over the island of Tortuga and the authority of the Pope as the head of the church, which fits neatly within the narratives that Irish Catholic indentured servants told in Spanish ports about escaping the hands of their cruel Protestant English overseers and pleading for the protection of their Spanish Catholic brethren.[19]

Morfo escaped to Cartagena, where the governor sent him to Santo Domingo. Once in the city, Morfo persuaded the interim governor of the opportunity that his knowledge of the defenses of Tortuga presented, and in 1635, an expedition of 300 soldiers and local Spanish militia from Santo Domingo conquered the buccaneer fortress of Tortuga, temporarily expelling its residents and capturing some treasure in the process. Morfo accompanied the expedition, performing admirably on the battlefield according to his superiors. Once back in Santo Domingo, Morfo stayed in Santo Domingo as a soldier of the garrison, where he accumulated merits and influenced local

---

[18] For more on the Irish diaspora in the Spanish Atlantic and the Caribbean, see Kristen Block and Jenny Shaw, "Subjects without an Empire: The Irish in the Early Modern Caribbean," *Past and Present*, vol. 210, n. 1 (2011): 33–60. Also, see Jenny Shaw, *Everyday Life in the Early English Caribbean: Irish, Africans, and the Construction of Difference* (Athens: University of Georgia Press, 2013); Natalie A. Zacek, *Settler Society in the English Leeward Islands, 1670–1776* (New York: Cambridge University Press, 2010); Igor Pérez Tostado and Enrique García Hernán, eds. *Irlanda y el Atlántico ibérico: movilidad, participación e intercambio cultural (1580–1830)* (Valencia: Albatros ediciones, 2010); Igor Pérez Tostado, "Por respeto a mi profesión: disciplinamiento, dependencia e identidad en la formación de las comunidades militares irlandesas e inglesas en los ejércitos hispanos," in Enrique García Hernán and Davide Maffi, eds., *Guerra y sociedad en la Monarquía Hispánica. Política, estrategia y cultura en la Europa moderna (1500-1700)* (Madrid: Centro Superior de Investigaciones Científicas, 2006), 681–706.

[19] For the entire memorial, dated in April 30, 1635, see AGI, 1, n. 255.

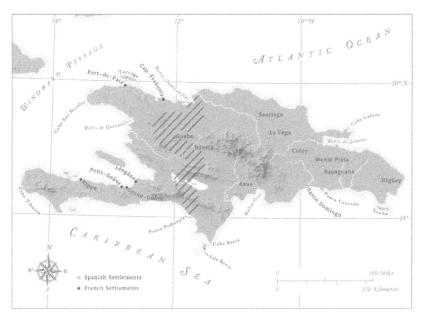

FIGURE 6.1 Main Spanish and French towns and villages of Hispaniola in the 1680s (Alexander Fries, University of Alabama Cartographic Research Laboratory).

affairs throughout his long military career. He fought alongside Spanish forces against the failed English invasion of Santo Domingo in 1655, and ultimately became a knight of the Order of Santiago.[20]

Juan Morfo would not be the last Irishman to attempt to settle in Hispaniola. In 1642, Richard Hackett, with a group of his countrymen, left Barbados and Montserrat looking to escape mistreatment by their English patrons and lords. Hackett and his men, who numbered near 300, settled in a port in northern Hispaniola where Hackett wrote to the governor of Santo Domingo with an emotional account of their travails under the English and asked for his protection and permission to serve the Catholic king. Both the *Cabildo* of Santo Domingo and the governor mistrusted the intentions of the Irish, however, and so they wrote to the Council of the Indies. Even though Hackett was compensated with 200

---

[20] Ibid. Morfo's certificate of knighthood, granted in 1650, is in AGI, Indiferente General, 115, N.28. For another account of Morfo's life and exploits, see Block and Shaw, "Subjects without an Empire," 44–49. Morfo is also mentioned in Kris E. Lane, *Pillaging the Empire: Piracy in the Americas, 1500–1750* (New York: M.E. Sharpe, 1998), 98.

234   *Islanders and Empire*

ducados, the numbers he commanded and his final intentions of settling in Hispaniola appeared suspicious. After a year in Hispaniola, those of Hackett's men who had survived were shipped back to Spain.[21] While Morfo individually had been able to convince the authorities of his good intentions, Hackett and his men posed too much of a threat to the limited defenses of Hispaniola, and his proposition to settle was rejected.

Despite Hackett's failure to persuade royal officials of his good intentions, Morfo's influence might have played a part in facilitating residency for other Irishmen in Santo Domingo. Since death or desertion was common among the soldiers in the garrison in Santo Domingo, the city was always in need of new recruits to augment its numbers. In 1648, the *alcaide* of the fortress in Santo Domingo, Pedro Pujadas complained that "of every four soldiers, three of them are Portuguese, and also the Irish, God only knows if they really are [Irish]. There are about nine or ten and they come and go into this fortress."[22] The *oidor* Francisco de Montemayor, writing in 1653, also reported that "on the entire island there are a great number of Irishmen, or so they claim, since it is not easy to ascertain the truth. They find the support of Juan Morfo ... and another soldier of this garrison who calls them Irish. I believe many of them pass [as Irish] without being so."[23] For both Pujadas and Montemayor, the impossibility of confirming that those claiming to be Irish soldiers were indeed Irish, and not English spies, seemed to have aroused a great degree of anxiety. Pujadas, himself a soldier seasoned in European battlegrounds, seemed to believe that those he saw as foreign mercenaries could not be trusted with the security of a Spanish fortress. Montemayor's dislike for the so-called Irish was rooted, first and foremost, in his deep dislike for Juan Morfo and, secondly, in the fact that there was no way to ensure the real origin or religion professed by these so-called Irish.

Royal officials were more vocal in their fears of treason at the hands of non-Spanish residents than most locals. This attitude was possibly part of their posturing to their superiors in Spain, who firmly believed in the

---

[21] For a complete and detailed account of Hackett's arrival to Hispaniola and the mistrust that generated, see Block and Shaw, 38–44.

[22] "Asimismo hay con plaza de soldados de cuatro partes las tres de portugueses, y en nombre de irlandeses, que sabe Dios si lo son, hay unos nueve o diez y estos entran en esta fuerza de guardia." *Alcaide* Pedro Pujadas Beaumonte to the Council of the Indies. October 20, 1648. AGI, SD. 7, n. 91.

[23] "En toda la isla hay sobrada cantidad de irlandeses que dicen serlo, y como no es fácil ajustar la verdad, y hallan apoyo en don Juan Morfo ... y en otro soldado que también sirve en él de esta nación que los califica por irlandeses. Juzgo que pasan muchos por tales sin serlo." Francisco de Montemayor y Cuenca to the Council of the Indies. December 14, 1653. AGI, SD 57, R. 6, n. 79.

necessity of keeping foreigners away from Spanish colonies. Local residents rarely complained about the presence of foreigners living in the city, even though there is ample evidence of their continued residency in Santo Domingo and other towns of the island with the complicity of their neighbors. In 1653, Juan Morfo, under the governor's orders, made an inspection of the city of Santiago and detained Nicolás Romero, a French silversmith who resided in the town. A carpenter called Juan Rodríguez, from Poland, also lived with Romero. Both of them seemed to have changed their names as a way to blend into local society. After their arrest, their properties were confiscated, and when asked who should keep them while the inquiries took place, Romero designated the *alcalde ordinario* of Santiago as his depository to keep all his possessions.[24] This case reveals, first of all, that Juan Morfo, despite being a foreigner, was trusted by some royal officials to carry out important assignments far from Santo Domingo where his activities could not be easily monitored. The fact that both Romero and Rodríguez were foreigners could not have passed unnoticed by other residents in Santiago. The men lived and interacted peacefully and productively with their Spanish neighbors, who did not seem to care about their birthplace. When troubled by the royal authorities, Rodríguez relied on local neighbors for help and support, just like any other resident would.

On March 24, 1640, Juan Morfo, always in touch with foreign residents and merchants in Santo Domingo, sent a written message to Governor Juan Bitrián about a conversation that he had with two Englishmen by the house of a Captain Limbres.[25] One of the Englishmen asked Morfo why there were so many people in arms in the streets of Santo Domingo, and Morfo replied it might be due to a sighting of enemy ships. The other Englishman replied that "the enemy" was not coming to Santo Domingo, but to a different port on the depopulated north of the island.[26] The complete normalcy with which this conversation took place, the fact that the Englishmen were not detained, and that Morfo was confident enough in his actions to report the conversation to Governor Juan Bitrián, points at how ordinary the presence of foreigners was in Santo Domingo.

---

[24] Inquiries conducted by Juan Morfo for Governor Andrés Pérez Franco in Santiago de los Caballeros. Initial date, April 30, 1654. AGI, SD. 58, R. 1, n. 11

[25] Captain Limbres' rank seems to indicate that he was either a soldier of the fortress or a captain of a merchant ship, though it is not entirely clear from the sources. Note from Juan Morfo to Governor Juan Bitrián, May 24, 1640. AGI, SD. 55, R. 20, n. 126.

[26] Ibid.

236 *Islanders and Empire*

Governor Bitrián was often accused of having allowed foreign ships to enter the port of Santo Domingo to trade. In fact, some members of the local elites were so happy with Juan Bitrián's tenure that Rodrigo Pimentel led the *Cabildo* of Santo Domingo into signing a petition addressed to Juan Bitrián's successor and judge in Bitrián's residency trial calling for him to be honored and treated justly. All the *regidores*, except for one, signed the petition.[27] On the other hand, Bitrián was the governor who refused Hackett and his group of Irishmen permission to settle on the island. Also, he often shipped out foreigners whom Spanish troops captured in the unpopulated parts of the island to Spain. These apparently contradictory behaviors likely reflected his attempt to balance his personal commercial interests in foreign trade with his superiors' efforts to manage a colonial possession. Also, the fact that Bitrián openly traded with foreigners did not necessarily mean that he allowed them to roam freely throughout Hispaniola, beyond his supervision.

In 1672, the documents of the Treaty of Madrid between Spain and England (signed in 1670) arrived in Santo Domingo. The governor sent these documents to Jamaica to establish diplomatic relations with the English neighbors. In turn, the Spanish envoy brought back letters written by the governor of Jamaica. In order to translate them, the authorities in Santo Domingo sought the help of Ricardo Ermenzon (perhaps Richard Emmerson?), who is described in the sources as "surgeon and *vecino*," that is, a permanent resident of the city. He managed to translate only part of the document, claiming that the ink was very dark and that "he had not exercised his tongue in over twenty years."[28] This episode shows that government officials selectively chose foreigners to incorporate rather than expel. The fact that Ermenzon's status as *vecino* was not challenged indicated the acceptance of his presence in Santo Domingo. His value as an English speaker, even if it was limited in this particular instance, and as a surgeon, points to the importance that some colonial officials attributed to foreigners as long-term residents on the island.

Life in the Spanish Caribbean borderlands required a certain flexibility in inhabitants and their assessments of the value of residents of non-Spanish birth. The peoples of Hispaniola, regardless of rank or race, saw foreigners living among them as ordinary members of their community, while many peninsular authorities either failed to understand this or

---

[27] Letter of the *Cabildo* of Santo Domingo, February 21, 1646. AGI, SD. 87. R. 3.
[28] "había más de veinte años que [la lengua] no la ejercitaba." January 27, 1672. AGI, SD. 62, R. 5, n. 31.

saw little benefit in expressing it to their superiors in Spain. In Hispaniola, as in many other places in Latin America, a person's belonging to a community was always implied, and it was only in very specific cases that a person's status was questioned.[29] This difference in judgment when thinking about foreigners is clearly represented in a petition made by the ecclesiastical *Cabildo*. In 1643, the religious authorities on the island petitioned the crown for permission to have Alejandro Glut, an English physician, reside on the island due to the lack of doctors.[30] The fact that Glut was already married with children shows that he was not a newcomer to the island. He had probably resided in Santo Domingo for years, and as a doctor he had befriended influential local residents. These people, through the religious institutions of the island, supported Glut's efforts to legalize his situation in Santo Domingo, thus protecting him against any future doubts about his social standing, while demonstrating that his value as a doctor trumped his non-Spanish birthplace.

BUCCANEERS, MARAUDERS, DISEASE, AND DESTRUCTION

While some foreigners who resided in Santo Domingo and other towns of Hispaniola maintained an ordinary relationship with their Spanish neighbors, other outsiders presented a much more direct threat. The arrival of northern European settlers to the island of Tortuga, and later to the mainland, forced Spanish residents of Hispaniola to defend their properties and land from encroachment. As explained in Chapter 3, the Spanish crown forcefully removed the Spanish population living in the lands of western Hispaniola during the depopulations (1604–6) to prevent them from dealing with northern European merchants and to protect the islanders from Protestant influence. In the decades that followed, as English and French settlers started to populate the Lesser Antilles, they also landed on the northern coast of Hispaniola, settling in temporary encampments where they hunted, living off the land and possibly planting small quantities of tobacco.[31] By the 1630s, these people, popularly known as

---

[29] Herzog, *Defining Nations*, 44.
[30] The Ecclesiastic *Cabildo* of the Archdiocese of Santo Domingo to the Council of the Indies. October 16, 1643. AGI, SD. 94, R. 4, n. 100.
[31] Michel Camus, *L'île de la Tortue au coeur de la Flibuste caraïbe* (Paris: L'Harmattan, 1997), 30, 38, 40, 47, 48. Cited in Robert D. Taber, "The Issue of the Union: Family, Law, Politics in Western Saint-Domingue, 1777 to 1789" (Ph.D. dissertation, University of Florida, 2015), 63. My thanks to Dr. Taber for kindly sharing his dissertation with me; Giovanni Venegoni, "Creating a Caribbean Colony in the Long Seventeenth Century:

238 *Islanders and Empire*

buccaneers due to their habit of cooking meat in an Arawak-style grill known as *boucan*, dedicated their time to hunting feral cattle and planting tobacco, which they would in turn take back to the island of Tortuga and sell to European merchants.

Situated at the northwestern tip of Hispaniola, Tortuga became the most important non-Spanish settlement from the 1630s to 1670s. As Tortuga became the organizing center of pirate raids into the Spanish mainland, it also attracted the attention of the Spanish governors in Santo Domingo, who feared foreign encroachment on Spanish territory and property. These so-called trespassers were killing feral cattle that, at least nominally, belonged to the Spanish residents of Hispaniola. In two separate instances, 1635 and 1652, the governors of Santo Domingo organized expeditions to expel the foreigners from Tortuga.[32] They were successful both times, but due to the Spanish inability to garrison Tortuga, or at least to populate the area with Spanish settlers, the French and English peoples who had been expelled from Tortuga soon returned.

By the late 1650s, northern Europeans had become a permanent fixture in the island's depopulated regions. Writing in 1653, a governor of Santo Domingo informed the Council of the Indies that his troops had captured English, Irish, Dutch, and French prisoners during their patrols through western Hispaniola.[33] Earlier that same year, an *oidor* from the *Audiencia* of Santo Domingo reported that, in the two years he had been on the island, fifty-seven foreigners, most of them French, had been apprehended, sent to Santo Domingo, and shipped to the Iberian Peninsula.[34] These prisoners only represented a small sample of those residing in the theoretically depopulated regions. By the middle of the seventeenth century, Hispaniola had become a contested borderland where Spanish authorities struggled to maintain control over their territorial claims while groups of northern Europeans tried to reap benefits from the uneven Spanish control over great parts of the island. This is the implied message in a travel narrative published in London in 1655, in which its author claimed that Hispaniola "is, for the fertility of the Soil, the richest and

---

Saint Domingue and the Pirates," in L. H. Roper, ed., *The Torrid Zone: Caribbean Colonization and Cultural Interaction in the Long Seventeenth Century* (Columbia: University of South Carolina Press, 2018), 145.

[32] As told above, Irishman Juan Morfo was one of the protagonists of 1635 attack.

[33] Governor Andrés Pérez Franco to the Council of the Indies. April 23, 1653. AGI, SD. 57, R. 5, n. 70.

[34] *Oidor* Francisco de Montemayor y Cuenca to the Council of the Indies. December 14, 1653. AGI, SD. 57, R. 5, n. 79.

Neighbors, Rivals, and Partners

most flourishing Countrie (one of them) in the World ... the Meadows and Pastures alwaies green, and of such excellent Herbage, that Cattel both breed and thrive there almost beyond beleef."[35] Such open invitations as this one to exploit the riches of the island may have increased the appeal of places as sparsely populated as Hispaniola at a time in which northern European monarchies were more interested than ever in expanding into the Caribbean at the expense of the Spanish monarchy. The English attack on Santo Domingo in 1655 is but one example of those aspirations, and it served as a powerful reminder to colonial administrators of the imminent and recurring danger that Spanish Caribbean possessions faced during these years.[36]

It was precisely the 1655 English attack that forced Spanish troops stationed in Tortuga since its capture in 1652, to return hurriedly to Santo Domingo, thus allowing French settlers to resume their lives on Tortuga. In the years that followed, the still unofficially French colony of Tortuga flourished. Its population of 900 people in 1660 jumped to 6,500 individuals in 1681 (2,012 of them black and 200 colored). A population estimate for that same year in the Spanish colony placed it at 6,312 individuals, including soldiers from the garrison, enslaved people, and free blacks. Of those, only 2,444 people were labeled as *españoles*, meaning that the rest of the population was comprised of enslaved Africans and free people of color.[37] Even though the Spanish estimates seem rather conservative, there is little doubt that the explosive growth of Tortuga represented a clear threat to the territorial integrity of the Spanish colony, particularly after 1670, with the foundation of Cap-Français on the northwest coast of Hispaniola. That settlement quickly became the most important port in the rising French presence on the island.

---

[35] N. N. Gent, *America: or an exact description of the West Indies: More especially of those provinces which are under the dominion of the king of Spain* (London, printed by Richard Hodgckinsonne for Edward Dod, 1655), 138.

[36] For a description of the 1655 English attack on Santo Domingo as well as the motivations behind it and its aftermath, see Carla Pestana, "English Character and the Fiasco of the Western Design." *Early American Studies: An Interdisciplinary Journal*, vol. 3, n. 1 (2005): 1–31; Carla Pestana, *The English Conquest of Jamaica: Oliver Cromwell's Bid for Empire* (Cambridge: Harvard University Press, 2017).

[37] French population data was extracted from Michel Camus, "Correspondance de Bertrand Ogeron, Gouverneur de l'île de la Tortue et costs de Saint-Domingue au XVIIe siècle." *Revue de la Société Haitienne d'Histoire et de Géographie*, vol. 43, n. 146 (March 1985). Cited in Philip P. Boucher, *France and the American Tropics to 1700: Tropics of Discontent?* (Baltimore: Johns Hopkins University Press, 2008), 238. The Spanish population data is extracted from Fray Domingo de Navarrete, Archbishop of Santo Domingo, to the Council of the Indies, April 30, 1681. AGI, SD. 93, R. 5, n. 241.

240 *Islanders and Empire*

As the French population grew, the Spanish colony faced its own internal troubles. Starting in the 1660s, there were reports of repeated waves of epidemics that devastated the population of Santo Domingo. Already in 1659, Governor Juan de Balboa believed that the city was prone to the spread of leprosy due to the constant contact between the sick and their relatives and their disregard for the advice of the local doctor.[38] The repeated outbreaks of smallpox and measles that ravaged the population throughout the 1660s were much more serious and affected both enslaved and free populations. In 1677, an already debilitated population faced a wave of dysentery that killed what seemed like a significant number of residents, although the testimony of the witnesses does not offer data on the number of deaths. The only numbers available are those offered by the archbishop, who documented the baptism of 638 children and the death of 780 individuals between 1677 and 1681. Therefore, during these years, the city of Santo Domingo had a negative growth rate, which probably also had a serious impact on the city's business and trade. It is unclear whether the waves of disease also affected the countryside and the other villages of the island, although it seems likely that they were spared.[39]

The diseases spreading through Santo Domingo were not limited to humans, but also attacked crops, including the valuable cacao trees. Cacao trees had been introduced in Hispaniola during the 1630s and 1640s as an alternative to the already declining profits of ginger cultivation. Cacao was embraced by the elites and religious institutions as the only viable cash crop and was produced extensively. By the late 1650s, Rodrigo Pimentel was planting a total of 38,000 cacao trees divided across several properties. His enslaved laborers harvested an average of 1,000 *cargas* of cacao annually, which earned him a reported 12,000 *pesos*.[40]

---

[38] Balboa could not know that most people are immune to leprosy, but prolonged close contact with someone with the disease might indeed propagate it among those who are not immune. Juan Balboa Mogrovejo to the Council of the Indies. November 7, 1659. AGI, SD. 58, R. 6, n. 80.

[39] The information regarding the measles and smallpox outbreaks are from February 3, 1669. AGI, SD. 76, R. 1. The report of the dysentery epidemic is contained in a letter of *oidor* Juan de Padilla to the Council of the Indies. August 24, 1677. AGI, 63, R. 3, n. 32, doc. 4. The demographic data comes from a letter by Archbishop Fray Domingo de Navarrete to the Council of the Indies. April 30, 1681. AGI, SD. 93, R. 5, n. 241. The archbishop did not specify how many of the dead were Spanish and how many were people of color, either enslaved or free.

[40] One *carga* amounts approximately to fifty pounds. AGI, Escribanía de Cámara, 22A, fol. 323v.

Planting cacao became a thriving business, and many residents dedicated their lands to its cultivation even if it meant eliminating crops needed for their own subsistence. Writing in 1659, the new governor Juan de Balboa noticed upon his arrival that "the interest in the sale of cacao is so big that local residents have dedicated their haciendas to growing it and they even displaced their lands planted with yuca ... the only bread of this island. ... A while ago hunger spread among the poor, soldiers and the local convents, which they eased eating bananas and other wild fruits."[41] The spread of cacao, while benefiting the pockets of wealthy landowners, appears to have affected the access of poor people to basic foodstuffs like cassava. Wealthy residents, who bought their wheat flour from merchants arriving from Caracas and New Spain, did not have to adjust their diets or go without bread.

In the 1660s, cacao was well on the way to becoming the cash crop that could revitalize the economy of the colony. As early as 1669 and certainly by 1671, such optimistic prospects had vanished. That year, numerous letters from Santo Domingo reported that cacao trees were falling prey to a disease that prevented them from producing fruit and eventually killed them.[42] A look at the tithe collected by the Archdiocese of Santo Domingo during these years seems to indicate this trend. In 1666, the Archdiocese collected almost 13,000 *pesos*. Only three years later, they managed to collect only 4,000 *pesos*.[43] Everyone in the colony, particularly those near the capital, felt the ruin of the cacao similar to that which afflicted the crops of contemporaries in Cuba and Jamaica. The disappearance of the crop interrupted the incipient trade that the port of Santo Domingo had begun to experience due to the cacao bonanza. Most planters were reduced yet again to practicing subsistence agriculture and cattle ranching.[44]

---

[41] "Hallando interés crecido en la venta del cacao se han dado en sembrarle de manera en sus haciendas que embarazaron y ocuparon las tierras de la yuca ... único pan de la isla ... Clamó a un tiempo el hambre entre los pobres, de los soldados y de los conventos de religiosas, supliendo esa falta en parte plátanos y otras frutas silvestres." Juan Balboa Mogrovejo to the Council of the Indies. November 7, 1659. AGI, SD. 58, R. 6, n. 80.

[42] For testimonies of the death of the cacao trees, see, for instance, the letter by Governor Ignacio de Zayas Bazán to the Council of the Indies, May 29, 1671. AGI, SD. 76, R.1; or letter by resident Manuel González Pallano to the Council of the Indies. May 2, 1675. AGI, SD. 90, R. 2.

[43] AGI, SD. 93 and 94.

[44] To see the effects of the disease in the neighboring Jamaica, see Janet Henshall Momsen and Pamela Richardson, "Caribbean and South America. Caribbean Cocoa: Planting and Production," in Louis Evan Grivetti and Howard-Yana Shapiro, eds., *Chocolate: History, Culture, and Heritage* (Hoboken: Wiley, 2009), 482.

242   *Islanders and Empire*

As if the diseases that affected both humans and crops were not enough, natural disasters also presented challenges to Hispaniola's residents. In 1673, a massive earthquake shook the island causing great destruction in the capital. Battered by years of torrential rain and hurricane winds, a third of all houses and private residences of Santo Domingo, many dating back to the early 1500s, could not withstand the 120 aftershocks over a period of forty days following the main earthquake and ended up collapsing.[45] Civil and religious buildings were also partially or completely destroyed. Writing almost twenty years later, in 1691, the governor of Santo Domingo reported that, with the exception of the cathedral, most of the buildings lining the main square laid in ruins following the earthquake.[46] The owners, possibly pressed by economic hardship, seemed to have been unwilling or unable to rebuild their houses. In 1680, a hurricane swept over the island causing even more destruction. Fortunately for the Spaniards, the hurricane also destroyed a French fleet of twenty-five ships in the proximity of Santo Domingo, which might have helped to maintain the status quo between the two colonies for the time being.[47]

BORDER PRESSURES

Even as the Spanish colony grew weaker as a consequence of diseases and natural disasters, the French settlements, under the control of Governor Bertrand d'Ogeron, flourished. Spanish authorities and many residents perceived the increasing presence of the French in the border regions as a constant threat to the security of the towns of the Hispaniola, especially Santiago, which was surrounded by some of the most fertile valleys in the north of the island and was many miles away from Santo Domingo's reinforcements. In an early attempt to fend off foreign marauders and buccaneers, in 1647, the crown authorized the recruitment of sixty soldiers in two groups of thirty to run through the northern and southern lands beyond the Spanish settlements to fight against foreign encroachment into the western part, which the crown and local residents still considered to be Spanish. These troops were led by career soldiers and formed by a mix of local whites and free people of color from Hispaniola,

[45] Antonio Gutiérrez Escudero, *Población y economía en Santo Domingo (1700–1746)* (Sevilla: Diputación Provincial de Sevilla, 1985), 17.
[46] Governor Ignacio Pérez Caro to the Council of the Indies. July 27, 1691. AGI, SD. 91, R. 4.
[47] Anonymous, *Relación verdadera en que se da cuenta del horrible huracán que sobrevino a la isla y puerto de Santo Domingo de los Españoles el día 15 de agosto de 1680* (Madrid: Lucas Antonio de Bedmar, printer,1680).

Neighbors, Rivals, and Partners

many of whom knew the land and whose lack of formal employment, at least in the eyes of crown officials, made them ideal candidates to perform these tasks. The troops also protected new Spanish settlers who had established themselves in the formerly depopulated lands. The valley of Guaba, where some of the most relevant events of the 1605 depopulations took place, was settled again with cattle ranchers and their families in order to secure the claim to the territory. Such settlements, far from Spanish populated centers, were particularly exposed to French attacks and depended on these troops for protection. The settlement in Guaba would be frequently raided by French forces. Despite such attacks, the population of the frontier region continued to grow, and the Spanish village of Bánica was large enough to have its own *Cabildo* by the 1680s.[48]

Troops patrolled continually in Hispaniola until the beginning of the governorship of Juan de Balboa in 1659, when he called the men to Santo Domingo and disbanded them. According to a witness, the governor pointed out that the troops were useless and that "His Majesty did not pay blacks or mulattoes," using race as an excuse for reneging on payment of the salaries owned to them.[49] Balboa's overt use of a racialized language also reveals the contrasts between the ideas about race and hierarchy held by many peninsular officials and the very different racial landscape that they encountered in remote frontier outposts like Hispaniola. In these places, racial boundaries, while harsh and very real, reveal a certain malleability in daily interactions.[50] Peninsular Spaniards, however, often interpreted this as a dangerous break in the colonial order. By the time Balboa disbanded these troops, the group of soldiers patrolling the north of the island had sixteen men: nine Spaniards and seven free men of African descent. The group monitoring the southern lands was formed of ten men: eight Spaniards and two free men of African descent.[51] This fraternization of white and black soldiers might have made the governor uncomfortable, so it is possible that his reasoning for disbanding the troops and pocketing the money reflected deeper concerns about social

---

[48] Manuel Hernández González, *La Colonización de la Frontera Dominicana, 1680–1795* (Santo Domingo: Academia Dominicana de la Historia, 2006), 133–35.

[49] "que su Majestad no pagaba a negros ni mulatos." This quote belongs to the testimony of Francisco de Luna, a veteran soldier with thirty-seven years serving in Hispaniola and the soldier in charge of the troop patrolling the northern lands of the island. He testified in Juan de Balboa's *residencia*. AGI, Escribanía, 12A, bundle 1.

[50] David J. Weber, *The Spanish Frontier of North America* (New Haven: Yale University Press, 1992), 328. Thanks to Chase MacCarter for this reference.

[51] *Residencia* of Governor Juan de Balboa, November 12, 1666. AGI, Escribanía, 12A, bundle 1, fol. 128–130r.

244   *Islanders and Empire*

order. It also seems clear, looking at the small number of soldiers among these men, that this was a hard, dangerous, and poorly remunerated job, so few people were willing to do it.

These troops also represented a first line of defense against any French attack, and, in their absence, French forces moved mostly unnoticed. In 1660, thirty men guided by a Spanish free black man attacked the settlers in Guaba, taking some of them as prisoners. That same year, a group of about 300 Frenchmen from Tortuga sacked the town of Santiago, forcing its inhabitants to flee to the mountains. More than 150 people were killed and injured, and some residents, including members of the *Cabildo*, were taken as prisoners and only released once the French forces had escaped aboard a ship they had stolen from a Spanish resident. *Oidor* Andrés Martínez de Amileta was sent north by Governor Balboa to help the people of Santiago, and he initiated an investigation into these events. According to Martínez de Amileta, the town had become complacent about its defense. Some of the French residents of Santiago took advantage of the attack to seek vengeance against those who had wronged them. A Frenchman called Luis Bilvo, who had resided in Santiago for a year and a half, was said to have gone house to house during the attack, calling the names of his enemies and committing "horrendous atrocities."[52] It is likely that Bilvo took advantage of the attack to seek retribution on a few specific individuals, but in general, the Spanish residents of Santiago did not treat the actions of one Frenchman as representative of all. Other French residents, apparently fearing no reprisal from their neighbors, stayed in Santiago after the attack. Martínez de Amileta found them in town when he arrived, which once again shows that non-Spaniards were not always judged by local residents based on their birthplace. The same can be said about crown officials, but in this case, the *oidor* decided to round up the French and send them to Santo Domingo so that they could be shipped out of the colony.[53]

These events forced Governor Balboa to establish a permanent garrison or *presidio* in the town of Santiago, drawing from soldiers in the garrison in Santo Domingo, although the specific number is unclear. Many of these soldiers established ties with local residents and married in Santiago. Others, faced with the prospect of being stationed for an undetermined amount of time in a frontier town like

---

[52] In the original, "horrendas atrocidades." *Oidor* Andrés Martínez de Amileta to Governor Juan de Balboa. April, 21, 1660. AGI, Escribanía, 12B, bundle 8, fol. 58r–61v.

[53] Ibid.

Neighbors, Rivals, and Partners

Santiago, fled their posts.[54] These available vacancies were filled by local residents, for whom working the land or tending their cattle had become almost impossible due to the constant risk of French attack. In their steady employment as soldiers, these men thus found a way to make a living while perhaps gaining certain social recognition.

During the 1670s, as the French settlements expanded over the western lands of the island and even across the northern coast of Hispaniola, the French attacks and Spanish counterattacks continued relentlessly. The successors of Governor Balboa once again mustered the troops, ordering them to patrol the frontier region between the Spanish and French settlements. This time, the troops were formed by local residents and led by professional soldiers from the garrison of Santo Domingo. Spanish forces attacked Cap-Français in December 1673 and burned half the houses, killing everyone in sight.[55] Despite the active presence of Spanish forces in the frontier region, French attacks over Spanish towns could not be completely stopped either. In 1674, the French went deep into Spanish territory and attacked the towns of Cotuy and La Vega, burning houses and killing some people and cattle. The town of Santiago, further north and more exposed, although better protected, also suffered the French advance. Many residents of Santiago were forced to abandon their lands, which extended along the coast of Hispaniola all the way to the site of the depopulated town of Bayahá.[56] In 1677, the governor of Santo Domingo had to send an expedition against a French settlement in the Samaná bay in the northeastern corner of the island. The French captain and other settlers were killed, and eleven French prisoners and eighteen enslaved Africans were captured; the former were sent to Spain, and the latter were sold at auction in the capital.[57]

In the meantime, the elites in Santo Domingo also struggled, or so they claimed. In 1679, the members of the *Cabildo* of Santo Domingo relayed to the crown the difficult economic circumstances in which the island was

---

[54] Lope de las Marinas y Nevares, alcalde mayor of Santiago, to Governor Balboa. July 4, 1661. AGI, Escribanía, 12B, bundle 8, fol. 65r.

[55] "Memoire concernant la colonnie françoise de la côte de Saint Domingue." September 20, 1676. AGI, SD. 63, R. 3, n. 32, doc. 6.

[56] For some descriptions of the challenges that the French settlers posed to Spanish residents, see Archbishop Francisco de la Cueva Maldonado to the Council of the Indies. March 15, 1666. AGI, SD. 93. R. 4, n. 198; Francisco Sánchez Calderón to the Council of the Indies. July 10, 1667. AGI, SD. 89. R. 3; and Francisco Sánchez Calderón to the Council of the Indies. Undated (very possibly, 1674). AGI, SD. 90, R. 2.

[57] Juan de Padilla to the Council of the Indies. August 23, 1677. AGI, SD. 63, R. 3, n. 32, doc. 1.

246   *Islanders and Empire*

immersed, referring to the colony as "the almost cadaverous ... body of the unhappy Hispaniola." The Council members requested a shipment of slaves to substitute for those who had died in the waves of diseases that had afflicted the island in previous years. They also requested that at least two ships be sent to Santo Domingo with clothing and other manufactured goods because the few merchants arriving in Santo Domingo sold their products "without fear from God ... at prices that provide them over 100% benefit, and against human and divine laws."[58] As we saw in Chapter 2, price gouging was a common practice among merchants doing business in Santo Domingo, and it is clear that local people suffered the consequences. However, some warned the crown that behind the real economic crisis affecting important sectors of the population, members of the *Cabildo* of Santo Domingo and others hid their own business interests. Archbishop Fray Domingo de Navarrete warned the crown that, despite the pleas for the importation of more enslaved Africans into the colony, many were being exported to other colonies: "A ship does not leave the port without blacks to be sold in the Spanish Main. Even married black men are sent, leaving their wives on the island."[59]

The sale of Africans outside the island might have been triggered by high market prices elsewhere and a new source of cheaper enslaved labor. The proximity of French settlements brought some unexpected benefits to some local Spanish residents and officials. The initial use of indentured servants or *engagés* by French settlers soon gave way to the progressive introduction of enslaved Africans for the cultivation of the land. Many of these African peoples, due to harsh treatment they received from their French masters and the harsh living conditions of the western Hispaniola borderlands, ran away to Spanish lands. These slaves were taken by crown officials and questioned to find out if they had previously belonged to Spanish owners and had been obtained in raids of Spanish Caribbean settlements. For example, in the aftermath of the fall of Veracruz in 1684, many slaves captured during that raid were taken to western Hispaniola

---

[58] "El cuerpo ... casi cadáver de la infeliz Española" and "Nos venden sin temor de Dios lo que le compraron a más de cien por ciento de ganancia y contra lo que prohiben las leyes divinas y humanas." Interestingly enough, this petition was signed by all the *alcaldes* and *regidores* of the *Cabildo* except for Rodrigo Pimentel. The *Cabildo* of Santo Domingo to the Council of the Indies. April 24, 1679, in Genaro Rodríguez Morel, ed., *Cartas del Cabildo de Santo Domingo en el siglo XVII* (Santo Domingo: 2007), 373.

[59] "Mucho se quejan en esta isla de la falta de negros. Por otra parte veo que no sale barco de aquí en que no envíen negros a vender a Tierra Firme. Y aún envían negros casados dejando las mujeres en la isla." Archbishop Fray Domingo de Navarrete to the Council of the Indies. April 4, 1679. AGI SD. 93, R. 5, n. 230.

Neighbors, Rivals, and Partners

and sold to French masters. Some of these enslaved Africans managed to escape to the Spanish part of the island. The Spanish authorities questioned them and sent word to their masters so they could claim them.[60] Once it was established that they were actually owned by French settlers, they were given in deposit to powerful local residents and crown officials to work in their households and lands, while their fate was decided. According to Jerónimo Chacón, a new *oidor* who arrived in 1675, some members of the elite (possibly those without access to the slaves) pressured to have the enslaved Africans sold at auction, but the crown officials and residents benefitting from having these enslaved men and women in deposit resisted their sale.[61] It was also the opinion of the *fiscal* of the *Audiencia*, Juan Garcés de los Fayos, that a decision had to be made between selling them to benefit the royal treasury or setting them free to reward their escape from French hands. For the moment, the crown chose an intermediate option, in which people with enslaved Africans in deposit would have to pay the crown a daily salary for their labor.[62]

The disputes about the future of these men and women started again in 1677, when twelve enslaved Africans arrived in Santo Domingo from French territory. Some residents, possibly the most affluent and with cash in hand, requested that they be sold at auction; others wanted the crown to own the slaves so they could benefit from their labor in exchange for wages paid to the treasury. The *Audiencia* saw the case, and after a disputed trial, it was decided that the enslaved Africans who escaped from their rightful French masters could not be considered slaves anymore, since they had escaped to Spanish lands on their own volition. Instead, the *Audiencia* decided to declare all African enslaved peoples escaped from French territory free, hoping that this would encourage other enslaved Africans to escape their French masters and come to Spanish

---

[60] See for instance, Governor Andrés de Robles to the Council of the Indies. November 24, 1684. AGI, SD. 64, R. 6, n. 156. For more on enslaved Africans captured on Spanish soil and taken to French Hispaniola, see Pablo Miguel Sierra Silva, "Afro-Mexican Women in Saint-Domingue: Piracy, Captivity, and Community in the 1680s and 1690s." *Hispanic American Historical Review*, vol. 100, n. 1 (2020): 3–34. Indigenous people were also a common target of the pirate raids of the Spanish mainland and were forced into servitude in western Hispaniola. See Arne Bialuschewski, "Slaves of the Buccaneers: Mayas in Captivity in the Second Half of the Seventeenth Century." *Ethnohistory*, vol. 64, n. 1 (2017): 41–63.

[61] *Oidor* Jerónimo Chacón Albarca to the Council of the Indies. June 6, 1675. AGI, SD. 63, R. 2, n. 14, document 6.

[62] *Fiscal* Juan Garcés de los Fayos to the Council of the Indies. January 22, 1675. AGI, SD. 63, R. 1, n. 1; Royal Decree, June 15, 1675. AGI, SD. 63, R. 2, n. 15.

248 *Islanders and Empire*

lands. Interim governor Juan de Padilla settled them near Santo Domingo, where they could cultivate the land and local residents could hire them for work. The settlement was named San Lorenzo de los Minas, possibly in reference to the fact that many of the first settlers of the village self-identified with the ethnonym *Mina*, signaling their origin in the African Gold Coast, and possibly, the Slave Coast.[63]

The application of a sanctuary policy for enslaved Africans escaping from other imperial orbits and their relocation into villages became a standard Spanish practice after 1693 across the Caribbean region, with one of its best known examples in San Agustín.[64] It allowed Spanish frontier regions to increase their labor pool and defense needs, while weakening rival colonies. At the same time, enslaved Africans who managed to escape found in this policy a new avenue to achieve freedom and a certain autonomy within the Spanish colonial world. The village of San Lorenzo de los Minas flourished during these years. By 1686, the initial settlement of 50 individuals was already home to over 150 African men and women who continued to arrive to Spanish lands, and the village expanded during the eighteenth century. Some governors also took steps to train the new settlers in the use of the spear, so they could be conscripted to aid in the defense of the territory.[65]

COEXISTENCE AND LOCAL COLLABORATION

Beginning in the 1680s, the diplomatic relationship between the crowns of Spain and France changed in important ways. The end of the Franco–Dutch War, in which Spain sided with the Dutch Republic, was

[63] For an interesting debate on the origin of this ethnonym, see Gwendolyn Midlo Hall, "African Ethnicities and the Meanings of 'Mina,'" in Paul E. Lovejoy and David R. Trotman, eds., *Trans-Atlantic Dimensions of Ethnicity in the African Diaspora* (London: Continuum, 2003), 65–81; Robin Law, "Ethnicities of Enslaved Africans in the Diaspora: On the Meanings of 'Mina' (Again)." *History in Africa*, 32 (2005): 247–67.

[64] Jane Landers, *Black Society in Spanish Florida* (Urbana: University of Illinois Press, 1999). See also Jane Landers, "Gracia Real De Santa Teresa De Mose: A Free Black Town in Spanish Colonial Florida." *American Historical Review*, vol. 95, n. 1 (1990): 11, 14. For a recent study on sanctuary policy, see Fernanda Bretones Lane, "Spain, the Caribbean, and the Making of Religious Sanctuary" (Ph.D. dissertation: Vanderbilt University, 2019). This work is currently being revised for publication.

[65] Since the case seen in the *Audiencia* about the freedom of these slaves has not been preserved, it is difficult to know what legal precedents the judges may have used to base their verdict. Juan de Padilla to the Council of the Indies. October 25, 1677. AGI, SD. 63, R. 3, n. 62; Governor Andrés de Robles to the Council of the Indies. December 9, 1686. AGI, SD. 303.

Neighbors, Rivals, and Partners

formalized in the Peace of Nijmegen in 1678. The signing of this treaty marked the beginning of a time of peace between France and Spain. The news of the peace agreement reached the Spanish officials in Santo Domingo in 1680, and the period of peace lasted until 1689. The governor of Santo Domingo decided to send an envoy to Tortuga to inform the French governor of the new peace between the two monarchies. The person chosen to carry out the mission was Juan Bautista Escoto, a cleric from Santiago. Escoto was well received, and the French schooled him in their colony's wealth, trading prowess, and strength of its military. He also observed that the island of Tortuga was a very busy port in which Spanish ships regularly stopped to trade illegally, as well as vessels from Italy and many other places. He also noted the frustration of French settlers with the Spanish policy of welcoming runaway enslaved Africans and French indentured servants into their lands, thus depriving the French of their labor.[66]

The reaction of the French governor of Tortuga to the news of the peace was tepid at best. Even though he acknowledged the treaty, he observed that the document did not make any reference to Hispaniola. He promised to do everything in his power "according to justice and reason" to keep French subjects from Spanish lands, but expected that Hispaniola's governors would still make provisions on the Spanish island for lands that French inhabitants had acquired "by right of conquest." He also expressed his desire to come to an agreement on the location of the borders.[67] The French governor thus intended to keep his options as open as possible while extracting some concessions from the Spanish.

The governors' mistrust of each other was evident, both in their handling of the peace as well as in the interpretation of each other's responses. On January 1, 1681, after Escoto had returned to Santo Domingo, the French governor sent four men with a letter to his Spanish counterpart. The men were intercepted in the north of the island and asked to return to French territory, due to fears that they might be encouraging trade between French and Spanish residents. Their letter was then taken to the governor in Santo Domingo. The members of the *Audiencia* did not like the fact that the French governor had sent the four men by land. Such an act was perceived as a discourtesy (instead of sending one single cleric, like

---

[66] Governor Francisco de Segura to the Council of the Indies. 1681. AGI, SD. 64, R. 3, n. 61.

[67] "todo lo que sea de justicia y razón"; "por derecho de conquista." Letter of Jacques N. de Pouançay, governor of Tortuga, to Governor Francisco de Segura [1681] translated into Spanish by *oidor* Antonio Cemillán Campuzano. Ibid.

250 *Islanders and Empire*

the Spanish had done) and an attempt to survey Spanish lands and defenses. In his communication, the governor of Tortuga defended the French visit with liberal interpretation of what was allowed under the peace treaty. He tried to convince the Spanish that the exchange of prisoners contained in the peace agreement signaled that the Spanish had to return the indentured servants and enslaved Africans who had escaped from French territory. In reply, the governor of Santo Domingo argued that he could not return those that had come by their own will.[68] These exchanges between the authorities of both colonies underscore the fragility of the Franco–Spanish peace in Hispaniola and the uses to which each side put the text of the peace agreement. While the Spanish saw it as an opportunity to stop French advances, the French interpreted it as a way to legitimize their territorial gains and recover some of their lost enslaved and indentured laborers.

From the north, others also raised the alarm about the French. Jerónimo de Robles, *alcalde mayor* of Santiago, declared that the four Frenchmen sent by the governor of Tortuga had said in his presence that removing the French settlers from the island was "impossible" and that "we [the Spanish] should erase the idea from our imagination." Robles also claimed that the French had all the provisions they desired from Europe, and they had become bolder since the time of the peace, going into territories that they would have never dared to enter during times of war. His letter was signed by all the officers serving in the northern region of the island to add credibility to his statement.[69] The urgency that the letter contains might also have been motivated by the soldiers' desire to highlight the risks of their job in order to receive their long-delayed salary, but the threat of French encroachment, as perceived by both peninsular and local royal officials, was nonetheless evident.

Not all officials saw French encroachment as a threat. When artillery general Andrés de Robles came to office as governor of Santo Domingo (1684–90) facing deep budgetary deficits, he decided to once again eliminate the two companies in charge of patrolling the frontier, claiming that during peace times such troops were no longer necessary.[70] His actions earned him a scathing rebuke from the Council of the Indies: "Regarding

---

[68] Ibid.

[69] "Dicen públicamente a los moradores de nuestra parte que es imposible su desarraigo y que se nos borre de la imaginación semejante parto." Jerónimo de Robles Cornejo, *alcalde mayor* de Santiago, to the Council of the Indies. June 28, 1681. AGI, SD. 294.

[70] Andrés de Robles to the Council of the Indies. April 24, 1687. AGI, SD. 65, R. 3, n. 44.

Neighbors, Rivals, and Partners

that island, treaties do not apply because, as I have informed you in numerous decrees, foreigners inhabiting those lands do it illegally, and they are merely tolerated."[71] From this reaction, there are at least a couple of conclusions to draw. First, the attitude of the crown here is very similar to that initial reaction of the governor of Tortuga when he received the news of the peace treaty. Both the Spanish crown and the governor of Tortuga contested the validity of the treaty for Hispaniola, even though both sides tried to use the treaty for their own advantage. Second, despite being inhabited by French settlers for decades, the crown refused to acknowledge the French presence as legitimate, and still held hopes of a future reunification of the island under Spanish control. The position of the royal officials on the ground was based on their perception of local circumstances and the very real financial constraints of the island. The crown, however, still held western Hispaniola as sovereign Spanish territory and expected its governor to behave accordingly, despite Madrid's continued inability to provide the means to make reunification a reality.

Military tensions along the border areas over land and cattle continued during these years, but the reality on the ground differed from the accounts of soldiers serving in Santiago or the imaginings of Spanish bureaucrats in Madrid. During the time of the peace, the French and Spanish attacks upon each other's territory halted, while commercial relations flourished. Commerce had undoubtedly existed before, but during these years, the documentary evidence of these exchanges is more abundant, which might indicate an increase. In fact, the excuse that the governor of Santo Domingo gave the governor of Tortuga about not allowing his four men to arrive in Santo Domingo was "the issue of prohibited trade."[72] It seems that the peace between France and Spain was interpreted by some French merchants as an opportunity to gain new customers in the eastern side of the island. In a letter addressed "to the Spanish gentlemen whose hands found this [letter] and to those from San Juan de Guaba," the French merchant Carlos de Orange informed his prospective customers that "observing that your very Christian king has made peace with ours, we are joyful and looking forward to meet you, ...

---

[71] "Respecto de que por lo que mira a esa isla no se entienden los tratados de ellas porque los extranjeros que las habitan están mal introducidos y sin derecho alguno. Sólo es una tolerancia la permitida, como os tengo remitido en diferentes cédulas." Royal Decree, January 29, 1690. AGI, Escribanía, 26C, R. 2, fol. 121r.

[72] "Por el tema de los comercios prohibidos." Francisco de Segura, governor of Santo Domingo to Jacques Nepveu de Pouançay, governor of Tortuga. January 25, 1681. AGI, SD. 64, R. 3, n. 61.

252   *Islanders and Empire*

you can come here safely as if you were with your own brothers." He insisted that the governor of Tortuga sanctioned these deals and that they would find everything they wished at a good price.[73] If it were true that the governor of Tortuga supported French merchants' attempts to expand their business into the Spanish colony, it might indicate that he embraced the peace as an opportunity to seek non-military avenues to benefit the French colony. There is evidence of at least one other letter like this one, but it is difficult to ascertain how many of these letters circulated and how many people read them shared their views.

The existing documentation seems to indicate that commercial interactions with French merchants became increasingly common during this period. Even among Spanish settlers at the border, where armed scuffles with French groups still existed, trade was unavoidable. This was the case in Bánica, founded in 1683 in the frontier region and in the vicinity of the nearby settlement of Lares de Guaba, established in the early 1650s in the ruins of a sixteenth-century Spanish town.[74] Talking about the Spanish residents of the settlement of Bánica, Governor Robles wrote that "even though they ordinarily trade with the enemies with great disorder and little faith, I have decided to leave them there because they maintain the enemies at a distance from their settlement." These settlers, the governor added, were "the worst vassals that Your Majesty has on this island."[75] The fact that, despite Robles' negative assessment of the settlers, he was willing to leave them be illustrates the importance of these populations to deter French advances. The behavior of these settlers (both combative and collaborative with the French) provides a window into the ambiguous experience of living in a porous borderland, where enemies and trading

---

[73] "A los señores españoles que la hallaren o a cuyas manos viniese y a los de San Juan de Guaba"; "Viendo que vuestro rey cristianísimo ha establecido la paz con el nuestro de que nos hallamos gozosos y deseando encontrados ... podéis venir aquí seguramente como con vuestros propios hermanos." Carlos de Orange, February 24, 1681. AGI, SD. 92.

[74] Manuel Hernández González, "Sociedad en la Española, 1492–1795," in Frank Moya Pons, ed., *Historia de la República Dominicana* (Madrid: Consejo Superior de Investigaciones Científicas, 2010), 221; Manuel Hernández González, "Bánica y Las Caobas, dos pueblos ganaderos de la frontera dominicana de fundación canaria." *El Pajar. Cuaderno de Etnografía Canaria*, 19 (2004), 62.

[75] "Aunque el trato y comercio con los enemigos es común y ordinario con ellos con gran desorden y poca fe, todavía los he dejado estar allí porque detienen los enemigos más cerca de sus poblaciones." Andrés de Robles to the Council of the Indies. May 5, 1687. AGI, SD. 65, R. 3, n. 49; "Los peores vasallos que Vuestra Majestad tiene en esta isla." Governor Andrés de Robles to the Council of the Indies. July 20, 1687. AGI, SD. 65, R. 3, n. 66.

Neighbors, Rivals, and Partners

partners were just roles that individuals and communities adopted according to necessity and opportunity.

By the end of the 1680s, commerce with the French was widespread. Governor Robles was informed that even some of the most respectable residents of the town of Santiago were engaged selling cattle, horses, and mules to the French, but it was impossible to find evidence because they protected each other. The governor only managed to arrest one *mulato* resident of Santiago and one of his brothers. Two members of the local militia denounced them for selling 150 heads of cattle for seven to ten *pesos* each to the French in 1686, and in 1687 they sold another 120. The two men who provided the information to the governor did so secretly because "it is true that [the informants] would have been speared if [Santiago residents] had known that they gave me the news." As punishment, the two brothers were exiled for six years to the Araya fortress on the Venezuelan coast.[76] The fact that these two brothers were of mixed race and quite successful in their illicit trade with the French might have made them an easy target for their neighbors. It is also relevant that the two individuals who reported the two brothers to the governor were both local militia captains, since there is ample evidence that both members of the *Cabildo* of Santiago and the local militia (whose leaders were often members of both bodies) were actively involved in illicit trade. Among those mentioned are Antonio Pichardo de Vinuesa and his nephew Pedro Morel de Santa Cruz, both of them protagonists in the events that opened this chapter. They were both members of the local elite, and both had served as *alcaldes* of Santiago on different occasions. The Pichardo family had resided in northern Hispaniola for over a century.[77]

Pichardo made a career as a militia captain and had led multiple expeditions against the French in the northwest, beyond the Dajabón river and the Guaba valley. According to the Archbishop of Santo

---

[76] "es cierto que los alancearían si supieran quién me había dado la noticia." Governor Andrés de Robles to the Council of the Indies. November 17, 1688. AGI, SD. 65, R. 4, n. 98.

[77] Pichardo's grandfather had been *alcalde ordinario* of the town of Puerto Plata in 1582. For a full list of merits and a family tree of Antonio Pichardo de Vinuesa, see AGI, Indiferente General, 127, n. 5. Pedro Morel de Santa Cruz was the son of one of Pichardo's sisters. For a recent genealogical study of the Pichardo and Morel de Santa Cruz families, see Roberto Cassá, *Rebelión de los capitanes: viva el rey y muera el mal gobierno* (Santo Domingo: Archivo General de la Nación: Facultad de Humanidades, Universidad Autónoma de Santo Domingo, 2011), 46–60.

254 *Islanders and Empire*

Domingo, Pichardo was "the knife and scourge of the French on this island."[78] Yet despite his accomplishments on the military front, the salaries of soldiers in the northern frontier were often delayed for years, if paid at all. Pichardo's salary was not an exception. Writing in 1688, he complained that he had not received any salary during the previous three years, and since his appointment of *cabo general* (highest ranking military officer in the northern frontier), he had only received a small fraction of his wages.[79] Unable to exert enough political influence in Santo Domingo, the needs of soldiers in general, and especially those in the northern frontier, were regularly ignored in the capital.

During the years of peace in the 1680s, as the northern residents of the island enjoyed a fluid trade with their French neighbors, the circulation of French and Spanish peoples and cattle across the frontier region could not have passed unnoticed by the militia or the soldiers patrolling the northern frontier. In most cases, they were active participants in this illicit trade. Governor Robles believed that French settlers were present at every cattle ranch in the north trading with their owners. He tried to persuade local authorities to act, but they claimed they did not know anything about these deals. The governor took this response as an excuse not to act. He also pointed out that the local judges and Pichardo were in these deals together and questioned how, on a ranch belonging to Pichardo's brother, local residents gathered 200 head to be sold to the French without his knowledge and collaboration.[80] The military elites in Santiago constituted the first line of defense against a possible French invasion, but at the same time, deprived of their salaries and supplies from Santo Domingo, they actively participated in trade deals with French settlers as their only means of survival.

SABOTAGING THE WAR EFFORT

The year 1689 brought this period of relative peace between the residents of the Spanish colony of Hispaniola and the French settlers living on the western shores of the island to an end, as France and Spain renewed hostilities in Europe in 1688 with the beginning of the Nine

[78] "Ha sido años ha el cuchillo y azote del francés en esta isla." Fray Domingo de Navarrete to the Council of the Indies. April 4, 1679. AGI, SD. 93, R. 5, n. 230.

[79] From 1669 to 1679, he only received seven and a half *pesos* per month of his salary. From 1679 to 1685, twelve and a half *pesos*. Antonio Pichardo de Vinuesa to the Council of the Indies. April 6, 1688. AGI, SD. 91, R. 3.

[80] Andrés de Robles to the Council of the Indies. April 13, 1688. AGI, SD. 65, R. 4, n. 120.

Years' War.[81] This is the context for the 1690 French attack on Santiago that opened this chapter took place. If colonial officials in Santo Domingo already had doubts about the ability or even the willingness of the garrison and militia from Santiago to defend the north of the island from French settlements, the events surrounding the 1690 battle confirmed their worst suspicions. Already in 1689, the viceroy of New Spain, the Count of Galve, had started the preparations for a Spanish assault to put an end to all French settlements on western Hispaniola. The offensive was planned as a dual attack: by land by the local militias and professional soldiers in the Spanish colony, and by sea with the help of the Spanish Caribbean fleet known as the *armada de Barlovento*. The battle was often retold as a great victory for the Spanish forces, and even the renowned jurist and scholar Carlos de Sigüenza y Góngora wrote a panegyrical account of the battle in 1691, which was in turn dedicated to the vicereine of New Spain as a flattering gesture toward her husband, one of the planners of the attack.[82] A close reading of some of the available documentation from Hispaniola, however, provides a very different view of the expedition and its outcome.

The *armada de Barlovento* arrived in Santo Domingo in November 1690. Governor Ignacio Pérez Caro called a meeting of the military captains of the island. Even though Pichardo was no longer commander of the northern forces, he attended as a captain along with his nephew Pedro Morel. The newly appointed commanders of the troops in Santiago and the captains of the forces patrolling the border were also in attendance, but according to a witness, they appeared very deferential to both Pichardo and Morel. Despite Morel's carelessness in the defense of Santiago that year, the governor initially appointed him head of the land forces. Apparently, the news only pleased Morel's allies, while the great majority of the other captains did not hide their dissatisfaction with the governor's choice. The governor was thus forced to reconsider, and he finally settled on Francisco de

---

[81] A Royal Decree sent to the governor of Santo Domingo in May 24, 1689, announced the start of the war with France. Governor Andrés de Robles acknowledged its receipt in September 15, 1689. Andrés de Robles to the Council of the Indies. AGI, SD. 65, R. 5, n. 187.

[82] Carlos de Sigüenza y Góngora, *Trofeo de la justicia española en el castigo de la alevosía francesa que al abrigo de la armada de Barlovento, ejecutaron los lanceros de la isla de Santo Domingo, en los que se aquella nación ocupan sus costas* (Mexico City: Herederos de la Viuda de Bernardo Calderón, 1691), published in Emilio Rodríguez Demorizi, *Relaciones Históricas de Santo Domingo*, vol. I (Ciudad Trujillo: Montalvo, 1942), 9–57.

256   *Islanders and Empire*

Segura y Sandoval. Segura had been governor of Santo Domingo
(1679–84) but was removed from his post and faced trial for his
collaboration with some members of the local elite over the escape
of a Dutch pirate from Santo Domingo. For such a grave infraction,
Segura was sentenced to death, but he had appealed his sentence and
been imprisoned in the fortress of Santo Domingo following his
removal from office. For Segura, this was an opportunity to prove
his military experience and his loyalty to the crown. The choice was
also very well received by the members of the *Cabildo* of Santo
Domingo. Segura was a popular choice, and having the support of
Hispaniola's local elites for the attack may have been an important
reason not to question the appointment. In the case of Pérez Caro, he
was appointed governor of Santo Domingo in exchange for monetary
compensation that the crown owed him. Perhaps more than any of
his predecessors, Pérez Caro was a merchant first and a bureaucrat
only a distant second. His time in office became a business venture
whose success depended on his good relationship with local elites.
Pedro Morel and Antonio Pichardo were then appointed Segura's
second- and third-in-command, respectively, to please the elites from
the north of the island.[83]

In January 1691, the area of Cap-Français and all its nearby settlements were surrounded by a Spanish land force of 1,200 soldiers and
the Hispaniola militia of 700, all of them supported from the sea by
the Spanish fleet. They killed 200 men and captured significant quantities of coin, textiles, and other valuables. In his letters to Madrid,
Pérez Caro, as well as his allies in the *Cabildo* of Santo Domingo,
wrote of the victory in self-aggrandizing (and mutually beneficial)
terms and made it sound like a great victory of Spanish arms against
the French aspirations in the region.[84] The reality, however, seemed to
be more complicated. Once the region was secure, the captains of the

---

[83] *Oidor* Fernando de Araujo Rivera to the Council of the Indies. April 24, 1691. AGI, SD.
65, R. 7, n. 229; Marc Eagle, "The Audiencia of Santo Domingo in the Seventeenth
Century" (Ph.D. dissertation, Tulane University, 2005), 93–94.

[84] For a taste of this self-congratulatory zeal, see Espino López, "Sobre La Creación De
Fronteras", 170–71. The accounts of the battle from the French perspective, which have
been widely accepted by the historiography, also speak of the defeat, Spanish killings, and
destruction in hyperbolic terms, which might have also been the convenient narrative to
report back to French authorities. Pierre-François-Xavier de Charlevoix, *Histoire de l'isle
Espagnole ou de S. Domingue*, vol. 2 (Paris: Chez F. Didot, 1730–31), 222–25. For an
example of historians that follow Charlevoix's account, see Nellis M. Crouse, *The French
Struggle for the West Indies, 1665–1713* (New York: Columbia University Press, 1943),

Neighbors, Rivals, and Partners

army gathered to discuss whether they should move west and attack Port-de-Paix. Citing a lack of ammunition and food, despite having captured ample amounts of both in Cap-Français, many of the captains refused to continue the attack.[85] *Sargento mayor* José de Piña, in a letter to an *oidor* of the *Audiencia* of Santo Domingo, described how Pedro Morel, who many considered the real commander, took every possible measure to slow down the attack and benefit from it. He gave quarter to prisoners in exchange for secret caches of money and jewels and protected the property of some French landowners from pillage. Morel accumulated a significant amount of loot that he shared with his uncle Pichardo and other relatives and allies, while leaving everyone else without a reward, proving once again that patronage networks were the most important avenue to success in Hispaniola society. Piña, who was the fourth in the line of command on the expedition, believed that the overwhelming momentum that the Spanish force had experienced could have led to the expulsion of the French from western Hispaniola. The accomplishment of the mission was, however, impeded by the unwillingness of the local militia to continue the campaign, preferring instead to concentrate their efforts on pillaging and accumulating loot acquired in the sack of Cap-Français. Piña did not mince words when describing the actions of Morel and his allies. He depicted the local elites as committed "to discredit our arms to cover their malice and cowardice." After two weeks in French territory, the Spanish force retreated, leaving the property and houses of many French settlers untouched, though Morel managed to take some of the loot. The rest was loaded into the fleet ships and sent to Veracruz, thus depriving members of the local militia outside of Morel's circle of any reward for the campaign.[86]

In 1692, Governor Pérez Caro organized a second expedition with the very clear goal of plundering the French territory above all other considerations. Two witnesses heard Juan Pérez Caro, son of the governor, declare that if the expedition did not gather at least 40,000 *pesos*

177–78; James Pritchard, *In Search of Empire: The French in the Americas, 1670–1730* (New York: Cambridge University Press, 2004), 314–15.

[85] *Oidor* Fernando de Araujo Rivera to the Council of the Indies. April 24, 1691. AGI, SD. 65, R. 7, n. 229.

[86] "deslucir nuestras armas por encubrir su mal obrar y cobardía." *Sargento mayor* of Santo Domingo José de Piña to *Oidor* Fernando de Araujo Rivera. January 25, 1691. Ibid.

258 *Islanders and Empire*

for his father, it would be useless.[87] In order to accomplish this, the governor mobilized the military forces at his disposal and gathered a total of 1,700 men, including 400 musketeers from the Spanish *armada de Barlovento* that had come to support the offensive and 200 men from the garrison of Santo Domingo, with the remainder taken from the local militias of the island.[88] This last group was very reticent to join due to the treatment they had received from Pedro Morel in the 1691 expedition. Pérez Caro had to resort to giving each man five *pesos* as an incentive to join the campaign. Many of them replied that they did not need the money to serve the king, but wanted an experienced commander who treated them well. As an added incentive, Pérez Caro gave them permission to take as much property from the French as they wanted as a reward, something that Morel had not allowed them to do in 1691. Still reluctant, the militia nonetheless gathered in Santo Domingo for the preparations.[89] Once the entire force was gathered in the capital, the governor announced that the commander of the expedition would be, once again, Pedro Morel, with some members of the *Cabildo* of Santo Domingo. This decision angered many soldiers of the fleet, who expected to be commanded by a professional soldier. It also disappointed many among the local militias, who saw themselves once again in the hands of a man they did not respect. Some members quit after the new commander was announced, but enough stayed on to depart with the army toward French territory.[90]

The army set up camp near the French settlements in anticipation of the attack. The local militia units were grouped according to their villages of origin. In his camp, Morel rearranged the units, separating men from their neighbors and trusted friends. He also removed local militia captains from the command of each unit. Following Pérez Caro's instructions, Morel appointed merchants of certain wealth but little military experience as captains, unknown to the militia forces, and without any knowledge of

[87] The testimony of Juan Pérez Caro, as heard by Juan Mieses Ponce de León and Captain Silverio Manzanilla, *alcaide* of the fortress of Santo Domingo, were gathered in an investigation that Pérez Caro's successor, Severino de Manzaneda, conducted in 1696. AGI, Escribanía, 26A. These investigations also revealed that much of the wealth that Pérez Caro had accumulated during his tenure was kept in the houses of many Santo Domingo residents, among them, the house of Rodrigo Claudio Maldonado, possibly the wealthiest man in Santo Domingo at the time.

[88] Ignacio Pérez Caro to the Council of the Indies, August 27, 1692. AGI, SD. 66, R. 1, n. 7.

[89] Unsigned letter (possibly written by the Fernando de Araujo Rivera, *oidor* of the *Audiencia* of Santo Domingo). April 18, 1692. AGI, SD. 66, R. 1, n. 1.

[90] Ibid.

Neighbors, Rivals, and Partners

the men and terrain in which they would be fighting. As if these changes were not enough to undermine the morale of the soldiers, Morel also prohibited members of the army from taking any property from the French with the exception of used clothing. This order clearly contradicted the promises the governor had made. The reorganization of the local militias, the substitution of local captains, and the prohibition to loot the enemies proved too much for the militias. That same evening, they left the camp en masse and returned to their homes. Morel attempted to continue without them, but deprived of the most experienced men and those with the best knowledge of the territory, he was forced to abort the campaign. A few days later, the expedition returned to Santo Domingo without having confronted the enemy.[91]

The official version of the events, as related by the governor, was very different. According to Pérez Caro, the local militia left the expedition because they were afraid of the news they were receiving from the front about the reinforcements that the French had received and the cannons protecting Port-de-Paix. This theory, according to an *oidor*, was the governor's own invention to justify his dealings and mismanagement of the expedition. In the aftermath of the Spanish withdrawal, Pérez Caro started a judicial process against the local militia for leaving their posts. The Archbishop of Santo Domingo convinced the local *Cabildos* of the island and the religious orders to write letters to the governor asking him to forgive the island residents who had fled, arguing that these men were needed to defend the island in case of invasion and had abandoned their posts out of ignorance. These letters seemed to satisfy the governor, since they exculpated him of any wrongdoing, and in July 1692, he issued a general pardon.[92]

The failed 1692 attack was not the final attempt to expel the French from Hispaniola. In 1695, an Anglo–Spanish alliance came together in what became the last real effort to take the western shores from the French setters.[93] The attack was a resounding victory, but limited exclusively to the northwest coast and the settlements of and around Cap-Français and

---

[91] Ibid.

[92] AGI, Escribanía, 26C.

[93] For two views on the formation of this alliance and the execution of the attack, see Espino López, "Sobre La Creación De Fronteras," 174–79; Carmen Maria Fernández Nadal, "La unión de las armadas inglesa y española contra Francia: La defensa de las Indias en la Guerra de los Nueve Años," in Enrique García Hernán and Davide Maffi, eds., *Guerra y sociedad en la monarquía hispánica: política, estrategia y cultura en la Europa moderna (1500–1700)*, vol. 1 (Madrid: Centro Superior de Investigaciones Científicas, 2006), 1025–42.

260 *Islanders and Empire*

Port-de-Paix. In a letter to Madrid, governor Pérez Caro praised the courage and valor of the local militia soldiers who only years before he had accused of cowardice and deserting the field on the eve of battle. The victory came despite the mistrust between English and Spanish troops, disagreements about the treatment of religious buildings, and the division of the spoils. Both the English and Spanish troops contracted fevers that forced them to retreat, leaving the territory to be retaken by the French soon afterwards. In 1697, the Treaty of Ryswick put an end to the Nine Years' War, and it also settled the future of western Hispaniola. Spain acknowledged France's possession of the West, thus giving up on its aspirations to unify the territory under Spanish control.

THE LIMITS OF EMPIRE

As French settlers consolidated their position in the western lands of Hispaniola in the second half of the seventeenth century, the place of the island within the geopolitical struggles of the Spanish and the French crowns were forever altered. The Spanish residents of the island had to protect their territory and property from French encroachment, but at the same time, they found in the presence of these new neighbors opportunities to trade and, to a certain degree, prosper in ways that it had been impossible for nearly a century. Throughout this period, the Spanish crown never gave up the hope of expelling the French from western Hispaniola and placing the entire island under its control. In order to carry out these plans, however, the crown needed the collaboration of royal officials on the ground and local residents.

The military expeditions against the French territory in Hispaniola failed due to the diverging objectives and interests of those who organized and participated in these attacks. This was patently obvious in the 1695 expedition, where, despite the victory in the battlefield, both the English and the Spaniards had their own aspirations in their participation of the incursion. The attack did not translate into a takeover of the territory, but instead was limited to a punitive expedition. The assaults of 1691 and 1692 were more revealing of underlying tensions within the Spanish forces. For Governor Pérez Caro, the expeditions were a commercial enterprise that promised wealth for him and his associates in Santo Domingo and Santiago. A sailor and merchant by trade, Pérez Caro used his position as governor of Santo Domingo to reap important benefits from the war between France and Spain. Pérez Caro's misuse of the crown's resources and his appointment of certain members of the local

Neighbors, Rivals, and Partners

elites as leaders of the expeditions provoked the ire of an important sector of the militias and undermined the military efforts that might have brought to an end to the French rule over western Hispaniola to an end.

At the same time, members of the local elites of the northern town of Santiago, like Pedro Morel, established commercial partnerships with their French neighbors during the peaceful 1680s and accumulated wealth and influence in their communities that they mobilized to their advantage during war. For Pedro Morel, the objective of the military actions against the French was not to expel them from the island, but extract as much wealth as possible in the course of these offensives to benefit his own small circle of relatives and allies. As a resident of Santiago in frontier territory, Pedro Morel understood the importance of adapting from times of peace to times of war. In both scenarios and despite the risks inherent in the proximity of this potential enemy, the French were a great source of wealth for these men and some members of their communities. Expelling the French from Hispaniola would isolate them even more, depriving them of commerce during times of peace and pillage during times of war.

In this context, the alliance between Pedro Morel and Pérez Caro, two men heavily invested in maneuvering the spaces between competing imperial agendas, made perfect sense. The constant transimperial competition in the Caribbean became the most reliable source of wealth for them. Their interests, however, differed in at least one important way. While Pérez Caro, as a royal official, might have benefitted from the complete expulsion of the French settlers by the Spanish forces with a substantial promotion, Pedro Morel did not have any interest in ending the French presence from Hispaniola. Morel's actions sought to maintain the complex instability that the island endured during those years.

The cozy relationships that some members of the local groups enjoyed with French settlers might have equaled treason in the eyes of crown officials in Madrid, but it made sense in the context of the fluid coexistence that residents in Hispaniola had maintained with non-Spanish Europeans throughout the second half of the seventeenth century. Although some royal officials were alarmed at the presence of foreigners on Spanish soil and tried to limit the presence of these individuals in Hispaniola, many of their colleagues saw opportunities in the language or professional skills of foreigners. It is only in those rare instances in which government officials complained about these foreigners that we are alerted to their presence in the archival sources. Although officials claimed that the foreign birth of these individuals was behind their complaints, the reasons appear to have been rooted instead in personal disputes about money or property, in which the officials deliberately exposed the birthplace of an adversary. These maneuvers represent the exception, rather than the norm. Most residents of Hispaniola lived side by side with non-Spaniards without ever showing any concern about these individuals. This peaceful coexistence with foreigners gave way, in the last decades of the seventeenth century, to a closer interaction with French settlers in the western part of Hispaniola at a time in which the Spanish imperial agenda pushed for an aggressive stance against French encroachment on the island.

Local Spanish residents defended their lands aggressively against French attacks when needed, but at the same time, many of them embraced the possibility of benefitting from the commercial partnerships with their non-Spanish neighbors. The small but steady stream of slave refugees also contributed to the defensive and labor needs of the colony. As French and Spanish imperial interests clashed in Hispaniola in the second half of the seventeenth century, local residents on both sides of the border found ways to collaborate beyond the often-rigid dictates of the Spanish crown. Inflexible imperial directives and aspirations became malleable in the hands of Spanish subjects in these borderlands. These individuals often had a crucial role in shaping the limits and conditions under which imperial rule took place, as well as in imperial expansion and contraction.

Conclusion

In the early days of 1694, tireless traveler Gregorio de Robles arrived at a bay on the northern coast of Hispaniola, where the town of Puerto Plata once stood. He journeyed on the ship of an *asiento* slave merchant, and once ashore, he encountered two Dutch sloops and an English one full of goods and openly trading. Locals had prepared 1,000 hides and the English and Dutch sailors went ashore "as if it was their own land," ready to exchange their wares for all kinds of agricultural products. Robles suggested that this port needed to be better defended and that the city of Santiago should have a "good commander" because vigilance was crucial to protect the region.[1] If Gregorio de Robles suspected that the local militias were involved in allowing this illicit trade, he was correct. Less than a century after the depopulations, the northern residents of Hispaniola had once again restored their transnational mercantile connections with the complicity of local militias and officials. These foreign contacts did not have to come all the way from northern Europe as in the late sixteenth century. Their ports of operations were just a few days away in Jamaica, Curaçao, the Lesser Antilles, or just across the border in western Hispaniola. Spaniards and Afrodescendants in the Spanish colony held on to illicit trade as their most precious asset to overcome their marginality within the Spanish empire. The stories behind their black market commerce indicate that, beyond being mere spectators or passive victims of pillage, the white and black inhabitants of the Spanish Caribbean played a crucial role as active participants and business

---

[1] "Como si fuesen en poblaciones suyas"; "un buen cabo." Gregorio de Robles, *America a fines del siglo XVII: noticias de los lugares de contrabando*, ed. Víctor Tau Anzoátegui (Valladolid: Casa-Museo de Colón y Seminario Americanista de la Universidad, 1980), 35.

264 *Islanders and Empire*

partners in the illicit transnational networks that facilitated the rise of English, French, and Dutch Atlantic empires in the region.

Within the confines of Hispaniola itself, at the dawn of the seventeenth century, the power and influence that the people of Hispaniola wielded locally were instrumental in the ambitions of, at the very least, two Atlantic empires in the Caribbean. The intervention of Hispaniola residents had stopped the expansion of French Saint-Domingue further east, but at the same time, they thwarted the Spanish crown's attempt to expel the French, reunify the island, and eliminate the center of operations of a powerful enemy in Caribbean waters. Imperial projects represented desires for unmitigated triumphs. The residents of Hispaniola, however, struggled to accommodate within the interstices of these two different imperial projects without granting either of them a complete victory. It was precisely in this ambiguous balance that Spanish Caribbean residents found the most profitable conditions for their prosperity.

In the Peace of Ryswick (1697), the division of the island was formalized. Spain recognized France's official possession of the western third of the island after minor skirmishes. On the ground, both sides continued their attempts to consolidate their control over the vaguely defined frontier between both colonies, and in the following years, the potential for illicit commercial exchanges expanded greatly. The authorities of Santo Domingo, with the support of the elites of the capital, tried once again to profit from the new *status quo,* impeding the trade of the rural residents of the north and west with a mix of fees and suppression. Even though these residents had suffered the brunt of French attacks for years and navigated the risks of creating these commercial contacts in the first place, Spanish authorities tried to wrest a questionably legal monopoly over the trade of cattle and hides.

As in the depopulations in the early seventeenth century, northern residents' response to Santo Domingo's attempts to suppress this extralegal commerce turned violent. In December of 1720, the town of Santiago rose in arms against Santo Domingo and its authorities with shouts of "long live the king," and "death to bad government." The local militias were the main protagonists of the rebellion, although the entire town was behind them. At the head of the militias were the local elites of Santiago, who had the ranks of *capitán* and *alférez,* which is why this episode is known as "the rebellion of the captains." As their last names indicate (Pichardo de Vinuesa, Morel de Santa Cruz, etc.) many of these officers were the children and descendants of the protagonists of the events in 1691 and 1692 (see Chapter 6), and they, just like their predecessors, had

Conclusion 265

strong family and patronage networks in Santiago. The rebellion was triggered by the attempts of the governor of Santo Domingo to restrict trade with the French neighbors while extorting cattle ranchers and thus benefit himself (and likely his network of allies of Santo Domingo) with this trade. The rebellion spread to the towns of Azua in the south and the newly founded town of Hincha in the frontier. In sharp contrast with the official response during the depopulations, this time the authorities showed a certain level of restraint. Even though officially the crown maintained the prohibitions to trade with the French neighbors, there were some notable concessions, such as free trade for ten years in the refounded town of Montecristi and regular permissions to sell cattle to Saint-Domingue.[2]

These concessions hid the fact that the crown had become unable to impede trade with Saint-Domingue and was not necessarily under the control of the local and royal elites in Santo Domingo. Rather, it was in the hands of those who lived in the north and interior of the island, which included a growing number of free Afrodescendants. Already by 1716, Saint-Domingue consumed approximately 3,000 head of cattle annually. All of them came from the Spanish colony, and this trade only expanded in the following decades as Saint-Domingue plantations grew and the enslaved population arrived in greater numbers.[3] Throughout the eighteenth century, Montecristi became an entrepôt for ships of all nations to trade illegally with Saint-Domingue, and the economy of the Spanish colony thrived in a symbiotic relation with that of its French neighbor. This nearby food supply was key for the high productivity of Saint-Domingue, and secured the brutal working, living, and dying conditions of the approximately 800,000 enslaved Africans who were forced into the fields of western Hispaniola in the eighteenth century.

Looking at Hispaniola's internal economic and political tensions during this long seventeenth century, the period is marked by the rise of

---

[2] The eighteenth century is marked by the brisk establishment of towns and villages near the French border and in the northern coast. Montecristi was refounded in 1751. See Antonio Gutiérrez Escudero, *Población y economía en Santo Domingo (1700–1746)* (Sevilla: Diputación Provincial, 1985), 72–75. For a detailed study on the rebellion, see Roberto Cassá, *Rebelión de los capitanes: viva el rey y muera el mal gobierno* (Santo Domingo: Archivo General de la Nación and Facultad de Humanidades, Universidad Autónoma de Santo Domingo, 2011). For a shorter account that includes a study of the high level of militarization of Hispaniola, see Margarita Gascón, "The Military of Santo Domingo, 1720–1764." *The Hispanic American Historical Review*, vol. 73, no. 3 (1993): 431–52.

[3] Cassá, *Rebelión de los capitanes*, 68.

266   *Islanders and Empire*

smuggling and the depopulations at the beginning of this period and the conflicts against the French in 1691 and 1692 at the end, with "the rebellion of the captains" as a coda and an omen of the stratified planta-tion system that was exploding in the west. The picture that emerges is one of great competition for social and economic primacy between center and periphery within Hispaniola: Santo Domingo, the seat of the Spanish Monarchy on the island and its main urban center, and the rural interior and north of the island. With Santo Domingo as the only legal port of entry and exit of goods and agricultural products on an island of nearly 30,000 square miles, the residents of most of the island turned to smuggling as the only possible way of subsistence and socioeconomic advancement. Smuggling allowed economic growth in ways that Santo Domingo could never aspire to after the decline of its nearby sugar plantations. The success of royal officials in suppressing contraband trade with the depopulations in 1604–5 only achieved an eighty-year reprieve, during which the city's local elites infiltrated and controlled every aspect of the city's institutions. Santo Domingo's elites became the most powerful group on the island, able to govern the *Audiencia*, hold the purse strings of the *situado*, and thus finance and direct the flow of illicit goods into the city and island.

The establishment of French settlers in western Hispaniola, as well as the more stable presence of northern Europeans in the Caribbean, drama-tically altered once again the brief but powerful hold that Santo Domingo's patronage networks had on smuggling. Rural Hispaniola, which by the end of the seventeenth century was home to an increasing number of enslaved and free Afrodescendants, became the most econom-ically active region of the island, to the chagrin of Santo Domingo mer-chants, elites, and crown administrators. The population grew steadily in the next century. Centering on the people in rural Hispaniola expands our understanding of the ways people in the countryside of the Spanish Caribbean adapted and contributed to the great transformation of the Atlantic world during this century. In their hands, smuggling defied and defined empires in ways that left an indelible mark on their societies and Caribbean culture for generations to come.

Hispaniola also provides a framework for understanding the enduring yet conflicted relationship of Spanish imperial borderlands with Madrid, particularly in the Caribbean region. Throughout this long seventeenth century, this relationship must be understood beyond simplistic ideas of loyalty to the Spanish crown or mere historical inertia. Since the colony was far from a priority for crown bureaucrats, elites on the island enjoyed

Conclusion

a great margin of maneuver within their social and political environment. Ironically, that independence became an important binding element in the relationship of Hispaniola as a peripheral colony with its imperial core. In Santo Domingo, local elites created wide patronage networks that cut across race and class and used them against their rivals for the control of local institutions. These conflicts were intimate and violent, and they often involved enslaved Africans, who were caught between obedience to their owners and fear of legal and personal reprisal. The highly controversial nature of ordering enslaved people to attack fellow Spaniards was precisely the allure of the practice for Santo Domingo elites. Having those at the lowest rung of the social ladder attack those at the top was meant to send a message to the victims, as well as their allies: to know their place and stop interfering in the business arrangements of others.

Santo Domingo's patronage networks successfully upended the system of colonial governance. Governors and members of the *Audiencia,* despite representing the king's authority, became defenders of local interests as well as their own. Despite some efforts by the crown to restore its control over these institutions through strongly worded decrees and *visitas,* colonial institutions remained under the unequivocal influence of local residents, who shaped them and continued to exert considerable authority over their daily functions. With their letters to Madrid, local groups fought to discredit their local rivals while presenting themselves as the king's most loyal servants. At times, their letters succeeded in shaping royal responses. On other occasions, the Council of the Indies, already overburdened by endless correspondence from the Spanish colonies, appears to have been paralyzed by these discordant versions of the reality on the ground, and amidst all the noise that these conflicting narratives created, royal ministers possibly chose to ignore them to focus on more pressing matters.[4]

Against the backdrop of the fierce imperial competition that we have come to expect in the early modern Caribbean, Hispaniola appears as a fluid space in which inter-imperial collaboration on the ground was often understood not only as reasonable, but quite possibly inevitable and perhaps even as moral. Recent arrivals from Spain often complained in their correspondence about the disloyal behavior of locals and other

---

[4] For examples of how colonial petitioners and correspondents influenced the Council's responses, see Adrian Masters, "A Thousand Invisible Architects: Vassals, the Petition and Response System, and the Creation of Spanish Imperial Caste Legislation." *Hispanic American Historical Review*, vol. 98, no. 3 (2018): 377–406.

officials who had become accustomed to such practices. The men and women of Hispaniola, just like their Caribbean neighbors, learned to coexist with high levels of violence in their daily lives. They knew that war was always a possibility. They also knew that it was in their best interest to find opportunities to maximize each other's resources, even if that meant to cross the invisible lines that separated imperial worlds. At times they appear to have seen these lines as highly porous, while at others, they treated them as fictions that they could (and had to) ignore to ensure their own fortunes. At the end of the day, smuggling may have been against the laws of the realm, but it contributed to the survival and prosperity of Hispaniola and other Caribbean colonies that kept the imperial dreams of European kings alive.

Glossary of Spanish Terms

Alcaide: castellan, person in charge of a fortification.

Alcalde or alcalde ordinario: each of the two annually elected local judges in every town or village.

Alcalde mayor: also known as *corregidor* in other parts of Spanish America; royal official in charge of a district that might encompass several towns and villages.

Alférez: junior officer in local militias and professional Spanish troops.

Alférez mayor: voting member of the *Cabildo* with the special honor of transporting the royal banner.

Alguacil mayor: city constable, in charge of keeping the peace and managing local prisoners.

Asiento: contract that different European merchants bought from the Spanish monarchy to introduce enslaved Africans in the Spanish colonies; often became a way for these merchants to introduce illicit trade in Spanish territories.

Audiencia of Santo Domingo: highest court of appeal for the islands of Hispaniola, Cuba, Puerto Rico, Margarita, and the coast of Venezuela from Caracas to Maracaibo, and judicially only second in importance to the Council of the Indies, in Spain, for these territories. It normally consisted of a president (who was also the governor of Santo Domingo), three *oidores*, one *fiscal*, all of them appointed in Spain, and a whole series of mid- and low-level officials.

Bohío: house or hut made of branches and wood.

Bozal (pl. Bozales): term that Spaniards used to designate enslaved Africans who were not familiarized with Spanish or Portuguese language and customs.

270 *Glossary of Spanish Terms*

Cabildo (secular): town or city council.

Cabildo (Ecclesiastical): cathedral chapter, which included the archbishop and all the cathedral prebendaries.

Cacique: political and religious leader of a Taíno polity; could be either men or women.

Calidad: an individual's social status as delineated by race as well as kinship, occupation, wealth, social peers, etc.

Censo: also known as *censo al quitar*, a mortgage on a piece of property in favor of ecclesiastical institution, such as a convent or monastery; in exchange of the principal, the recipient of the mortgage agreed to pay the religious institution an annuity (between 5 percent and 7.5 percent of the mortgaged amount) in perpetuity. Censos would be passed on to heirs or whomever owned the mortgaged property.

Confraternities: catholic voluntary organizations, organized around the cult of certain sacred images and the promotion of pious works; also mutual-aid institutions, helping their poorest deceased members with burial costs and other needs.

Contador: one of the officers (along with the other *oficiales reales*) entrusted with the custody of the royal treasury.

Criollo: Spaniard born in the American colonies.

Cuartos: also known as *vellón*; copper currency, worth half of its silver currency equivalent or less.

Demora: extension of the work obligations of Native Americans working under the *encomienda* system.

Ducados: in the late sixteenth and early seventeenth century, unit of account equivalent to 375 *maravedíes*.

Encomienda: system of forced labor whereby the Indians residing in a territory were assigned to a Spaniard (*encomendero*) to work for him for a specific time during the year in exchange of religion instruction. The system led to systemic abuses and exploitation of the indigenous laborers.

Escribano: notary.

Escribano de Cámara: notary of the *Audiencia*.

Estancia: farm.

Estanciero: Person in charge of an *estancia* or farm.

Fanega: old Spanish unit of volume commonly used for grain and other dry products. It equals approximately 12.6 gallons.

Fiscal: crown attorney within an *Audiencia*.

Juicio de residencia: see *Residencia*.

Glossary of Spanish Terms

Ladino/a: when used to refer to enslaved Africans, someone familiar with Spanish language and customs.

Legua: unit of length equal to approximately 2.7 miles.

Maestre de campo: high military rank in the Spanish army; in areas where there was not an active war, it was second to the *capitán general*, which was the military rank of governors.

Maestre de la plata: person entrusted with bringing the *situado* to Santo Domingo.

Maravedí: smallest unit of account in Spain in the sixteenth and seventeenth century.

Maroon: runaway indigenous or African enslaved men and women who sought refuge in inhabited areas and formed their own communities beyond the control of Spanish colonial society.

Mayorazgo: entailment.

Mayordomo: secular person in charge of the financial accounts and properties of a convent.

Mulato: person of mixed African and Spanish ancestry.

Oficiales reales: officials in charge of the royal treasury.

Oidor (pl. Oidores): judge and member of the Audiencia.

Peninsular (pl. Peninsulares): Spaniards born in the Iberian Peninsula.

Peso (de a ocho): known in English as "piece of eight"; silver coin worth eight *reales* or 272 *maravedíes*.

Pieza (from Portuguese, peça): unit of value used in the Transatlantic slave trade and applied also to Native American slaves; an enslaved man or woman between fifteen and twenty-five years old was considered a *pieza*. Older, or younger enslaved laborers or those with physical disabilities were given a fractional value: half a *pieza*, three quarters of a *pieza*, etc.

Quintal: unit of weight equivalent to approximately 46 kg.

Real (pl. Reales): silver currency worth 34 *maravedís*.

Regidor (pl. Regidores): voting member of a town council, councilman.

Relator (pl. Relatores): secretaries appointed by the *Audiencia* in charge of writing the briefs of the cases coming to court and reading them to the *oidores*.

Repartimiento: division of the native labor force among Spanish colonists.

Residencia: also known as *juicio de residencia*, it was a trial that every governor, *oidor*, or any other appointed royal official had to go through at the end of their tenure to prove that he had been a good administrator; trial was conducted by the official's successor and involved the testimony of local witnesses.

Glossary of Spanish Terms

Situado: annual subsidy the Spanish crown sent to some colonies to pay for its administrative and military maintenance when local revenue was unable to meet these costs.

Socorro: small sums of money paid weekly to soldiers, royal ministers, and bureaucrats to cover their most basic necessities when there was not enough money to pay complete salaries; balances were normally paid with the arrival of the new *situado*.

Vecino: free male or female head of household, a property owner in a Spanish town or city.

Visita: extraordinary inspection of a district, institution, or royal official.

Visitador: royal inspector in charge of a *visita*.

Bibliography

Abello Vives, Alberto, and Ernesto Bassi. "Un Caribe por fuera de la ruta de la plantación," in *Un Caribe sin plantación: Memorias de la Cátedra del Caribe Colombiano*, edited by Alberto Abello Vives. San Andrés: Universidad Nacional de Colombia, sede Caribe, Observatorio del Caribe Colombiano, 2006, 11–43.

Adorno, Rolena, and Patrick Charles Pautz, eds. *The Narrative of Cabeza De Vaca*. Lincoln: University of Nebraska Press, 2003.

Aizpurua, Ramón. *Curazao y la costa de Caracas: introducción al estudio del contrabando de la provincia de Venezuela en tiempos de la compañía guipuzcoana, 1730–1780*. Caracas: Academia Nacional de Historia, 1993.

Alegría, Ricardo E. *Juan Garrido, el conquistador negro en las Antillas, Florida, Mexico y California*. San Juan: Centro de Estudios Avanzados de Puerto Rico y El Caribe, 2004.

Altman, Ida. "The Revolt of Enriquillo and the Historiography of Early Spanish America." *The Americas* vol. 63, n. 4 (2007): 587–614.

"Marriage, Family, and Ethnicity in the Early Spanish Caribbean." *The William and Mary Quarterly* vol. 70, n. 2 (2013): 225–50.

Altman, Ida, and David Wheat, eds. *The Spanish Caribbean & the Atlantic World in the Long Sixteenth Century*. Lincoln: University of Nebraska Press, 2019.

Anderson-Córdova, Karen Frances. *Surviving Spanish Conquest: Indian Fight, Flight, and Cultural Transformations in Hispaniola and Puerto Rico*. Tuscaloosa: The University of Alabama Press, 2017.

Andrews, Kenneth R. *English Privateering Voyages to the West Indies, 1588–1595; Documents Relating to English Voyages to the West Indies From the Defeat of the Armada to the Last Voyage of Sir Francis Drake*. Cambridge [Eng.]: Published for the Hakluyt Society at the University Press, 1959.

The Spanish Caribbean: Trade and Plunder, 1530–1630. New Haven: Yale University Press, 1978.

Bibliography

Andrien, Kenneth J. "The Sale of Fiscal Offices and the Decline of Royal Authority in the Viceroyalty of Peru, 1633–1700." *The Hispanic American Historical Review* vol. 62, n. 1 (1982): 49–71.

Andújar Castillo, Francisco, and Pilar Ponce Leiva, eds. *Debates sobre la corrupción en el mundo ibérico, Siglos XVI–XVIII.* Alicante: Biblioteca Virtual Miguel de Cervantes, 2018.

Anonymous. *Relación verdadera en que se da cuenta del horrible huracán que sobrevino a la isla y puerto de Santo Domingo de los españoles el día 15 de agosto de 1680.* Madrid: Lucas Antonio de Bedmar, 1680.

Aram, Bethany. "Caribbean Ginger and Atlantic Trade, 1570–1648." *Journal of Global History* vol. 10, n. 3 (2015): 410–30.

Araúz Monfantes, Celestino Andrés. *El contrabando holandés en el Caribe durante la primera mitad del siglo XVIII.* Caracas: Academia Nacional de la Historia, 1984.

Armitage, David. "Three Concepts of Atlantic History," in *The British Atlantic World, 1500–1800,* edited by David Armitage and Michael J. Braddick, 11–27. New York: Palgrave McMillan, 2002.

Barcia Paz, Manuel. *The Great African Slave Revolt of 1825: Cuba and the Fight for Freedom in Matanzas.* Baton Rouge: Louisiana State University Press, 2012.

Barriera, Darío G. *Abrir puertas a la tierra: microanálisis de la construcción de un espacio político: Santa Fe, 1573–1640.* Rosario: Museo Histórico Provincial, 2017.

Bassi, Ernesto. *An Aqueous Territory: Sailor Geographies and New Granada's Transimperial Greater Caribbean World.* Durham: Duke University Press, 2016.

Bataillon, Marcel. "Santo Domingo 'era Portugal'," in *Historia y sociedad en el mundo de habla española. Homenaje a José Miranda,* edited by Bernardo García, 113–20. Mexico: Colegio de Mexico, 1970.

Bayle, Constantino. *Los Cabildos seculares en la América española.* Madrid: Sapientia, 1952.

Belmonte Postigo, Jose Luis. "Bajo el negro velo de la ilegalidad. Un análisis del mercado de esclavos dominicano, 1746–1821," *Nuevo Mundo Mundos Nuevos.* Online publication, 2016. https://journals.openedition.org/nuevomundo/69478

"Tratando de gobernar lo ingobernable. Leyes y proyectos esclavistas en Santo Domingo durante la centuria ilustrada," in *El ocaso del Antiguo Régimen en los imperios ibéricos,* coordinated by Scarlett O'Phelan and Margarita Rodríguez, 205–30. Lima: Pontificia Universidad Católica del Perú, Fondo Editorial, 2017.

"Esclavitud y status social en Santo Domingo y Puerto Rico durante la diáspora de la Revolución Haitiana," in *Formas de Liberdade. Gratidão, condicionalidade e incertezas no mundo escravista nas Americas,* edited by Jonis Freire and María Verónica Secreto, 71–102. Rio de Janeiro: Ed. Mauad, 2018.

"Sobre esclavitud y otras formas de dominio. Gradaciones de libertad y estatus social en Santo Domingo a fines del periodo colonial," in *Gente de color entre esclavos,* edited by José Antonio Piqueras and Imilcy Balboa Navarro, 159–78. Granada: Editorial Comares, 2019.

Bibliography

Benjamin, Thomas. *The Atlantic World: Europeans, Africans, Indians and Their Shared History, 1400–1900.* New York: Cambridge University Press, 2009.

Bennett, Herman L. *Africans in Colonial Mexico: Absolutism, Christianity, and Afro-Creole Consciousness, 1570–1640.* Bloomington: Indiana University Press, 2003.

Bertrand, Michel. "En torno a una problemática de la administración colonial: la real hacienda de Nueva España (1680–1770)." *Anuario de Estudios Americanos* 46 (1989): 195–217.

Bialuschewski, Arne. "Slaves of the Buccaneers: Mayas in Captivity in the Second Half of the Seventeenth Century." *Ethnohistory* vol. 64, n. 1 (2017): 41–63.

Bigges, Walter, and Thomas Gates. *A Summarie and True Discourse of Sir Francis Drakes West-Indian Voyage. Accompanied With Christopher Carleill, Martin Frobusher, Francis Knollis, With Many Other Captains and Gentlemen. Wherein Were Taken, the Townes of Saint Jago, Sancto Domingo, Cartagena and Saint Augustine.* Imprinted at London: Roger Ward, 1589.

Block, Kristen. *Ordinary Lives in the Early Caribbean Religion, Colonial Competition, and the Politics of Profit.* Athens: University of Georgia Press, 2012.

Block, Kristen, and Jenny Shaw. "Subjects Without an Empire: The Irish in the Early Modern Caribbean." *Past and Present* vol. 210, n. 1 (2011): 33–60.

Blumenthal, Debra. "Defending Their Masters' Honor: Slaves as Violent Offenders in Fifteenth-Century Valencia," in *"A Great Effusion of Blood"? Interpreting Medieval Violence,* edited by Mark D. Meyerson, Daniel Thiery, and Oren Falk, 34–56. Toronto: University of Toronto Press, 2004.

Blumenthal, Debra. *Enemies and Familiars: Slavery and Mastery in Fifteenth-Century Valencia.* Ithaca: Cornell University Press, 2009.

Bosh, Juan. *De Cristobal Colón a Fidel Castro: el Caribe, frontera imperial.* Madrid: Alfaguara, 1970.

Boucher, Philip P. *France and the American Tropics to 1700: Tropics of Discontent.* Baltimore: Johns Hopkins University Press, 2008.

Boulind, Richard. "Shipwreck and Mutiny in Spain's Galleys on the Santo Domingo Station, 1583." *The Mariner's Mirror* vol. 58, n. 3 (1972): 297–330.

Bourdieu, Pierre. "The Forms of Capital," in *Handbook of Theory and Research for the Sociology of Education,* edited by John G. Richardson, 241–58. New York: Greenwood Press, 1986.

Brading, D.A. "Government and Elite in Late Colonial Mexico." *The Hispanic American Historical Review* vol. 53, n. 3 (1973): 389–414.

Bretones Lane, Fernanda. "Spain, the Caribbean, and the Making of Religious Sanctuary." Ph.D. diss., Vanderbilt University, 2019.

Bryant, Sherwin K. *Rivers of Gold, Lives of Bondage: Governing Through Slavery in Colonial Quito.* Chapel Hill: University of North Carolina Press, 2014.

Burns, Kathryn. *Into the Archive: Writing and Power in Colonial Peru.* Durham: Duke University Press, 2010.

Burset Flores, Luis Rafael. "¿'cosas indebidas' o 'siembra de mala voz'? Los conflictos internos de la Real Audiencia de Santo Domingo, 1605–1608." *CLIO* 189 (2015): 96–153.

Bibliography

El ejercicio del poder a dos manos: el capital social del licenciado Francisco Manso De Contreras. Ediciones Bayamo: Bayamo, 2018.

Callaci, Emily. "On Acknowledgments." *The American Historical Review* vol. 125, n. 1 (February 2020): 126–31.

Camp, Stephanie M. H. *Closer to Freedom: Enslaved Women and Everyday Resistance in the Plantation South*. Chapel Hill: University of North Carolina Press, 2004.

Camus, Michel. "Correspondance De Bertrand Ogeron, Gouverneur De L'île de La Tortue et Costs de Saint-Domingue au Xviie Siècle." *Revue de la Société Haitienne d'Histoire et de Géographie* vol. 43, n. 146 (1985).

L'Île de La Tortue au coeur de la Flibuste Caraïbe. Paris: Editions L'Harmattan, 1997.

Cañeque, Alejandro. *The King's Living Image: The Culture and Politics of Viceregal Power in Colonial Mexico*. New York: Routledge, 2004.

Cassá, Roberto. *Los taínos de la Española*. Santo Domingo: Editora de la Universidad Autónoma de Santo Domingo, 1974.

Historia social y económica de la República Dominicana. Santo Domingo: Alfa y Omega, 1983.

Rebelión de los capitanes: viva el rey y muera el mal gobierno. Santo Domingo: Archivo General de la Nación: Facultad de Humanidades, Universidad Autónoma de Santo Domingo, 2011.

Cavanaugh, Stephanie M. "Litigating for Liberty: Enslaved Morisco Children in Sixteenth-Century Valladolid." *Renaissance Quarterly* vol. 70, n. 4 (2017): 1282–320.

Céspedes del Castillo, Guillermo. "La avería en el comercio de Indias." *Anuario de Estudios Americanos* vol. 2 (1945): 515–698.

Chang-Rodríguez, Raquel. "Colonial Voices of the Hispanic Caribbean," in *A History of Literature in the Caribbean*, vol. 1, *Hispanic and Francophone regions*, edited by Albert James Arnold et al., 111–37. Amsterdam: John Benjamins Publishing, 1994.

Charlevoix, Pierre-François-Xavier de. *Histoire de l'isle Espagnole ou de S. Domingue*. Paris: Chez F. Didot, 1730.

Chasteen, John Charles, and James A. Wood. *Problems in Modern Latin American History: Sources and Interpretations: Completely Revised and Updated*. Wilmington: SR Books, 2004.

Checa Cremades, Fernando, and Laura Fernández-González, eds. *Festival Culture in the World of the Spanish Habsburgs*. Farnham: Ashgate, 2015.

Chueca Saldías, Ignacio. "El Caribe portugués: sobre políticas imperiales, redes planetarias y la presencia de portugueses en el Caribe durante el gobierno de Felipe III (1598–1621)." *Iberoamérica Social* volumen especial 2 (2018): 27–45.

Coleman, David. *Creating Christian Granada: Society & Religious Culture in an Old-World Frontier City, 1492–1600*. Ithaca: Cornell University Press, 2003.

Cook, Karoline P. *Forbidden Passages: Muslims and Moriscos in Colonial Spanish America*. Philadelphia: University of Pennsylvania Press, 2016.

Cook, Noble David. "Disease and the Depopulation of Hispaniola, 1492–1518." *Colonial Latin American Review* vol. 2, n. 1–2 (1993): 213–45.

Bibliography

Cordero Michel, Emilio. "Hernando Gorjón, Hombre de Empresa Y De Presa." *Clío* 155 (1996): 93–113.

Cromwell, Jesse. "More Than Slaves and Sugar: Recent Historiography of the Trans-imperial Caribbean and Its Sinew Populations." *History Compass* vol.12, n. 10 (2014): 770–83.

"Illicit Ideologies: Moral Economies of Venezuelan Smuggling and Autonomy in the Rebellion of Juan Francisco De León, 1749–1751." *The Americas* vol. 74, n. 3 (2017): 267–97.

The Smugglers' World: Illicit Trade and Atlantic Communities in Eighteenth-Century Venezuela. Williamsburg, Omohundro Institute of Early American History and Culture; Chapel Hill: University of North Carolina Press, 2018.

Crouse, Nellis M. *The French Struggle for the West Indies, 1665–1713.* New York: Columbia University Press, 1943.

CUNY Dominican Studies Institute. *First Blacks in the Americas: The African Presence in the Dominican Republic.* www.firstblacks.org/en/

Curcio, Linda Ann. *The Great Festivals of Colonial Mexico City: Performing Power and Identity.* Albuquerque: University of New Mexico Press, 2004.

Curtin, Philip D. *The Rise and Fall of the Plantation Complex: Essays in Atlantic History.* New York: Cambridge University Press, 1990.

Daniels, Christine, and Michael V. Kennedy, eds. *Negotiated Empires: Centers and Peripheries in the Americas, 1500–1820.* New York: Routledge, 2002.

Dawdy, Shannon Lee. *Building the Devil's Empire: French Colonial New Orleans.* Chicago: University of Chicago Press, 2008.

Dean, Carolyn. *Inka Bodies and the Body of Christ: Corpus Christi in Colonial Cuzco, Peru.* Durham: Duke University Press, 1999.

Deive, Carlos Esteban. *La Española y la esclavitud del indio.* Santo Domingo: Fundación García Arévalo, 1995.

Tangomangos: contrabando y piratería en Santo Domingo, 1522–1606. Santo Domingo: Fundación Cultural Dominicana, 1996.

Los guerrilleros negros: esclavos fugitivos y cimarrones en Santo Domingo. Santo Domingo, República Dominicana: Fundación Cultural Dominicana, 1989.

"Las Devastaciones de 1605 y 1606," in *Historia general del pueblo dominicano*, tomo II, coordinated by Raymundo González de Peña, 67–68. Santo Domingo: Academia Dominicana de la Historia, 2018.

Del Río Moreno, Justo L. "Comercio y transporte en la economía del azúcar antillano durante el siglo XVI." *Clío* 179 (2010): 15–54.

Del Río Moreno, Justo L., and Lorenzo E. López y Sebastián. "El jenjibre: historia de un monocultivo caribeño del siglo XVI." *Revista complutense de historia de América* 18 (1992): 63–88.

Diccionario enciclopédico hispano-americano de literatura, ciencias y artes: Edición profusamente ilustrada con miles de pequeños grabados intercalados en el texto y tirados aparte, que reproducen las diferentes especies de los reinos animal, vegetal y mineral, vol. 12. Barcelona: Montaner y Simón Editores, 1893.

Domínguez Ortiz, Antonio, and Bernard Vincent. *Historia de los moriscos: vida y tragedia de una minoría.* Madrid: Revista de Occidente, 1978.

Bibliography

Eagle, Marc. "The Audiencia of Santo Domingo in the Seventeenth Century." Ph.D. diss., Tulane University, 2005.

"Beard-Pulling and Furniture Rearranging: Conflict within the Seventeenth-Century Audiencia of Santo Domingo." *The Americas* vol. 68, n. 4 (2012): 467–93.

"Restoring Spanish Hispaniola, the First of the Indies: Local Advocacy and Transatlantic Arbitrismo in the Late Seventeenth Century." *Colonial Latin American Review* vol. 23, n. 3 (2014): 384–412.

"Portraits of Bad Officials: Malfeasance in Visita Sentences from Seventeenth-Century Santo Domingo," in *Corruption in the Iberian Empires: Greed, Custom, and Colonial Networks*, edited by Christopher Rossmüller, 139–60. Albuquerque: University of New Mexico Press, 2017.

"The Early Caribbean Trade to Spanish America: Caribbean Pathways, 1530–1580," in *The Spanish Caribbean & the Atlantic World in the Long Sixteenth Century*, edited by Ida Altman and David Wheat, 139–60, Lincoln: University of Nebraska Press, 2019.

Egerton, Douglas R., Alison Games, Jane G. Landers, Kris Lane, and Donald R. Wright. *The Atlantic World: A History, 1400–1888*. Wheeling: Harlan Davidson, 2007.

Espino López, Antonio. "Sobre la creación de fronteras. El caso de la Española y las guerras del reinado de Carlos II, 1673–1697." *Anuario de estudios americanos* vol. 75, n. 1 (2018): 157–84.

Ferguson, James. *A Traveller's History of the Caribbean*. New York: Interlink Books, 1999.

Fernández Albaladejo, Pablo. *Fragmentos de monarquía: trabajos de historia política*. Madrid: Alianza, 1992.

Fernández de Oviedo y Valdés, Gonzalo. *Historia general y natural de las Indias, islas y Tierra Firme del mar Océano*. Asunción: Guaranía, 1944.

Fernández Nadal, Carmen María. "La unión de las armadas inglesa y española contra Francia: la defensa de las Indias en la guerra de los nueve años," in *Guerra y sociedad en la monarquía hispánica: política, estrategia y cultura en la Europa moderna*, edited by Enrique García Hernán and Davide Maffi, 1025–42. Madrid: Centro Superior de Investigaciones Científicas, 2006.

Floyd, Troy S. *The Columbus Dynasty in the Caribbean, 1492–1526*. Albuquerque: University of New Mexico Press, 1973.

Foucault, Michel. *Discipline and Punish*. New York: Pantheon, 1977.

Franco, Franklin J. *Historia del pueblo dominicano*. Santo Domingo: Instituto del Libro, 1992.

Fuente, Alejandro de la (in collaboration with César del Pino García and Bernardo Delgado Iglesias). *Havana and the Atlantic in the Sixteenth Century*. Chapel Hill: University of North Carolina Press, 2008.

Fuentes, Marisa J. *Dispossessed Lives: Enslaved Women, Violence, and The Archive*. Philadelphia: University of Pennsylvania Press, 2016.

García, Guadalupe. *Beyond the Walled City: Colonial Exclusion in Havana*. Berkeley: University of California Press, 2015.

Gelman, Jorge Daniel. "Cabildo y élite local. El caso de Buenos Aires en el siglo XVII." *HISLA* 6 (1985): 3–20.

Bibliography

Gent, N. N. *America: Or an Exact Description of the West-Indies More Especially of Those Provinces Which Are Under the Dominion of the King of Spain.* London: Richard Hodgkinsonne for Edward Dod, 1655.

Gerhard, Peter. "A Black Conquistador in Mexico." *The Hispanic American Historical Review* vol. 58, n. 3 (1978): 451–59.

Germeten, Nicole von. *Violent Delights, Violent Ends: Sex, Race, & Honor in Colonial Cartagena de Indias.* Albuquerque: University of New Mexico Press, 2013.

Gil-Bermejo García, Juana. "El Burlador de Sevilla (Posible origen histórico en las Antillas)." *Archivo Hispalense* 60 (1977): 173–84.

La Española: anotaciones históricas, 1600–1650. Sevilla: Escuela de Estudios Hispanoamericanos, CSIC, 1983.

Gil, Juan, and Consuelo Varela. "La conquista y la implantación de los españoles," in *Historia General Del Pueblo Dominicano*, vol. 1, edited by Genaro Rodríguez Morel, 243–314. Santo Domingo: Academia Dominicana de la Historia, 2013.

Gómez, Pablo F. *The Experiential Caribbean: Creating Knowledge and Healing in the Early Modern Atlantic.* Chapel Hill: University of North Carolina Press, 2017.

González Gutiérrez, Pilar. "Importación y acuñación de moneda circulante en la Española durante el siglo XVI." *Estudios de historia social y económica de América* 13 (1996): 25–45.

González, Raymundo. *De esclavos a campesinos: vida rural en Santo Domingo colonial.* Santo Domingo: Archivo General de la Nación, 2011.

Goodall, Jamie L. H. "Tippling Houses, Rum Shops and Taverns: How Alcohol Fueled Informal Commercial Networks and Knowledge Exchange in the West Indies." *Journal for Maritime Research*, vol. 18, n. 2 (2016), 97–121.

Greene, Jack P., and Philip D. Morgan. *Atlantic History: A Critical Appraisal.* New York: Oxford University Press, 2009.

Guilmartin, John Francis. *Gunpowder & Galleys: Changing Technology & Mediterranean Warfare at Sea in the 16th Century.* Victoria & Albert Publications, 2003.

Guitar, Lynne. "Cultural Genesis: Relationships Among Indians, Africans, and Spaniards in Rural Hispaniola, First Half of the Sixteenth Century." Ph.D. diss., Vanderbilt University, 1998.

"Willing It So, Intimate Glimpses of Encomienda Life in Sixteenth Century Hispaniola." *Colonial Latin American Historical Review* vol. 7, n. 3 (1998): 244–63.

"Boiling It Down: Slavery on the First Commercial Sugar Ingenios in the Americas (Hispaniola, 1530–45)," in *Slaves, Subjects, and Subversives: Blacks in Colonial Latin America*, edited by Jane G. Landers and Barry M. Robinson, 39–82. Albuquerque: University of New Mexico Press, 2006.

Gutiérrez Escudero, Antonio. *Población y economía en Santo Domingo, 1700–1746.* Sevilla: Diputación Provincial, 1985.

Hall, Gwendolyn Midlo. "African ethnicities and the meanings of 'Mina,'" in *Trans-Atlantic Dimensions of Ethnicity in the African Diaspora*, edited by Paul E. Lovejoy and David R. Trotman, 65–81. London: Continuum, 2003.

Hamm, Brian. "Between Acceptance and Exclusion: Spanish Responses to Portuguese Immigrants in the Sixteenth-Century Spanish Caribbean," in

280   *Bibliography*

The Spanish Caribbean & the Atlantic World in the Long Sixteenth Century, edited by Ida Altman and David Wheat, 113–38. Lincoln: University of Nebraska Press, 2019.

Hanna, Mark G. *Pirate Nests and the Rise of the British Empire, 1570–1740*. Chapel Hill: University of North Carolina Press, 2015.

Haring, Clarence Henry. *Trade and Navigation Between Spain and the Indies in the Time of the Hapsburgs*. Cambridge: Harvard University Press, 1918.

Harvey, L. P. *Muslims in Spain, 1500–1614*. Chicago: University of Chicago Press, 2005.

Haskett, Robert S. "Santiago De La Paz: Anatomy of a Sixteenth-Century Caribbean Sugar Estate." *UCLA Historical Journal* 1 (1980): 51–79.

Henríquez Ureña, Pedro. *La cultura y las letras coloniales en Santo Domingo*. Buenos Aires: Imprenta de la Universidad de Buenos Aires, 1936.

Henshall Momsen, Janet, and Pamela Richardson. "Caribbean and South America. Caribbean Cocoa: Planting and Production," in *Chocolate: History, Culture, and Heritage*, edited by Louis Evan Grivetti and Howard-Yana Shapiro, Hoboken: Wiley, 2009.

Hernández González, Manuel. "Bánica y Las Caobas, dos pueblos ganaderos de la frontera dominicana de fundación canaria." *El Pajar. Cuaderno de etnografía canaria* 19 (2004): 61–66.

"Santo Domingo: formación y desarrollo de una sociedad de frontera (1680–1795)." *Iberoamericana Pragensia – Suplementum* 19 (2007): 405–14.

"Sociedad en la Española, 1492–1795," in *Historia de la República Dominicana*, edited by Frank Moya Pons, 205–62. Madrid: Consejo Superior de Investigaciones Científicas, 2010.

Hernández Tapia, Concepción. "Despoblaciones de la isla de Santo Domingo en el siglo XVII." *Anuario de Estudios Americanos* XXVII (1970): 281–320.

Herzog, Tamar. *La administración como un fenómeno social: la justicia penal de la ciudad de Quito, 1650–1750*. Madrid: Centro de Estudios Constitucionales, 1995.

Defining Nations: Immigrants and Citizens in Early Modern Spain and Spanish America. New Haven: Yale University Press, 2003.

Higman, B. W. *A Concise History of the Caribbean*. New York: Cambridge University Press, 2011.

Hodges, William H., and Eugene Lyon. "A General History of Puerto Real," in *Puerto Real: The Archaeology of a Sixteenth-Century Spanish Town in Hispaniola*, edited by Kathleen Deagan, 83–112. Gainesville: University Press of Florida, 1995.

Hodges, William H., Kathleen Deagan, and Elizabeth J. Reitz. "The Natural and Cultural Settings of Puerto Real," in *Puerto Real: The Archaeology of a Sixteenth-Century Spanish Town in Hispaniola*, edited by Kathleen Deagan, 51–82. Gainesville: University Press of Florida, 1995.

Hoffman, Paul E. *The Spanish Crown and the Defense of the Caribbean, 1535–1585: Precedent, Patrimonialism, and Royal Parsimony*. Baton Rouge: Louisiana State University Press, 1980.

Hofman, Corinne, Angus Mol, Menno Hoogland, and Roberto Valcárcel Rojas. "Stage of Encounters: Migration, Mobility and Interaction in the Pre-Colonial

Bibliography

and Early Colonial Caribbean." *World Archaeology* vol. 46, n. 4 (2014): 590–609.

Incháustegui Cabral, J. Marino. *Reales cédulas y correspondencia de gobernadores de Santo Domingo: de la regencia del cardenal Cisneros en adelante*. 5 volumes. Madrid: Gráficas Reunidas, 1958.

Jarvis, Michael J. *In the Eye of All Trade: Bermuda, Bermudians, and the Maritime Atlantic World, 1680–1783*. Williamsburg: Omohundro Institute of Early American History and Culture; Chapel Hill: University of North Carolina Press, 2010.

Johnson, Julie Greer. "Cristóbal de Llerena and His Satiric Entremés." *Latin American Theatre Review* vol. 22, n. 1 (1988): 39–45.

Kagan, Richard L., and Fernando Marías. *Urban Images of the Hispanic World, 1493–1793*. New Haven: Yale University Press, 2000.

Karras, Alan L. *Smuggling: Contraband and Corruption in World History*. Lanham: Rowman & Littlefield Publishers, inc., 2010.

Klooster, Wim. *Illicit Riches: Dutch Trade in the Caribbean, 1648–1795*. Leiden: KITLV Press, 1998.

The Dutch Moment: War, Trade and Settlement in the Seventeenth-Century Atlantic World. Ithaca: Cornell University Press, 2016.

Landers, Jane. "Gracia Real De Santa Teresa De Mose: A Free Black Town in Spanish Colonial Florida." *American Historical Review* vol. 95, n. 1 (1990): 9–30.

Black Society in Spanish Florida. Urbana: University of Illinois Press, 1999.

"Cimarrón and Citizen: African Ethnicity, Corporate Identity, and the Evolution of Free Black Towns in the Spanish Circum-Caribbean," in *Slaves, Subjects, and Subversives: Blacks in Colonial Latin America*, edited by Jane Landers and Barry M. Robinson, 111–46. Albuquerque: University of New Mexico Press, 2006.

Lane, Kris E. *Pillaging the Empire: Piracy in the Americas, 1500–1750*. Armonk, NY: M.E. Sharpe, 1998.

"Africans and Natives in the Mines of Spanish America," in *Beyond Black and Red: African-Native Relations in Colonial Latin America*, edited by Matthew Restall, 159–63. Albuquerque: University of New Mexico Press, 2005.

Las Casas, Bartolomé de. *Historia de las Indias*. Santo Domingo: Sociedad Dominicana de Bibliófilos, 1987.

Law, Robin. "Ethnicities of Enslaved Africans in the Diaspora: On the Meanings of 'Mina' (Again)." *History in Africa* 32 (2005): 247–67.

Livi-Bacci, Massimo. "Return to Hispaniola: Reassessing a Demographic Catastrophe." *The Hispanic American Historical Review* vol. 83, n.1 (2003): 3–51.

Lockhart, James, and Stuart B. Schwartz. *Early Latin America: A History of Colonial Spanish America and Brazil*. New York: Cambridge University Press, 1983.

López y Sebastián, Lorenzo E., and Justo L. Del Río Moreno. "La ganadería vacuna en la isla española (1508–1587)." *Revista Complutense de Historia de América* 25 (1999): 11–49.

Bibliography

Lorenzo Sanz, Eufemio. *Comercio de España con América en la época de Felipe II*. Valladolid: Servicio de Publicaciones de la Diputación Provincial, 1979.

MacDonald, Lauren Elaine. "The Hieronymites in Hispaniola, 1493–1519." MA thesis, University of Florida, 2010.

Machiavelli, Nicolo, trans. by W. K. Marriott. *The Prince*. Project Guttemberg, 2016.

Mangan, Jane E. *Transatlantic Obligations: Creating the Bonds of Family in Conquest-Era Peru and Spain*. New York: Oxford University Press, 2016.

Martínez-Fernández, Luis. *Key to the New World: A History of Early Colonial Cuba*. Gainesville: University of Florida Press, 2018.

Marzahl, Peter. *Town in the Empire: Government, Politics and Society in Seventeenth-Century Popayán*. Austin: Institute of Latin American Studies, University of Texas, 1978.

Masters, Adrian, "A Thousand Invisible Architects: Vassals, the Petition and Response System, and the Creation of Spanish Imperial Caste Legislation." *Hispanic American Historical Review* vol. 98, n. 3 (2018): 377–406.

Mena, Miguel D. *Iglesia, espacio y poder: Santo Domingo (1498–1521), experiencia fundacional del Nuevo Mundo*. Santo Domingo: Archivo General de la Nación, 2007.

Midlo Hall, Gwendolyn. "African Ethnicities and the Meanings of 'Mina,'" in *Trans-Atlantic Dimensions of Ethnicity in the African Diaspora*, edited by Paul E. Lovejoy and David R. Trotman, 68–81. New York: Continuum Int'l Publishing Group, 2003.

Mira Caballos, Esteban. *El indio antillano: repartimiento, encomienda y esclavitud (1492–1542)*. Bogotá: Muñoz Moya, 1997.

———. *Nicolás de Ovando y los orígenes del sistema colonial español, 1502–1509*. Santo Domingo: Patronato de la Ciudad Colonial de Santo Domingo, Centro de Altos Estudios Humanísticos y del Idioma Español, 2000.

———. *La Española, epicentro del Caribe en el siglo XVI*. Santo Domingo: Academia Dominicana de la Historia, 2010.

———. "La consolidación de la colonia," in *Historia General Del Pueblo Dominicano*, edited by Genaro Rodríguez Morel, 315–74. Santo Domingo: Academia Dominicana de la Historia, 2013.

———. "Otros sectores productivos y económicos," in *Historia General Del Pueblo Dominicano*, edited by Genaro Rodríguez Morel, 425–72. Santo Domingo: Academia Dominicana de la Historia, 2013.

Mittelstrass, Jürgen. "Nature and Science in the Renaissance," in *Metaphysics and Philosophy of Science in the Seventeenth and Eighteenth Centuries*, edited by R. S. Woolshouse, 17–43. Springer, 1988.

Montemayor y Cuenca, Juan Francisco de. *Relación de la victoria que han tenido las armas de Su Majestad (Dios le guarde) en la ciudad de Santo Domingo, isla Española, contra la Armada Inglesa de Guillermo Pen, enviada por el señor don Bernardino de Meneses Bracamonte, conde de Peñalba, presidente de la Real Audiencia de aquella ciudad, gobernador y capitán general de la isla*. Sevilla: Juan Gómez de Blas, 1655.

Moscoso, Francisco. *Caguas en la conquista española del siglo 16*. Río Piedras, Puerto Rico: Publicaciones Gaviota, 2016.

Bibliography

Moutoukias, Zacarías. *Contrabando y control colonial en el siglo XVII: Buenos Aires, El Atlántico y el espacio peruano.* Buenos Aires: Centro Editor de América Latina, 1988.

Moya Pons, Frank. *Historia colonial de Santo Domingo.* Santiago, República Dominicana: UCMM, 1976.

Después de Colón: trabajo, sociedad y política en la economía del oro. Madrid: Alianza, 1987.

La otra historia dominicana. Santo Domingo: Buho, 2008.

The Dominican Republic: A National History. Princeton, NJ: Markus Wiener Publishers, 2010.

"La población taína y su desaparición," in *Historia de la República Dominicana,* edited by Frank Moya Pons, 19–28. Madrid: Consejo Superior de Publicaciones Científicas, 2010.

Mumford, Jeremy Ravi. *Vertical Empire: The General Resettlement of Indians in the Colonial Andes.* Durham, NC: Duke University Press, 2012.

Muro Romero, Fernando. "El beneficio de oficios públicos con jurisdicción en Indias. Notas sobre sus orígenes." *Anuario de Estudios Americanos,* 35 (1978): 1–67.

Nessler, Graham T. *An Islandwide Struggle for Freedom: Revolution, Emancipation, and Reenslavement in Hispaniola, 1789–1809.* Chapel Hill: The University of North Carolina Press, 2016.

Nesvig, Martin Austin. *Promiscuous Power: An Unorthodox History of New Spain.* Austin: University of Texas Press, 2018.

O'Malley, Gregory E. *Final Passages: The Intercolonial Slave Trade of British America, 1619–1807.* Williamsburg: Omohundro Institute of Early American History and Culture; Chapel Hill: University of North Carolina Press, 2014.

Palmié, Stephan, and Francisco A. Scarano. *The Caribbean: A History of the Region and Its Peoples.* Chicago; London: The University of Chicago Press, 2011.

Parry, J. H. *The Sale of Public Office in the Spanish Indies under the Hapsburgs.* Berkeley: University of California Press, 1953.

Pasquariello, Anthony M. "The Entremés in Sixteenth-Century Spanish America." *Hispanic American Historical Review* (1952): 44–58.

Pazos, María Luisa. *El ayuntamiento de la ciudad de México en el siglo XVII: continuidad institucional y cambio social.* Sevilla: Diputación Provincial de Sevilla, 1999.

Peña Pérez, Frank. *Antonio Osorio, monopolio, contrabando y despoblación.* Santiago: UCMM, 1980.

Pérez Montás, Eugenio. *La ciudad del Ozama: 500 años de historia urbana.* Santo Domingo: Patronato de la Ciudad Colonial de Santo Domingo, 1998.

Pérez Tostado, Igor. "Por respeto a mi profesión: disciplinamiento, dependencia e identidad en la formación de las comunidades militares irlandesas e inglesas en los ejércitos hispanos," in *Guerra y sociedad en la monarquía hispánica. Política, estrategia y cultura en La Europa moderna (1500–1700),* edited by Enrique García Hernán and Davide Maffi, 681–706. Madrid: Centro Superior de Investigaciones Científicas, 2006.

Pérez Tostado, Igor, and Enrique García Hernán. *Irlanda y el Atlántico ibérico: movilidad, participación e intercambio cultural (1580–1830).* Valencia: Albatros Ediciones, 2010.

Bibliography

Pérez-Mallaína Bueno, Pablo Emilio, trans. by Carla Rahn Phillips. *Spain's Men of the Sea: Daily Life on the Indies Fleets in the Sixteenth Century*. Baltimore: Johns Hopkins University Press, 1998.

Perry, Mary Elizabeth. *The Handless Maiden: Moriscos and the Politics of Religion in Early Modern Spain*. Princeton: Princeton University Press, 2005.

Pestana, Carla Gardina. "English Character and the Fiasco of Western Design." *Early American Studies: An Interdisciplinary Journal* vol. 3, n. 1 (2005): 1–31.

The English Conquest of Jamaica: Oliver Cromwell's Bid for Empire. Cambridge: The Belknap Press of Harvard University Press, 2017.

Polanco Brito, Hugo Eduardo. *Los escribanos en el Santo Domingo colonial*. Santo Domingo: Academia Dominicana de la Historia, 1989.

Ponce Leiva, Pilar. *Certezas ante la incertidumbre: élite y Cabildo de Quito en el siglo XVII*. Quito: Abya-Yala, 1998.

Ponce Vázquez, Juan José. "Casting Traitors and Villains: The Historiographical Memory of the 1605 Depopulations of Hispaniola," in *Sites of Memory in Spain and Latin America*, edited by Marina Llorente, Marcella Salvi, and Aída Díaz de León, 151–66. Lanham: Lexington Press, 2015.

"Atlantic Peripheries: Diplomacy, War, and Spanish–French Interactions in Hispaniola, 1660s–1690s," in *The Atlantic World*, edited by D'Maris Coffman, Adrian Leonard, and William O'Reilly, 300–18. New York: Routledge, 2015.

"Unequal Partners in Crime: Masters, Slaves and Free People of Color in Santo Domingo, C. 1600–1650." *Slavery & Abolition* vol. 37, n. 4 (2016): 704–23.

Prado, Fabricio. "The Fringes of Empires: Recent Scholarship on Colonial Frontiers and Borderlands in Latin America." *History Compass* vol. 10, n. 4 (2012): 318–33.

Edge of Empire: Atlantic Networks and Revolution in Bourbon Rio De La Plata. Oakland: University of California Press, 2015.

Premo, Bianca. *The Enlightenment on Trial: Ordinary Litigants and Colonialism in the Spanish Empire*. New York: Oxford University Press, 2017.

Pritchard, James. *In Search of Empire: The French in the Americas, 1670–1730*. New York: Cambridge University Press, 2004.

Ramírez, Susan Elizabeth. *The World Upside Down. Cross-Cultural Contact and Conflict in Sixteenth-Century Peru*. Stanford: Stanford University Press, 1996.

Ramos, Frances L. *Identity, Ritual, and Power in Colonial Puebla*. Tucson: University of Arizona Press, 2012.

Reeder, Tyson. *Smugglers, Pirates, and Patriots: Free Trade in the Age of Revolution*. Philadelphia: University of Pennsylvania Press, 2019.

Reichert, Rafal. "El situado novohispano para la manutención de los presidios españoles en la region del golfo de México y el Caribe durante el siglo XVII." *Estudios de Historia Novohispana* 46 (2012): 47–81.

"Gastos militares que sufragó la Nueva España para mantener los presidios en la región del circuncaribe durante el reinado de Carlos II, 1665–1700." *Jahrbuch für Geschichte Lateinamerikas* 49 (2012): 58–81.

Sobre las olas de un mar plateado: la política defensiva española y el financiamiento militar novohispano en la región del Gran Caribe, 1598–1700. Mexico City: Universidad Nacional Autónoma de México, 2013.

Bibliography 285

Rivas, Christine D. "Power, Race, Class and Gender in Colonial Santo Domingo: An Analysis of Spanish Dominican Marital Patters in the Archbishopric of Santo Domingo, 1701, 1801." Ph.D. diss., Carleton University, 2008.

Robles, Gregorio de, *America a fines del siglo XVII: noticias de los lugares de contrabando*, edited by Víctor Tau Anzoátegui. Valladolid: Casa-Museo de Colón y Seminario Americanista de la Universidad, 1980.

Rodríguez Demorizi, Emilio. *Relaciones históricas se Santo Domingo*, vol. I. Ciudad Trujillo: Editora Montalvo, 1942.

Relaciones históricas de Santo Domingo, vol. II. Ciudad Trujillo: Editora Montalvo, 1945.

Rodríguez Morel, Genaro. *Cartas del Cabildo de la ciudad de Santo Domingo en el siglo XVI*. Santo Domingo: Centro de Altos Estudios Humanísticos y del Idioma Español, 1999.

Cartas de los Cabildos eclesiásticos de Santo Domingo y la Vega en el siglo XVI. Santo Domingo: Patronato de la Ciudad Colonial de Santo Domingo, 2000.

"The Sugar Economy in Hispaniola in the Sixteenth Century," in *Tropical Babylons: Sugar and the Making of the Atlantic World, 1450–1680*, edited by Stuart B. Schwartz, 85–114. Chapel Hill: University of North Carolina Press, 2003.

Cartas del Cabildo de la ciudad de Santo Domingo en el siglo XVII. Santo Domingo: Archivo General de la Nación, Academia Dominicana de la Historia, 2007.

"Desarrollo económico y cambio demográfico en la Española. Siglos XV-XVII." *Boletín del Archivo General de la Nación* XXXII, n. 117 (2007): 79–144.

Orígenes de la economía de plantación en la Española. Santo Domingo: Editora Nacional, 2012.

"El sector azucarero," in *Historia general del pueblo dominicano*, edited by Genaro Rodríguez Morel, 375–424. Santo Domingo: Academia Dominicana de la Historia, 2013.

Rogozinski, Jan. *A Brief History of the Caribbean: From the Arawak and the Carib to the Present*. New York: Plume, 2000.

Roorda, Eric, Lauren H. Derby, and Raymundo González. *The Dominican Republic Reader: History, Culture, Politics*. Durham: Duke University Press, 2014.

Rosenmüller, Christoph. *Corruption in the Iberian Empires: Greed, Custom, and Colonial Networks*. Albuquerque: University of New Mexico Press, 2017.

Rubio, Fray Vicente, and María Ugarte. *Semana Santa en la ciudad colonial de Santo Domingo*. Santo Domingo: Comisión Permanente para la Celebración del Quinto Centenario del Descubrimiento y Evangelización de América, 1992.

Ruiz Rivera, Julián and Ángel Sanz Tapia, eds. *La venta de cargos y el ejercicio del poder en Indias*. León: Universidad de León, 2007.

Ruiz, Teofilo F. *Spanish Society, 1400–1600*. New York: Longman, 2001.

A King Travels: Festive Traditions in Late Medieval and Early Modern Spain. Princeton: Princeton University Press, 2012.

Rupert, Linda Marguerite. *Creolization and Contraband: Curaçao in the Early Modern Atlantic World*. Athens: The University of Georgia Press, 2012.

Bibliography

Sáez, José Luis. *La Iglesia y el negro esclavo en Santo Domingo: una historia de tres siglos*. Santo Domingo: Patronato de la Ciudad Colonial de Santo Domingo, 1994.

Libro de bautismos de esclavos, 1636–1670. Santo Domingo: Archivo General de la Nación, 2008.

Sagás, Ernesto, and Orlando Inoa. *The Dominican People: A Documentary History*. Princeton: Markus Wiener Publishers, 2003.

Santos-Granero, Fernando. *Vital Enemies: Slavery, Predation, and the Amerindian Political Economy of Life*. Austin: University of Texas Press, 2009.

Sanz Tapia, Ángel. "La venta de oficios de hacienda en la Audiencia de Quito (1650–1700)." *Revista de Indias* vol. 63, n. 229 (2003): 633–48.

Schmitt, Casey. "Centering Spanish Jamaica: Regional Competition, Informal Trade, and the English Invasion, 1620–62." *The William and Mary Quarterly* vol. 76, n. 4 (2019): 697–726.

"Virtue in Corruption: Privateers, Smugglers, and the Shape of Empire in the Eighteenth-Century Caribbean." *Early American Studies, An Interdisciplinary Journal* vol. 13, n. 1 (2015): 80–110.

Schneider, Elena A. *The Occupation of Havana: War, Trade, and Slavery in the Atlantic World*. Williamsburg: Omohundro Institute of Early American History and Culture; Chapel Hill: University of North Carolina Press, 2018.

Schwaller, Robert C. *Géneros de Gente in Early Colonial Mexico: Defining Racial Difference*. Norman: University of Oklahoma Press, 2016.

"Contested Conquests: African Maroons and the Incomplete Conquest of Hispaniola, 1519–1620." *The Americas* vol. 75, n. 4 (2018): 609–38.

Schwartz, Stuart B. *Sugar Plantations in the Formation of Brazilian Society: Bahia, 1550–1835*. New York: Cambridge University Press, 1985.

"Spaniards,'Pardos', and the Missing Mestizos: Identities and Racial Categories in the Early Hispanic Caribbean." *New West Indian Guide/Nieuwe West-Indische Gids* vol. 71, n. 1–2 (1997): 5–19.

All Can Be Saved: Religious Tolerance and Salvation in the Iberian Atlantic World. New Haven: Yale University Press, 2008.

Serrano Álvarez, José. *Ejército y fiscalidad en Cartagena de Indias. Auge y declive en la segunda mitad del siglo XVII*. Bogotá: El Áncora, 2006.

Sevilla Soler, Ma Rosario. *Santo Domingo Tierra de Frontera (1750–1800)*. Sevilla: Escuela de Estudios Hispanoamericanos, 1980.

Shaw, Jenny. *Everyday Life in the Early English Caribbean: Irish, Africans, and the Construction of Difference*. Athens: The University of Georgia Press, 2013.

Sierra Silva, Pablo Miguel. "Afro-Mexican Women in Saint-Domingue: Piracy, Captivity, and Community in the 1680s and 1690s." *Hispanic American Historical Review* vol. 100, n. 1 (2020): 3–34.

Sigüenza y Góngora, Carlos de. *Trofeo de la justicia española en el castigo de la alevosía francesa que al abrigo de la armada de Barlovento, ejecutaron los lanceros de la isla de Santo Domingo, en los que se aquella nación ocupan sus costas*. México: Herederos de la viuda de Bernardo Calderón, 1691.

Silverblatt, Irene. *Modern Inquisitions: Peru and the Colonial Origins of the Civilized World*. Durham: Duke University Press, 2004.

Bibliography

Soria Mesa, Enrique. *Los últimos moriscos: Pervivencias de la población de origen islámico en el reino de Granada (siglos XVII–XVIII)*. Valencia: Universidad de Valencia, 2014.

Stone, Erin. "America's First Slave Revolt: Indians and African Slaves in Española, 1500–1534." *Ethnohistory* vol. 60, n. 2 (2013): 195–217.

"Indian Harvest: The Rise of the Indigenous Slave Trade and Diaspora from Española to the Circum-Caribbean, 1492–1542." Ph.D. diss., Vanderbilt University, 2014.

"Slave Raiders Vs. Friars: Tierra Firme, 1513–1522." *The Americas* vol. 74, n. 2 (2017): 139–70.

"War and Rescate: The Sixteenth-Century Circum-Caribbean Indigenous Slave Trade," in *The Spanish Caribbean & the Atlantic World in the Long Sixteenth Century*, edited by Ida Altman and David Wheat, 47–68. Lincoln: University of Nebraska Press, 2019.

Studnicki-Gizbert, Daviken. *A Nation Upon the Ocean Sea: Portugal's Atlantic Diaspora and the Crisis of the Spanish Empire, 1492–1640*. New York: Oxford University Press, 2007.

Taber, Robert D. "The Issue of the Union: Family, Law, Politics in Western Saint-Domingue, 1777 to 1789." Ph.D. diss., University of Florida, 2015.

Taylor, William B. "Between Global Process and Local Knowledge: An Inquiry Into Early Latin American Social History, 1500–1900," in *Reliving the Past: The Worlds of Social History*, edited by Olivier Zunz, 115–90. Chapel Hill: University of North Carolina Press, 1985.

Tomás y Valiente, Francisco. *La venta de oficios en Indias (1492–1606)*. Madrid: Instituto de Estudios Administrativos, 1972.

Torres Ramírez, Bibiano. *La armada de Barlovento*. Sevilla: Escuela de Estudios Hispano-Americanos, 1981.

Utrera, Cipriano de. *Santo Domingo. Dilucidaciones Históricas*, tomo 1. Santo Domingo: Imprenta de Dios y Patria, 1927.

"Sor Leonor de Ovando." *Boletín del Archivo General de la Nación* 68 (1951): 120–50.

Varela, Consuelo, and Isabel Aguirre. *La caída de Cristóbal Colón: el juicio de Bobadilla*. Madrid: Marcial Pons Historia, 2006.

Vega, Bernardo. *La derrota de Penn y Venables en Santo Domingo, 1655*. Santo Domingo: Academia Dominicana de la Historia, 2013.

Venegoni, Giovanni. "Creating a Caribbean Colony in the Long Seventeenth Century: Saint Domingue and the Pirates," in *The Torrid Zone: Caribbean Colonization and Cultural Interaction in the Long Seventeenth Century*, edited by L. H. Roper, 132–46. Columbia: *The University of South Carolina Press*, 2018.

Vicioso, Abelardo G. *Santo Domingo en las letras coloniales (1492–1800)*. Santo Domingo: Universidad Autónoma de Santo Domingo, 1979.

Vidal Ortega, Antonino. *Cartagena de Indias en la articulación del espacio regional Caribe, 1580–1640: la producción agraria*. Lebrija: Agrija Ediciones, 1998.

"Barcos, velas y mercancias del otro lado de mar. Cartagena de Indias a comienzos del siglo XVII." *XIII Congreso de Colombianistas* (2003): 45–60.

Bibliography

Villalobos, Sergio R. *Comercio y contrabando en el Río de la Plata y Chile: 1700–1811*. Buenos Aires: Editorial Universitaria de Buenos Aires, 1965.

Walker, Tamara J. "'He Outfitted His Family in Notable Decency': Slavery, Honour and Dress in Eighteenth-Century Lima, Peru." *Slavery and Abolition* vol. 30, n. 3 (2009): 383–402.

　Exquisite Slaves: Race, Clothing, and Status in Colonial Lima. New York: Cambridge University Press, 2017.

Warsh, Molly A. *American Baroque: Pearls and the Nature of Empire, 1492–1700*. Williamsburg: Omohundro Institute of Early American History and Culture; Chapel Hill: University of North Carolina Press, 2018.

Weber, David J. *The Spanish Frontier in North America*. New Haven: Yale University Press, 1992.

Wernke, Steven A. *Negotiated Settlements: Andean Communities and Landscapes Under Inka and Spanish Colonialism*. Gainesville: University Press of Florida, 2013.

Wheat, David. "Mediterranean Slavery, New World Transformations: Galley Slaves in the Spanish Caribbean, 1578–1635." *Slavery and Abolition* vol. 31, n. 3 (2010): 327–44.

　"*Nharas* and *Morenas Horras*: A Luso-African Model for the Social History of the Spanish Caribbean, c. 1570–1640." *Journal of Early Modern History* 14 (2010), 119–50.

　Atlantic Africa and the Spanish Caribbean, 1570–1640. Williamsburg: Omohundro Institute of Early American History and Culture; Chapel Hill: University of North Carolina Press, 2016.

Williams, Eric Eustace. *From Columbus to Castro: The History of the Caribbean, 1492–1969*. London: Deutsch, 1970.

Wilson, Samuel M. *Hispaniola: Caribbean Chiefdoms in the Age of Columbus*. Tuscaloosa: University of Alabama Press, 1990.

Wright, Irene A. "Rescates: With Special References to Cuba, 1599–1610." *Hispanic American Historical Review* (1920): 333–61.

Zacek, Natalie. *Settler Society in the English Leeward Islands, 1670–1776*. New York: Cambridge University Press, 2010.

Index

Acuña, Diego de, 193–194
Africans, 7–10, 44, 227
  Angola, 69, 141–142
  in depopulations, 1604–6, 114, 115–116,
    119–121, 125–127, 131–132
  elites and enslaved, 134–135, 136–137,
    155–159, 162–169, 170, 246–248
  ethnonyms of, 50, 141–142, 248
  French, trade with, and, 265
  from French settlements, slaves fleeing,
    246–250, 262
  frontier soldiers of, 242–244
  Garrido, 32
  labor performed by, types of, 142–143
  ladino/a, 33–38, 119–120, 271
  maroons, 6–7, 34–38, 41–42, 54, 78–79,
    271
  in Mexico City, enslaved, 157–158
  Pimentel, R., selling enslaved, 197–198
  of Pimentel, R., enslaved, 134–135, 136,
    137, 158–159, 164–169, 183–184,
    240–241
  population of, 77–78, 141–143,
    148–149, 155, 239–240
  regidores and, 158–159
  resistance of, indigenous and, 34–38, 54
  in San Lorenzo de los Minas, 248
  Santo Domingo, religious processions of,
    50
  Santo Domingo, relocations to, and,
    141–143
  from Santo Domingo, Havana importing,
    157

  in Santo Domingo, 32–34, 50, 53, 55,
    134–135, 136–137, 155–159,
    162–169, 170, 245–248
  sexual abuse of enslaved, 128–129
  in smuggling, work of, 64, 77–79, 83,
    84–85
  smuggling in enslaved, 63, 65–66, 69,
    86–87, 119–120
  social importance of enslaved, 155–159
  in sugar economy, 30–31, 32–34, 35–36,
    38, 39–42, 49, 54, 142–143
  in violence, masters using enslaved,
    159–162, 164–169, 170, 183–184,
    266–267
Agüero Bardeci, Jerónimo, 116–117
Agustín, Juan, 169
Alarcón Coronado, Francisco de, 189–190,
    195–196, 198–201, 230
alcabala (sales tax), 164–165, 181–182
alcaide (castellan), 195–196, 201, 258, 269
  Pimentel, R., and, 188–190, 210–211
  Pujadas, 188–190, 234
alcalde. See alcalde ordinario
alcalde mayor, 269
  Hernández, in depopulations, 1604–6,
    123–125
  Rodríguez Franco as, 180–181
  of Santiago de los Caballeros, Robles, J.,
    250
  smuggling, investigation of, and, 81–82
alcalde ordinario, 64–65, 134–135,
    163–164, 269
  Fernández de Castro, 205–206

Index

alcalde ordinario (cont.)
  Llerena on, 56–58
  of Monte Plata, 183–184
  Pérez Franco, will of, and, 205–206
  Pimentel, R., as, 179–180
  smuggling, investigation of, and, 83
Alcázar, Simón de, 71
alférez, 264–265, 269
alférez mayor, 146, 269
alférez real, 106–107
alguacil mayor, 60, 146, 269
Aliaga, Francisco de, 80–81
Aliaga, Juan de, 166–168
Alpujarras, wars of, 99, 104–105
Andes, 103–104, 106
Angola, 69, 141–142
Anti-Haitianism, 101
Arawak, 3–4, 25, 237–238
archbishops
  Dávila Padilla, 73–75
  Navarrete, 220–221, 245–246, 253–254
  Ramos, N., 72–73
  of Santo Domingo, 44–45, 58, 72–75,
    94–95, 181–182, 217–218, 219–221,
    245–246, 253–254, 259, 270
  of Toledo, Cisneros, 29–30, 103
  Torres, F., 181–182
Archivo General de Indias, Spain, 20
Archivo General de Simancas, Spain, 20
armada de Barlovento, 178–179, 255–256
arribadas (unscheduled arrivals), 60–61
asiento, 263–264, 269
Atlantic islands, 30–31
attorney, powers of, 185–186, 187
Audiencia, Quito, 75
Audiencia of Santo Domingo, 2–3,
    162–163, 238–239. *See also oidores*
  arribadas and, 60–61
  buildings of, 48–49, 52, 76, 189
  Cabildo, secular, and, 76–77, 144–146,
    147–148, 150–154
  depopulations, 1604–6, and, 100–101,
    109–113, 115–117, 121–122, 127–128
  escribano de cámara of, 63, 79, 106–107,
    109, 204, 270
  fiscal in, 44, 80–81, 115–116, 146, 152,
    154, 161, 189–190, 193, 195–196,
    198–201, 210, 213–214, 215–216,
    218–219, 230, 246–247, 269
  French and, 249–250, 259
  galleys and, 88–90

ginger economy and, 45
governor and, 12–13, 176–178, 179, 202,
    205–206, 208–209
graffiti on, 172
jurisdiction of, 12–13
maestre de la plata and, 193–194,
    195–197
offices, sale of, and, 146, 147–148,
    150–154, 210
oidor in, 13, 38–39, 269, 271
patronage networks and, 173–175
Pérez Franco and, 202, 205–206
Pimentel, R., and, 165–168, 169,
    172–176, 179–180, 181–182,
    183–188, 189–190, 198–201,
    203–205, 209, 210, 211, 212–214,
    218–219, 221–222
  on Portuguese residents, 199, 228–231
relatores in, 186–188, 271
Rodríguez Franco and, 180–181
  on runaway slaves, 246–248
Santiago de los Caballeros, attack on,
    and, 224
Sevillian merchants and, 59–61
situado and, 195–197
smuggling and, 61, 75–79, 80–87, 88–90,
    91, 98–99, 106, 107–109, 180–181,
    188, 189–191, 193, 195–196,
    198–201, 213–214, 215–216, 222,
    265–266
sources on, 19–21
Spanish crown and, 173–175, 222
Zúñiga and, 208–209
Ayala, Franco de, 86–87
Ayala, Gregorio de, 94–95

Bahoruco, War of, 34–37, 54
Balboa Mogrovejo, Juan de, 240, 241
  frontier troops disbanded by, 243–244
  Pimentel, R., and, 214–215, 217–218
  Santiago de los Caballeros garrison
    established by, 244–245
  Ubilla and, 213–216, 217–218
Bánica, 252–253
Bastida Peñalosa, Rodrigo de la, 134–136
Bitrián, Juan
  extortion under, 194–195
  foreign ships and, 235–236
  maestre de la plata, election of, and,
    194–196
  patronage networks of, 190–192

Index

291

Pimentel, R., and, 181–182, 185, 191–192, 197–198, 236
residencia of, 185
situado and, 178–179, 194–196, 197–198
smuggling and, 190–192, 194–196, 198–199
Blumenthal, Debra, 158–159
bohío, 117, 269
Bourdieu, Pierre, 156
bozales, 33–34, 269
Bryant, Sherwin, 136
buccaneers, 237–238, 242–243
El burlador de Sevilla y convidado de piedra (Molina), 128
Bushnell, Amy Turner, 11

Caballero, Andrés, 209, 213–214
Cabildo (ecclesiastical), 45, 46, 49, 212–213, 237, 270
Cabildo (secular), 38, 143–144, 270. *See also* offices, sale of; *regidores*
alférez mayor in, 146, 269
Audiencia of Santo Domingo and, 76–77, 144–146, 147–148, 150–154
Bitrián and, 236
in depopulations, 1604–6, 100–101, 113–115, 121–122, 128–132
in depopulations, 1604–6, aftermath of, 130–132
disputes within, 134–136, 144–145, 165–168
families in, rivalries among, 134–136, 150
French, war with, and, 256, 258, 259
galleys and, 88–89
on Irish, 233–234
Llerena on, 56–58
López de Castro in, 106–107
of Monte Plata, 183–184
patronage networks and, 150, 151–152, 165
Pérez Franco, death of, and, 205–206
Pimentel, R., and, 134–136, 162, 171, 179–180, 181–182, 188, 196–197, 200–201, 212–213, 222
prices, regulation of, and, 43–44
regidores perpetuos in, 145–146
seats in, inherited, 145–146
seats in, power of, 143–145
seats in, sale of, 136–137, 146–148, 150–155
on smuggling, 73

Spanish crown and, 145–148, 151, 245–246
cacao, 240–241
caciques, 27–29, 102–103, 270
Colón, C., arrival of, and, 25
Enrique, 34–37, 54
calidad, 17–18, 270
Camp, Stephanie M. H., 158–159
Canary Islands, 30–31
Cañeque, Alejandro, 18–19, 150
de capa y espada ministers, 109–110
Cap-Français, 239–240, 245, 256–257, 259–260
capitán general, 271
Caracas, Venezuela, 13, 187, 196–197, 241, 269
Caribbean, Spain and, 5, 8, 173–174, 266–267
Caribs, 31–32
Cartagena, 10–11, 151–152, 178–179, 192–193, 196–197
Carvajal, Pedro de, 214, 217–219
castellan (*alcaide*). *See* alcaide
Castilians, 25–26, 38–39, 40–41, 43, 74–75, 231
Fuenteovejuna, 79–80
moriscos and, 98–99, 104–105
with Portuguese, union of, 61–62, 228
Castillo, Isabel del, 159–162
Castillo Vaca, Damián del, 200–201, 206–207, 213, 215, 218–219
Castro Rivera family, 152–153
Cateau-Cambrésis, treaty of, 61–62
Catholicism. *See* Christianity
cattle, 143
depopulations, 1604–6, and, 113–114, 117, 119–122, 125, 126–127, 132–133
French, trade with, and, 253, 254, 265
growth in, 46–47, 54, 55, 59–60
slaves and, 142–143
smuggling and, 73, 107–108, 119–120
censo, 43–44, 123–125, 270
census (1606), 143, 149
Africans in, 77–78, 141–143, 148–149
vecinos in, 77–78, 148–149
Chacón Albarca, Jerónimo, 246–247
Chaves Osorio, Gabriel de, 180, 193–194
Christianity
church, Pimentel, R., and, 182, 217, 219–221, 222

292   *Index*

Christianity (cont.)
  depopulations, 1604–6, and, 100–101,
    117–118, 122–123, 124–126, 130–132
  Lutherans, 3, 64, 73–74, 114
  non-Spaniards and, 227–227, 229, 232,
    233–234
  population relocations, Spanish,
    motivated by, 102–106
  Protestantism, fear of, 3, 59, 64,
    72, 73–74, 96–97, 105–106, 114,
    227, 232
  smuggling and, 70–75, 96–97, 99, 114
Cisneros, Francisco Jiménez de, 29–30, 103
Cobo, Alonso de, 71
Colón, Cristóbal (Christopher Columbus),
  3–4, 25–26, 32, 34
Colón, Diego, 35–36, 38–39, 48–49
Columbus, Christopher. *See* Colón,
  Cristóbal
confraternities, 50, 66, 270
contador, 191, 193, 198–199, 203, 270
contraband. *See* smuggling
Córdoba, Pedro de, 29
corregidor. *See* alcalde mayor
corruption
  arribadas and, 60–61
  smuggling and, 17–19, 61
  as term, 17
Cortés, Hernán, 32
Council of the Indies, 20–21, 60, 68, 267,
  269
  cases appealed to, 17–18, 20
  depopulations, 1604–6, and, 100, 106,
    107–109, 111–113, 122–123
  on frontier patrols, Robles, A., ending,
    250–251
  galleys approved by, 88–89
  ginger and, 44–45
  López de Castro and, 107–109
  on Melgarejo, 192
  on offices, sale of, 151, 152–153
  for patrol ships, requests ignored by,
    98–99
  Pimentel, R., and, 181–182, 185,
    213–214, 216–217, 219–220
criollo, 71–72, 142–143, 270
Cromwell, Jesse, 2, 58–59
cuartos, 43, 270
Cuba, 241
  in depopulations, 1604–6, flight to, 126,
    127–128, 130, 132

Havana, 10–11, 43–44, 157
Santiago, smuggling in, 126
from Santo Domingo, slaves imported
  into, 157
Cuello, Antonio, 229–230
Cuello, Silvestre, 159–162
Cueva, Francisco de la, 214, 217–218,
  219–220
Cumaná, 189–190
currency, standardization of, 43–44

Dávila Padilla, Agustín, 73–75
debt, 38–39
demora, 270
depopulations, 1604–6, 264–265
  Africans in, 114, 115–116, 119–121,
    125–127, 131–132
  in aftermath, narrative of, 128–133
  aftermath of, 4, 111, 128–133, 135–136,
    137–138, 169–170, 176, 177–178,
    265–266
  Audiencia of Santo Domingo and,
    100–101, 109–113, 115–117,
    121–122, 127–128
  Cabildo, secular, and, 100–101,
    113–115, 121–122, 128–132
  cattle and, 113–114, 117, 119–122, 125,
    126–127, 132–133
  Christianity and, 100–101, 117–118,
    122–123, 124–126, 130–132
  Council of the Indies and, 100, 106,
    107–109, 111–113, 122–123
  Cuba, flight to, in, 126, 127–128, 130,
    132
  as *las devastaciones*, 101
  in Dominican historiography, 101
  Dutch and, 116–117, 119, 121, 122
  fiscal, *Audiencia* of Santo Domingo, on,
    115–116
  Hernández in, 123–125
  La Yaguana in, 3, 110, 116–117,
    125–127
  López de Castro in, 107–110, 111–113,
    117–118, 132, 138–139
  Manso de Contreras in, 110–113,
    115–117, 121, 127–129
  mestizos in, 114, 115–116,
    131–132
  Montoro in, 119–121
  mulatos in, 114, 115–116, 119–121,
    131–132

Index

in north, resistance to, 119–132,
137–138, 242–243
oidores in, 110–113, 115–117, 127–128
Osorio, A., in, 100–101, 109–110,
112–115, 116–118, 119–125,
126–129, 131–132, 138–139, 177
preliminaries to, 109–118
runaway slaves in, 126–127
Santo Domingo, primacy of, after, 133,
135–136, 137–142
to Santo Domingo, relocation after,
137–143
Spanish crown and, 3, 100–101,
122–123, 130–132
Spanish population relocations compared
with, 100–102, 106
las devastaciones (the devastations). *See*
depopulations, 1604–6
Díaz de Mendoza, Ruy, 89–90
disease
in Santo Domingo, 201, 240–242,
245–246
smallpox epidemics, 29–30, 31–32, 103,
240
Dominican order, 29–30, 49–50
Don Juan Tenorio (fictional character), 128
Drake, Francis. *See also* piracy
Langton and, 92
Santo Domingo attack by, 22–24, 47–48,
54–55, 57–58, 61–62, 68–69, 91–92,
106–107, 109–110
Santo Domingo attack by, aftermath of,
23–24, 55, 92, 109–110, 176
ducados, 54–55, 270
Dutch, 211, 263–264
depopulations, 1604–6, and, 116–117,
119, 121, 122
Spain and, 227, 248–249
West India Company, 61–62, 149–150

encomienda system, 26–30, 270
demora in, 270
dismantling of, Jeronymite friars
attempting, 102–103
Enrique and, 34–35
sugar economy and, 30–31, 38
English, 87–88, 213–214
Drake, Santo Domingo attacked by,
22–24, 47–48, 54–55, 57–58, 61–62,
68–69, 91–92, 106–107, 109–110, 176
in Hispaniola, settlers of, 232, 236–238

Irish and, 232, 233–234, 235
Langton, raids by, 92–95
of Santo Domingo, failed 1655 invasion
of, 177, 206–208, 210–211, 232–233,
239
smuggling and, 67–68, 72, 92–95, 96,
137–138, 215–216, 263–264
Spain and, 61–62, 67–68, 109–110, 227,
236, 259–260
Enrique (*cacique*), 34–37, 54
entailment (*mayorazgo*), 38–39, 271
entremés, 56–58
Ermenzon, Ricardo, 236
Escoto, Bautista, 248–250
escribano, 80–81, 270
office of, transferring, 147–148
Pimentel, R., and, 186–188
escribano de cámara, 270
López de Castro as, 106–107, 109
Méndez, 204
Torres, J., 63, 79
estancia, 270
estanciero, 160, 270
ethnonyms, African, 50, 141–142, 248
expeditions, sixteenth century, 26–27,
31–32

Facundo Carvajal, Francisco, 209–210
fanega, 270
Felipe II (king), 52, 61–62, 109,
228
Felipe III (king), 109, 121
Felipe IV (king), 121, 213–214
Fernández de Castro, Baltasar, 205–206
Fernández de Córdoba, Luis, 200–201
Fernández de Oviedo, Gonzalo, 34, 47,
106–107
Fernández de Torrequemada, Francisco,
134–136, 162, 165
Fernando V (king), 29–30, 33–34
Figueroa y Castilla, Baltasar de, 200–201,
215
fiscal, 270
fiscal, *Audiencia* of Santo Domingo, 161,
269
Alarcón, 189–190, 195–196, 198–201,
230
Aliaga, F., 80–81
on depopulations, 1604–6, 115–116
Garcés, 246–247
Herrera, on *situado*, 193

294 Index

fiscal, Audiencia of Santo Domingo (cont.)
  Larrieta, 44
  offices, sale of, and, 146, 152, 154, 210
  Pimentel, R., and, 189–190, 198–201,
    213–214, 218–219
  smuggling and, 80–81, 189–190, 193,
    195–196, 198–201, 213–214, 215–216
  Trigo de Figueroa, 210
fiscal, Council of the Indies, 151, 152–153
fleet system, 42–43, 95–96
Florida, 178, 248
Foucault, Michel, 37
Franciscan order, 29, 34–35, 36, 49–50, 182
Franco de Quero, Diego, 163–164
Franco–Dutch war, 248–249
French, 233, 234–235. *See also* Nine Years'
  War; Northern Europeans
  African slaves fleeing, 246–250, 262
  Cap-Français, 239–240, 245, 256–257,
    259–260
  cattle and trade with, 253, 254, 265
  corsairs of, 87–88
  in Guaba, attacks of, 242–243, 244–245
  mulatos and trade with, 253
  Port-de-Paix, 256–257, 259–260
  Saint-Domingue, 3–4, 9–10, 264–265
  Santiago de los Caballeros and, 242–243,
    245, 250, 253
  Santiago de los Caballeros attacked by,
    223–225, 254–256
  smuggling and, 3–4, 61–62, 63–65, 71,
    79, 81–82, 89–91, 96, 98, 99, 119–120,
    186, 225, 264–266
  with Spain, peace of, 3–4, 227, 248–255,
    259–260, 264
  with Spain, war of, 223–225, 254–262,
    264, 265–266
  with Spanish residents, coexistence of,
    242, 248–255
  with Spanish residents, conflict of,
    184–185, 223–225, 242–243,
    244–245, 251–262, 264, 265–266
  with Spanish residents, trade of, 14, 225,
    227, 246–248, 251–253, 254, 260,
    261–262, 264–266
  in Tortuga, 232–233, 237–238, 239–240,
    248–252
  Treaty of Ryswick with, 3–4, 259–260,
    264
frontier patrols, 242–244, 250–251
Fuente, Alejandro de la, 157

Fuenteovejuna (Vega Carpio), 80
Fuenteovejuna, Castilla, 79–80

Gage, Thomas, 157–158
galleys, 88–92, 96
Garabito family, 134–135, 215, 218–219
Garcés de los Fayos, Juan, 246–247
Garrido, Juan, 32
garrisons
  Santiago de los Caballeros, 244–245
  Santo Domingo, 177–178, 202, 228–229,
    232–233, 234, 244–245
General History of the Indies (Fernández de
  Oviedo), 47
ginger, 44–45, 53, 54, 55, 59–60
  decline of, 45–46, 132–133, 240
  smuggling and, 45–46
Glut, Alejandro, 237
gold, 25–26, 27–29, 30–31, 49, 53–54,
  102–103
Gómez de Sandoval, Diego, 128–130, 132,
  137–138
  offices, sale of, under, 151
  regidores and, 143–144, 181
  Santo Domingo relocations and, 138–140
  situado and, 193
González de Cuenca, Gregorio, 81–82
Gorjón school, 50
governor, Santo Domingo, 52, 81–82,
  173–175, 207
  Acuña, 193–194
  Audiencia of Santo Domingo and, 12–13,
    176–178, 179, 202, 205–206, 208–209
  Balboa, 213–216, 217–218, 240, 241,
    243–245
  Bitrián, 178–179, 181–182, 185,
    190–192, 194–196, 197–199, 235–236
  Carvajal, 214, 217–219
  Fernández de Córdoba, 200–201
  garrison, Santo Domingo, under,
    177–178, 244–245
  Gómez de Sandoval, 128–130, 132,
    137–140, 143–144, 151, 181, 193
  on Irish, 233–234
  maestre de la plata, election of, and,
    192–197
  Melgarejo as interim, 188–190, 191–192,
    198–201, 202, 216–217, 231
  Montemayor as interim, 205–206
  on non-Spaniard settlers, 238–239
  office of, changes to, 175–180

Index

oficiales reales and, 179, 191
Osorio, A., 100–101, 109–110, 112–115,
  116–118, 119–125, 126–129,
  131–132, 138–140, 150–151, 156, 177
Osorio, A., census of, 77–78, 141–143,
  148–149
Ovalle, 60, 66–67
Ovando, 26–27, 34, 46, 47–48
Padilla as interim, 248
Peñalba, 206–208, 209–210, 213
Pérez Caro, I., 224–225, 255–261
Pérez Franco, 202–206
Pimentel, R., and, 173, 179–180,
  181–182, 184–185, 188–190,
  191–192, 197–201, 202–210, 211,
  212–215, 216–219, 221–222, 236
Robles, A., 221, 250–251, 252–253, 254
Rodríguez Franco and, 180–181
situado and, 178–179, 193, 194–196,
  197–198
Vega Portocarrero, 77–79, 176
Zúñiga, 208–210, 211, 212–214
graffiti, 172, 181
Granada, 98–99, 104–105
Guaba valley
  French attacking, 242–243, 244–245
  rebels in, 119–125, 126–127, 128–129,
    130, 132, 137–138, 242–243
Guitar, Lynne, 41–42
Guzmán, Juan de, 125–126

Hackett, Richard, 233–234, 236
Haitians
  Anti-Haitianism, 101
  Haitian Revolution, 9–10
Havana, Cuba, 10–11, 43–44, 157
Hernández, Bartolomé, 123–125
Herrera, Jerónimo de, 193
Herzog, Tamar, 75, 186, 226
Hispaniola. *See specific topics*
Hurtado, Alonso de, 180–181,
  193–194

indigenous peoples
  Andean, 103–104, 106
  Arawak, 3–4, 25, 237–238
  caciques of, 25, 27–29, 34–37, 54,
    102–103, 270
  Colón, C., and, 25–26, 34
  demora for, 270
  enslavement of, 25–26, 27–29, 31–32

gold production and, 25–26, 27–29,
  53–54, 102–103
Jeronymite friars and, 29–30, 31–32,
  102–103
labor of, 25–30, 34–35, 39–40, 44,
  47–48, 53–54, 102–103
pirate raids targeting, 247
pueblos tutelados for, 102–103
resistance of, 34–38, 54
smuggling and, 79
with Spanish, mixed families of, 28–29
Taíno, 25–30, 34–37, 47–48, 53–54,
  102–103, 270
Inca Empire, 103–104
Irish, 227, 229, 232–235
Isabel I (queen), 26

Jamaica, 213–214, 236, 241, 263–264
Jeronymite friars, 29–32, 38, 102–103
Jiménez, Francisco, 64–65, 82–85
John Carter Brown Library, Rhode Island,
  20
juicio de residencia. See residencia
Justinian, Pedro Juan, 93
Juvel, Luis, 158–159, 160–162, 169

La Yaguana, 147
  in depopulations, 1604–6, 3, 110,
    116–117, 125–127
  smuggling and, 14, 61–63, 64–65, 67–68,
    79, 81–82
labor
  indigenous, 25–30, 34–35, 39–40, 44,
    47–48, 53–54, 102–103
  indigenous, Andean, 103–104
  on plantations, 39–42
  types of, 142–143
ladino/a, 33–38, 119–120, 271
Landrobe, Rodrigo, 159–162
Langton, James, 92–95
Larrieta, Juan de, 44
Las Casas, Bartolomé de, 29–30, 36,
  102–103
Ledesma, Antonio de, 196–199, 203–205
legua, 271
Lemba, 36–38
leprosy, 240
lieutenant captain general (*teniente de
  capitán general*), 184–185, 188–189
Llerena, Cristóbal de, 56–58, 96–97
López de Brenes, Diego, 118

296 *Index*

López de Castro, Baltasar
  in depopulations, 1604–6, 107–110,
    111–113, 117–118, 132, 138–139
  as *escribano de cámara*, 106–107, 109
López de Luaces Otañez, Juan, 164–168,
  181–182
Lutherans, 3, 64, 73–74, 114

machina mundi, 173
maestre de campo, 206–207, 224, 271
maestre de la plata, 192–193, 271
  Audiencia of Santo Domingo and,
    193–194, 195–197
  Bitrián and election of, 194–196
  governor and, 192–197
  patronage networks and election of,
    193–194
  Pimentel, R., and, 196–199, 203–204,
    210
Maldonado, Rodrigo Claudio, 258
Mangan, Jane, 28
Manso de Contreras, Francisco, 110–113,
  115–117, 121, 127–129
Manzaneda, Severino de, 258
maravedí, 43, 44, 271
Margarita, 68, 110–112, 189–190
maroons, 37, 271
  plantation economy and, 6–7, 34–38,
    41–42, 54
  resistance of, 34–38, 41–42, 54
  smuggling and, 78–79
Martínez, Diego, 137–138
masquerade, Santo Domingo, 52
mayorazgo (entailment), 38–39, 271
mayordomo, 182, 219–220, 271
Mejías de Villalobos, Gonzalo, 112, 128
Melchor Luis (slave), 142–143, 159–162
Melgarejo Ponce de León, Juan, 196–197
  as interim governor, 188–190, 191–192,
    198–201, 202, 216–217, 231
  Pimentel, R., and, 184–186, 188–190,
    191–192, 198–201, 202, 216–217
  Portuguese discharged by, 199, 200–201,
    231
  residencia of, 192, 199–201
Méndez, Diego, 204
Meneses, Simón de, 85–87, 92
Mesa, Bernabé de, 200–201
mestizos, 28–29, 114, 115–116, 131–132
methodology, 19–21
Mexica Empire, 32

Mexico City, slaves in, 157–158
military, 126–127, 211
  frontier patrols, 242–244, 250–251
  Osorio, A., career in, 109–110
  Pimentel, R., controlling, 210–211,
    212–213
  Portuguese soldiers, 199, 200–201,
    202–203, 228, 231
  Santiago de los Caballeros garrison,
    244–245
  Santo Domingo garrison, 177–178, 202,
    228–229, 232–233, 234, 244–245
  situado funding for, 178, 191, 192–193,
    194–195, 196, 197–198, 201, 272
Molina, Tirso de, 128
Monte Plata, 183–184
Montecristi
  in depopulations, 1604–6, 3, 108–109,
    110, 113–115, 117–119, 140–141
  refounding of, 264–265
  smuggling and, 61–63, 64, 71, 83
Montemayor y Cuenca, Juan Francisco de,
  205–206, 208, 212–213, 234
Montero, Juan, 93
Montesinos, Antonio de, 29–30
Montoro, Hernando, 119–121
Morales, Luis de, 162–163
Morel de Santa Cruz, Pedro, 223–225, 253,
  255–259, 261
Moreno, Juan (Juan Prieto), 32
Morfo, Juan, 232–235
moriscos, 98–99, 104–106, 108–109
Morla, Lope de, 163–164, 167, 169
Mosquera, Diego de, 210–211
mulatos, 163–164, 271
  in depopulations, 1604–6, 114, 115–116,
    119–121, 131–132
  French trade with, 253
  Montoro, 119–121
  Pimentel, Alonso, 165–169
municipal offices, sale of. *See* offices, sale of
Muslims, 98–99, 104–106

narrative exclusion, of Hispaniola, 6–12
Navarrete, Domingo de, 220–221,
  245–246, 253–254
Navarro, Rodrigo, 219–220
New Granada, 2–3
Nieto, María, 183–184
Nine Years' War, 255, 260
  armada de Barlovento in, 255–256

Index

French settlements attacked in, 254–262, 265–266
Santiago de los Caballeros attacked in, 223–225, 254–256
Treaty of Ryswick ending, 3–4, 259–260, 264
non-Spaniards, Hispaniola, 227, 238–239, 261–262
Bitrián and, 235–236
Christianity and, 227, 229, 232, 233–234
English settlers, 232, 236–238
Irish, 227, 229, 232–236
Portuguese, 199, 200–201, 202–203, 228–231
in Santo Domingo, 199, 200–201, 202–203, 225–226, 227–237
in Tortuga, 232–233, 237–238, 239–240, 248–252
Northern Europeans
privateering of, 149–150
smuggling with, 61–68, 71, 72, 73–74, 79, 81–82, 89–90, 96, 116–117, 186, 211, 215–216, 263–266
in Tortuga, 232–233, 237–238, 239–240, 248–252

offices, sale of, 136–137, 169–170
Audiencia of Santo Domingo and, 146, 147–148, 150–154, 210
Council of the Indies on, 151, 152–153
fiscal, Audiencia of Santo Domingo, and, 146, 152, 154, 210
under Gómez de Sandoval, 151
under Osorio, A., 150–151
price of, fluctuations in, 150–155
Spanish crown and, 143–144, 145–148, 151, 152–153
oficiales reales, 146, 177–178, 271
contador, 191, 193, 198–199, 203, 270
governors and, 179, 191
situado and, 192–193
Ogeron, Bertrand d', 242–243
oidores, 13, 162–163, 269, 271
backgrounds of, 17–18
Chacón, 246–247
corruption of, 61
Cuello, A., and, 229–230
in depopulations, 1604–6, 110–113, 115–117, 127–128
on foreigners, apprehension of, 238–239

in French conflict, 259
local elites and, 75–77, 176–177
maestre de la plata and, 193–194
Manso de Contreras, 110–113, 115–117, 121, 127–129
Melgarejo and, 184–186, 200–201
Montemayor, 205–206, 208, 212–213, 234
in offices, sale of, 154
Orozco, D., 203–204
Pérez Franco and, 202, 205–206
Pimentel, R., and, 166, 169, 172–176, 181–182, 184–188, 203–204, 209, 210, 213–214, 221–222
relatores and, 271
Rodríguez Franco and, 180–181
Sáenz de Morquecho, 98–99, 106, 108–109
smuggling and, 61, 75–77, 80–81, 85–87, 98–99, 106, 108–109
in sugar economy, 38–39
Zúñiga and, 208–209
Orozco, Alonso de, 82–85
Orozco, Diego de, 203–204
Osorio, Antonio, 139–140, 150–151, 156
census of, 1606, 77–78, 141–143, 148–149
in depopulations, 1604–6, 100–101, 109–110, 112–115, 116–118, 119–125, 126–129, 131–132, 138–139, 177
residencia of, 128–129
Osorio, Diego de, 90–91, 95
Ottoman Empire, 105–106
Ovalle, Cristóbal de, 60, 66–67
Ovando, Nicolás de, 26–27, 34, 46, 47–48

Padilla, Juan de, 248
palace, Santo Domingo, 48–49
patronage networks, 150, 151–152, 265–267
Audiencia of Santo Domingo and, 173–175
of Bitrián, 190–192
López de Luaces Otañez, assassination attempt on, and, 181–182
maestre de la plata, election of, and, 193–194
of Pimentel, R., 165, 172–176, 180–188, 196–197, 200–201, 204–205, 206, 208–211, 214–215, 220–222

Index

patronage networks (cont.)
Rodríguez Franco and, 180–181
in Santiago de los Caballeros, 264–265
Pedro (slave), 159–162
Peñalba, Count of, 206–208, 209–210, 213
peninsulares, 158, 271
Pérez Caro, Ignacio, 224–225, 255–261
Pérez Caro, Juan, 257–258
Pérez Franco, Andrés, 202–206
Peru, 85, 103–104, 106
peso (de a ocho) (piece of eight), 271
Pichardo de Vinuesa, Antonio, 223–225,
253, 255–256
piece of eight. See peso (de a ocho)
pieza, 271
pigs, 143
Pimentel, Alonso, 165–169
Pimentel, Álvaro, 199–200, 203, 210
Pimentel, Pedro Serrano, 182
Pimentel, Rodrigo
Agustín and, 169
Alarcón and, 189–190, 198–201
alcaide and, 188–190, 210–211
Audiencia of Santo Domingo and,
165–168, 169, 172–176, 179–180,
181–182, 183–188, 189–190,
198–201, 203–205, 209, 210, 211,
212–214, 218–219, 221–222
Balboa and, 214–215, 217–218
Bitrián and, 181–182, 185, 191–192,
197–198, 236
Cabildo, secular, and, 134–136, 162, 171,
179–180, 181–182, 188, 196–197,
200–201, 212–213, 222
cacao production of, 240–241
Carvajal and, 214, 217–219
Chaves Osorio and, 180
church and, 182, 217, 219–221, 222
city markets and, 212–213
Council of the Indies and, 181–182, 185,
213–214, 216–217, 219–220
English invasion, 1655, and, 206–207
exiles of, 204–206, 215, 216–219
family of, 179–180, 201, 222
Figueroa y Castilla and, 200–201
fiscal, Audiencia of Santo Domingo, and,
189–190, 198–201, 213–214, 218–219
governors and, 173, 179–180, 181–182,
184–185, 188–190, 191–192,
197–201, 202–210, 211, 212–215,
216–219, 221–222, 236

as lieutenant captain general, 184–185,
188–189
López de Luaces Otañez and, 164–168,
181–182
maestre de la plata and, 196–199,
203–204, 210
Melgarejo and, 184–186, 188–190,
191–192, 198–201, 202, 216–217
military controlled by, 210–211, 212–213
Navarro investigating, 219–220
oidores and, 166, 169, 172–176,
181–182, 184–188, 203–204, 209,
210, 213–214, 221–222
Orozco, D., and, 203–204
pardon for, 216–218
patronage networks of, 165, 172–176,
180–188, 196–197, 200–201,
204–205, 206, 208–211, 214–215,
220–222
Pérez Franco and, 202–206
Pimentel, Alonso, and, 165–169
as port, Santo Domingo of, 211–213
powers of attorney and, 185–186, 187
prosecution, imprisonment of, 203–205,
214–215, 216–217
as regidor, 179–180, 181–182
return of, 1661, 217
revenge of, 218–219
situado and, 196–199, 201, 203–204,
206, 210
slaves of, 134–135, 136, 137, 158–159,
162, 164–169, 183–184, 240–241
slaves sold by, 197–198
smuggling and, 135–136, 171, 175–176,
186, 188–190, 191–192, 196–199,
201, 213–214, 219–220, 222
smuggling and absence of, 215–216
Spanish crown on, 213–214, 219–220
treasury controlled by, 209–211,
212–213
Ubilla and, 214–215, 216, 217–219
Velasco and, 184, 185, 188
visitadores and, 166, 169, 214–215, 216,
217–219
Zúñiga and, 208–210, 211, 212–214
Pimentel Enríquez, Francisco, 179–180
piracy, 95–96
English, Langton, 92–95
indigenous targeted by, 247
privateering, Northern European, 149–150
smuggling and, 87–88, 92–95

Index

on sugar mills, raids, 92–93, 94–95
plague, 1651, Santo Domingo, 201
plantations
  ginger, 44–46, 53
  labor on, 39–42
  maroons from, 6–7, 34–38, 41–42, 54
  sugar, 30–34, 38–42, 44–45, 53–54,
    92–93, 94–95, 142–143, 265–266
population
  African, 77–78, 141–143, 148–149, 155,
    239–240
  in census, 1606, 77–78, 141–143, 148–149
  before Colón, C., 25
population relocations, Spanish, 100–106
Port-de-Paix, 256–257, 259–260
Portuguese
  Castilian union with, 61–62, 228
  Cuello, A., 229–230
  Cuello, S., 159–162
  rebellion of, 199, 228
  in Santo Domingo, 199, 200–201,
    202–203, 228–231
  in Santo Domingo, re-enlisting, 202–203
  Santo Domingo discharging, 199,
    200–201, 228, 231
  in smuggling, 65–68, 74–75, 79
  in sugar economy, 42
  trade with, 61–62, 108–109
Premo, Bianca, 17–18
prices, regulation of, 43–44
Prieto, Juan. *See* Moreno, Juan
prime mover, 172–173
privateering, 149–150
Protestantism
  fear of, 3, 59, 64, 72, 73–74, 96–97,
    105–106, 114, 227, 232
  Lutherans, 3, 64, 73–74, 114
public spectacles, 50–53
pueblos tutelados, 102–103
Puerto Rico, 26–27, 67–68, 82, 126–127,
    178, 269
  ginger in, 45–46
  Pimentel, R., in, 204–205
Pujadas, Pedro de, 188–190, 234

quintal, 45, 271
Quito, 75, 151–152, 213

raiding. *See* piracy
Rama, Angel, 186
Ramírez, Susan Elizabeth, 104

Ramos, Frances, 135–136
Ramos, Nicolás de, 72–73
real, 43, 271
reducciones, 103–104, 106
regidor, 271
regidores, 73, 144–145, 206
  Ayala, G., Langton and, 94–95
  Bitrián and, 236
  Cuello, A., and, 229–230
  Gómez de Sandoval and, 143–144, 181
  oidores and, 76–77
  in patronage networks, 150, 151–152,
    165
  Pimentel, R., as, 179–180,
    181–182
  posts of, 143–146
  posts of, selling, 136–137, 146–148,
    150–155
  rivalries among, 134–136, 150,
    165–168
  Rodríguez Franco as, 180–181
  slaves held by, 158–159
  Spanish crown on, 145–148, 151
  visitadores and, 94–95, 145–146
regidores perpetuos, 145–146
relatores, 186–188, 271
repartimiento, 271
residencia (juicio de residencia), 20–21,
    86–87, 271
  of Bitrián, 185
  of Melgarejo, 192, 199–201
  of Osorio, A., 128–129
Reyes, Pedro de los, 215–216
Ribero, Rodrigo, 66–67, 79–80, 81–82,
    145–146, 155–158
Rio de la Plata, 15–16
Robles, Andrés de, 221, 250–251, 252–253,
    254
Robles, Gregorio de, 263–264
Robles, Jerónimo de, 250
Rodríguez, Juan, 234–235
Rodríguez, Tomé, 67–68
Rodríguez Franco, Francisco, 180–181
Romero, Nicolás, 234–235
ruralization, 39
Ryswick, Treaty of (1697), 3–4, 259–260,
    264

Sáenz de Morquecho, Pedro, 98–99, 106,
    108–109
Saint-Domingue, 3–4, 9–10, 264–265

300 *Index*

Salazar, Pedro Luis de, 172–173, 186–188, 201, 229–230
sales tax (*alcabala*). *See alcabala*
San Agustín, Florida, 178, 248
San Francisco, monastery of, 134–135, 182
San Lorenzo de los Minas, 248
Sánchez Aragonés, Juan, 199–200
Santa Clara, convent of, 182, 219–221
Santa María de la Encarnación, cathedral of, 49, 51
Santiago, Cuba, 126
Santiago de los Caballeros, 234–235
  with French, commerce of, 253
  French attack on, 223–225, 254–256
  French threat and, 242–243, 245, 250
  garrison in, 244–245
  patronage networks of, 264–265
  Robles, J., *alcalde mayor* of, 250
  smuggling and, 4, 263–264
  uprising of, 1720, 264–266
Santo Domingo, 4–5, 30–31, 57. *See also* governor, Santo Domingo
  African slaves and elites of, 134–135, 136–137, 155–159, 162–169, 170, 246–248
  African slaves and relocations to, 141–143
  Africans in, 32–34, 50, 53, 55, 134–135, 136–137, 155–159, 162–169, 170, 245–248
  armada de Barlovento in, 255–256
  buildings in, 47–50, 52, 76, 135, 189
  as center, 12–13, 54
  city markets of, 212–213
  currency and merchants in, 43–44
  after depopulations, 1604–6, primacy reaffirmed, 133, 135–136, 137–142
  after depopulations, 1604–6, relocation to, 137–143
  disease in, 201, 240–242, 245–246
  Drake attacking, 22–24, 47–48, 54–55, 57–58, 61–62, 68–69, 91–92, 106–107, 109–110, 176
  English in, 235, 236–237
  English invasion of, failed, 177, 206–208, 210–211, 232–233, 239
  fleet system and, 42–43, 95–96
  garrison of, 177–178, 202, 228–229, 232–233, 234, 244–245
  gates of, 189
  ginger economy and, 45
  Havana importing slaves from, 157

  Llerena on, 56–58
  natural disasters in, 242
  non-Spaniards in, 199, 200–201, 202–203, 225–226, 227–237
  patronage networks and economy of, 221–222, 265–266
  as periphery, 10–14
  as port, Pimentel, R., and, 211–213
  Portuguese in, 199, 200–201, 202–203, 228–231
  privateering, increasing, and, 149–150
  public spectacles in, 50–53
  raids and, 92–95, 149–150
  with rural Hispaniola, tension of, 14, 265–266
  Santiago uprising against, 1720, 264–266
  Sevillian merchants and, 59–61
  situado for, 178–179, 191, 192–199, 201, 203–204, 206, 210, 265–266, 271–272
  sixteenth century expansion centered in, 26–27
  smuggling accepted in, 69–70
  as stage, 50–53
Santo Domingo, *Audiencia* of. *See Audiencia* of Santo Domingo
Schwaller, Robert C., 37
Schwartz, Stuart B., 226
Second War of the Alpujarras, 99, 104–105
Segura y Sandoval, Francisco de, 255–256
seventeenth century, long, 1–2, 5
Sevilla, Spain, 42–43, 44, 45–46, 59–61, 74
sheep, 143
Sigüenza y Góngora, Carlos de, 255
Simón (enslaved man), 162–163
situado, 191, 272
  Bitrián and, 178–179, 194–196, 197–198
  governors, Santo Domingo, and, 178–179, 193, 194–196, 197–198
  maestre de la plata bringing, 192–199, 203–204, 210, 271
  Pimentel, R., and, 196–199, 201, 203–204, 206, 210
  smuggling and, 192–199, 201, 265–266
slaves, 7–10, 44, 227. *See also* Africans; labor
  in depopulations, 1604–6, 114, 119–120, 125–127
  elites and, 134–135, 136–137, 155–169, 170, 183–184, 246–248, 266–267
  ethnonyms of, 50, 141–142, 248

Index

301

indigenous, 25–26, 27–29, 31–32
ladino/a, 33–38, 119–120, 271
maroons, 6–7, 34–38, 41–42, 54, 78–79,
  271
in Mexico City, 157–158
pieza for, 271
Pimentel, R., selling, 197–198
of Pimentel, R., 134–135, 136, 137,
  158–159, 162, 164–169, 183–184,
  240–241
population of, 77–78, 141–143,
  148–149, 155, 239–240
regidores and, 158–159
resistance of African, indigenous and,
  34–38, 54
runaway, from French settlements,
  246–250, 262
runaway, in depopulations, 1604–6,
  126–127
Santo Domingo, relocation to, and,
  141–143
from Santo Domingo, Havana importing,
  157
in Santo Domingo, 32–34, 50, 53, 55,
  134–135, 136–137, 159, 162–169,
  170, 245–248
sexual abuse and, 128–129
in smuggling, work of, 64, 77–78, 83,
  84–85
smuggling of, 63, 65–66, 69, 86–87,
  119–120
social importance of, 155–159
in sugar economy, 30–31, 32–34, 35–36,
  38, 39–42, 49, 54, 142–143
in violence, masters using, 159–162,
  164–169, 170, 183–184, 266–267
smallpox epidemics, 29–30, 31–32, 103,
  240
smuggling, 1–3, 4–6, 14–15, 189
acceptance of, 69–70, 79–80, 267–268
Africans in, 64–65, 77–79, 83, 84–85
Audiencia of Santo Domingo and, 61,
  75–79, 80–87, 88–90, 91, 98–99, 106,
  107–109, 180–181, 188, 189–191,
  193, 195–196, 198–201, 213–214,
  215–216, 222, 265–266
Bitrián and, 190–192, 194–196, 198–199
Cabildo, secular, on, 73
cattle and, 73, 107–108, 119–120
Christianity and, 70–75, 96–97, 99, 114
clergy on, 70–75

conciliatory approach to, 95
corruption and, 17–19, 61
depopulations, 1604–6, and, 3, 100, 114,
  177–178
after depopulations, 1604–6, 137–138,
  177–178
eighteenth century, 15–16
English and, 67–68, 72, 92–95, 96,
  137–138, 215–216, 263–264
fiscal, *Audiencia* of Santo Domingo, and,
  80–81, 189–190, 193, 195–196,
  198–201, 213–214, 215–216
fleet system and, 95–96
French and, 3–4, 61–62, 63–65, 71, 79,
  81–82, 89–91, 96, 98, 99, 119–120,
  186, 225, 264–266
galleys policing, 88–92
ginger and, 45–46
indigenous and, 79
institutionalization of, 2–3, 59
Llerena on, 56, 58, 96–97
maroons and, 78–79
moral economy of, 2, 58–59
with North European traders, 61–68, 71,
  72, 73–74, 79, 81–82, 89–90, 96,
  116–117, 186, 211, 215–216, 263–266
Ovalle and, 66–67
Pérez Franco and, 203
Pimentel, R., absence of, and, 215–216
Pimentel, R., and, 135–136, 171,
  175–176, 186, 188–190, 191–192,
  196–199, 201, 213–214, 219–220, 222
piracy, pillaging, and, 63–64, 87–88,
  92–95
Portuguese in, 65–68, 74–75, 79
of Reyes, 215–216
Ribero on, 66–67, 79–80, 81–82
Rodríguez Franco and, 180–181
in Santiago, Cuba, 126
Santiago de los Caballeros and, 4,
  263–264
situado and, 192–199, 201, 265–266
of slaves, 63, 65–66, 69, 86–87, 119–120
Spain curbing, failure of, 3, 4–5, 59,
  82–87, 89–91, 95, 96–99, 107–109
in transimperial world, 14–16
Venezuela and, 2–3, 186, 189–190
Villagrá and, 81, 86–87
visitador and, 66–67, 79–80, 81–82,
  86–87
social capital, 155–156

302 *Index*

socorro, 191, 194, 272
sources, 19–21
Spain, 10–14, 222. *See also* Council of the Indies
  archives in, 20
  Audiencia of Santo Domingo and, 173–175, 222
  Cabildo, secular, and, 145–148, 151, 245–246
  with Caribbean, relationship of, 5, 8, 173–174, 266–267
  Castilian, 25–26, 38–39, 40–41, 43, 61–62, 74–75, 79–80, 98–99, 104–105, 228, 231
  depopulations, 1604–6, and, 3, 100–101, 122–123, 130–132
  Dutch and, 227, 248–249
  English and, 61–62, 67–68, 109–110, 227, 236, 259–260
  French peace with, 3–4, 227, 248–255, 259–260, 264
  French war with, 223–225, 254–262, 264, 265–266
  Fuenteovejuna, 79–80
  galleys sent by, 88–92, 96
  moriscos in, removal of, 98–99, 104–106, 108–109
  offices, sale of, and, 143–144, 145–148, 151, 152–153
  Osorio, A., fighting for, 109–110
  on Pimentel, R., 213–214, 219–220
  population relocations by, 100–106
  Portuguese union with, 61–62, 228
  Sevilla, 42–43, 44, 45–46, 59–61, 74
  situado of, 178–179, 191, 192–199, 201, 203–204, 206, 210, 265–266, 271–272
  of smuggling, failure to curb, 3, 4–5, 59, 82–87, 89–91, 95, 96–99, 107–109
Spanish Succession, War of, 15–16
Suárez, Gonzalo, 69–71
Suazo, Simón de, 195–196, 198
sugar economy, 132–133
  African slavery in, 30–31, 32–34, 35–36, 38, 39–42, 49, 54, 142–143
  decline of, 42, 44–45, 53, 54, 55, 59–60, 155–156, 265–266
  encomienda system and, 30–31, 38
  plantations in, 30–34, 38–42, 44–45, 53–54, 142–143, 265–266
  raiding on, 92–93, 94–95

Taíno
  caciques of, 25, 27–29, 34–37, 54, 102–103, 270
  Colón, C., and, 25–26, 34
  gold and, 25–26, 27–29, 53–54, 102–103
  labor of, 25–30, 34–35, 47–48, 53–54
  resistance of, 34
  with Spanish, mixed families of, 28–29
Taylor, William, 19
teniente de capitán general (lieutenant captain general), 184–185, 188–189
TePaske, John Jay, 12
Thompson, E. P., 2, 58–59
Tierra Firme, expedition to, 26–27
Toledo, Francisco de, 103–104
Tomás y Valiente, Francisco, 146
Torres, Facundo de, 181–182
Torres, Jerónimo de, 63, 79
Tortuga, 232–233, 237–238, 239–240, 248–252
treasury
  contador of, 191, 193, 198–199, 203, 270
  oficiales reales of, 146, 177–178, 179, 191, 192–193, 198–199, 203, 270, 271
  Pimentel, R., controlling, 209–211, 212–213
  in Veracruz, 178–179
Trigo de Figueroa, Bernardo, 210
Trujillo, Rafael Leónidas, 101

Ubilla, Sancho de, 213–216, 217–219
unscheduled arrivals (*arribadas*), 60–61

Varela, Fernando, 82–87
vecinos, 191, 272
  in census, 77–78, 148–149
  depopulations, 1604–6, aftermath of, and, 130–132, 140
  Ermenzon, 236
  Pimentel, R., and, 213–214
  situado and, 196, 210
  sugar economy and, 30–31
Vega Carpio, Lope de, 80
Vega Portocarrero, Lope de (governor), 77–79, 176
Velasco, Nicolás de, 184, 185, 188
vellón. See cuartos
Venezuela, 185
  Caracas, 13, 187, 196–197, 241, 269
  smuggling and, 2–3, 186, 189–190
Veracruz, 178–179, 192–193

Index

Villafañe, Diego de, 123–125
Villagrá, Francisco Alonso de, 76–77, 81, 86–87, 94–95
Villegas, Lope de, 120–122
visita, 20–21, 267, 272
visitador, 272
  Hurtado, 180–181, 193–194
  Pimentel, R., and, 166, 169, 214–215, 216, 217–219
  regidores and, 94–95, 145–146
  Ribero, 66–67, 79–80, 81–82, 145–146, 155–158

smuggling and, 66–67, 79–80, 81–82, 86–87
Ubilla, 213–216, 217–219
Vega Carpio, 80
Villagrá, 76–77, 81, 86–87, 94–95

Walker, Tamara, 156
Wheat, David, 78, 141–142
Wolof, 35–36

Zúñiga Avellaneda, Felix de, 208–210, 211, 212–214

Other Books in the Series (continued from page ii)

108. *The Mexican Revolution's Wake: The Making of a Political System, 1920–1929*, Sarah Osten
107. *Latin America's Radical Left: Rebellion and Cold War in the Global 1960s*, Aldo Marchesi
106. *Liberalism as Utopia: The Rise and Fall of Legal Rule in Post-Colonial Mexico, 1820–1900*, Timo H. Schaefer
105. *Before Mestizaje: The Frontiers of Race and Caste in Colonial Mexico*, Ben Vinson III
104. *The Lords of Tetzcoco: The Transformation of Indigenous Rule in Postconquest Central Mexico*, Bradley Benton
103. *Theater of a Thousand Wonders: A History of Miraculous Images and Shrines in New Spain*, William B. Taylor
102. *Indian and Slave Royalists in the Age of Revolution*, Marcela Echeverri
101. *Indigenous Elites and Creole Identity in Colonial Mexico, 1500–1800*, Peter Villella
100. *Asian Slaves in Colonial Mexico: From Chinos to Indians*, Tatiana Seijas
 99. *Black Saint of the Americas: The Life and Afterlife of Martín de Porres*, Celia Cussen
 98. *The Economic History of Latin America since Independence, Third Edition*, Victor Bulmer-Thomas
 97. *The British Textile Trade in South American in the Nineteenth Century*, Manuel Llorca-Jaña
 96. *Warfare and Shamanism in Amazonia*, Carlos Fausto
 95. *Rebellion on the Amazon: The Cabanagem, Race, and Popular Culture in the North of Brazil, 1798–1840*, Mark Harris
 94. *A History of the Khipu*, Galen Brokaw
 93. *Politics, Markets, and Mexico's "London Debt," 1823–1887*, Richard J. Salvucci
 92. *The Political Economy of Argentina in the Twentieth Century*, Roberto Cortés Conde
 91. *Bankruptcy of Empire: Mexican Silver and the Wars Between Spain, Britain, and France, 1760–1810*, Carlos Marichal
 90. *Shadows of Empire: The Indian Nobility of Cusco, 1750–1825*, David T. Garrett
 89. *Chile: The Making of a Republic, 1830–1865: Politics and Ideas*, Simon Collier
 88. *Deference and Defiance in Monterrey: Workers, Paternalism, and Revolution in Mexico, 1890–1950*, Michael Snodgrass
 87. *Andrés Bello: Scholarship and Nation-Building in Nineteenth-Century Latin America*, Ivan Jaksic
 86. *Between Revolution and the Ballot Box: The Origins of the Argentine Radical Party in the 1890s*, Paula Alonso
 85. *Slavery and the Demographic and Economic History of Minas Gerais, Brazil, 1720–1888*, Laird W. Bergad
 84. *The Independence of Spanish America*, Jaime E. Rodríguez

83. *The Rise of Capitalism on the Pampas: The Estancias of Buenos Aires, 1785–1870*, Samuel Amaral
82. *A History of Chile, 1808–2002, Second Edition*, Simon Collier and William F. Sater
81. *The Revolutionary Mission: American Enterprise in Latin America, 1900–1945*, Thomas F. O'Brien
80. *The Kingdom of Quito, 1690–1830: The State and Regional Development*, Kenneth J. Andrien
79. *The Cuban Slave Market, 1790–1880*, Laird W. Bergad, Fe Iglesias García, and María del Carmen Barcia
78. *Business Interest Groups in Nineteenth-Century Brazil*, Eugene Ridings
77. *The Economic History of Latin America since Independence, Second Edition*, Victor Bulmer-Thomas
76. *Power and Violence in the Colonial City: Oruro from the Mining Renaissance to the Rebellion of Tupac Amaru (1740–1782)*, Oscar Cornblit
75. *Colombia before Independence: Economy, Society and Politics under Bourbon Rule*, Anthony McFarlane
74. *Politics and Urban Growth in Buenos Aires, 1910–1942*, Richard J. Walter
73. *The Central Republic in Mexico, 1835–1846, "Hombres de Bien" in the Age of Santa Anna*, Michael P. Costeloe
72. *Negotiating Democracy: Politicians and Generals in Uruguay*, Charles Guy Gillespie
71. *Native Society and Disease in Colonial Ecuador*, Suzanne Austin Alchon
70. *The Politics of Memory: Native Historical Interpretation in the Colombian Andes*, Joanne Rappaport
69. *Power and the Ruling Classes in Northeast Brazil, Juazeiro and Petrolina in Transition*, Ronald H. Chilcote
68. *House and Street: The Domestic World of Servants and Masters in Nineteenth-Century Rio de Janeiro*, Sandra Lauderdale Graham
67. *The Demography of Inequality in Brazil*, Charles H. Wood and José Alberto Magno de Carvalho
66. *The Politics of Coalition Rule in Colombia*, Jonathan Hartlyn
65. *South America and the First World War: The Impact of the War on Brazil, Argentina, Peru and Chile*, Bill Albert
64. *Resistance and Integration: Peronism and the Argentine Working Class, 1946–1976*, Daniel James
63. *The Political Economy of Central America since 1920*, Victor Bulmer-Thomas
62. *A Tropical Belle Epoque: Elite Culture and Society in Turn-of-the-Century Rio de Janeiro*, Jeffrey D. Needell
61. *Ambivalent Conquests: Maya and Spaniard in Yucatan, 1517–1570, Second Edition*, Inga Clendinnen
60. *Latin America and the Comintern, 1919–1943*, Manuel Caballero
59. *Roots of Insurgency: Mexican Regions, 1750–1824*, Brian R. Hamnett

58. *The Agrarian Question and the Peasant Movement in Colombia: Struggles of the National Peasant Association, 1967–1981,* Leon Zamosc

57. *Catholic Colonialism: A Parish History of Guatemala, 1524–1821,* Adriaan C. van Oss

56. *Pre-Revolutionary Caracas: Politics, Economy, and Society 1777–1811,* P. Michael McKinley

55. *The Mexican Revolution, Volume 2: Counter-Revolution and Reconstruction,* Alan Knight

54. *The Mexican Revolution, Volume 1: Porfirians, Liberals, and Peasants,* Alan Knight

53. *The Province of Buenos Aires and Argentine Politics, 1912–1943,* Richard J. Walter

52. *Sugar Plantations in the Formation of Brazilian Society: Bahia, 1550–1835,* Stuart B. Schwartz

51. *Tobacco on the Periphery: A Case Study in Cuban Labour History, 1860–1958,* Jean Stubbs

50. *Housing, the State, and the Poor: Policy and Practice in Three Latin American Cities,* Alan Gilbert and Peter M. Ward

49. *Unions and Politics in Mexico: The Case of the Automobile Industry,* Ian Roxborough

48. *Miners, Peasants and Entrepreneurs: Regional Development in the Central Highlands of Peru,* Norman Long and Bryan Roberts

47. *Capitalist Development and the Peasant Economy in Peru,* Adolfo Figueroa

46. *Early Latin America: A History of Colonial Spanish America and Brazil,* James Lockhart and Stuart B. Schwartz

45. *Brazil's State-Owned Enterprises: A Case Study of the State as Entrepreneur,* Thomas J. Trebat

44. *Law and Politics in Aztec Texcoco,* Jerome A. Offner

43. *Juan Vicente Gómez and the Oil Companies in Venezuela, 1908–1935,* B. S. McBeth

42. *Revolution from Without: Yucatán, Mexico, and the United States, 1880–1924,* Gilbert M. Joseph

41. *Demographic Collapse: Indian Peru, 1520–1620,* Noble David Cook

40. *Oil and Politics in Latin America: Nationalist Movements and State Companies,* George Philip

39. *The Struggle for Land: A Political Economy of the Pioneer Frontier in Brazil from 1930 to the Present Day,* J. Foweraker

38. *Caudillo and Peasant in the Mexican Revolution,* D. A. Brading, ed.

37. *Odious Commerce: Britain, Spain and the Abolition of the Cuban Slave Trade,* David Murray

36. *Coffee in Colombia, 1850–1970: An Economic, Social and Political History,* Marco Palacios

35. *A Socioeconomic History of Argentina, 1776–1860,* Jonathan C. Brown

34. *From Dessalines to Duvalier: Race, Colour and National Independence in Haiti,* David Nicholls

33. *Modernization in a Mexican ejido: A Study in Economic Adaptation,* Billie R. DeWalt.
32. *Haciendas and Ranchos in the Mexican Bajío, Léon, 1700–1860,* D. A. Brading
31. *Foreign Immigrants in Early Bourbon Mexico, 1700–1760,* Charles F. Nunn
30. *The Merchants of Buenos Aires, 1778–1810: Family and Commerce,* Susan Migden Socolow
29. *Drought and Irrigation in North-east Brazil,* Anthony L. Hall
28. *Coronelismo: The Municipality and Representative Government in Brazil,* Victor Nunes Leal
27. *A History of the Bolivian Labour Movement, 1848–1971,* Guillermo Lora
26. *Land and Labour in Latin America: Essays on the Development of Agrarian Capitalism in the Nineteenth and Twentieth Centuries,* Kenneth Duncan and Ian Rutledge, eds.
25. *Allende's Chile: The Political Economy of the Rise and Fall of the Unidad Popular,* Stefan de Vylder
24. *The Cristero Rebellion: The Mexican People Between Church and State, 1926–1929,* Jean A. Meyer
23. *The African Experience in Spanish America, 1502 to the Present Day,* Leslie B. Rout, Jr.
22. *Letters and People of the Spanish Indies: Sixteenth Century,* James Lockhart and Enrique Otte, eds.
21. *Chilean Rural Society from the Spanish Conquest to 1930,* Arnold J. Bauer
20. *Studies in the Colonial History of Spanish America,* Mario Góngora
19. *Politics in Argentina, 1890–1930: The Rise and Fall of Radicalism,* David Rock
18. *Politics, Economics and Society in Argentina in the Revolutionary Period,* Tulio Halperín Donghi
17. Marriage, Class and Colour in Nineteenth-Century Cuba: A Study of Racial Attitudes and Sexual Values in a Slave Society, Verena Stolcke
16. *Conflicts and Conspiracies: Brazil and Portugal, 1750–1808,* Kenneth Maxwell
15. *Silver Mining and Society in Colonial Mexico: Zacatecas, 1546–1700,* P. J. Bakewell
14. *A Guide to the Historical Geography of New Spain,* Peter Gerhard
13. *Bolivia: Land, Location and Politics Since 1825, J. Valerie Fifer,* Malcolm Deas, Clifford Smith, and John Street
12. *Politics and Trade in Southern Mexico, 1750–1821,* Brian R. Hamnett
11. *Alienation of Church Wealth in Mexico: Social and Economic Aspects of the Liberal Revolution, 1856–1875,* Jan Bazant
10. *Miners and Merchants in Bourbon Mexico, 1763–1810,* D. A. Brading
9. *An Economic History of Colombia, 1845–1930,* by W. P. McGreevey
8. *Economic Development of Latin America: Historical Background and Contemporary Problems,* Celso Furtado and Suzette Macedo

7. *Regional Economic Development: The River Basin Approach in Mexico,*
   David Barkin and Timothy King
6. *The Abolition of the Brazilian Slave Trade: Britain, Brazil and the Slave
   Trade Question, 1807–1869,* Leslie Bethell
5. *Parties and Political Change in Bolivia, 1880–1952,* Herbert S. Klein
4. *Britain and the Onset of Modernization in Brazil, 1850–1914,*
   Richard Graham
3. *The Mexican Revolution, 1910–1914: The Diplomacy of Anglo-
   American Conflict,* P. A. R. Calvert
2. *Church Wealth in Mexico: A Study of the "Juzgado de Capellanias" in the
   Archbishopric of Mexico 1800–1856,* Michael P. Costeloe
1. *Ideas and Politics of Chilean Independence, 1808–1833,* Simon Collier

Lightning Source UK Ltd.
Milton Keynes UK
UKHW010814101120
373118UK00004B/12